ב"ה

April 1999.

To David
    Fond good wishes for a
splendid birthday,
    Happy 60th,
With affection,
    Shalom,
        Ruth & Mel & family.

ArtScroll Judaica Classics®

Rabbi Nosson Scherman / Rabbi Meir Zlotowitz

General Editors

ליקוטים מספר דרך חיים

Avos

*A commentary
based on selections from
Maharal's Derech Chaim*

RABBI TUVIA BASSER

A PROJECT OF THE

Mesorah
Heritage
Foundation

Maharal of Prague

PIRKEI

Published by

Mesorah Publications, ltd

FIRST EDITION
First Impression . . . May 1997

Published and Distributed by
MESORAH PUBLICATIONS, Ltd.
4401 Second Avenue
Brooklyn, New York 11232

Distributed in Europe by
J. LEHMANN HEBREW BOOKSELLERS
20 Cambridge Terrace
Gateshead, Tyne and Wear
England NE8 1RP

Distributed in Israel by
SIFRIATI / A. GITLER — BOOKS
10 Hashomer Street
Bnei Brak 51361

Distributed in Australia & New Zealand by
GOLDS BOOK & GIFT CO.
36 William Street
Balaclava 3183, Vic., Australia

Distributed in South Africa by
KOLLEL BOOKSHOP
22 Muller Street
Yeoville 2198, Johannesburg, South Africa

ARTSCROLL JUDAICA CLASSICS®
MAHARAL OF PRAGUE: PIRKEI AVOS
© *Copyright 1997, by* MESORAH PUBLICATIONS, Ltd.
4401 Second Avenue / Brooklyn, N.Y. 11232 / (718) 921-9000

ISBN:
0-89906-109-5 (hard cover)
0-89906-100-1 (paperback)

Typography by CompuScribe at ArtScroll Studios, Ltd.
4401 Second Avenue / Brooklyn, N.Y. 11232 / (718) 921-9000

Printed in the United States of America by Edison Lithographing and Printing Corp.
Bound by Sefercraft Inc., Quality Bookbinders, Brooklyn, N.Y.

בן חמשים לעצה
(Avos 5:25)

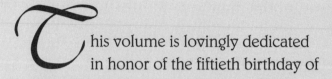 his volume is lovingly dedicated
in honor of the fiftieth birthday of

Eric Austein

As a loving husband and father, he offers
wise counsel and much, much more.

His dedication to his family,
to friends and neighbors, and to
countless worthy causes of Klal Yisrael
have made him an admired and
cherished role model to all who know him.

To us, he is the foundation and anchor of our home,
the source of direction,
the constant fount of joy and security.

In the merit of the profound wisdom and guidance
that pulse through every page of this work —
Ethics of the Fathers and the commentary of Maharal —
May Hashem Yitbarach bless him with
decade after decade of good health and
accomplishment, and may we be blessed
with his company and inspiration until 120.

Joyce Austein
Ilana and Avi, Michael, Jonathan, Adam, Eytan

Rabbi Aaron M. Schechter   אהרן משה שכטר

ב"ה
עש"ק פ' שמיני כ"ו אדר השני תשנ"ז

תורתו של המהר"ל דומה לנו כאותו אור אשר נגנז לצדיקים לע"ל, כן הלביש
המהר"ל גניזותיו מתחת דבריו המאירים. אין סוף לעומק כוונת דבריו, ובב"א
ניצוצי אור בוקעים ומזהירים מתוכם בעדנו להאיר עיניו בתורת ה' ולרומם
השגותנו ונשמותנו, להוליכנו בארח חיים למעלה למשכיל.
וכפי רוממותם מעולם היו דבריו מיוחדים לבעלי מעלה המסוגלים.-אמנם
בהשגחת ה' עלינו, אחרי אשר לוקח מאתנו בזמן האחרון "רובי-תורתי" עם
הקודש שתפארת התורה שכנה בתוכם, נתעורר רוח ממרום וימים באים, וזעיר
שם זעיר שם, לבבות נפתחים, וכמה אנפי צמאון לדבר ה' מופיעים. וכתוצאה
מזה נמצאים כאלה אשר עיקר שליטתם הוא בשפת המדינה ועם כל זה
משתוקקים לטעום מהרוממות של דרך החיים המוביל לעץ חיים.
וראוי להזכיר דברי המהר"ל שיסוד ענין שנים מקרא ואחד תרגום הוא בהא
דהתורה נתנה בסיני ונשנית באהל מועד ונשתלשה בערבות מואב, אשר שם
הואיל משה באר את התורה בע' לשון של האומות. והוסיף בזה כי התורה על
הכל. ואם שהאומות לא קבלוה, מ"מ עצם מעלת התורה היא לכל, וכפי
מהותה מעוטרת היא בבאר היטב בתרגום.-ויתכן דאחד מתוצאות הגלות היא
אשר בכל מקום מהפכים אנו כלי הגלות שמטילים עלינו לשמש כלים בעדנו
לדברי תורה, וגברת נצחון היא לנו שגם שפת מדינת גלותנו, שכל כך רחוק
מדרכי הקדושה של תורתנו, יתהפך בידנו כלי ביאור לרוממות תורת המהר"ל.
כי ישראל קדושים כן קבלו לעשות מהכל דברי תורה.
ומעתה, בא ונחזיק טובה לאיש יקר, משכיל ונלהב לכבוד ה' ותורתו, הרב
טוביה אליהו באסער שליט"א אשר מתוך עוצם עונג הדברי תורה שהטעים בו
פגישתו עם דברי המהר"ל ותוקף הכרת הקדושה והיראה שהטיל עליו, קיים בה
אחזתיו ולא ארפנו. ולימודיו גבר עליו והכריחו לקיים בהם גם "ללמדה". כי
ליקט מניצוצות "דרך-החיים" ונבלעו הדברים בדמיו, ודם נעכר ונעשה חלב
להניק לאלו אשר לשונם לשון הגלות הזה, שגם מתוכה יאיר להם אור מופלא
בטעם עליון וקדוש.-אמנם הכיר כי הדרך הצלחה בזה לא יהיה כי אם בצירוף
מלאכת מחשבת לקיים "תשים-לפניהם", וביֵרר וסידר הדברים לערוך השלחן
שיהא מוכן וקרוב לנפשם ודעתם של הלומדים מתוך דבריו.
באמונה ובירֵאה עשה וחפץ ה' בידו יצליח להרחיב גבולת הכרת הקודש ויאיר
בתוכנו אור העליון אשר לא פסק המהר"ל ללמדה, ואשר חשק המחבר היא
להמשיכה, כי שמים וארץ אחד הם, ועמך ישראל גוי אחד בארץ הם המעידים
על זה.

אהרן משה שכטר

⌐§ Author's Introduction

In the final century of the Second Temple, Yonasan ben Uziel made public the Aramaic translation of the books of Prophets. It was more than just a literal translation; it revealed details of Scriptural allusions that only the elite of Torah scholars had known. The Rabbis tell us [*Megillah* 3a]:

> "When Yonasan ben Uziel made public the Aramaic translation of Prophets, handed down from Haggai, Zechariah and Malachi, the land of Israel shook.
>
> "A voice went out from heaven and said, 'Who has revealed My secrets to the people?' Yonasan ben Uziel stood up and said, 'It is I who has revealed Your secrets to the people. It is revealed and known to You that I did not do this for my honor nor for the honor of my ancestors, but for Your honor, to avoid contention within Israel.' "

Yonasan ben Uziel realized that publicizing the insights of earlier sages might bring honor to himself and to his ancestors, but he testified that his motivation was purely to promote God's honor and the spiritual welfare of His people.

This story has two parallels with the present work. The first is Yonasan ben Uziel's wish to promote God's honor. In this secular age, God's honor must be restored as well as enhanced and Maharal's *Derech Chaim* is a powerful vehicle to achieve that goal. Maharal's writings fairly glow with an intense awareness of God's presence, engaging us with the immediacy of His wisdom and His will.

Yonasan ben Uziel also wished to avoid the "contention within Israel" that arose from differing interpretations of the Prophets. Today, speakers and authors often confuse Maharal's principles with those of other Kabbalists and philosophers and it is hoped that this work will clarify points of Maharal's philosophy for the layman and public figure alike.

There is yet one more point of relevance. Yonasan ben Uziel recognized that publishing a work of Torah would unavoidably bring honor to the author and his ancestors. I dedicate any honor that may accrue from this work to those who were the greatest influence on my life.

May God grant me a measure of the integrity and sincerity
that I saw in my father

אבא מורי יעקב דוד בן צבי זאב באסער ע״ה

Yaakov David Basser

and a measure of the dedication to His service that I saw in my *Rebbi*

רבי מובהק בהלכה הרב הגאון הרב גדלי׳ ב״ר צבי פעלדער ז״ל

Rabbi Gedalia Felder

I dedicate this book to their memory.

◆§ Acknowledgments

Maharal is noted for the conceptual depth that underlies his words, and so the task of simplifying his writings accurately is not to be taken lightly. It demands constant vigilance and the reassurance of an objective opinion to be certain of remaining faithful to Maharal's intent and philosophy. In this regard, I wish to express my appreciation to Rabbi Aaron Moshe Schechter *shlita, Rosh Yeshivah* of Mesivta Chaim Berlin, for the opportunity to discuss Maharal's writings and for the enlightenment I have received from him. I also feel privileged and grateful to have received guidance, advice and above all encouragement from the noted *Rosh Yeshivah* and author, Rabbi Zev Hoberman *shlita.*

The task of casting Maharal's system of thought into an English style that would be comfortable for the contemporary reader was a formidable challenge, and I am grateful to those who helped in that endeavor. In particular, I am highly indebted to Mrs. Sherri Wise of Toronto for the generous amount of time that she spent reviewing the manuscript and coaching me, frankly but respectfully, in style, completeness of content, flow and relevance. I am grateful also to her husband Chanina (Kenny) Wise, who frequently gave of his time to share his impressions of the manuscript. May God bless them and their family with good health, prosperity, success in their many community activities, and continuing *nachas* from their children.

I also thank Mr. Michael Halbert and Mr. Hayyim Oliver for their many helpful suggestions; and Mr. Moshe Podolsky for his review of Chapter One.

I conclude these acknowledgments with a special note of appreciation to my wife Esther *shetichyeh,* for it is she who provided the initial encouragement to express my love for Maharal through writing. She also reviewed the draft manuscript and offered valuable stylistic critique. This book is the fruit of labors which were rooted in and nourished by her wisdom and sensitivity.

✎ Author's Note

The intention of this work is to share with the reader my appreciation of Maharal's insights into the essence of life.

This book is intended as an entry point to the concepts of Maharal. It is expected that the reader will be inspired by the vitality and cogency of Maharal's approach to our relationship with God, and it is hoped that the advanced reader will feel encouraged to study the original *Derech Chaim*.

There is a popular style that uses *Pirkei Avos* as a vehicle for inspirational anecdotes. These have universal appeal, and they are consumed quickly and in large quantity. In contrast, Maharal's commentary is like a fine liqueur. It can be appreciated only when savored slowly and deliberately, a sip at a time. Each paragraph of Maharal's writings has a fresh and profound thought that warrants reflection.

✎ Rav Yehudah Loew

Moreinu HaRav Yehudah Loew of Prague, known as Maharal Me-Prague, lived over 400 years ago, from 1512 to 1609. He was a contemporary of Rav Yosef Karo, author of the *Shulchan Aruch,* and the master of Torah's secrets, Rav Yitzchok Luria, *Ari'zal.* Maharal taught a metaphysical system that draws upon the *Zohar* and later Kabbalistic works. Using that method, his explanations of Talmudic and Midrashic homiletics are systematic, consistent and relevant. Maharal's teachings have provided a framework for authentic Jewish philosophy down to our own generation.

✎ Maharal's Style

The distinctive and engaging feature of Maharal's style is his gift for reaching the very essence of a subject. His messages are captivating and inspiring.

The traditional commentaries explain *Avos* by defining and clarifying details of the content. In contrast, Maharal considers the relationships between the *mishnayos*; the themes that evolve from them collectively; the metaphysical system that underlies the *mishnayos*; and the history of rabbinical leadership as reflected in the development of *Avos*. In short, Maharal explains the Rabbis' statements within the context of history and of the spiritual universe that we inhabit.

✎ Maharal's Philosophy

Maharal's commentary is built on Kabbalistic principles, although direct allusions to *Kabbalah* are rare. The following is a skeletal outline of Maharal's focus on the flow of existence from the Creator to the creation, and its implications for human conduct.

- God is perfect (*shaleim*) and an aspect of perfection is the ability to create *ex nihilo*. To remain only potentially able to create falls short of perfection: God actually does create.
- God's greatness as Creator is especially manifested by creating human beings for we, in a sense, are also creators. We have self-determination, for He gave us the freedom to revere Him or to reject Him.
- He created two worlds for mankind to inhabit: a predominantly spiritual world and a predominantly physical world. People have the native intelligence to succeed in the physical world; however, only the wisdom of Torah opens the doors to prosper in the spiritual world.
- Only the spiritual world properly reflects His perfection; that world is termed, from our current perspective, the World to Come. In that world God's Presence is manifest and it endows the human soul with consummate serenity.
- Because the World to Come is an eternal and hence unchanging existence, God also created this physical world so that human beings can develop and prepare for eternal life. By way of comparison, we know that we can prepare for Shabbos only on a weekday, because the Shabbos rest itself precludes shopping and cooking. Similarly, it is only in this world that we can develop the spiritual substance that is the essence of our existence in the World to Come.

    Because physical things can change, the greatness of the human being comes out only in this physical world. It is here that we can exercise a choice to grow spiritually. However, a world of change is inherently temporal and must eventually end.
- A world devoid of God's Presence would not have been worth creating; it would have been a sterile, pointless creation, rather than a vehicle for spiritual growth as it was intended. Rather, God associates His presence with this world, and in doing so He reveals specific Divine qualities.
- The world serves and reveals the Holy One, and that fact is the essence of the giving of the Torah. Torah directs mankind to know the Holy One and what He desires of him. It (a) enlightens him in the pursuit of increasing holiness in the conduct of his life and (b) further enlightens him to the truth of all being, so that he recognizes the Holy One in all existence.

    The first level is incumbent on all. The second level varies according to the level of holiness one has attained in the pursuit of the Holy One. At the height of this knowledge are the Kabbalistic teachings. Esoteric in nature, they are really intended for the *b'nei aliyah* (those who are eminently righteous and immersed in the pursuit of understanding the

Creator and His ways), who are very few in number. The uniqueness of Maharal is the presentation of Torah through his profound intellect and holiness, in a language all his own, which the educated student will recognize is rooted in *Kabbalah*. [1]

- The human being lives at the focal point of the links between God and the physical world. At the personal level, these links appear in our relationships with God, with other people and within ourselves. At the social level, the connections between God and mankind are implemented through the institutions of the Rabbinical Court, the Monarchy and the Priesthood. Indeed, there are three fundamental links that appear in many realms and dimensions of religious human life, as discussed in Maharal's commentary to *Avos* 1:2. Human beings bind the spiritual and physical planes together by following the mandates of the Torah, and they undermine creation by violating the Torah.

- Although we have the *ability* to choose good or evil, we do not have the *right* to choose evil. If we contravene the dictates of Torah, we ultimately destroy God's creation and are held accountable. Conversely, if we support the dictates of Torah, we maintain — and indeed fortify — His creation and we are deserving of reward.

- We perceive God as He appears through such Divine qualities as kindness and might. Maharal takes the Kabbalistic position that God's "knowledge" is another of the Divine qualities. In this, he disagrees with Rambam's well-known opinion that God and His knowledge are one. The ramifications of this debate are discussed, among other places, in Maharal's commentary to *Avos* 5:8.[2] The Divine qualities are listed in his commentary to *Avos* 5:7,[3] although I have omitted them from this English adaptation on the basis that detailed Kabbalistic teachings are the domain of the advanced Torah scholar.

- Our relationship with God is frequently illustrated through the metaphor of a King. Everything is His. He sets laws and He judges; He rewards compliance with the law and decrees consequences for noncompliance. He supports the world with material and spiritual sustenance. As King, He is distinct from the nation, yet intimately concerned with the people's welfare.

- He is the Source of all existence, and we are totally dependent on Him,

1. The points contained in these two paragraphs were contributed by Rabbi Aaron Schechter *shlita,* for which the author is extremely grateful.

2. Such is the numbering in the *Siddur* and in this work. In the numbering scheme employed in the *Mishnah,* and in the original *Derech Chaim,* this *mishnah* is 5:6.

3. In the *Mishnah,* and in the original *Derech Chaim,* this *mishnah* is 5:5. See previous footnote.

for there is no existence other than His creation. The recognition of His munificence is the source for our love of God. The recognition of how utterly dependent we are on Him is the essence of our reverence of God, generally referred to in literal translation as the "fear" of God.

◄§ Elements of Maharal's Philosophy

The study of Maharal cultivates a deep, intense and immediate awareness of God, as Maharal presents the systematic study of the principles and structure of existence as it flows from God, to mankind and to all creation. *Derech Chaim,* and indeed all of Maharal's works, will be better understood with the following explanations of Maharal's principles. The Hebrew terms will be included as a reference vocabulary for those who wish to pursue Maharal's writings in the original.

Maharal introduces the basic elements of an ontological system by comparing Creation to building a house.[1] There are four elements in the construction of a house: a builder (*po'eil*); physical materials (*chomer*) such as bricks and mortar; the architect's vision of what the house will look like (*tzurah*) and the purpose (*tachlis*) for which the house is built. The house would not be built if even one of these factors were absent.

◄§ Form and Substance

Referring again to the metaphor of a house, the **form** lies in the architect's vision of the house, and is realized in the **substance** of the bricks. Nothing could be qualitatively more different than these two, yet they are inseparable for most objects.

The contrast of form, *tzurah,* and substance, *chomer,* and their synthesis are recurring themes in Maharal's works and deserve extra definition.

Substance, *chomer,* like the bricks of the house, is physical: It takes up space and is tangible; it is passive, and accepts form; it is specific; it is finite; it deteriorates. Substance takes on one form at a time. Because substance can always change, it is never fully complete. This characteristic is called *chaseir,* which we have translated "deficient."

Form, *tzurah,* like the architect's vision of the house, is conceptual. Form does not occupy space; it is not tangible; it does not accept change. It is active, spawning change by imposing itself upon substance. It does not have physical limitations; it does not age. It is general: One "form," such as a chair, has innumerable realizations in specific chairs. Since form does not change, it is complete, *shaleim.*

As can be seen, the characteristics of form and substance are mutually exclusive. Maharal uses the term *nivdal* to describe this relationship.

---

1. Maharal's *Drush l'Shabbos HaGadol*, p.195, found in the back of the *Haggadah Shel Pesach*, London edition.

Nonetheless, form and substance are intimately bound together in every object.

Form is considered a higher level than substance, for it constrains substance and is universal rather than specific. For example, law has the characteristic of form, shaping society, whereas the conduct of each individual is akin to substance.

Physical, material existence is the diametric opposite of spiritual, conceptual existence. Creation spans the full spectrum between the two extremes of the physical and the conceptual.

Success in living up to Torah's mandates will come through a personality that can balance these components so that they are complementary rather than antagonistic. Intellect without action is sterile, while thoughtless action is brutish. Only through intellectually directed, purposeful action can the human being mature towards eternal spiritual life.

⊷§ *The Human Being: Body and Soul*

The soul has characteristics of form: It is abstract; it is eternal; it gives purpose and character to the body. The body is substance: It is tangible; it is finite; it gives expression to the soul. The soul is imposed upon the body as form is imposed on substance.

Clearly, the human being is both a physical and spiritual being. A person is as physical a creature as an animal: He is mortal, selfish, changeable and dependent on his environment. The human being also has spiritual, Godly characteristics: Man has awareness, creativity, self-discipline and initiative.

⊷§ *Levels of Existence*

A human being lives at three hierarchical levels, called *chomer, tzurah* and *tzelem.*

The lowest level, *chomer,* is the level of our physical existence, including our physical drives.

The middle level is *tzurah.* It manifests itself as the aspect of our personality that seeks to impose form and structure on objects, people or ourselves. *Tzurah* is the origin of the human drive to influence and to dominate. The faculty of speech, which formulates into words our abstract longings and thoughts, is another example of human life at the level of *tzurah.*

The highest level, *tzelem,* is a reference to mankind's being created in the "image of God." If we consider *tzurah* as the quality of the foot soldier, subduing opposition and enforcing allegiance, we may consider *tzelem* as the qualities of the king: majesty, dominion, leadership and inspiration. Whereas *tzurah* is only form, *tzelem* is beauty. It is associated with the radiance of life that shines in a person's face and that exudes from the independent spirit of individual existence.

The full personality integrates all three levels of *chomer*, *tzurah* and *tzelem*. The spiritual person elevates the lower levels to serve his Creator, whereas the spiritually defective person subjugates the higher levels to serve his physical drives.

◄§ Sechel

This key concept has been translated "intellect" or "concept," according to context. *Sechel* is conceptual as opposed to tangible. The term embraces all forms and degrees of conceptual grasp, knowledge and insight. *Sechel* is a primary characteristic of Torah, of the elevated human being and indeed of all spiritual entities. It is "spiritual" — eternal, divine, intangible, influential. Because *sechel* is non-physical, the physical element of human existence is an impediment to exercising *sechel*.

A person acquires *sechel*; he is not born with it. Although *sechel* is closely associated with the soul, it is an acquisition and not the soul itself.

◄§ Torah

Maharal uses the word "Torah" with many different connotations. The most common use is Torah as a system of values and relationships. Torah determines the positive actions by which we can elevate ourselves to eternal life and the negative activities that may undermine our being worthy of eternal existence.

Torah can also refer to:

• The Ten Commandments
• The 613 commandments
• All commandments, including rabbinical ordinances
• The study of Torah
• The Talmud (reasons and principles underlying the *Mishnah*)
• The definition of all existence and relationships

It is evident that Torah is the system that regulates human life. It is true, albeit not evident, that Torah also embraces the systems within which the universe, the world and mankind exist.

Torah is pure intellect, *sechel*. Unlike human intellect, it is completely independent, *nivdal* of physical existence, *chomer*.

Within the metaphor of the Tree of Life,[1] Torah is rooted in God's essence. It is the link between God and mankind, through which life flows from Him to us.

---

1. *Mishlei* 3:18.

Maharal of Prague

Pirkei Avos

◆§ Maharal's Introduction

◆§ „כִּי נֵר מִצְוָה וְתוֹרָה אוֹר וְדֶרֶךְ חַיִּים תּוֹכְחוֹת מוּסָר" ◆§
**"For a lamp is the commandment and Torah is light and
the way to life[1] is admonitions of correction"** (*Mishlei* **6:23).**

"Light" is the Biblical and Rabbinic metaphor for intellect. As light reveals our surroundings, horizons and pathways, so the light of intellect can illuminate a goal and the necessary steps to achieve it. Mankind is naturally endowed with an intellect that is adequate only to succeed at worldly goals. Human intellect alone cannot fulfill the human potential for eternal existence, because it cannot by itself discover and succeed at spiritual goals.

The human being is confined in a body that he will leave behind all too soon. He gropes in darkness for the portal to eternal life, but the meager light of human intelligence is inadequate to find the way. Only the light of *mitzvos* (commandments), Torah and *mussar* (constructive admonitions) can illuminate the path to eternity.

◆§ „כִּי נֵר מִצְוָה", — *"For a* lamp *is the commandment*

The physical practice of *mitzvos* is likened to a "lamp." The point of the metaphor is that a wick, oil and container form a physical base for an ethereal flame. Likewise, our physical practice of *mitzvos* is the basis for a Divine light to settle upon us, as we dedicate our thought and action to the commandments and will of our Creator.

◆§ וְתוֹרָה אוֹר — *and Torah is* light

The study of Torah is compared to light. As light is intangible, so Torah is entirely free of physical limitations. Unlike *mitzvos*, which are physical actions and hence fixed in time and limited in effect, Torah is not limited in time or impact.

---

1. *Derech Chaim,* the title of the original work by Maharal.

◆§ "וְדֶרֶךְ חַיִּים תּוֹכְחוֹת מוּסָר" — *and the way to life is* admonitions of correction."

"The way to **life**" refers to the eternal life of the World to Come. The verse tells us that even the lamp of *mitzvos* and the light of Torah may not be enough for us to succeed in reaching the World to Come. We also require practical common sense, based on experience and wisdom, to keep us on the path to eternity. "Admonitions of correction" refers to the guidance of parents and teachers who have gained wisdom through experience, study and guidance from their own teachers.

◆§ דֶּרֶךְ חַיִּים — *the way to life (derech chaim)*

"The way to life" in the quoted verse means "the way to the Tree of Life." That is Scripture's metaphor for the essence of Torah, which originates in the highest spiritual realm. Indeed, Torah is like a massive, unshakable tree, for it is rooted in the very source of life: God. The way to the Tree of Life is bounded on the right and on the left by תּוֹכְחוֹת מוּסָר, *tochachos mussar,* admonitions to counter the pull of desire and physical distractions. The path to eternal life must be followed directly, for deviation leads to failure and death.

In summary, the practice of *mitzvos*, and study of the Divine wisdom of Torah are vehicles that bring us to eternal life. *Mussar*, admonition, keeps us away from the death that lurks behind the distractions of physical desire. The tractate of *Pirkei Avos*, small in size and immense in value, is a complete manual of sage guidance to keep us focused on Torah and *mitzvos*.

The Talmud tells us,[1]

> Rav Yehudah said: He who wishes to be **pious** should fulfill the matters contained in tractate *Nezikin* (laws of liability and damages). Rava said: [He should fulfill] the matters contained in tractate *Avos*; while others say: the matters contained in tractate *Berachos* (laws of blessings and prayers).

The Hebrew word for "pious" — חָסִיד, *chasid* — denotes a person who does more than the strict letter of the law requires. To be truly pious, a person must go beyond simple duty in life's three basic relationships: the relationship with others; the relationship with oneself; and the relationship with God.

---

1. *Bava Kamma* 30a.

In the above passage, each of the opinions emphasizes one of these relationships. Rav Yehudah promotes the relationship with others as the primary focus of piety. He recommends fulfilling the requirements of *Nezikin* which require us to avoid causing financial harm to others, even indirectly or through negligence.

Rava maintains that the relationship with oneself is the most important element of piety. Hence, he recommends fulfilling the words of *Avos*, which focus on personal development. Finally, *Berachos* stresses the relationship with God through blessings and prayer.

The three opinions differ only as to where to place our emphasis, but all opinions agree that *Avos* is a guide to personal spiritual excellence.

A Note to the Reader:

Pirkei Avos is an anthology of practical advice, guiding each generation towards spiritual success. Maharal's commentary shows the larger context surrounding each *mishnah*: What did the author of each *mishnah* wish to accomplish with his advice? How will the advice help? What does each Rabbi's advice reveal about his personality and about the people to whom he is talking? How are the *mishnayos* of each chapter related to each other?

Maharal's commentary will show that the chapter consists of one fabric, with tightly woven messages. It will demonstrate how the advice of *Pirkei Avos* is cogent, complete and effective. The commentary shows, as well, the parallels between the development of *Pirkei Avos* and the history of Torah, the nation and the sages.

פרק ראשון &

Chapter One

כָּל יִשְׂרָאֵל יֵשׁ לָהֶם חֵלֶק לָעוֹלָם הַבָּא,
שֶׁנֶּאֱמַר: „וְעַמֵּךְ כֻּלָּם צַדִּיקִים; לְעוֹלָם
יִירְשׁוּ אָרֶץ; נֵצֶר מַטָּעַי, מַעֲשֵׂה יָדַי לְהִתְפָּאֵר."

It is customary to recite this *mishnah* before studying the weekly
chapter of *Avos* on Shabbos afternoon.[1] Afterwards we recite the
mishnah, "Rabbi Chanania ben Akashia says: The Holy One, Blessed is
He, wished to confer merit upon Israel; therefore He gave them Torah
and *mitzvos* in abundance."[2]

◆§ וְעַמֵּךְ כֻּלָּם צַדִּיקִים; לְעוֹלָם יִירְשׁוּ אָרֶץ — *your people*
are all righteous; they shall inherit the land forever

The term *land* is associated with life, as in the expression,[3] "in the land
of the living." The phrase refers to the land of eternal life, namely, the
World to Come. The people of Israel are all citizens[4] of the World to
Come; they do not have to earn the right to enter.[5]

The danger does exist of individuals forfeiting citizenship, by losing
their identification as members of the nation of Israel. This can happen
in a number of ways; for example, if their sins outweigh their merits or
if they renounce citizenship by breaking ties with the Jewish nation. As
a nation, however, "Your people are all righteous" innately; therefore
"they shall inherit the land forever."

◆§ נֵצֶר מַטָּעַי — *the stem of My plantings*

The stem is that straight, vertical branch which first comes out of the
ground, before it develops side branches that extend in different
directions. Eternity is symbolized by the straight and true, and hence the
nation of Israel is called the "*stem of my plantings*," for it is directed
towards God. That early trunk is the primary structure of the tree and it
defines the direction of a tree's growth. This metaphor contrasts Israel
with the other nations who, like side branches turning from the trunk,

---

1. Between Pesach and Shavuos, or Pesach and Rosh Hashanah in other communities.
2. *Makkos* 23b.
3. *Yeshayahu* 38:11. Similar expressions are found in *Yeshayahu* 53:8; *Yechezkel* 26:20
and elsewhere.
4. Author's paraphrase of *Rashi*, quoted by Maharal.
5. *Sanhedrin* 110b: A child is destined for eternal life even from the moment of birth; i.e.,
without doing anything to earn it.

A ll Israel has a share in the World to Come, as it
is said (*Yeshayahu* 60:21): "And your people
are all righteous; they shall inherit the land
forever; they are the stem of My plantings, My
handiwork, in which to take pride."

---

become sidetracked from the quest for eternity.

מַעֲשֵׂה יָדַי לְהִתְפָּאֵר ⋄ — My handiwork, in which to take pride

---

A finite creation such as this world does not adequately reflect God's
greatness. Only the eternal World to Come can evince the perfection of
the eternal Creator. Since Israel completes the World to Come, as its
primary citizens, they are a principal part of that world's tribute to God's
greatness.

The Sages established the custom of reciting this *mishnah* to encourage the people of Israel throughout this long and bitter exile. The
mishnah, "All Israel has a share in the World to Come," confirms the lofty
spiritual core of every Jew. It is fitting as a preparation for the study of
Pirkei Avos, which leads to elevated qualities of conduct. Such refinement of behavior leads in turn to the highest national treasure, the
Torah, which is the subject of the concluding *mishnah*, "He gave them
Torah and *mitzvos* in abundance."

Shabbos is a fitting time for these reflections, for the reason illustrated
by the following *Midrash*:

> "Three testify about each other. Shabbos and Israel testify to the
> unity of God. God and Shabbos testify that Israel is one nation.
> God and Israel testify that Shabbos is a day of rest."[1]

The phrase "that Shabbos is a day of rest" means that Shabbos also is
"one" in the sense of being complete, unique and foremost of the days
of the week.[2]

Shabbos, Israel and the Creator reflect each other's preeminence.
Hence, Shabbos is the optimum time for Jews to study *Avos*, the
practical advice which guides them to their privileged portion, namely,
God's presence in the World to Come.

---

1. Quoted in *Tosafos* to *Chagigah* 3b.
2. It is appropriate to rest only when something is complete; otherwise there is continuing development. The day of rest is therefore "one" in the sense of self-contained
perfection, as well as being unique and foremost among the days of the week.

[א] **מֹשֶׁה** קִבֵּל תּוֹרָה מִסִּינַי, וּמְסָרָהּ לִיהוֹשֻׁעַ; וִיהוֹשֻׁעַ לִזְקֵנִים; וּזְקֵנִים לִנְבִיאִים, וּנְבִיאִים מְסָרוּהָ לְאַנְשֵׁי

Mishnah 1

ৰ§ **מֹשֶׁה קִבֵּל תּוֹרָה מִסִּינַי, וּמְסָרָהּ לִיהוֹשֻׁעַ** — *Moshe received the Torah from Sinai, and transmitted it to Yehoshua*

Torah is primarily law. In contrast, *Pirkei Avos* is a compilation of rabbinical wisdom and practical advice. Why begin it by chronicling the transmission of Torah?

In truth, it is precisely because this tractate deals with advice directed towards each generation's needs, and not with absolute law, that the *mishnah* begins with the history of Torah leadership. As we will see, this opening *mishnah* establishes the right and the responsibility of the sages to give advice, and our responsibility to heed it.

Avos, which means fathers, begins with the chain of those who provided the world with spiritual life. They taught the love and the practice of Torah and enriched the world with its wisdom and values. They prepared successors to be the leaders who would guide the next generation. These people were truly the fathers of Torah society, and for this reason the tractate is called *Avos*.

As fathers of the nation, they must provide guidance for the survival and the success of the nation. Scripture teaches about this relationship in the verse,[1]

"Listen, my son, to your 'father's advice,' and do not forsake the Torah of your mother."

This passage implies that it is both the father's right and responsibility to provide guidance. Moreover, the verse says that we must not only listen to but moreover heed the advice of our fathers.

ৰ§ **מֹשֶׁה קִבֵּל תּוֹרָה מִסִּינַי** — *Moshe received the Torah* from Sinai

---

We would certainly expect the first step in the chain of Torah transmission to be phrased as 'Moshe received the Torah *from God*." The expression "Moshe received the Torah *from Sinai*" is used instead, out of

---

1. *Mishlei* 1:8.

1.   **M**oshe received the Torah from Sinai, and transmitted it to Yehoshua; and Yehoshua to the Elders; the Elders to the Prophets; and the Prophets transmitted it to the Men

---

respect for the Creator of the Universe, for it would be highly inappropriate to include God in a list of human beings. The phrase "from Sinai" emphasizes the significance of Torah revelation, for a special place in the world was set aside for that cosmic event.

We might argue that Mount Sinai also does not fit into a list of human beings. There is, however, one point in common. God Himself designated Sinai as the geographical origin of the Torah, and He designated Moshe as His ambassador to humanity. The Torah conveys this fact by calling Mount Sinai הַר הָאֱלֹקִים, *Har HaElokim,* [1] the mountain of God — and by calling Moshe אִישׁ הָאֱלֹקִים, *Ish HaElokim,* [2] the man of God.

◆§ מֹשֶׁה קִבֵּל תּוֹרָה מִסִּינַי, וּמְסָרָהּ לִיהוֹשֻׁעַ — *Moshe received the Torah from Sinai, and transmitted it to Yehoshua*

After using the term "received" in regard to Moshe, the *mishnah* uses the term "transmitted" for each link up to the Men of the Great Assembly and reverts to the expression "received" for the rabbinical leaders after Shimon HaTzaddik beginning with Antignos, leader of Socho.[3] Why does the *mishnah* alternate between the term "receive" and the term "transmit"?

The terms "received" and "transmitted" are used to describe different degrees of success in transmitting Torah at each link in the chain of Tradition. A teacher attempts to impart his knowledge in its entirety, and the student attempts to grasp this knowledge without loss. The term "transmitted" is used to express that the knowledge was completely transmitted. If the student grasped less than everything that was taught, then there remains only what was "received." The *mishnah* tells us that Moshe could only "receive" the Torah, for it exceeds total human comprehension. Conversely, Moshe, Yehoshua and the generations up to and including the Men of the Great Assembly were successful in "transmitting" all that they knew. As we will see, the generations after

---

1. *Shemos* 24:13.
2. *Devarim* 33:1.
3. *Infra*, mishnah 3.

that were not able to grasp all of the Torah that their predecessors could teach. Thus, the following *mishnayos* say that the Torah was only "received."

---

§ **הֵם אָמְרוּ שְׁלֹשָׁה דְבָרִים** — *They said three things:*

The Men of the Great Assembly flourished prior to the Second Temple and in its early days. The "things" that they said are *mussar*.[1] *Mussar* is distinct from Torah, which is a system of law, and it is different from *mitzvos*, which are the practice of Torah law. It is advice that supports both the study and the practice of Torah. *Mussar* strengthens the ability of mere human beings to live within a Divine system.

During the thousand years in which the Torah was transmitted from Moshe to the Men of the Great Assembly, none of these bearers and transmitters of Torah gave *mussar* to the nation. The pronouncements they issued were restatements of Torah, not the advice of *mussar*. What prompted the Men of the Great Assembly to dispense *mussar*?

In the time of the Men of the Great Assembly, persecution and exile had taken their toll on scholarship and the intellectual fabric of the nation was starting to wear thin. Intellect, *sechel*,[2] had declined with regard to the power of its presence and influence. Since Torah is conceptual in nature, the grasp of Torah was weakening and was in need of reinforcement. From that time on, rabbinical leaders found it necessary to give advice on how to deal with the changes that were taking place in society.

We will now see how the advice of the Men of the Great Assembly fortifies the intellect, *sechel*, and thereby promotes the understanding and practice of Torah law and facilitates life at each stratum within Torah society (see chart on facing page).

Benefit to the Intellect

The advice of the Men of the Great Assembly fortifies the three components of intellect: wisdom, *chachmah;* understanding, *binah;* and discerning, *daas*.

---

1. Cor.structive criticism. This work translates the word as **advice**, which is actually too mild an expression. The English language falls short of a translation that adequately conveys the obligatory weight of *mussar* and the positive, nurturing intent with which it is given and received.
2. *Sechel*, שֵׂכֶל, is translated as intellect. The term embraces all forms and degrees of conceptual grasp, knowledge and insight.

of the Great Assembly. They [the Men of the Great Assembly] said three things:

OBJECTS OF THE MEN OF THE GREAT ASSEMBLY'S ADVICE			
OBJECTS	ADVICE		
	Be patient in judgment	Many students	Fence for the Torah
Intellect	Wisdom, *chachmah*	Understanding, *binah*	Discerning, *daas*
Law	*Mishpatim*	General *Mitzvos*	*Chukim*
Society	Judges	Scholars	Lay people

- Wisdom, *chachmah,* refers to factual knowledge, including a sense of the relevance of those facts.
- Understanding, *binah,* refers to seeing implications beyond the facts.
- *Daas* refers to discerning the essential distinguishing characteristics of things. This is the faculty we use to analyze and organize information, to group similar items and to distinguish between categories.

Wisdom, *understanding* and *discerning* are independent aspects of the intellect, although they work together.[1] Therefore, advice that restores one of these may not be effective for the others, and the Rabbis had to prescribe a separate remedy for each.

"Be patient in judgment" strengthens wisdom, *chachmah.* For example, a judge is called upon for his wisdom, and patience nurtures wisdom. The judge needs time to resolve conflicting principles, to reflect on the consequences of a decision and to feel confident in the conclusion reached.

"Develop many *students"* fortifies understanding, *binah.* Interaction and discussions among scholars enhance their *understanding* of Torah.

"Make a *fence* for the Torah" compensates for weakened *daas,* discernment. The "fence" refers to rabbinical enactments that avoid the need to differentiate between permitted actions and similar but forbidden actions. For example, Torah law forbids boiling the flesh of an animal in milk, but permits boiling the flesh of fowl in milk. The rabbis enacted a "fence" for these laws by forbidding us to boil any kind of meat — animal or fowl — in milk.

---

1. This may be understood by comparison to the independent dimensions of length, width and height. Those dimensions are clearly distinguishable, but there is no part of an object that is only one or two of them.

הֱווּ מְתוּנִים בַּדִּין; וְהַעֲמִידוּ תַלְמִידִים הַרְבֵּה;
וַעֲשׂוּ סְיָג לַתּוֹרָה.

Benefit to Torah Practice

The three pieces of advice of the Great Assembly also fortify the three categories of Torah law: *mishpatim*, *chukim* and *mitzvos*.

- *Mishpatim* are laws that are obviously essential to the smooth functioning of society. Simple common sense can see and apply the system and method of *mishpatim*.
- *Chukim* are the opposite; they are laws which are beyond human ability to rationalize into a system. Although we do not know the ultimate reason that God decreed any of the commandments, we can usually posit principles that guide us to the application of the law in specific situations. *Chukim* defy formulating such principles, and hence are difficult to arrange into a methodical system that can be practiced through the use of guidelines.
- All other laws are in the category of *mitzvos*, which are not as intuitively grasped as *mishpatim*, but which can be organized, through analysis and insight, by their underlying principles.

"Be deliberate in *judgment*" supports *mishpatim*, i.e., ensuring fairness and integrity in laws that deal with social issues, such as torts and damages.

"Develop *many disciples*" strengthens *mitzvos*, the general body of Torah law. The study and analysis of many people discussing Torah among themselves help to develop an understanding of the principles and system behind these laws.

"Make a *fence* for the Torah" protects *chukim*, those laws that are difficult to cast into a logical system, such as forbidden marriage relationships. Because there is no systematic principle to determine which relative we may marry and which we may not, one could easily enter into a forbidden marriage. One of the earliest "fences" was instituted by Shlomo HaMelech who, by disallowing marriage to yet other relatives, produced a system that is easily and reliably applied.

Benefit to Social Roles

Because the human being is an intellectual being, advice to remedy different parts of the intellect also addresses different parts of society.

1/1 Be deliberate in judgment; develop many disciples; and make a fence for the Torah.

8§ הֱווּ מְתוּנִים בַּדִּין — Be deliberate in judgment

In a Torah-based society, judges are rabbis. The advice to "be deliberate in judgment" strengthens the social institutions of the court and of rabbinical leadership and develops the judges and rabbis to become proficient in those roles.

8§ וְהַעֲמִידוּ תַלְמִידִים הַרְבֵּה — develop many disciples

This advice promotes another important segment of Torah society, the rabbinical scholars. Their interaction with the rabbis and with the general population benefits both of those groups. Scholars sharpen their teachers with questions and problems, and they disseminate Torah to the general population.

8§ וַעֲשׂוּ סְיָג לַתּוֹרָה — and make a fence for the Torah

This advice benefits the general population, who are not well versed in the details of Torah law. The "fence for the Torah" is a system of rabbinical enactments that helps people to avoid confusing the forbidden with the permitted. Such additional restrictions make the law more consistent and thus easier to remember and to apply. The example used above is that the rabbis prohibited cooking any type of meat with milk, since the common person does not distinguish between meat that is animal flesh and the meat of fowl.

The "fence for the Torah" is a set of restrictions that is over and above the letter of Torah law. The entire population undertook these extra constraints lovingly, in reciprocation of the Creator's loving kindness.

The Significance of the Number "Three"

It seems superfluous for the *mishnah* to count how many things were said; after all, we can easily count them ourselves. The *mishnah* states "They said *three* things" to teach that the remedy consists of precisely three parts. No less would be adequate and no more are required.

The number three is characteristic of a complete entity. An entity consists of three parts: two opposite extremes and an intermediate part that joins with those extremes to form a unified whole.

13 / MAHARAL: PIRKEI AVOS

Consider a house. Inside is a haven of refuge and tranquillity; outside lies danger and the harsh elements; and the structure joins these extremes. We can fortify a house in all three dimensions. We can protect it from outside forces with a windbreak and good water drainage. We can protect the inside by eliminating fire hazards, and we can brace the structure of the house itself. All of those areas must be fortified, and there is no other area available for improvement.

This principle of a three-dimensional creation appears in many facets of Jewish thought:

- The three forefathers, Avraham, Yitzchak and Yaakov, left a legacy for the Jewish nation in the dimensions of kindness, strictness and the balanced synthesis of these opposites.
- A human being is the synthesis of the spiritual and physical planes of existence.
- This *mishnah* addresses the three areas that encompass all of Torah law: *mishpatim*, *mitzvos* and *chukim*. At one extreme are *mishpatim* — intuitive civil law. At the other extreme are *chukim* — laws that defy systematic rationale. And in between those extremes are all other *mitzvos*, which have systematic principles that require significant effort to discover.

Much of *Pirkei Avos* provides three-dimensional solutions to three-dimensional problems.

The Relationship of Mishnah 1 to the Mishnayos That Follow

The wisdom of the early rabbis is expressed in *Pirkei Avos* as practical advice that brings the full force of Torah into daily life. That wisdom, which has guided Torah society to this day, is built upon their grasp of the essence of Creation. Chapter 1 starts with the most general fundamentals of Creation and continues with increasingly specific elements of human life.

Mishnah 1 addresses all of society. It intends to strengthen the Torah, which is the foundation of meaningful existence. The next *mishnah* will explore the three primary relationships of human life. Subsequent topics will deal with a variety of social relationships and then discuss personal values for self-improvement.

The role and the character of each author manifests itself in the scope

2. Shimon HaTzaddik was among the survivors of the Great Assembly. He used to say: The world depends on three things: on

---

and perspective of his advice. The *mussar* of *mishnah* 1 comes from the Men of the Great Assembly. That sacred body of 120 sages and prophets was very close to the source of existence. Their advice reflects that perspective, by addressing the needs of the nation at the very source of its existence; namely, the Torah.

Mishnah 2

Nothing exists apart from God; rather, existence flows from God to the world at every moment. Shimon HaTzaddik reveals a striking fact: We are the link between this world and God, and hence the world relies on our deeds for continued existence.

---

§⊷ עַל שְׁלֹשָׁה דְבָרִים הָעוֹלָם עוֹמֵד — *The world depends on three things:*

When after each stage of Creation God declared that it was "good,"[1] He meant that it merited to be created and to continue to exist because of its goodness. Conversely, anything that did not merit continued existence was not called "good." For that reason the declaration of "good" was withheld from the second day's creation, because dissension was created on the second day[2] and, while a dispute may be necessary, it is not sustained indefinitely.[3]

The major categories of Creation, such as plants, were designated "good" even though each tree and flower must wither and die. The category itself continues on, however, and it is to this that the term "good" applies.

Mankind was a different order of creation, because man must cultivate his goodness. The declaration of "good" was not explicitly applied to the creation of mankind, but was ambiguously included in the statement "and behold, it was very (מְאֹד)." The Hebrew word מְאֹד has the letters of אָדָם — man — rearranged, for the choice to become good lies within us.[4]

---

1. *Bereishis* Chapter 1.
2. *Bereishis Rabbah* 1.
3. *Avos* 5:20: "Any dispute. . .that is not for the sake of Heaven will not endure." Maharal explains that even disputes that are "for the sake of Heaven" endure by special Divine intervention and not because of any inherent durability.
4. *Bereishis Rabbah* 9.

The world was created for man to use in his mission to become "good." If we turn our back on this mission, the rest of the world has no relevance; therefore, all existence depends on mankind. This was manifested at the time of the Flood, when not only the people were destroyed but the animals and birds as well.

Of this the Midrash[1] says,

> There is a parable of a king who was marrying off his son and built a bridal chamber for him. He plastered it and cemented it and painted it. The king subsequently became angry at his son and had him killed. He entered the bridal chamber and began to break the supports, to remove the partitions and to rip the curtains. The king said, "Did I build this for any reason other than my son? My son is destroyed; shall this endure?" Similarly, the Flood was sent to destroy not only people, but the animals and birds as well.

When mankind is deserving of existence, the rest of creation fulfills its purpose and is maintained by the Creator. So it is that the world's existence truly depends upon our worthiness, as earned through Torah, the service of God and acts of kindness.

---

§ עַל הַתּוֹרָה וְעַל הָעֲבוֹדָה וְעַל גְּמִילוּת חֲסָדִים — *on Torah study, on the service [of God],* [2] *and on kind deeds*

A person relates to his world in three dimensions. One interacts with:

- oneself
- God
- and other people.

As will soon be explained, we maintain these relationships in our daily life through:

- Torah study
- the service of God
- and kind deeds.

The "three things" of the *mishnah* are vehicles to acquire "goodness" in each of these relationships.

---

1. *Bereishis Rabbah* section 28.
2. Prayer and, in the era of the Temple, sacrifice.

Torah study provides personal worth. The study of Torah builds spiritual, eternal beings out of mortals. The physical body is finite; it must come to an end. In contrast, Torah imbues a person with conceptual attributes: values and morals; principles and reason. Since these are not physical, they are not finite and they never come to an end.

Personal worth comes through internalizing the values and principles of Torah and in no other way. It is in this way that Torah is a pillar of existence, for it molds us into whole and worthy beings.

The service of God refers primarily to the Temple service of sacrifices, but it includes the service of God through the performance of all *mitzvos*. The service of God is a pillar of the world's existence; it gives worth and wholeness to human existence in the context of the relationship with the Creator. Since the only existence is that of God, everything else must relate back to His own existence, and we provide that linkage through the service of God.

Kind deeds, the third pillar, corresponds to the third dimension of life: being integrated with others and good to them. To perform an act of kindness, without personal gain, is the highest degree of pure and enduring human worth. Kind deeds between one person and another induce a corresponding flow of kindness from God that sustains the world.

Historical Illustration

The world was destroyed in the generation of the Flood[1] only when the people had sinned against all three of the pillars on which the world stands. When they had swung to the complete reverse of these principles, the world was destroyed from mankind down to the animals.

People sinned through the worship of other gods, which is the contrary of the service of God.

They engaged in perverse sexual practices,[2] which is the antithesis of Torah. Torah is intellect; it elevates us from a physical plane of life to a spiritual plane. In contrast, the pursuit of sexual immorality reduces a person to a level where he is little better than a mere animal.

They were also thieves,[3] which is the opposite of kind deeds: They took from others, rather than giving to others.

---

1. *Bereishis* 6:7: "And God said, 'I will destroy mankind, whom I have created, from the face of the earth; from man to animal, to creeping things and to the bird of the sky.' "
2. *Sanhedrin* 57a. Adultery and homosexuality were eschewed since the time of Adam.
3. *Bereishis* 6:11.

When that generation had completely undermined the three pillars upon which the world stands, there was no basis for support and therefore destruction came to the world.

Halachic Illustration

The rabbis say,[1]

> If miscreants tell one, "Transgress and you will not be killed," then one should transgress any commandment of the Torah to avoid being killed, except for the worship of other gods, sexual immorality and murder.

It is better to forgo one's life than to commit any of these three transgressions because they are the opposite of the three pillars upon which the world stands. Sexual immorality is the antithesis of Torah because it debases rather than elevates. Serving other gods is the opposite of serving God; and murder is the opposite of kind deeds. It is better to be killed because transgressing these sins controverts the three pillars of human existence. If one nevertheless succumbs and commits any of these transgressions rather than be killed, he in any event has forfeited genuine existence. Therefore, these actions are really a form of death, and it is preferable to die in innocence, rather than die burdened with such sins.

The Three Pillars Personified

The forefathers Avraham, Yitzchak and Yaakov were the foundations of the Torah world. They personally embodied the three foundations of the world: Torah, service and kindness. Kind deeds were the outstanding characteristic of Avraham, who is noted for his hospitality to guests. Yitzchak, who willingly approached the sacrificial altar, exemplifies the service of God. Scripture associates the Torah nation with Yaakov, as it says,[2]

> Moshe commanded to us the Torah, the inheritance of the Congregation of Yaakov.

---

§≈ עַל שְׁלֹשָׁה דְּבָרִים ≈§ — *on three things*

The *mussar* of the Men of the Great Assembly and of Shimon Ha-Tzaddik consists of three components, as do many of the statements in

---

1. *Sanhedrin* 74a.
2. *Devarim* 33:4 Although Avraham observed all of the commandments (*Yoma* 28b), Yaakov was noted for study of the Torah and was the source of merit through which the Torah was given to the nation of Israel.

this tractate. This is because three elements embrace the total perspective: Everything has two opposite extremes and a middle that unifies those extremes into a whole. For example, the pillars of existence are: the animal sacrifices of the Temple service[1] and its opposite, kindness, and Torah that binds them into a total, balanced system.

Kabbalistic Basis of the "Three Things"

God has infused this material world of rock, plants and animals with sanctity, through the Torah's commandments and values. The words and ideas of Torah are abstract rules and principles; it takes people to put them into practice. In this light, Torah may be seen as the vehicle to introduce God's sanctity into this world.

The One God appears to us with three primary attributes: the extremes of strict justice and kindness, and the integrated spectrum of how we perceive God through this world. These attributes are respectively expressed through the Divine Names א-להים, א-ל and י-ה-ו-ה, *Elokim, Kel* and *Hashem.* Since God continuously maintains the entire world, we can expect to see manifestations of these primary attributes wherever we look. As examples, these attributes appear in the commandments of Torah as *mishpatim, chukim* and general *mitzvos,* [2] and they appear in the concepts of Torah as wisdom, understanding and discernment.

In *mishnah* 1, the Men of the Great Assembly restored the vitality of Jewish life through measures that strengthened Torah in each of these primary dimensions. They advocated patience in judgment to address Torah as the vehicle of strict judgment. They initiated a fence for the Torah, which expresses our loving kindness towards God by doing more than He asks of us. And they encouraged a broader base of scholarship to maintain Torah in general.

Shimon HaTzaddik was a member of the Great Assembly and his *mussar* further strengthened the flow of existence through God's attributes to His Creation. Whereas the Men of the Great Assembly addressed God's association with this world at the level of rules and principles, Shimon HaTzaddik addressed the link between mankind and

---

1. The primary reference of *avodah,* service, is to the Temple service of sacrifices. Although the term includes prayer and *mitzvos*, these are also a form of offering to God our own effort, time, energy and dedication.

2. See commentary to 1:1 *supra*.

Mishpatim are the laws that build and maintain society and are a manifestation of God's quality of strict justice, conveyed by referring to Him as Elokim. The human response to *chukim* is to safeguard their observance by voluntarily doing more than strictly required and that is a human kindness that corresponds to God's kindness, as conveyed by the Name א-ל, *Kel*. The general body of *mitzvos* corresponds to God's general appearance which we convey by the Tetragrammaton

א/ג

[ג] אַנְטִיגְנוֹס אִישׁ סוֹכוֹ קִבֵּל מִשִּׁמְעוֹן
הַצַּדִּיק. הוּא הָיָה אוֹמֵר: אַל תִּהְיוּ
כַּעֲבָדִים הַמְשַׁמְּשִׁין אֶת הָרַב עַל מְנָת לְקַבֵּל

God through the *practice* of Torah. He identified the areas of human action that link our existence to God's attributes. The "service of God" refers to the sacrificial service and that seemingly harsh commandment is a link to God's attribute of strict justice. The two areas are so interrelated that the Sanhedrin — the Rabbinical Supreme Court — convened in the Temple, which also housed the Altar. The opposite quality is "kindness" and human kindness evokes the flow of Divine kindness. "Torah" is the total body of Torah and links us to the full manifestation of God in this world.

The Relationship of Mishnah 2 to the Other Mishnayos

Shimon HaTzaddik is described as one of the *remaining* members of the Great Assembly because he lived in an era when most of the Men of the Great Assembly had already passed on. The chain of Torah no longer resided with that community of righteous men, whose association was inherently graced by a special sanctity. Shimon's role in the chain of Torah tradition now rested on his personal righteousness, as would be the case for all of those leaders who would follow after him.

The *mussar* issued in each generation is a reflection of the rabbis who imparted that *mussar*. In the era of the Great Assembly, leadership was provided by a community of rabbis. Fittingly, their *mussar* was extensive in scope and restored the wholeness of mankind by strengthening Torah.[1] The *mussar* of Shimon HaTzaddik, as a member of that assembly, was equally extensive in scope but it was proferred from the perspective of the world that Torah supports. His *mussar* served as the basis of the *mussar* of Antignos and the subsequent pairs of leaders, who addressed our service of the Creator more specifically.

Mishnah 3

With the metaphor of "servants who serve their master," Antignos of Socho addresses our service of God. His *mussar* applies to everything we do, because all of our activities should be directed towards serving God.

---

1. Torah is rooted in God's essence. It is the link between God and mankind, through which life flows from Him to us. Hence, Torah is higher than this world, for it embraces and influences this world.

3. Antignos, leader of Socho, received the tradition from Shimon HaTzaddik. He used to say: Be not like servants who serve their master for the sake of

---

⊷§ **אַל תִּהְיוּ כַּעֲבָדִים הַמְשַׁמְּשִׁין אֶת הָרַב עַל מְנָת לְקַבֵּל פְּרָס** — *Be not like servants who serve . . . for the sake of receiving a reward*

How can Antignos say, "Be not like servants who serve . . . for the sake of receiving a reward," when the Torah itself is replete with offers of reward for observing *mitzvos*? One of many examples is the verse,[1]

> "Honor your father and your mother . . . in order that (לְמַעַן, *l'ma'an*) your days may be lengthened and in order that (*l'ma'an*) it may go well with you."

We may resolve this question by explaining that although the word *l'ma'an* is usually translated "in order that," it actually means *in consequence whereof*.[2] Therefore, the phrase לְמַעַן יִיטַב לָךְ correctly means, "in consequence whereof it will go well with you." Scripture means that good things will flow from God, and not that we should serve God for that reason.

We should serve God out of full-hearted love without regard to the concomitant reward, come as it may.

⊷§ **הֱווּ כַּעֲבָדִים הַמְשַׁמְּשִׁין אֶת הָרַב שֶׁלֹּא עַל מְנָת לְקַבֵּל פְּרָס** — *be like servants who serve their master not for the sake of receiving a reward*

This *mishnah* appears to be at odds with a Talmudic dictum[3] that implies there is nothing improper with doing a *mitzvah* in the hope of receiving a favorable result:

> If one says, "[I donate] this money to charity in order that my son will live" or "in order that I will merit life in the World to Come," that person [remains] fully righteous.

---

1. *Devarim* 5:16.

2. Maharal proves that the correct translation of לְמַעַן is *in consequence whereof*, from the verse לְמַעַן סְפוֹת הָרָוָה (*Devarim* 29:18) . To translate the verse "*in order that* the accidental sins be added to the deliberate sins" would be untenable. The verse surely means "*in consequence whereof*, the accidental sins will be added to the deliberate sins." See Ramban *ad loc*.

3. *Bava Basra* 10b.

א/ג פְּרָס; אֶלָּא הֱווּ כַּעֲבָדִים הַמְשַׁמְּשִׁין אֶת הָרַב שֶׁלֹּא עַל מְנָת לְקַבֵּל פְּרָס; וִיהִי מוֹרָא שָׁמַיִם עֲלֵיכֶם.

The Talmud means that it is minimally acceptable to serve God and hope for a benefit. At the other end of the spectrum, Antignos tells us that serving God out of love is the principal way to serve Him. The Talmud does not consider it wrong to serve God for such rewards as a long and good life, because God wants us to have those good things. Similarly, the intention that his son might live, or that he himself might share in eternal life, also aligns with God's will. Therefore, a person who wants good health in return for his donation to charity is pursuing God's will and remains fully righteous.

Although this person has not compromised his righteousness or piety, he has not enhanced it, either. Such a person does not achieve the lofty stature of one who serves God purely out of love, as Antignos advocates.

---

§ הֱווּ כַּעֲבָדִים הַמְשַׁמְּשִׁין אֶת הָרַב שֶׁלֹּא עַל מְנָת לְקַבֵּל פְּרָס —
*be like servants who serve their master not
for the sake of receiving a reward*

Antignos uses this metaphor to convey that the proper motive for serving God is the love of God, but why did he not explicitly tell us to serve God out of love? The reason is that some kinds of love are self-centered. Indeed, even love that comes from kindnesses already received falls short of the mark. Although love that is based on kindnesses received or expected is truly love, this *mishnah* promotes a higher ideal; namely, that the basis of service should be one's love for God. Fulfilling His commandments should be done with a love that is based upon recognition of His greatness; namely, that He is truth and His words and *mitzvos* are truth.

---

§ וִיהִי מוֹרָא שָׁמַיִם עֲלֵיכֶם — *And let the awe of Heaven be upon you.*

Our love of God must not be allowed to compromise our fear of God. When we love someone our heart is so tightly bound to the one we love that feelings of fear are dissolved. For example, a person who loves the Holy One will feel happiness when he hears His Name. That joy will nullify any fear, but in fact we *should* be fearful and alarmed upon

22 / פרקי אבות

receiving a reward; instead be like servants who
serve their master not for the sake of receiving a
reward. And let the awe of Heaven be upon you.

---

hearing His Name. Therefore Antignos says: "Although I have advocated
love, do not consider the Lord, Blessed is He, as your friend with
Whom you are familiar; but consider that He is in the Heavens and you
are on earth."

The love of God and the fear of God are different aspects of the same
thing and therefore they should go hand in hand.[1] In practice, however,
it is difficult to feel both love and fear at the same time, and as we
develop our love of God, we must reinforce our fear of God as well.

⋅§ וִיהִי מוֹרָא שָׁמַיִם עֲלֵיכֶם — *And let the awe of* **Heaven** *be upon you.*

Why did he choose the expression "the awe of *Heaven,*" rather than
"the awe of *God*"?

The feeling of awe comes with the realization that God, on Whom we
depend for our existence, is extremely distant. When we consider that
the Holy One, Blessed is He, is in the Heavens, while we are on the earth,
then the fear of Heaven grips us and the love of God will not nullify it.

Fear of God is often called "Fear of Heaven" (*yiras shamayim*)
because the remoteness of Heaven instills fear. We never refer to the love
of God as the "love of Heaven" (*ahavas shamayim*) because feelings of
love come from envisioning ourselves as clinging to Him.

The Relationship of Mishnah 3 to the Other Mishnayos

Antignos of Socho received the chain of Torah transmission from
Shimon HaTzaddik, and his teachings logically follow those of his
teacher. In *mishnah* 2 Shimon HaTzaddik identified the pillars of the
world, a world which was created for use by mankind to serve the
Creator. In *mishnah* 3 Antignos clarifies that we must serve the Creator
with both love and fear. Ultimately, love of God and fear of God share a
common root[2] and should not be separated.

It is noteworthy that Antignos is the one to stress that serving God

---

1. Love of God is based on the recognition that He is the source of all existence. Fear
of God is based on the recognition that our existence is inherently and totally
dependent on Him (*Nesivos Olam*, *Nesiv Yiras Hashem*, Chapter 1).
2. Namely, the awareness that He is the source of existence and our existence flows
from Him.

[ד] יוֹסֵי בֶּן יוֹעֶזֶר, אִישׁ צְרֵדָה, וְיוֹסֵי בֶּן יוֹחָנָן,
אִישׁ יְרוּשָׁלַיִם, קִבְּלוּ מֵהֶם. יוֹסֵי בֶּן יוֹעֶזֶר,
אִישׁ צְרֵדָה, אוֹמֵר: יְהִי בֵיתְךָ בֵּית וַעַד
לַחֲכָמִים; וֶהֱוֵי מִתְאַבֵּק בַּעֲפַר רַגְלֵיהֶם; וֶהֱוֵי
שׁוֹתֶה בַצָּמָא אֶת דִּבְרֵיהֶם.

requires a combination of love and fear. He was the last one in the chain
of Torah transmission who personally embraced the service of God in its
entire scope, from love to fear. Subsequent generations in the chain of
Torah transmission continued to decline in stature, until spiritual leadership had to be provided by *pairs* of rabbis. As we shall see in the
following *mishnayos*, one of the pair always directs his *mussar* toward
the love of God and the other directs his *mussar* toward the fear of God.
Antignos is the last person who fully integrated the love and fear of God.

Mishnah 4

The Decline of the Generations

The Men of the Great Assembly, which included Shimon HaTzaddik,
were a link in the chain of Torah transmission, both collectively and as
individuals. After they had passed on, Shimon HaTzaddik carried on in
this role alone. The Torah then passed to Antignos, who had never been
a member of the Great Assembly, and he fulfilled the role of Torah transmission entirely on his own. The next link in the Torah tradition consists
of a *pair* of rabbis, who share the role jointly and not individually.

The change in leadership mirrored the ongoing decline in national
unity. The role that had been filled by a unified leadership was now a
divided and shared responsibility. This divided leadership, shared by
pairs of rabbis, was fitting for the era of the Second Temple, a time that
was marked by growing factionalism within society.

The advice of these great personalities reflected their stature. Antignos, who served as leader by himself, gave advice[1] that addressed the
individual in and of himself. The rabbis of this *mishnah* shared the
leadership responsibility and their advice is in the context of the family
unit. No one fulfills his entire role in life alone; one needs a house, a
wife,[2] and members of the household.

---

1. *Supra, mishnah* 3.
2. The reference is to Yose ben Yochanan's statement in the next *mishnah*.

4. Yose ben Yoezer, leader of Tz'redah, and Yose ben Yochanan, leader of Jerusalem, received (the Torah) from them. Yose ben Yoezer says: Let your house be a meeting place for sages; and sit in the dust of their feet; and drink in their words thirstily.

---

§ יְהִי בֵיתְךָ בֵּית וַעַד לַחֲכָמִים — *Let your house be a meeting place for sages*

Yose ben Yoezer enjoins that one's household should be a repository of wisdom. The home is a model of the human being and the wisdom of sages enhances the home just as wisdom enriches a person. Indeed, a home that is holy, Godly and honorable is a firm foundation for our own worthiness.

---

§ וֶהֱוֵי מִתְאַבֵּק בַּעֲפַר רַגְלֵיהֶם — *and sit in the dust of their feet*

Unless you are a scholar of equal stature, do not depreciate the prestige (honor) of scholarship by treating the sages as peers; rather, you should subordinate yourself to them. The feet are the lowest part of a person, and the image of sitting by their feet conveys that anything you have in common with them is at the simplest level. You are only associating with them and not joining them on an equal basis.

---

§ וֶהֱוֵי שׁוֹתֶה בַצָּמָא אֶת דִּבְרֵיהֶם — *and drink in their words thirstily.*

A person who is thirsty is חָסֵר, *wanting, in need.* By drinking, this need is met and he is שָׁלֵם, *complete.* In the same way, a person who lacks knowledge is חָסֵר, and with knowledge he becomes שָׁלֵם. We should satisfy our intellectual thirst with the same degree of enthusiasm that we apply to satisfying our physical thirst.

Summary

Yose ben Yoezer enjoins that our house should be a place of wisdom and wise people. In this way, the house parallels the physical body that is home to the intellect. The intellectual need for wisdom must be pursued as vigorously as the physical need for water.

An additional message of this *mishnah* is that the Torah scholar fulfills an intrinsic need of society just as the intellect fulfills an intrinsic need of the individual.

[ה] יוֹסֵי בֶּן יוֹחָנָן, אִישׁ יְרוּשָׁלַיִם, אוֹמֵר: יְהִי
בֵיתְךָ פָּתוּחַ לָרְוָחָה; וְיִהְיוּ עֲנִיִּים בְּנֵי בֵיתֶךָ;
וְאַל תַּרְבֶּה שִׂיחָה עִם הָאִשָּׁה. בְּאִשְׁתּוֹ אָמְרוּ,
קַל וָחֹמֶר בְּאֵשֶׁת חֲבֵרוֹ. מִכַּאן אָמְרוּ חֲכָמִים: כָּל
הַמַּרְבֶּה שִׂיחָה עִם הָאִשָּׁה גּוֹרֵם רָעָה לְעַצְמוֹ,
וּבוֹטֵל מִדִּבְרֵי תוֹרָה, וְסוֹפוֹ יוֹרֵשׁ גֵּיהִנֹּם.

Mishnah 5

This *mishnah* continues the theme of how to sanctify our home. The advice in this *mishnah* builds the sanctity of the home on three fronts. It deals with those who are outside the household; with the makeup of the household itself; and with the innermost core of the household, namely, one's wife.

יְהִי בֵיתְךָ פָּתוּחַ לָרְוָחָה — *Let your house be open wide*

Opening our doors to those who are outside the household brings merit into the home. Neighbors feel comfortable to come in for company or to borrow things. Merchants who pass by will find a welcome at this house as they try to earn a livelihood.

וְיִהְיוּ עֲנִיִּים בְּנֵי בֵיתֶךָ — *treat the poor as members of your household*

Members of the household also bring merit to the home. When we invite the poor into our home regularly, they become like part of the household and can be supported with honor and dignity.

וְאַל תַּרְבֶּה שִׂיחָה עִם הָאִשָּׁה — *and do not converse excessively with a woman*

The third and principal element of the household is one's wife.
The premise of this *mishnah* is that a holy person orients his life towards God, and not towards himself. Talking with women is self-centered because men enjoy interaction with women. Therefore a man's sanctity is maintained by not talking excessively with his wife.
Talking "excessively" means talking without a need. Talking with one's wife as necessary is not at all negative.

5. Yose ben Yochanan, leader of Jerusalem, says: Let your house be open wide; treat the poor as members of your household; and do not converse excessively with a woman. They said this even about one's own wife; surely it applies to another's wife. Consequently, the Sages said: Anyone who converses excessively with a woman causes evil to himself, neglects Torah study, and will eventually inherit Gehinnom.

◆§ בְּאִשְׁתּוֹ אָמְרוּ; קַל וָחֹמֶר בְּאֵשֶׁת חֲבֵרוֹ ◆§ — *They said this even about one's own wife; surely it applies to another's wife.*

This statement is a commentary by the redactor of the *mishnah*, on the earlier enactment, "do not converse excessively with a woman." That original enactment was necessary despite the wife's central role in the family. How much more so must a man avoid excessive talk with other women, who do not contribute to his household.

◆§ הַמַּרְבֶּה שִׂיחָה עִם הָאִשָּׁה . . . וּבוֹטֵל מִדִּבְרֵי תוֹרָה ◆§ — *Anyone who converses excessively with a woman . . . neglects Torah study*

All idle talk results in neglecting Torah study; what is the point of this particular example?

In fact, excessive conversation with women causes a man to neglect Torah study more than other idle speech does. When one is finished with idle speech, he can return to his studies. In contrast, a man finds it difficult to return to Torah study after lengthy conversation with a woman, because man cleaves to woman by nature.[1]

◆§ כָּל הַמַּרְבֶּה שִׂיחָה עִם הָאִשָּׁה גּוֹרֵם רָעָה לְעַצְמוֹ ◆§ — *Anyone who converses excessively with a woman causes evil to himself*

What is the nature of the "evil" that he causes? Evil is that which negates existence. It is the opposite of "good," which implies that something is worthy of enduring existence.[2]

---

1. *Bereishis* 2:24: "Therefore, a man . . . will cleave to his wife."
2. See *supra*, commentary to *mishnah* 2 for more detail.

How can talking excessively with his wife create evil for a man?

Men and women each have a unique role to fulfill. The husband, through his knowledge of Torah, establishes the spiritual guidelines for the household, while the wife engages in bringing those principles to life within the home. The *mishnah* does not imply that the wife's role is an inferior one at all;[1] however, the man who neglects his own role, being drawn into his wife's role through superfluous conversation, will fall short of his purpose in life.

Purpose is an essential characteristic of existence.[2] The definitive characteristic of evil is that it negates existence; it opposes life. The "evil" that he causes himself is that of not living up to the purpose for which he was created. He betrays his special potential.

There are areas in which the husband gives direction and other areas in which the wife gives direction.[3] He should accept his wife's advice on matters regarding the household, since she is the principal of the home. He should also consider his wife's opinion on worldly matters, since they share that domain. In spiritual matters, however, he must be careful not to compromise Torah principles in deference to her opinion.

The *mishnah* does not intend to diminish a man's love for his wife, for he should love her as he loves himself.

---

§ וְסוֹפוֹ יוֹרֵשׁ גֵּיהִנָּם — *and will eventually inherit Gehinnom*

What is so detrimental about talking to women that it would cause a person to inherit *Gehinnom*?

The word *Gehinnom* refers to a deficiency in existence and our existence is ultimately defined by our purpose in life.[4] *Gehinnom* is the destiny of one who has compromised his purpose in life;[5] it is the destiny of one who has been distracted by and influenced by matters that are not intended for him. The female presence is a powerful force of distraction for men. For example, the sages say[6] that it is better for a

---

1. See Maharal's *Drush al HaTorah*. He states that women are inherently more suited towards and predisposed to the World to Come than are men and hence they achieve eternal reward more readily than men.
2. See the author's introduction, "Elements of Maharal's Philosophy."
3. *Bava Metziah* 59a.
4. See the author's introduction, "Elements of Maharal's Philosophy."
5. See Maharal's *Nesivos Olam*, *Nesiv Yiras HaShem*, Chapter 4 page 32, for a fascinating application of this definition of *Gehinnom* as a reference to not fulfilling one's potential: One who studies Torah and does not fulfill the *mitzvos* is in the *Gehinnom* of not performing *mitzvos* which everyone is capable of; and in the *Gehinnom* of not practicing *mitzvos* in accordance with his advanced knowledge of Torah.
6. *Berachos* 61a. The physical risk of the lion is a metaphor for the spiritual risk of sexual desire; the point of contrast is the likelihood of hazard.

man to walk behind a lion than to walk behind a woman. They mean that the danger posed by a lion is circumstantial: It may or may not attack. By contrast, it is certain that a man's absorption with spiritual matters will be broken when walking behind a woman.

The Home as a Metaphor for the Human Being

As noted before, this pair of rabbinical leaders advises us to organize our household in a manner that parallels the human being. Yose ben Yoezer adjures us to foster an intellectual atmosphere at home by inviting sages to meet in our house. That corresponds to the intellect, *sechel*, that governs the body and the very subject parallels Yose ben Yoezer's own position as President, ruling over the Rabbinical Court.

Yose ben Yochanan continues that theme by comparing the master of the house to the spirit that animates the body. The head of the house should help outsiders such as neighbors, and support the poor by bringing them into the household. This parallels the spirit, which maintains the vitality of the body and brings life to both the external limbs and to the internal organs.

Although the spirit is closely linked to the limbs, it is not the same entity as the body. In the same way, it is inappropriate for the husband to be excessively attached to his wife through superfluous and idle talk. If the spirit were to somehow merge with the body, it would no longer be a spirit! So too, the man who permits his role in the household to merge with his wife's role causes serious spiritual harm to himself.

The Relationship of Mishnah 5 to the Following Mishnayos

Yose ben Yoezer and Yose ben Yochanan were now the leaders of the generation and they filled that role together, as a pair. As would be the case for the four subsequent pairs of leaders as well, they were respectively the *Nasi*, President, and the *Av Beis Din*, Head of the Supreme Rabbinical Court. Their advice set the paradigm for the pairs of rabbis in each generation, in the following way. The first of the pair directs his comments at strengthening the service of God through the love of God, while the other strengthens it through the fear of heaven. Taken together, the pair provides advice that covers the service of God completely.

It is not always obvious how to distinguish whether advice is directed towards the love of God or the fear of God, and the following rule is helpful. *Love* of God leads to active performance of *mitzvos*. *Fear* of God occasions caution and concern not to transgress a forbidden act.

Of each pair of rabbis, the President of the Rabbinical Court provides positive leadership, encouraging us to fulfill *mitzvos* out of love, while the Head of the Court warns against transgressions. For example, Yose

[ו] יְהוֹשֻׁעַ בֶּן פְּרַחְיָה וְנִתַּאי הָאַרְבֵּלִי קִבְּלוּ **א/ו**
מֵהֶם. יְהוֹשֻׁעַ בֶּן פְּרַחְיָה אוֹמֵר: עֲשֵׂה לְךָ
רַב; וּקְנֵה לְךָ חָבֵר, וֶהֱוֵי דָן אֶת כָּל הָאָדָם
לְכַף זְכוּת.

ben Yoezer promotes the love of wisdom and of sages, which supplements the love of God.[1]

Yose ben Yochanan advises opening up our house to neighbors, guests and the poor. Such advice reflects the fear of God, because one who fears God is humble and sensitive to the needs of the poor — whom life has humbled — and to the needs of itinerant guests. If one is not moved to help the poor, he is a sinful person who has cast off the fear of God. Yose ben Yochanan's *mussar* averts the sin of stinginess, for one who begrudges sharing his wealth sins against man and God. He also cautions against excessive talk with women, since that act of levity is a rejection of the fear of Heaven.

Mishnah 6

The preceding pair of rabbis focused on the household, the inner circle of our relationships. This pair of rabbis broadens their teachers' theme, as they address relationships outside the home.

> ⋟ עֲשֵׂה לְךָ רַב; וּקְנֵה לְךָ חָבֵר, וֶהֱוֵי דָן אֶת כָּל הָאָדָם לְכַף זְכוּת ⋞
> *Accept a* Torah teacher *upon yourself; acquire a*
> friend *for yourself, and judge* everyone *favorably.*

How are these three things — establishing a teacher, acquiring a friend, and judging people charitably — related to each other? These three pieces of advice deal with close relationships. The closest relationship outside of family is with one's *Rav*, the teacher of Torah; the next is a friend; and then comes all other people.

Alternatively, the three parts of the *mishnah* can be seen as directing our interactions with three relative segments of society. There are those who are accomplished above our own level, who could be suitable as a teacher. There are those at our own level, our peers. Finally, there are those who are less accomplished than we are, and we must assess them favorably and not disparagingly.

---

1. *Kesubos* 111b: "Cling to the sages and their students, and it is as if you cling to the Divine Presence."

פרקי אבות / 30

6. Yehoshua ben Perachyah and Nittai of Arbel received the tradition from them. Yehoshua ben Perachyah says: Accept a Torah teacher upon yourself; acquire a friend for yourself, and judge everyone favorably.

⧳ עֲשֵׂה לְךָ רַב; וּקְנֵה לְךָ חָבֵר — Accept a Torah teacher upon yourself; acquire a friend for yourself

---

We should be receptive to learn from a Torah scholar who has something to offer, even if he is not learned enough to serve as our main teacher. It is worth the effort required to accept that person as a teacher, whether we learn much or little from him.

Why is the word "acquire" used in connection with getting a friend, whereas "accept" is used in connection with getting a Torah teacher?

A friend is "acquired" in the sense that he will do things for his friend and *vice versa*. In other words, the friendship is owned in partnership between the two friends. By contrast, the relationship between a Torah teacher, *Rav*, and his student is never such that the *Rav* could be called an acquisition of the student.

In both cases, the use of an active expression, such as "accept" or "acquire," carries a powerful message. The *mishnah* tells us: Make the effort to create the "friend" or "teacher" relationship, even with a person who is not so well suited to you that a relationship would form naturally. It is better to have a friend than to be alone.

⧳ וֶהֱוֵי דָן אֶת כָּל הָאָדָם לְכַף זְכוּת — and judge everyone favorably

---

We should give a positive overall evaluation to all people, and be prepared to overlook things when necessary. Do not rebuff a person by saying that he is unworthy.

⧳ עֲשֵׂה לְךָ רַב; וּקְנֵה לְךָ חָבֵר, וֶהֱוֵי דָן אֶת כָּל הָאָדָם לְכַף זְכוּת — Accept a Torah teacher upon yourself; acquire a friend for yourself, and judge everyone favorably.

Another approach explains the *mishnah* as referring to one's principal *Rav* and to a lifelong friend, and the expression "judge everyone favorably" also refers to those two people. In this interpretation, the use of the strong terms "accept" and "acquire" teaches that it takes effort to

[ז] נִתַּאי הָאַרְבֵּלִי אוֹמֵר: הַרְחֵק מִשָּׁכֵן רָע, וְאַל תִּתְחַבֵּר לָרָשָׁע, וְאַל תִּתְיָאֵשׁ מִן הַפֻּרְעָנוּת.

cultivate and maintain a close relationship. Judge your teacher and your friend favorably and overlook those offenses that are bound to arise when people spend so much time together. By assuming the best of your friend or your teacher, you will prevent a rift and preserve the relationship.

Summary

This *mishnah* deals with general social conduct, for we live as part of a kindred people, whether rabbis, peers or others. Successful participation in society flows from the love of God, as we draw people close because our love for God includes the love of the people He created.

In practice, this means that we should accept our religious superior as a *Rav*, even if he is not perfect. We should accept our peers as companions, even if they do not completely meet our own standards. Finally, we should not judge another as evil because of a religious or other shortcoming. Rather, judge everyone favorably and do not let such differences keep you apart.

The basic rule is: Draw people near and do not rebuff them.

Mishnah 7

In the previous *mishnah* Yehoshua ben Perachyah promoted stronger social ties, based on the love for people that is part of the love of God. In this *mishnah*, Nittai of Arbel complements the *mussar* of his colleague from the perspective of the fear of Heaven and advises that we avoid harmful relationships.

The *mishnah* warns that one will be harmed by associating with bad people.

୶§ הַרְחֵק מִשָּׁכֵן רָע — *Distance yourself from a bad neighbor*

This is a reference to the rabbinical dictum,[1] "Woe to an evil person and woe to his neighbor."

---

1. *Nega'im* 12:6.

7. Nittai of Arbel says: Distance yourself from a bad neighbor, and do not associate with a wicked person, and do not despair of retribution.

וְאַל תִּתְחַבֵּר לָרָשָׁע — *and do not associate with a wicked person*

This point is illustrated by the verse,[1]

Then Eliezer ben Dodavahu of Mareshah prophesied against Yehoshafat, saying: "Because you have joined yourself (כְּהִתְחַבֶּרְךָ) with (the evil) Ahazyahu, God will destroy what you have done." And the ships were wrecked and they were not able to go to Tarshish.

הַרְחֵק מִשְּׁכֵן רָע וְאַל תִּתְחַבֵּר לָרָשָׁע — *Distance yourself from a bad neighbor, and do not associate with a wicked person*

We can avoid *association* with a "wicked person" by just keeping away from him. A "bad neighbor" must be actively *distanced*, since he will come to you even if you do not associate with him.

Maharal now presents two different ways to understand the phrase "and do not despair of retribution."

וְאַל תִּתְיָאֵשׁ מִן הַפֻּרְעָנוּת — *and do not despair of retribution*

One explanation sees "do not despair of retribution" as the reason behind the first part of the *mishnah*: "Distance yourself from a bad neighbor, and do not associate with a wicked person."

You might associate with evil people and think that all is well. However, the consequences could strike so suddenly that it will be too late to save yourself. Therefore, "distance yourself from an evil neighbor and do not associate with a wicked person" now, before it is too late.

וְאַל תִּתְיָאֵשׁ מִן הַפֻּרְעָנוּת — *and do not despair of retribution*

Another explanation of this statement would translate הַפֻּרְעָנוּת as referring to any harmful situation, not necessarily a retributive punishment. According to this interpretation, the entire *mishnah* tells us to be cautious and avoid danger, whether that means avoiding evil people or avoiding harmful situations.

---

1. *Divrei HaYamim II* 20:37.

א/ ח־ט

[ח] יְהוּדָה בֶּן טַבַּאי וְשִׁמְעוֹן בֶּן שָׁטַח קִבְּלוּ מֵהֶם. יְהוּדָה בֶּן טַבַּאי אוֹמֵר: אַל תַּעַשׂ עַצְמְךָ כְּעוֹרְכֵי הַדַּיָּנִין; וּכְשֶׁיִּהְיוּ בַּעֲלֵי הַדִּין עוֹמְדִים לְפָנֶיךָ, יִהְיוּ בְעֵינֶיךָ כִּרְשָׁעִים; וּכְשֶׁנִּפְטָרִים מִלְּפָנֶיךָ, יִהְיוּ בְעֵינֶיךָ כְּזַכָּאִין, כְּשֶׁקִּבְּלוּ עֲלֵיהֶם אֶת הַדִּין.

[ט] שִׁמְעוֹן בֶּן שָׁטַח אוֹמֵר: הֱוֵי מַרְבֶּה לַחֲקוֹר אֶת הָעֵדִים; וֶהֱוֵי זָהִיר בִּדְבָרֶיךָ, שֶׁמָּא מִתּוֹכָם יִלְמְדוּ לְשַׁקֵּר.

Nittai warns us to be vigilant against the death and destruction that are an integral part of this physical world. Indeed, the potential for harm presents a more imminent threat than any human neighbor because it hovers over us constantly.

We should not trust that wealth will save us from difficult times, as Haman did, for his success was reversed in the blink of an eye.

The *mishnah* tells us judiciously to **not give up** on harmful events, rather than telling us to **worry** about harmful events, because worrying about impending danger is itself an undesirable trait.

Mishnah 8

The Hebrew term translated as "lawyer" refers to anyone who tutors litigants with regard to how to formulate their arguments, or who presents the litigants' case to the judges. The *mishnah* is directed to judges, warning them not to coach the litigants in any way. Such conduct is strictly forbidden, because it could modify the outcome of a judgment.

This admonition is critical to the fair administration of justice, because it is likely, and indeed not uncommon, for a judge to be more sympathetic to one litigant than to the other.

וּכְשֶׁיִּהְיוּ בַּעֲלֵי הַדִּין עוֹמְדִים לְפָנֶיךָ, יִהְיוּ בְעֵינֶיךָ כִּרְשָׁעִים — ***and when the litigants stand before you, consider them [both] as guilty***

It is a grave error to assume that one litigant is more likely to be innocent or that one is more likely to be dishonest. Rather, the judge must consider them equally likely to be guilty or innocent. It is preferable for the judge to consider them both dishonest, because he will

8. Yehudah ben Tabbai and Shimon ben Shatach received the tradition from them. Yehudah ben Tabbai says: [When serving as a judge] do not act as a lawyer; and when the litigants stand before you, consider them [both] as guilty; but when they are dismissed from you, consider them [both] as innocent, provided they have accepted the judgment.

9. Shimon ben Shatach says: Interrogate the witnesses extensively; and be cautious with your words, lest through them they learn to lie.

---

then scrutinize each one's claims and probe the case in depth.

---

§• יִהְיוּ בְעֵינֶיךָ כְּרַבָּאִין — *consider them [both] as innocent*

Maharal seems to have had an alternative text[1] which reads: 'יִהְיוּ בְעֵינֶיךָ כְּצַדִּיקִים, *consider them [both] as righteous."*

Every respectable citizen comes to court in the belief that his case is just. Therefore it takes a truly righteous person to accept that an unfavorable judgment has been just.

How can a judge reasonably consider both parties guilty and then consider them both righteous?

While the case is in progress both parties are equally likely to be guilty, because there is no reason to consider one litigant different from the other and they are both engaged in the dispute. When the case has been settled without antagonism, and the litigants have accepted the judgment, the judge can see that the monetary dispute was an honest and dispassionate misunderstanding and that they have been righteous from the beginning.

Mishnah 9

Shimon ben Shatach continues to address the point of the previous *mishnah,* as he advocates the pursuit of righteous judgment. It is important to be thorough when examining a witness, for he might embellish a detail or withhold a detail upon which everything depends. If the judge does not choose his words carefully, a witness could discern

---

1. Cambridge manuscript, cited in שנויי נוסחאות *ad loc.* This version provides a more consistent parallel between the terms כְּצַדִּיקִים and כְּרְשָׁעִים.

[י] שְׁמַעְיָה וְאַבְטַלְיוֹן קִבְּלוּ מֵהֶם. שְׁמַעְיָה אוֹמֵר: אֱהַב אֶת הַמְּלָאכָה; וּשְׂנָא אֶת הָרַבָּנוּת; וְאַל תִּתְוַדַּע לָרָשׁוּת.

the direction of the examination from the questions and alter the testimony to suit his purpose.

We said before that the first rabbi of each pair advises from the perspective of the love of God, and enjoins some positive action. The second of the pair brings the perspective of the fear of Heaven and cautions against violating a *mitzvah*. This pair of rabbis follows that pattern as well, since judgment has aspects of both love and fear.

Yehudah ben Tabbai focused on the love of God in his statement: "when the litigants stand before you, consider them [both] as guilty; but when they are dismissed from you, consider them [both] as innocent." This supports the *mitzvah* "in righteousness shall you judge your neighbor."[1]

Shimon ben Shatach focused on the fear of God in his statement: "Interrogate the witnesses extensively; and be cautious with your words, lest through them they learn to lie." This advice avoids the transgression "You shall not commit a perversion of justice in judgment."[2]

Mishnah 10

The *mussar* of this pair of rabbis is directed toward the spiritual leaders, so that their conduct will fortify the love and fear of God within the community.

◆§ שְׁמַעְיָה וְאַבְטַלְיוֹן — *Shemayah and Avtalyon*

Shemayah and Avtalyon were descended from converts to Judaism.[3] Those[4] who say that they themselves were converts are mistaken, for then they would not have qualified for appointment to the offices of President and Head of the Rabbinical Court.[5] Rather, they were descended from converts, but their mothers were of Israelite descent.

1. *Vayikra* 19:15.
2. *Ibid.*
3. *Gittin* 57b; *Yoma* 71b.
4. *Rambam, Introduction to Mishneh Torah.*
5. *Yevamos* 45b: All appointments must be from your brethren.

10. Shemayah and Avtalyon received [the Torah] from them. Shemayah says: Love work; despise holding office; and do not become overly familiar with the government.

⊷§ — אֱהַב אֶת הַמְּלָאכָה; וּשְׂנָא אֶת הָרַבָּנוּת §⊷
Love work; despise holding office

Shemayah deals first with the love of God, as the Rabbis say,[1]

Heaven should be beloved through you. A man should study the Written and Oral Law, and apprentice to scholars; he should speak gently with people. His purchasing and business dealings should be pleasant; he should conduct his business in good faith. What do people say of such a person? Fortunate is this one who learned Torah! How beautiful are his ways, how proper is his conduct!

Similarly, a Torah scholar brings honor to Torah and honor to God and he inspires the love of God, when he is not dependent on people.

The Rabbis tell us[2] that people were highly resentful of Moshe Rabbeinu, claiming that he was living comfortably through use of public funds. In truth, he was independently wealthy, but if people could unjustly resent Moshe, how do you think they view rabbinical leaders who actually are supported by public funds! Communal support undermines the honor of the Torah, and if Torah scholars did not accept this support, the esteem for Torah among the community at large would rise to great heights. Furthermore, rabbis would not show favoritism and they would be able to reprove the public, whose transgressions are their responsibility. Now,[3] however, because they are dependent on the community, every rabbi has acquired for himself a master.

⊷§ — אֱהַב אֶת הַמְּלָאכָה; וּשְׂנָא אֶת הָרַבָּנוּת §⊷
Love work; despise holding office

Positions of authority result in the opposite of loving work, for it shortens life in this world. The Rabbis said,[4]

---

1. *Yoma* 86a.

2. *Shekalim,* Chapter 5, *halachah* 2.

3. Maharal lived over 400 years ago. Maharal himself did maintain his independence and did repeatedly reprove the community on matters of *lashon hara* and of drinking non-kosher wine.

4. *Pesachim* 87b.

Woe to authority, for it buries those who hold it; there is not a single prophet who did not outlive four kings.

Furthermore, Rabbi Yochanan said,[1]

Why did Yosef die before his brothers?[2] Because he conducted himself in a position of authority.

⊷§ אֱהַב אֶת הַמְּלָאכָה — Love work

Do not imagine that work is dishonorable. Just the opposite is true, for labor brings a person honor. The Rabbis said,[3]

Rabbi Yehudah used to carry a jug on his shoulder (to sit on) when he went to the *Bais HaMedrash.* He would say, "Great is work, for it honors the worker."

In other words, a leader should not think that laboring for his own needs is beneath his dignity. Such labor actually brings honor, and spares him the disgrace of being despised by the people on whom he would have been dependent.

⊷§ אֱהַב אֶת הַמְּלָאכָה — Love work

The sages extolled the virtue of labor, especially when we love to work rather than just accepting it. The Rabbis said:[4]

Greater is the one who enjoys the effort of his own hands than one who fears Heaven. It is written regarding one who benefits from his own efforts, "You eat of the labor of your hands; you will be happy and it will be well with you,"[5] meaning that "you will be happy" in this world and "it will be well with you" in the World to Come. By contrast, of the one who fears Heaven, it is written only, "Happy is the man who fears God."[6]

The person who is self-reliant and self-supporting — who is satisfied and happy with what God has granted him to earn and accomplish — is not in need of other people for support and not in need of additional possessions. That person lacks nothing and is by definition complete, שָׁלֵם.

We exist in two worlds: this world and the World to Come. The quality

---

1. *Sotah* 13b.
2. Although he was the second youngest of 12 sons.
3. *Nedarim* 49b.
4. *Berachos* 8a.
5. *Tehillim* 128:3.
6. *Ibid.* 112:1.

of self-sufficiency is integral to our fullest possible existence, because the more dependent we are on others, the less complete is our personal existence. Consequently, a person who is self-sufficient is fully satisfied with this world, for he does not want more than he can earn by himself. Furthermore, he has developed the personal substance that is the essence of existence in the World to Come.

Why is a person who enjoys the effort of his own hands greater than one who fears Heaven? Because the joy that comes from personal fulfillment fosters love for He Who is the Source of happiness, and the love of God is superior to the fear of God.[1] If we know only the fear of God, without the love of God that accompanies well-earned joy, we are only partly alive in either world.

In summary, the message of "love work" is: "Enjoy and find complete satisfaction in the fruit of your own labor," for this is the key to happiness in this world and in the World to Come.

וּשְׂנָא אֶת הָרַבָּנוּת — *despise holding office*

Community leadership develops the incumbent to some extent, but there are also negative consequences to the position. For one, labor brings a person honor and saves him from many sins,[2] while holding office is an obstacle to working and it brings about many sins.[3] Furthermore, leaders are accountable for every misdemeanor of the community, deliberate or accidental, that they could have prevented.

וְאַל תִּתְוַדַּע לָרָשׁוּת — *and do not become overly familiar with the government*

This *mishnah* discusses social relationships which are less personal than those addressed above, such as a judge and litigants.[4] Although

---

1. With regard to love of God it is written (*Shemos* 20:6): "Performing kindness for thousands of generations of those who love Me."

With regard to fear of God it is written (*Devarim* 7:9): "He keeps. . . kindness. . . for a thousand generations, for those who guard His *mitzvos*." The word "*guard*" implies fear of transgression, and the reward endures for only 1,000 generations. Therefore, love has at least twice the reward of fear, as the minimum implication of the word "thousands," in the first passage, is 2,000.

2. These are not specified, but would include: receiving honor at another's expense; undermining the honor of Torah; receiving something to which he has no right; and the general loss of self-sufficiency, which is an important quality.

3. These also are not specified but would include, in addition to those listed above: hearing slanderous talk, slighting people's feelings, seeking his own and not God's glory, flattering important people, harboring suspicions and giving incorrect advice.

4. *Supra, mishnah* 8 and *mishnah* 9.

[יא] אַבְטַלְיוֹן אוֹמֵר: חֲכָמִים, הִזָּהֲרוּ בְדִבְרֵיכֶם, שֶׁמָּא תָחוּבוּ חוֹבַת גָּלוּת וְתִגְלוּ לִמְקוֹם מַיִם הָרָעִים. וְיִשְׁתּוּ הַתַּלְמִידִים הַבָּאִים אַחֲרֵיכֶם וְיָמוּתוּ, וְנִמְצָא שֵׁם שָׁמַיִם מִתְחַלֵּל.

---

that is a fairly impersonal relationship, the judicial system does seek the welfare of the community. In contrast, this *mishnah* discusses our relationship with people in power, who seek only their own welfare. Furthermore, the power and intimidation they exercise over their subordinates minimize the closeness of any relationship with them.

◆§ **וְאַל תִּתְוַדַּע לָרָשׁוּת** — *and do not become overly familiar with the government*[1]

Since officials seek only that which is to their own benefit, no good will come of associating with them, but evil will. Office is an entity unto itself, and hence those in power are concerned with themselves and stand aloof from those who are not in power.

Consequently, people in power approach an individual only when it is to their own benefit. That person can be certain that he will not gain from such an affiliation.

Love work; despise holding office; and do not become overly familiar with the government.

The progression of these ideas is:

- Work makes a person whole, in this world and the next.
- Holding a position of authority also rounds out a person, but it shortens existence in this world and the benefit is canceled by the loss.
- Associating with the government is never a worthwhile consideration, as we find[2] that those in government strike up a close relationship with a person solely for their own benefit and not at all for the best interests and welfare of that individual.

---

1. The author wishes to observe that the nature of government assumed in the *mishnah* and the commentary is more characteristic of governments and power structures that are not held accountable to the people and perhaps less characteristic of contemporary democracy where those in power must depend on pleasing their constituents in order to remain in office.

2. *Infra,* 2:3. Beware of rulers, for they befriend someone only for their own benefit; they act friendly when it benefits them, but they do not stand by someone in his time of need.

11. Avtalyon says: Scholars, be cautious with your words, for you may incur the penalty of exile and be banished to a place of evil waters [heresy]. The disciples who follow you there may drink and die, and consequently the Name of Heaven will be desecrated.

Mishnah 11

As we noted previously, the first rabbi of each pair gives positive advice, relevant to the love of God, while the second gives advice to avoid a transgression, in the spirit of fearing God. When Shemayah advised rabbis, in *mishnah* 10, to love labor and not to benefit from others, he wished to foster people's love for God and His Torah. In this *mishnah,* Avtalyon rounds out that advice by cautioning against behavior that could cause His Name to be profaned.

◈§ חֲכָמִים, הִזָּהֲרוּ בְדִבְרֵיכֶם — *Scholars,*
be cautious with your words

The concern lies with teaching students who do not have proper qualities of character. They may distort the *Rav*'s words, and the Name of God will ultimately be profaned.

◈§ שֶׁמָּא . . . וְתִגְלוּ לְמְקוֹם מַיִם הָרָעִים — *for you may . . .*
be banished to a place of evil waters [heresy]

"Evil waters" is a metaphor for unworthy students. This concern is associated specifically with being exiled, because that is where students of unrefined character are likely to be encountered. Furthermore, in his home town the *Rav* would be in a position to be more discriminating and selective in accepting only students of upright character.

◈§ וְיִשְׁתּוּ הַתַּלְמִידִים הַבָּאִים אַחֲרֵיכֶם וְיָמוּתוּ — *the disciples*
who follow you there may drink and die

The metaphor of *drinking* evil waters refers to the next generation of students, who will learn distorted versions of the *Rav*'s words from the first group of unworthy students. The metaphor of dying means that they

א/יב

[יב] הִלֵּל וְשַׁמַּאי קִבְּלוּ מֵהֶם. הִלֵּל אוֹמֵר: הֱוֵי
מִתַּלְמִידָיו שֶׁל אַהֲרֹן, אוֹהֵב שָׁלוֹם וְרוֹדֵף
שָׁלוֹם, אוֹהֵב אֶת הַבְּרִיּוֹת וּמְקָרְבָן לַתּוֹרָה.

---

will depart from the Torah's teachings and cause God's Name to be profaned.[1]

People will not be disillusioned when they see that first generation of students depart from Torah values, because they know that those students are not worthy of being Torah scholars. Avtalyon is concerned for the students of those students, who could well be of good character and therefore cause God's Name to be profaned through the corrupted doctrines they received.

Mishnah 12

This world is prone to division and dissension by its very nature. Kayin and Hevel brought conflict into the world[2] from the earliest days of human creation and conflict flourishes still today. Therefore, Hillel says, we must continually improve the world through the pursuit of peace. When strife and divisiveness do occur, one should respond by uniting the adversaries.

❧ הֱוֵי מִתַּלְמִידָיו שֶׁל אַהֲרֹן — *Be among the disciples of Aharon*

This phrase begs for explanation.

• If not for this *mishnah* itself, there is no reason for us to associate these qualities with Aharon. Since Scripture does not explicitly[3] portray him as a man of peace, why choose Aharon as the model peacemaker?

• Even if a person would have these qualities, why call him a disciple of Aharon, whose distinction lies in being the holy High Priest?

• Why does Hillel say, "*Be of the disciples of Aharon,* loving peace and pursuing peace"? It would have been sufficient to start directly with "Love peace and pursue peace."

---

1. By the time of Avtalyon, such distortions of rabbinical teachings had already occurred, with far-reaching impact on Jewish history. In *mishnah* 3, Antignos taught, "Be not like servants who serve their master for the sake of receiving a reward." The students corrupted that statement as representing a denial of the World to Come. The rejection of that cardinal doctrine ultimately split the nation with factions that denied rabbinic authority (see *Bartenura*).

2. *Bereishis*, Chapter 4.

3. The principal reference is in *Malachi* 2:6: "he walked with Me in peace and uprightness, and turned many away from iniquity."

12. Hillel and Shammai received the tradition from them. Hillel says: Be among the disciples of Aharon, loving peace and pursuing peace, loving people and bringing them closer to the Torah.

The answer lies in understanding that the role of the High Priest is to unite and bind Israel into a unified nation. For example, the Rabbis of the *midrash* tell us that Israel's unity is reflected in the fact that there is only one Temple, one Altar, and one High Priest.[1] The High Priest was always a model of peace and love, who actively united the Jewish people by resolving disputes and promoting harmony. He brought Israel close to God through the Temple service.

Hillel uses Aharon as the role model precisely *because* he was the High Priest. The mission of every High Priest is to bring harmony among the people, and between Israel and their Father in Heaven. We know that Aharon must have been the best suited and most capable personality to fulfill that role, for God designated him as High Priest. It was for these reasons that Hillel chose Aharon as the quintessential champion of peace.

---

§ אוֹהֵב שָׁלוֹם וְרוֹדֵף שָׁלוֹם — *loving peace and pursuing peace*

The phrase "**loving** peace" refers to preventing disputes from arising. The phrase "**pursuing** peace" refers to restoring a harmonious relationship if a dispute did arise. Hillel uses the term "pursuing" in this context because people who quarrel keep at a distance from each other, and anything at a distance requires pursuit.

The ability to restore peace is so characteristic of *kedushah*, holiness, that Peace, שָׁלוֹם, is one of God's Names. Since *kedushah* lies in the spiritual realm, outside the constraints of time, peacemaking must be undertaken with instant pursuit as befits this spiritual endeavor.[2]

---

§ אוֹהֵב אֶת הַבְּרִיּוֹת — *loving people*

What kind of person will be effective in bringing about harmony? Someone who loves people and seeks their best interests. Only when we

---

1. *Bereishis Rabbah,* Section 18.
2. Maharal's full point is that *kedushah* is *nivdal* (see Author's Introduction) and not subject to time. Therefore, in the spiritual realm, things can happen instantaneously and in this case also peace-making should be initiated without delay.

love people so genuinely that we feel at one with them can we succeed in drawing people together to be at one with each other.

---

§ וּמְקָרְבָן לַתּוֹרָה — *and bringing them closer to the Torah*

Just as we should create harmony among people, so we should create harmony and unity between Israel and their Father in Heaven, and that is done by drawing near those who are at a distance from God's Torah and *mitzvos.*

It is clear that Hillel's advice is based on loving God's creation, which itself is founded on the love of God. As in the previous *mishnayos,* the first mentioned of each pair of rabbis is the President of the Rabbinical Court, and his advice addresses the love of God.

The Relationship of Mishnah 12 to the Following Mishnayos

In this *mishnah,* Hillel advocates the pursuit of peace. In the following *mishnayos,* he advises against pursuing fame, cautions against benefiting from one's Torah scholarship, and he accents personal accountability and responsibility. What is the connection between the statements of Hillel in this *mishnah* and those of the following *mishnayos*?

The flow of the *mishnayos* is based on the theme of humility.[1] A person who "loves peace and pursues peace" must be humble and unpretentious and go to the quarrelers, because they certainly will not come to him on their own. By contrast, a person who lacks humility will consider it beneath his dignity to appeal to them in the pursuit of peace.

Humility is a prerequisite to loving humanity and to a concern for total social harmony. Those who seek power are opposite in nature. They are concerned with themselves and unconcerned about others, because they do not recognize the value of other people. This accounts for the style of powerful people who keep to themselves and do not mingle with general society.

Hillel himself was meek and humble.[2] His advice in the following *mishnayos* continues to promote the quality of humility, as he warns

---

1. An inadequate translation of the Hebrew *anavah.* *Anavah* means that one considers other people important, while not assessing his own importance. The English word "humility" conveys a negative evaluation of oneself, rather than the positive evaluation of others implied by *anavah.*
2. *Shabbos* 31a.

13. He used to say: He who seeks renown loses his reputation; he who does not increase [his Torah learning] decreases it; and he who

against the domineering character of those who seek fame and power, for that is the antithesis of humility.

Mishnah 13

◆§ נְגִיד שְׁמָא אֲבַד שְׁמֵהּ — *He who seeks renown loses his reputation*

This translation follows Rambam's interpretation of the word שְׁמָא as meaning "reputation." He explains that once a person's fame has spread far and wide, that itself is a harbinger of imminent decline. This explanation is in accordance with the words "Pride goes before destruction."[1]

Maharal offers a different translation, understanding the word שְׁמָא as Aramaic for "name" and נְגִיד as a position of authority and power.

Therefore, Maharal renders נְגִיד שְׁמָא אֲבַד שְׁמֵהּ as: Power is its name? Destruction is its name!

High office carries an aura of permanence and security, but the truth is that holding office leads to one's ruin. As the Rabbis said,[2]

> Woe to authority, for it buries those who hold it; there is not a single prophet who did not outlive four kings.

The reason that authority "buries those who hold it" is that human beings receive life and support from God, may His Name be blessed. He is אֱ־לֹהִים חַיִּים, the God of life, from Whom life and sustenance flow towards all existence. Everyone who enters into this relationship on the receiving side, as a humble dependent, is in fact worthy of receiving life from God. By contrast, one who seeks power to rule over another does not enter relationships in a dependent role, but in a dominant role, and that is not conducive to receiving life from its Source.

◆§ וּדְלָא מוֹסִיף יָסֵף — *he who does not increase [his Torah learning] decreases it*

In contrast to power, which interferes with the flow of life from above, Torah study creates a bond with God. Hence Torah is the substance of

---

1. *Mishlei* 16:18.
2. *Pesachim* 87b.

life, as it says,[1] "for it is your life and the length of your days." Therefore, one who does not continue to be occupied with Torah study will die before his time.

Mankind's existence is inherently a physical one: finite and limited. We can reverse this and acquire a spiritually intellectual existence, but it requires the hard work of laboring in Torah study. The meaning of the *mishnah* is this: "One who does not work hard at making the intellectual component of life dominate the physical component, even if he studies Torah at his leisure, will suffer the finiteness of physical existence and therefore die earlier [than his allotted time]."[2]

---

§⇢ **וּדְלָא יָלֵיף קְטָלָא חַיָּב** — *and he who refuses to teach [Torah] deserves death*

If a person does not study Torah at all, he actively brings death upon himself,[3] for he distances himself from Torah and opposes it.

---

§⇢ **וּדְאִשְׁתַּמַּשׁ בְּתָגָא חֲלָף** — *and he who exploits the crown of Torah shall fade away*

One who makes personal use of the holy Torah is liable to death through Divine intervention, which is the penalty for deriving personal benefit from any sacred object.

Why is death the consequence of benefiting from holy objects? A physical entity that merges with a spiritual entity[4] cannot continue to exist, because the result is neither physical nor spiritual. Specifically, we exists on a physical plane and holiness exists on a non-physical (*nivdal*)[5] plane. If we make personal use of a sacred article, we are attempting to

---

1. *Devarim* 30:20.

2. It seems that the "life" under discussion is a life of *value*. "Death" is not having value in life. However, there is still an implication, at the literal level, that actual longevity is associated with living a worthy life, relative to one's potential life span.

3. As explained *infra* in Maharal's commentary to 6:2, this statement is directed only to those who can study but do not. It does not apply to a person who cannot study due to illness or a lack of education and teachers. Lack of study for those reasons does not imply opposition to Torah.

4. Which is not part of the body itself; i.e., the spirit that is part of our human existence does not fall within this rule. Spirit and body stand in a synergistic relation as form and substance, rather than merging.

5. *Nivdal* is a category of existence which does not share the attributes of physical existence: it is not tangible, nor susceptible to change nor constrained by time.

bring a non-physical entity into our physical domain. The physical entity is necessarily displaced, since it cannot be both physical and *nivdal.*

Therefore, one who derives personal benefit from the Torah passes away, for he has attempted to bring the *nivdal* crown of Torah into the human domain.

By way of metaphor, the crown worn upon the king's head qualitatively distinguishes the monarch from the body of the nation. Similarly, the crown of Torah graces the head, the home of spiritual intellect, which rules our lives.[1] Any subject of the king who would place the king's crown upon his own head can surely expect to be put to death, and likewise the death penalty befits anyone who would misappropriate the crown of Torah for personal benefit.

The sages say,[2]

> Rabbi Tarfon was eating figs which he thought to be abandoned and unowned, when the watchman found him, put him into a sack and brought him to the river to throw him in. [Rabbi Tarfon said,] "Woe to Tarfon, whom that man is about to kill." The watchman heard this, left him and ran away (upon realizing that he had attacked a Torah scholar). Rabbi Abuha said in the name of Rabbi Chananiah, "All the days of that righteous man (Rabbi Tarfon) he was distressed about this matter. He would say, "Woe to me, that I used the crown of Torah."[3]

&❧ וּדְאִשְׁתַּמֵשׁ בְּתָגָא חֲלָף &— *and he who exploits the crown of Torah shall fade away*

This statement can also be viewed in the context of the opening words of the *mishnah* — "Power is its name? Destruction is its name!" — which caution against seeking a position of authority. The crown of Torah is the essence of authority; it is a sacred crown above all other crowns and must not be exploited.

---

1. For this reason, the Talmud (*Gittin* 62a) says that Torah scholars are called "kings" as it is written (*Mishlei* 8:15), "Through me (a personification of Torah) kings reign."
2. *Nedarim* 62a.
3. The watchman had incorrectly suspected Rabbi Tarfon of being a thief who had been stealing figs throughout the season. Rabbi Tarfon was wealthy enough to save himself by offering to pay for all of the figs that had been stolen. Thus he had not used the honor of Torah scholarship to save his life, but to save his money.

[יד] הוּא הָיָה אוֹמֵר: אִם אֵין אֲנִי לִי, מִי לִי? וּכְשֶׁאֲנִי לְעַצְמִי, מָה אֲנִי? וְאִם לֹא עַכְשָׁו, אֵימָתַי?

The ideas presented in this *mishnah* belong together. Not extending one's Torah studies; not studying Torah at all; and misusing the crown of Torah share in common the punishment of early death. Death follows from sinning against any sacred article and so it is the inescapable consequence for compromising the sanctity of Torah.

Mishnah 14

Hillel continues the theme of humility, saying that we should never consider ourselves adequately accomplished in spiritual growth or in Torah scholarship. That way, we will always feel the need for self-improvement by acquiring Torah.

◆§ אִם אֵין אֲנִי לִי, מִי לִי — *If I am not for myself, who will be for me?*

If we do not put forth our own effort to perfect ourselves through Torah and *mitzvos,* whose Torah and *mitzvos* **will** contribute to our spiritual growth? If our father learned Torah, we do not inherit a single word of it. Wealth can be accumulated and given as a gift to someone who did not earn it, and sometimes people inherit a fortune. Other material needs, also, can come to an entire community through the merit of a single person, such as rain[1] or sustenance.[2] By contrast, our portion in the eternal world can be acquired only through our own efforts, for one person's deeds cannot spiritually elevate another person.[3]

◆§ וּכְשֶׁאֲנִי לְעַצְמִי מָה אֲנִי — *And if I am for myself, what am I?*

Hillel means: "Even if I fulfill my obligation to perform *mitzvos,* I am but flesh and blood and I cannot put in the amount of effort that the soul requires." In other words, we can effect only a little spiritual growth at a time, and yet there is no spiritual plateau that we would accept as "good enough" for all eternity.

---

1. *Taanis* 7a.
2. *Berachos* 17b: "The entire world receives sustenance on the merit of Chanina."
3. However, a child can elevate the soul of a deceased parent. Perhaps this is not really an exception, since children are referred to as the "good deeds" of the parent.

14. He used to say: If I am not for myself, who will be for me? And if I am for myself, what am I? And if not now, when?

Hillel's message is conveyed in the Midrash:[1]

"All the labor of Man is for his mouth."[2] Rabbi Shmuel bar Yitzchak said: [This verse means that] that all a person achieves through *mitzvos* and good deeds is only for his own mouth and not for the mouth of his son or his daughter.

Moreover, "and the soul is not filled."[3] [This verse means that] the soul is never satisfied because it knows that all of its accomplishments accrue to itself (i.e., it can never have enough, because there is no limit to how refined the soul can become).

Rabbi Levi said: [To what are the body and the soul comparable?] To a villager who marries a princess. Even if he provides her with delicacies from around the world, it will not satisfy her, because she comes from royalty. Similarly, whatever a person does for his soul is not enough, because it derives from a higher world.

שׁ‎ וְאִם לֹא עַכְשָׁו, אֵימָתָי — *And if not now, when?*

The third limitation to achievement is that life is very short. If we do not act now, when else is there?

In summary, we need to awaken from our lethargy to do *mitzvos* and good deeds, because:

- There is no one else to rely on for spiritual achievement.
- Even one's fullest efforts at *mitzvos* and good deeds fall short of the spiritual needs and potential of the soul.[4]
- One must act now, for one's days are short; suddenly he is taken and is no more.

These statements have been placed together because they all reflect Hillel's own humility.

---

1. *Vayikra Rabbah,* Section 4.

2. *Koheles* 6:7

3. *Ibid.* This is the continuation of the verse.

4. The intention is to avoid losing one's motivation through an exaggerated sense of accomplishment. Justified humility maintains motivation. Unjustified complacency robs people of their motivation.

Mishnah 15

Of each pair of leaders, the President offers *mussar* that stems from the love of God, and the Head of the Rabbinical Court offers *mussar* that stems from the fear of God. So too the *mussar* of Hillel and Shammai, in general, is complementary and fully subscribed to by each of them.

To a certain extent, however, their advice also reflects a difference of perspective on life and, as we shall see, there are situations in which Hillel would disagree with the application of Shammai's *mussar*, presented in this *mishnah*.

Each embodied his philosophy of life in his own personality. Hillel maintained a forgiving and tolerant personality. He did not insist that others do things his way and he tried to find a way to accommodate other views within the scope of Torah.[1] Hillel's view is crystallized in his admonition to pursue peace,[2] for that requires telling the disputing parties to forgive what the other has done and not to insist on their own terms. Those qualities must underlie Hillel's *mussar*, for how could we ask others to be forgiving and tolerant unless we ourselves are that way.

Although Shammai agreed that a tolerant attitude is proper for worldly matters such as quarrels, when it came to matters of religious practice he was exacting and adamant in his standards. He embedded that approach in his personality and maintained that in the realm of Torah study and *mitzvos*, one must firmly enforce one's standards and beliefs without compromise.

Hillel vs. Shammai — A Philosophical Analysis[3]

Change is a physical characteristic and therefore it befits physical beings to change and adjust to each other. The logical conclusion is that, to the degree that we are physical beings, we should be accommodating and flexible.

Conversely, intellect, *sechel*, is non-physical, and hence it is not susceptible to change or accommodation. Therefore, to the extent that we treat ourselves as non-physical intellectual beings, we should stand firm by our opinions and not be influenced by others' opinions.

---

1. *Shabbos* 31a.

2. *Supra, mishnah* 12.

3. Based on Maharal's commentary here and *infra,* Chapter 2, pp. 89 (left column, bottom half) -90 in the original Hebrew text.

With this background, we are ready to understand the central point of contention between Hillel and Shammai's views of life.

Hillel maintains that the guiding principle in determining how to bring Torah values into practice is to consider people as physical beings, in all situations. True, we have intellectual and physical components, but the combination of those two is still a physical human being. Since Hillel considers only our physical nature in determining conduct, he maintains that tolerance and patience should always prevail.

Shammai maintains that the guiding principle is to recognize both the spiritual intellect — *sechel* — and the physical makeup of the human being, as appropriate to the situation. Shammai agrees with Hillel that, in the realm of worldly matters, it is appropriate to be forgiving and accommodating, because that matches the physical nature of this world. However, Shammai maintains that the realm of Torah and *mitzvos* requires an approach on its own terms, and then we should be unmovable and uncompromising, according to the characteristics of *sechel*.

The result is that Hillel agrees with Shammai's *mussar* within the context of guarding against transgression, just as all the previous pairs of rabbis agreed with each other. However, Hillel disagrees with Shammai's *mussar* when taken to an extreme that demands a single perspective to the exclusion of others.

⋖§ עֲשֵׂה תוֹרָתְךָ קֶבַע ⋗ — *Make your Torah study a fixed practice*

Shammai guards against transgression, warning us not to compromise the centrality of Torah study, and Hillel agrees with this.

Hillel and Shammai differ on the issue of whether the Torah should be so "fixed" that there is no room for differing practices.

According to Bartenura,[1] Shammai goes so far as to mean: Do not be strict for yourself and lenient with others, or vice versa. In matters such as Torah, we must be consistent and uncompromising.

Hillel did not agree that Torah had to be a "fixed practice" in that regard, but was strict on himself even when lenient with others.[2]

---

1. Although Maharal does not explicitly provide Bartenura's interpretation, Maharal's disciple R' Yom Tov Lipman Heller in *Tosafos Yom Tov* uses Bartenura's interpretation to bring out the point that Hillel would not agree with Shammai's *mussar*. Since that is Maharal's very point here, we may assume that Maharal agrees with Bartenura.
2. Commentary of *Tosafos Yom Tov, ad loc*.

א/טו

אֱמֹר מְעַט וַעֲשֵׂה הַרְבֵּה; וֶהֱוֵי מְקַבֵּל אֶת כָּל הָאָדָם בְּסֵבֶר פָּנִים יָפוֹת.

§ **אֱמֹר מְעַט וַעֲשֵׂה הַרְבֵּה** — *say little and do much*

Shammai warns against committing to do too much and then transgressing one's own word, and with this too Hillel concurs.

However, in the context of Torah study, "say little" means[1] that you should say only the law (*halachah*) as you intend to practice it. It is the converse of saying much and doing little; i.e., exposing academic possibilities and opinions that you do not intend to practice. Shammai maintains that our actions should not differ from our words, for just as Torah is not subject to change, so Torah study should not accommodate variations.

This is another point of contention between Hillel and Shammai. Shammai taught only what he practiced, to the exclusion of other opinions.[2] Hillel taught the halachic opinions of Shammai as well as his own, for he respected them, even though in practice he followed his own view and not Shammai's.

§ **וֶהֱוֵי מְקַבֵּל אֶת כָּל הָאָדָם בְּסֵבֶר פָּנִים יָפוֹת** —
and receive everyone with a cheerful face

Shammai's advice stems from the fear of God, for it avoids slighting people, and that complements Hillel's opinion that we must energetically pursue harmony.

The difference in approach between these two schools of thought is visible in this admonition also, for Hillel would not agree that it is mandatory to "receive everyone with a cheerful face." Hillel maintains that the other person should not care if he does not receive a cordial greeting, because he should not be particular whether people's conduct conforms to his personal preferences. Consequently, we need not unfailingly "receive **everyone** with a cheerful face."

Shammai agrees that the one being greeted should not care about being greeted pleasantly. However, he maintains that the one doing the greeting must be particular to greet each individual in a pleasant manner because that is an absolute standard of conduct, and the recipient's attitude is irrelevant to our conduct.

---

1. Author's understanding of an obscure passage in Maharal.
2. Author's amplification.

practice; say little and do much; and receive everyone with a cheerful face.

Torah Transmission up to Hillel and Shammai

This *mishnah* concludes the *mussar* of the fifth and last of the rabbinical pairs who formally transmitted the Torah from one generation to the next. From this point onward, there no longer were designated recipients in the chain of Torah transmission, for the students of Shammai and Hillel did not apprentice adequately[1] to synthesize the full spectrum of Torah principles. Therefore it is appropriate to pause and reflect upon the development of Torah and rabbinical leadership from Moshe to Hillel and Shammai.

The revelation of Torah at Mount Sinai set the paradigm for Torah dissemination over the next 1,200 years. Just as Torah was proclaimed at Sinai with five sounds,[2] which spread throughout the world,[3] so Torah spread through each historical era in five stages. We find that there were five stages of Torah transmission in the period from Moshe until the Great Assembly,[4] and there were five pairs of rabbinical leaders again in the era of the Second Temple.[5]

Furthermore, just as the five sounds at Mount Sinai spread Torah throughout the world and then subsided, so the first five groups spread Torah throughout the era prior to the Second Temple, and then it began to wane. At the time of the Second Temple the vitality of Torah was restored, as the pairs of rabbis acted together and strengthened each other in complementary roles. True to the paradigm, this renewed transmission of Torah also lasted for five stages and then subsided.

Antignos served, by himself, in the chain of Torah transmission, linking the era of the Great Assembly and the era of the rabbinical pairs.[6]

The institution of shared rabbinical leadership was a definitive characteristic of the Second Temple. The Rabbis tell us[7] that the Temples were established by both "hands" of the Creator, symbolizing the synthesis of two opposing yet complementary forces. Respectively, the

---

1. Due to the government's wariness of the power of the rabbinate.
2. *Berachos* 6b. The sounds emanated to each of the four directions and the fifth sound was in the center.
3. Similar to *Shemos Rabbah,* Section 5.
4. Listed in *mishnah* 1.
5. Identified in *mishnah* 4 through to *mishnah* 12.
6. Shimon HaTzaddik, although singled out for mention in *mishnah* 2, was nonetheless part of the Great Assembly.
7. *Kesubos* 5a.

[טז] רַבָּן גַּמְלִיאֵל הָיָה אוֹמֵר: עֲשֵׂה לְךָ
רַב, וְהִסְתַּלֵּק מִן הַסָּפֵק; וְאַל תַּרְבֶּה
לְעַשֵּׂר אֲמָדוֹת.

"right hand" and the "left hand" of the Creator are symbolic of the Divine attributes of Kindness and Strict Justice. During the Second Temple, those attributes came to appear as being more distinct than integrated. The impact of that shift was felt in the institution of shared leadership by the President and the Head of the Rabbinical Court, for their roles were derived from these two Divine attributes. In this light, it was most fitting that their admonitions expressed the love of God and the fear of God, in resonance with the attributes of Kindness and Strict Justice.

Development of Mussar from Antignos to Hillel and Shammai

As Torah leadership became diffuse, the rabbis' *mussar* addressed a more diffuse set of relationships, as we shall now see. Antignos' *mussar* addressed the person himself, advocating that we serve God out of love while maintaining the fear of Heaven. He was followed by the rabbinical pairs, each of which would extend the advice of the preceding generation. The first pair of rabbis addressed conduct within the household,[1] which is our closest of relationships. The second pair strengthened the relationship with one's *Rav*, one's friends and one's neighbors,[2] relationships which are progressively less close. The third pair addressed judges,[3] who are charged with an aspect of community leadership. The fourth pair addresses the conduct of those in power,[4] whose authoritative role renders them distant and distinct from the community. The fifth pair established rules of conduct for the community at large, so that the bond of peace should not be breached.[5]

The rabbis had addressed the full scope of relationships, from the individual to the general community, when the chain of Torah transmission as it had been known throughout history ultimately lapsed.

---

1. They advised one to open his house to sages, neighbors and the poor; and that he and his wife should fulfill the religious mandate of their respective roles by refraining from excessive conversation..

2. They advised one to secure a *Rav* and a friend; and to avoid bad neighbors.

3. They advised judges against acting as lawyers for those they are judging and to act in a manner which is objective and charitable to both litigants equally.

4. They advised people to love honest labor, avoiding holding an office of authority; and that a Rabbi must exercise care in selecting his words when addressing students.

5. They advised the pursuit of peace; being reliable and promoting a feeling of acceptance among people.

16. Rabban Gamliel used to say: Accept a Torah teacher upon yourself and remove yourself from uncertainty; and do not give excess tithes by estimating [instead of measuring].

Mishnah 16

These three statements of Rabban Gamliel comprise a single point: Every aspect of human activity should be executed with certainty and be free from doubt, as befits the *sechel,* intellect, that we were given. *Sechel* is more than academic intelligence, for it also includes the intellectual competence to do what is right. By contrast, Scripture refers to a fool as one who walks in the dark:[1]

> Then I saw that wisdom is superior to foolishness as light is superior to darkness. The wise person's eyes are in his head and the fool walks in darkness.

Uncertainty arises in three areas: theory, fact and practice, which is the application of theory to fact.

1. Doubt can arise in the grasp of guiding principles, when there are several possible ways to understand a point.
2. Factual doubt can arise in a specific situation, quite aside from any doubt about the rules.[2]
3. Doubt can arise in the application of principles to a specific situation, and that is of concern in the performance of a *mitzvah.*

The advice of the *mishnah* corresponds to each category of doubt:

1. "Accept a Torah teacher" so that one's knowledge will be acquired with certainty, leaving no area in doubt.
2. ". . . and remove yourself from uncertainty"; i.e., from every situation that is doubtful. It goes without saying that matters that could possibly result in transgression, such as a doubt as to whether food is kosher or not,[3] must be treated as definitely forbidden. We furthermore must remove risk from situations of potential danger or loss, as well. In summary, it is inappropriate for a rational human being to enter into a questionable situation.
3. ". . . and do not give excess tithes by estimating." Do not perform **any** *mitzvos* by estimation. Even though tithing by estimate is in fact

---

1. *Koheles* 2:13-14.
2. Maharal's point is that the three areas of doubt cover all aspects without overlap.
3. Author's illustration.

א/יז **[יז]** שִׁמְעוֹן בְּנוֹ אוֹמֵר: כָּל יָמַי גָּדַלְתִּי בֵּין
הַחֲכָמִים, וְלֹא מָצָאתִי לַגּוּף טוֹב אֶלָּא

permissible[1] it should not become a regular practice. The Torah
permitted it only if you need the food tithed immediately and there is
no time to measure it accurately. Torah law considers estimation to
be almost as reliable as certainty, but nonetheless we should refrain
from even a marginal doubt and do everything with precision and
certitude, as befits our intelligence.

Such conduct helps to perfect our character and avoids many problems that arise from doing things that we are not sure of.

Yehoshua ben Perachyah already advised in *mishnah* 6 that one
should establish a *Rav*, Torah teacher. However, he was concerned with
the need to avoid errors in halachic practice, whereas this *mishnah* is
concerned with the quality of Torah studies, aside from any practical
application. Rabban Gamliel advocates studying with a *Rav* because that
will ensure a conclusive understanding of the Torah and avoid the
ambiguity that results from studying without a *Rav*.

Unlike previous *mishnayos* in this chapter, this *mishnah* does not say
that Rabban Gamliel "received the Torah," because the chain of designated Torah transmission continued only up to Hillel and Shammai. The
Talmud says,[2]

> When there were many disciples of Shammai and Hillel who
> had not adequately apprenticed, there were many [halachic]
> disagreements within Israel and the Torah became like two
> Torahs.

Consequently, the *mishnah* no longer says that rabbis in the generations after Hillel and Shammai "received the Torah."[3]

Mishnah 17

The Rabbis frequently extol the virtue of minimizing extraneous
speech. Discussing Torah, however, is to be encouraged.[4]

---

1. *Bechoros* 58b. A *Levi* is obligated to give to the *Kohen* a tenth part of the tithes that
he himself receives from the people. That tenth may be figured by estimation and
therefore, explains Maharal, it is certainly permissible for people to give tithes to the
Levi by estimation.

2. *Sanhedrin* 88b.

3. The exception in *Avos* 2:9 [Rabban Yochanan ben Zakkai received from Hillel and
Shammai] is explained in the commentary to that *mishnah*, near the end.

4. This opening statement is the author's clarification.

17. Shimon his son says: All my days I have been raised among the Sages, and I found nothing better for the body than silence;

We have both intellectual and physical abilities. In the previous *mishnah* Rabban Gamliel gave advice to improve our judgment. In this *mishnah* his son Shimon offers insights to refine our physical nature.

⊷§ כָּל יָמַי גְּדַלְתִּי בֵּין הַחֲכָמִים — *All my days I have been raised among the Sages*

What is the point of the introductory words, "All my life I have been raised among the Sages"? Rashi explains this statement to mean, "I observed that the Sages practice silence and I have found that it is good even for them [although they have wise things to say]. Therefore, how much more so is silence suitable for ordinary people, who are not sages."

⊷§ וְלֹא מָצָאתִי לַגּוּף טוֹב אֶלָּא שְׁתִיקָה — *and I found nothing better for the body than silence*

We would expect the *mishnah* to say that silence is good for a *person*. Why does it say that silence is good especially for the *body*?

Shimon regards speech as a physical faculty, in that it is not purely cognitive. It is true that speech can be the handmaiden of emotional and creative thinking;[1] however, the *mishnah* is concerned with directed, analytical thought. Because speech occupies our concentration, we are more likely to err while talking than while given solely to reflection. This does not imply that talking itself is wrong; Shimon advocates silence only because it allows the intellect to function to its fullest potential. The statement that silence is "good for the body" means that the body becomes a valuable partner in the rational process, simply by not interfering. The discipline of refraining from speech makes the body a "tail of a lion."[2]

Conversely, when talking dominates our mental energy then the intellectual faculty becomes a "tail of a fox."[3]

---

1. Author's clarifying sentence.
2. *Avos* 4:16: "Be a tail of lions and not a head of foxes." The meaning is that it is better to have a subordinate relationship with something worthy than to dominate something that is unworthy.
3. An extension of the preceding reference. To be subordinated to something which itself is of little value is the worst of all possibilities.

א/יז שְׁתִיקָה; וְלֹא הַמִּדְרָשׁ הוּא הָעִקָּר, אֶלָּא הַמַּעֲשֶׂה; וְכָל הַמַּרְבֶּה דְּבָרִים מֵבִיא חֵטְא.

The *mishnah* assumes that analysis and insight engage the higher reaches of intellect, whereas the faculty of speech is more instinctive. Indeed, we may observe that children master speech well before their minds are developed enough to analyze and theorize. The *ability* to articulate thought is an intellectual function. However, the act of speech itself is largely a physical action that distracts us from reflection.

Since speech interferes with the faculty of reason, silence helps to prevent confusion and error.

Because talking interferes with reflection, it follows that fools are likely to be talkative. A wise person exercises the intellect rather than the faculty of speech.

────────────────────────────

⛤ וְלֹא הַמִּדְרָשׁ הוּא הָעִקָּר אֶלָּא הַמַּעֲשֶׂה — *not study,*
but practice is the main thing

────────────────────────────

This thought is parenthetical to the flow of the *mishnah,* and is intended to avoid a possible misconception. The first part of the *mishnah* stated that the discipline of maintaining silence is appropriate, because one should exercise the intellect instead of the body. One might erroneously conclude from this that the exposition of the Torah, מִדְרָשׁ, is primary and that its practice, מַעֲשֶׂה, is secondary.

The truth is that, while study is great, practice is the foundation on which intellectual achievement must be built. One can acquire the highest level of intellect only by building, a level at a time, on this firm foundation. This concept is dealt with in Chapter 3, *mishnah* 12: "Anyone whose good deeds exceed his wisdom, his wisdom will endure."

────────────────────────────

⛤ וְכָל הַמַּרְבֶּה דְּבָרִים מֵבִיא חֵטְא — *and everyone*
who talks excessively brings on sin

────────────────────────────

This *mishnah* is not a mere repetition of the verse, "In a multitude of words sin will not cease."[1] That passage means that one cannot avoid wasted words and foolishness in a large volume of speech.

Our *mishnah* makes a different point. Good judgment is the result of aligning our decisions and actions with a clear grasp of what is right.

────────────

1. *Mishlei* 10:19.

not study, but practice is the main thing; and everyone who talks excessively brings on sin.

Since talking too much distracts us from analytical reasoning, it subverts our insight and good judgment, leaving us more prone to sin in general.

Although our *mishnah* stated a preference for thinking rather than talking, it did not mean that talking too much is itself a sin. Speech is a human faculty in its own right; it is not a sin to use it rather than giving over all of one's attention to reflection.

The beginning of the *mishnah* tells us that talking in excess causes the faculty of speech to dominate the intellect. The conclusion of the *mishnah* states the result: When the power of the intellect is compromised, sin is likely to follow.

Mishnah 18

Author's Introduction

God continuously sustains the existence of the world. *Mishnah 2* stated that the world exists to support mankind's goodness. *Mishnah 18* informs us that mankind not only *warrants* the world's existence but is also a vehicle to *maintain* its existence.

Maharal provides several analyses of this *mishnah,* three of which will be presented here:

- The first analysis focuses on how the institutions of "justice, truth and peace" maintain the primary aspects of human society.
- The second analysis demonstrates how "justice, truth and peace," which *sustain* the world, correspond one-for-one with Torah, service of God and kindness, which *warrant* sustained existence, as stated in *mishnah 2.*
- The third explanation takes an entirely different approach. It shows how "justice, truth and peace" correspond to the basic elements of creation: the Creator, the created and the purpose of Creation.

A human being is only that which he is born with: a body and a soul. Everything else is acquired as he grows up, for wealth and even knowledge are only acquisitions. In total, a person is made up of three components: the person himself; material possessions such as money; and spiritual possessions such as intellect, *sechel.* The "three things" of this *mishnah* are directed at these three components of human existence.

א/יח

[יח] רַבָּן שִׁמְעוֹן בֶּן גַּמְלִיאֵל אוֹמֵר: עַל שְׁלֹשָׁה דְבָרִים הָעוֹלָם קַיָּם – עַל הַדִּין, וְעַל הָאֱמֶת וְעַל הַשָּׁלוֹם, שֶׁנֶּאֱמַר: ,,אֱמֶת וּמִשְׁפַּט שָׁלוֹם שִׁפְטוּ בְּשַׁעֲרֵיכֶם.''

❀ ❀ ❀

The world endures on three things — justice, truth and peace

How do these "three things" influence human life? The institution of "justice" maintains an orderly system of personal wealth. The pursuit of "truth" enriches the intellect. The pursuit of "peace" enhances our personal existence by ensuring that one person's domain of existence does not encroach on his neighbor's existence. We will now explain these in detail.

◆§ הָעוֹלָם קַיָּם – עַל הַדִּין — *The world endures . . . on justice*

The Creator has allocated possessions to each of us and it is improper for one person to take what God has intended for another. Competent "justice" maintains proper allocation of material possessions and enables the world to endure in the way that God planned for each person.

Without the justice system, the property of one person would come into the hands of someone else and the "material possessions" component of human existence would be abrogated.

◆§ וְעַל הָאֱמֶת — *on truth*

When one pursues "truth," intellect emerges into the world. When falsehood prevails, the intellectual side of life is abrogated.

◆§ וְעַל הַשָּׁלוֹם — *and on peace*

"Peace" addresses the human being himself. The world requires peace to endure, because it is an intrinsic part of human nature to conflict with other people. Each of us believes from birth that "everything is mine" and conflict arises because the very existence of other people interferes with "me and mine".

In summary, the world supports human existence in three categories: material possessions, intellect and the person himself. Judgment,

18. Rabban Shimon ben Gamliel says: The world endures on three things — on justice, on truth and on peace; as it is said (*Zechariah* 8:16): "Truth and the verdict of peace are you to adjudicate in your gates."

❦ ❦ ❦

---

truth and peace secure these three things and prevent the world from collapsing.

Second Analysis: The world endures on three things — justice, truth and peace

Shimon HaTzaddik, in *mishnah* 2, listed three pillars that are the origin and foundation of the world, for they support the flow of existence from God as follows. The "service of God" links mankind to the Creator. "Torah" makes people worthy of existence, and the flow of "acts of kindness" from one to another induces the flow of kindness from God to the world. Why is his list different than Rabban Shimon ben Gamliel's list in this *mishnah* here?

Rabban Shimon ben Gamliel lists the things through which God *maintains* the world. However, we will now show that the three pillars of the world's *origin* correspond directly to the three components of the world's *maintenance.*

• "Service of God" corresponds to "justice." [1]
  The Rabbis say:[2]

> Every judge who judges a sincere case correctly becomes a partner with the Holy One, Blessed is He, in creation.

Just as the service of God in prayer and *mitzvos* establishes a link with the Creator, so too does honest justice maintain a partnership with the Creator.

There are other examples of the close association between justice and the sacrificial service. For example:[3]

> Why was the portion in the Torah of judgments, מִשְׁפָּטִים, placed next to the portion that deals with the Altar? To teach that the Sanhedrin (Supreme Court) convenes near the Altar.

---

1. Both of these activities serve God, as opposed to enriching the person himself or bestowing a kindness upon others.
2. *Shabbos* 10a.
3. Rashi to *Shemos* 21:1.

Conversely, the Rabbis considered incompetent judgment to be similar to serving idols:[1]

> One who appoints an improper judge ... in a place of Torah scholars is like one who plants an *asheirah* (tree worshiped by idolaters) beside the Altar.

- "Torah" corresponds to "truth." Torah itself is truth and there is no truth like the Torah. Just as Torah improves the person himself, so does the pursuit of truth perfect a person.
- "Acts of kindness" corresponds to "peace," because kindness brings peace among people. Just as the goodness of acts of kindness makes the world worthy of existence, so does the pursuit of peace keep this world a place of goodness.

Third Analysis: The world endures on three things — justice, truth and peace

There are three elements to a constructive act. There is the creator; there is the created; and there is the purpose of creation. The three things of this *mishnah* may be understood as a reference to each of these elements of God's Creation.

"Justice"[2] addresses the world from the aspect of the Creator, Who decrees change as a judge issues decrees that must be followed. For this reason, the Divine Name, *Elohim,* which denotes a judge, is used throughout the Biblical narrative of Creation.[3]

The institution of justice maintains the decrees by which the world was created, as the Rabbis said:[4]

> Every judge who judges a true case correctly becomes a partner with the Holy One, Blessed is He, in creation.

Therefore, if the world did not embody justice, it would inevitably collapse.

"Truth" refers to the structure that He imposed on Creation. It addresses the world from the aspect of the created, which runs according to the consistent and equitable rules of Creation.

The decree of the true Judge is truth itself. The world, which is the object of God's decree, must embody truth or collapse.

"Peace" is achieved when all is complete and there is no need for any further development or change. This fact is seen in the common root of

---

1. *Sanhedrin* 7b.
2. I.e., effecting change based on a system of rules, as explained above.
3. *Bereishis* Chapter 1.
4. *Shabbos* 10a.

the Hebrew words for peace, שָׁלוֹם, and complete, שָׁלֵם. Peace is the purpose of Creation, just as peace is the purpose and fulfillment of justice.

At the conclusion of the six days of Creation and continuous development, God instilled into creation the ability to desist from change. Peace arrived when Creation was complete. The narrative of Creation says:[1]

> And He concluded on the seventh day His work that He had done and He rested on the seventh day from all the work that He had done.

The *Midrash* deals with the paradox that Creation was advanced yet further on the seventh day, although God rested on the seventh day:[2]

> What was created after He rested? Tranquillity, repose, peace and quiet.

Rashi[3] highlights that Creation became a stable entity when he comments:

> What did the world lack? Rest. When Shabbos comes, rest comes.

Peace is not a part of Creation itself, because Shabbos is not included among the days of Creation. Therefore peace, which is a spiritual entity, occupies a higher level in the hierarchy of existence than does the physical world.[4]

A world with no peace would collapse. This is the third aspect of Creation; namely, "peace" as it fulfills the "purpose" of Creation.

Relationship of the Closing Mishnayos to the Rest of Chapter 1

The advice of the earlier rabbis of this chapter — the pairs who were the "fathers" of the world — aimed to perfect the very substance of life, which is our love and fear of God. Rabban Gamliel then offered advice aimed at perfecting the person himself, in all three degrees of intellect: abstract intellect (שֵׂכֶל נִבְדָּל), practical intelligence, and planning or imagination. Similarly, Shimon[5] gave advice to perfect man as a physical being. Neither of these rabbis dealt with the love and fear of God but with the perfection of the person himself.

With the development of the human personality completed, Rabban

---

1. *Bereishis* 2:2.

2. *Midrash Rabbah, Bereishis,* Section 10.

3. To *Bereishis* 2:2.

4. Just as Shabbos is a higher level than the weekdays. The physical world is subject to change. Peace denotes completeness and stability which is akin to שֵׂכֶל *nivdal.*

5. *Supra, mishnah* 17.

Shimon ben Gamliel describes how mankind's existence is the basis of the world's existence.

The Missing Generations

The history of Torah transmission, from Moshe to after the destruction of the Second Temple, is traced in this chapter. Following the five pairs of rabbinical leaders, there are two omissions. Hillel's own son Shimon is not mentioned in this chapter. Shimon's son Gamliel is the author of *mishnah* 16. Gamliel's grandson Rabban Gamliel, who lived at the time of Rabbi Akiva, is first mentioned in Chapter 2.

Maharal gives several reasons for these omissions. One reason is that each of the two omitted leaders served concurrently with another leader, who was not a descendant of Hillel. The *mishnah* chose, in this chapter, not to delve into the leadership in that degree of complexity.

With the omission of these two rabbis, Chapter 1 has exactly ten generations, just as God created the world with ten statements.[1] Shimon HaTzaddik in *mishnah* 2 lists the three pillars that are the source of existence and that corresponds to the beginning of the week of Creation. The statement of Rabban Shimon ben Gamliel, at the conclusion of the chapter, lists three bases for sustaining the Creation when it was completed at the first Shabbos. Just as there were ten statements of Creation from the beginning until the first Shabbos, so there are ten stages of rabbinical statements from Shimon HaTzaddik until Rabban Shimon ben Gamliel.

It is significant that the first chapter of *Avos* provides ten sets of statements of the world's fathers, corresponding to the ten statements of the world's Creator.[2]

Summary of Chapter 1

The structure of Creation unfolds through this chapter. The Holy One, Blessed is He, is above all, and His Torah is above the world in the hierarchy of existence, for it is the very beginning of existence.[3] For this reason, the Men of the Great Assembly initiated the *mussar* of *Pirkei Avos* with advice to strengthen Torah. Shimon HaTzaddik then enumerated the foundations on which the world stands: Torah study, service of God and kind deeds.

Next, Antignos focused on the human being as the starting point for

---

1. *Infra*, 5:1.

2. Chapter 5 will deal thoroughly with the significance of numbers and the messages they convey.

3. *Bereishis Rabbah*, Chapter 1: בְּרֵאשִׁית (In the beginning) refers to Torah, which is called רֵאשִׁית, the beginning of His way, the first of His works of old, in *Mishlei* 8:22.

the world, for mankind is the justification of all other existence. By strengthening the love and fear of God, Antignos improved mankind as the single basis of the world, just as Shimon HaTzaddik had addressed the world on a general level.

The subsequent pairs of leaders aimed at improving the quality of mankind's existence from the closest relationships to the most distant, addressing family, teachers, friends and subordinates. Their advice strengthened all aspects of the love and fear of God, from the most direct to the most subtle. The later generations then turned to perfecting the person himself, with advice to strengthen the intellectual and finally the physical components of the human being.

As we said, Shimon HaTzaddik identified the three things through which the foundations of the source of the world are connected to the Creator. By contrast, the three things mentioned by Rabban Shimon ben Gamliel at the end of the chapter support the world by virtue of its completeness and fulfillment of purpose. This world comes from God and returns to Him when it is complete. Therefore it requires pillars to support it at its origin and at its completion.

Peace is achieved when all parts are finally brought into harmony. Peace is the ultimate plateau, and hence comes only at the end. For this reason, the priestly blessing and the daily prayers conclude with the blessing of peace, and this chapter, too, appropriately concludes with the pinnacle of all Creation — peace.

רַבִּי חֲנַנְיָא בֶּן עֲקַשְׁיָא אוֹמֵר: רָצָה הַקָּדוֹשׁ
בָּרוּךְ הוּא לְזַכּוֹת אֶת יִשְׂרָאֵל;
לְפִיכָךְ הִרְבָּה לָהֶם תּוֹרָה וּמִצְוֹת, שֶׁנֶּאֱמַר:

It is customary to study *Pirkei Avos* each Shabbos afternoon from
Pesach until Shavuos (or until Rosh Hashanah in many localities). The
mishnah "All Israel has a share in the World to Come..." is recited
before each chapter, and this *mishnah* of "Rabbi Chanania ben
Akashia..." is recited after each chapter.

⊷ רָצָה הַקָּדוֹשׁ בָּרוּךְ הוּא לְזַכּוֹת אֶת יִשְׂרָאֵל; לְפִיכָךְ הִרְבָּה לָהֶם
תּוֹרָה וּמִצְוֹת — *The Holy One, Blessed is He, wished to*
confer merit upon Israel; therefore He gave them
Torah and mitzvos in abundance

Some ask that the reverse seems to be more reasonable, because the
abundance of commandments just creates more opportunities to transgress God's will. It would appear that Israel would be better off if they had
to keep fewer *mitzvos*!

Rambam resolves this question as follows. He writes[1] that one of the
fundamental beliefs in Torah is that one can merit the World to Come
through even one *mitzvah*, if it is performed properly, without worldly
benefit but for the sake of Heaven; i.e., out of love. Since there are so
many *mitzvos*, it is unlikely that in a lifetime he will not perform even
one of them completely, in its proper way, and thereby merit the World
to Come. Such are his words.

Reason does not bear this interpretation. Most likely, Rambam himself
wrote these words only to draw the heart of the nation to the Torah, as
we explained previously.[2] It was an attempt to encourage people to
fulfill *mitzvos*, since one could merit the World to Come through even
one *mitzvah*.

It must be admitted that one can indeed merit the World to Come
through one *mitzvah*, for all Israel has at least a nominal portion in the
World to Come. Indeed, even one *mitzvah* is not necessary to merit the
World to Come for one who has no sins, or for someone such as a child[3]
who is not obligated in *mitzvos*.

---

1. Rambam's *Commentary to the Mishnah, Makkos* 3:16.
2. See *supra,* the end of Maharal's commentary to 6:11.
3. See *Sanhedrin* 110b.

Rabbi Chanania ben Akashia says: The Holy One, Blessed is He, wished to confer merit upon Israel; therefore He gave them Torah and *mitzvos* in abundance, as it is said

However it is impossible to suggest, as Rambam does, that one who has more sins than *mitzvos* will merit more than the minimum portion in the World to Come, which every Israelite receives automatically. If one has more sins than *mitzvos*, the reward for his *mitzvos* is received in this world, not the Next. Furthermore, there is no need for Rambam's condition that a *mitzvah* be performed fully and without other benefit. Finally, it is an error to think that the *mishnah* refers only to merit for the World to Come. God wished to confer merit upon Israel in both this world and the Next, and Rambam himself would agree that the goodness of *mitzvos* is felt in this world as well.

Rambam's approach was a response to the argument that giving us more *mitzvos* was not a kindness but an obstacle to gaining eternal life. However, the truth is that the *mishnah* does not mean that God gave many *mitzvos* so that people will accomplish at least one *mitzvah*. The *mishnah* means just what it appears to mean: God gave many *mitzvos* so that Israel could have much merit. It matters not that so many commandments increase the likelihood to have more sins than *mitzvos* — God wishes to bestow goodness upon good people, and good people are better off with many *mitzvos*. They can perfect themselves through the 613 commandments and God wishes to ennoble good people.

Those who question why God did not give great merit with just a few *mitzvos* do not understand the connection between a *mitzvah* and its reward. Reward is commensurate with the goodness inherent in the performance of the *mitzvah* and no more.[1]

---

§ רָצָה הַקָּדוֹשׁ בָּרוּךְ הוּא לְזַכּוֹת אֶת יִשְׂרָאֵל — *The Holy One, Blessed is He, wished to confer merit upon Israel*

The philosophers' interpretation of this *mishnah* is fundamentally in error for another reason. The *mishnah* does not mean that God wished to do Israel a favor, so He gave them many *mitzvos* and much Torah. If that were so, *mitzvos* would be for our benefit and hence *mitzvos* would

---

1. I.e., the reward of a *mitzvah* is not arbitrary, but integral to the performance of the *mitzvah*.

„יהוה חָפֵץ לְמַעַן צִדְקוֹ, יַגְדִּיל תּוֹרָה
וְיַאְדִּיר."

be optional. It is a halachic fact that *mitzvos* are not for our benefit,[1] and *mitzvos* are emphatically not optional.

The *mishnah* means that God wished to confer merit upon Israel whether or not they agree to it. God is righteous and He wants mankind to likewise be extremely worthy and to have much merit. He gave many *mitzvos* and much Torah to accomplish that purpose, and as a result Torah and *mitzvos* are compulsory. It is God's will that we have much merit, and therefore *mitzvos* are not optional, for there is no escaping what His will has mandated.

⧏ רָצָה הַקָּדוֹשׁ בָּרוּךְ הוּא לְזַכּוֹת אֶת יִשְׂרָאֵל — *The Holy One, Blessed is He, wished to confer merit upon Israel*

How does Chanania ben Akashia know that *mitzvos* were mandated to give Israel merit? Perhaps *mitzvos* are arbitrary decrees?

He bases his position on the fact that Hashem desired Torah to be great and glorious **for the sake of His righteousness.** Because God is

---

1. *Rosh Hashanah* 28a states that one may fulfill the *mitzvah* of hearing the *shofar* through the *shofar*-sounding of a person from whom he has forsworn any benefit. The reason given is that *mitzvos* are not considered a benefit.

(*Yeshayahu* 42:21): "Hᴀꜱʜᴇᴍ desired, for the sake of His righteousness, that the Torah be made great and glorious."

righteous, He loves righteousness, and He gave an abundance of Torah and *mitzvos* so that His people would likewise also be righteous.

Maharal, in *Derech Chaim,* opens our eyes to the spiritual structure of Creation. He explains that Torah is the tree of life rooted in God's existence, and that Torah study and practice cause beauty and worth to flow into our lives. Torah imbues life with the continuous potential to establish a multifaceted relationship with God, which will be the basis of our eternal existence in the World to Come. Although the opportunity to spend eternity in God's close presence is a foreboding challenge, the Rabbis of the *Mishnah* and Talmud have provided us with the knowledge and guidance we need to achieve this ultimate spiritual success.

❧ ה' חָפֵץ לְמַעַן צִדְקוֹ יַגְדִּיל תּוֹרָה וְיַאְדִּיר ,, — Hᴀꜱʜᴇᴍ *desired, for the sake of His righteousness, that the Torah be made great and gloriouss."*

"That the Torah be made great" means that He gave much Torah. **"And glorious"** refers to an abundance of *mitzvos.*

פרק שני ֍
Chapter Two

כָּל יִשְׂרָאֵל יֵשׁ לָהֶם חֵלֶק לָעוֹלָם הַבָּא,
שֶׁנֶּאֱמַר: ,,וְעַמֵּךְ כֻּלָּם צַדִּיקִים; לְעוֹלָם יִירְשׁוּ
אָרֶץ; נֵצֶר מַטָּעַי, מַעֲשֵׂה יָדַי לְהִתְפָּאֵר.''

All Israel has a share in the World to Come, as it is said (*Yeshayahu* 60:21): "And your people are all righteous; they shall inherit the land forever; they are the stem of My plantings, My handiwork, in which to take pride'.'

[א] **רַבִּי** אוֹמֵר: אֵיזוֹ הִיא דֶרֶךְ יְשָׁרָה שֶׁיָבֹר לוֹ הָאָדָם? כָּל שֶׁהִיא תִפְאֶרֶת לְעֹשֶׂיהָ וְתִפְאֶרֶת לוֹ מִן הָאָדָם.

Mishnah 1

Rabbi Yehudah HaNasi was President of the Rabbinical Court and the leader of all Jewry. He was the son of Rabbi Shimon ben Gamliel, author of the previous *mishnah*.

Chapter 1 chronicled the rabbinical dynasty of Hillel's descendants as far as Rabbi Shimon ben Gamliel. Rabbi Yehudah HaNasi's words could well have been joined to his father's words at the end of that chapter. However, the comprehensive scope of this *mussar* and the eminence of its author serve best as the start of a new chapter.

אֵיזוֹ הִיא דֶרֶךְ יְשָׁרָה — *Which is the proper path* ⋅§

Maharal understands the Hebrew *derech yesharah* (proper path) to describe a path that is the proper balance of a range of perspectives.

Following the path of the Torah leads to eternal life in the World to Come. Torah, however, is not like a railroad track that guides a train automatically to its destination. It is, rather, like a map, which requires human ingenuity to navigate, by selecting a path among many possible paths, each of which is paved with Torah and *mitzvos*. [1]

A path is defined by boundaries that constrain movement to ensure that one keeps within the path. The left side excludes everything to the left; the right side excludes everything to the right. The path is the narrow space between those two sides.

This *mishnah* tells us that there is a "balanced path," defined on one side by subjective opinion of what is proper, and on the other side by external perceptions of what is proper. To choose the right path is to do the right thing in the right way, by testing the integrity of our choices against personal and public standards.

כָּל שֶׁהִיא תִפְאֶרֶת לְעֹשֶׂיהָ וְתִפְאֶרֶת לוֹ מִן הָאָדָם — *Whatever is* ⋅§
a credit to himself and earns him the esteem of fellow men.

The choice of the "balanced path" must be confirmed by the judgment of other people.

---

1. Of course, there are countless non-Torah paths that lead to a dead end.

1. Rabbi says: Which is the proper path that a man should choose for himself? Whatever is a credit to himself and earns him the esteem of fellow men.

We may ask: If a person does that which he knows to be good, why does he need to consider the opinion of others? The answer is that behavior must be acceptable to the community as well as to God. Behavior can be truly upright and yet arouse suspicion or contempt. For example, a modest person might ensure that no one ever knows of his generous donations to charity. Yet if no one sees him giving charity, people may suspect him of not donating at all.[1] Although this person might choose to conceal the extent of his generosity, he should not keep all of his charitable acts under cover.

A Torah scholar in particular must be careful. He could desecrate God's Name by acting in a way that may appear to be improper or unpleasant. For example,[2] people could suspect a Torah scholar of trying to avoid payment if he buys groceries on credit from a store-keeper who is lax about collecting debts. Since a Torah scholar is the living model of God's word, God's Name could be defamed as a result of this innocent act.

Therefore, when we choose a proper path we must consider how others will perceive our behavior.

⧉§ כָּל שֶׁהִיא תִפְאֶרֶת לְעֹשֶׂיהָ וְתִפְאֶרֶת לוֹ מִן הָאָדָם — *Whatever is a credit to himself and earns him the esteem of fellow men.*

Conversely, we may ask: If others approve of his actions, why must he himself consider his deeds honorable as well? The reason is that the proper path must originate in the sincere pursuit of goodness, and an external observer cannot ascertain sincerity.

A sincere person directs his acts for the sake of Heaven. A person who wishes to gain approval by appearing to be righteous is not on the "proper path." One's actions must *receive* public esteem, but must not be *motivated* by it.

⧉§ מִן הָאָדָם — *of fellow men*

The choice of the Hebrew *adam* for "fellow men" connotes refined and discerning people, in contrast to the more general term *briyos*. Those

---

1. Author's example.
2. Author's example, based on *Yoma* 86a.

who know and discern laudable behavior set the standard of what is commendable; the opinion of coarse people does not provide a standard.

In summary, a proper path can be discerned when these factors are present together:

- The action arises from sincere religious motivation.
- One personally considers it a proper path.
- It is pleasing to refined and discerning people.
- It is not *motivated* by the fact that it is pleasing to others.

⊰ שֶׁיָּבֹר לוֹ הָאָדָם . . . וֶהֱוֵי זָהִיר ⊱ —
that a man should choose . . . Be as scrupulous

The shift in voice from the third person: "that a man should choose" to the imperative: "Be as scrupulous" signals a shift from the realm of personal choice — a proper path — to the realm of mandatory observance of *mitzvos*. There are many ways to do the right thing and we **should** choose the best way according to circumstances. Torah law, by contrast, is mandatory, and the *mishnah* adjures us to **be** as careful to perform a minor *mitzvah* as a major one. There is no room here for personal choice, to pick and choose among *mitzvos*.

Rabbi Yehudah HaNasi addresses both the subjective and the absolute aspects of religious life. He advocates that we do what we believe is right, in a way that takes social sensibilities into consideration; and he calls for compliance with all Torah law. Upright behavior comes first in the *mishnah,* because proper social conduct should precede Torah observance.[1]

⊰ וֶהֱוֵי זָהִיר בְּמִצְוָה קַלָּה כְּבַחֲמוּרָה ⊱ — *Be as scrupulous in*
performing a "minor" mitzvah as in a "major" one

Although all *mitzvos* must be observed with equal diligence, some *mitzvos* do defer to other *mitzvos* when a conflict arises. For example, burying a deceased person when there is no one else to tend to the funeral takes precedence over such major *mitzvos* as the Pesach sacrifice or ritual circumcision. This fact does not contradict our *mishnah,*

---

1. Based on *Vayikra Rabbah,* Section 9: "Proper social conduct (*derech eretz*) preceded the Torah by 26 generations." This point is dealt with more fully in the commentary to the next *mishnah.*

2/ 1   Be as scrupulous in performing a "minor" *mitzvah* as in a "major" one, for you do not know the reward given for the respective *mitzvos.*

because the Torah's order of precedence is not determined by which *mitzvah* offers the greater reward. It is very possible that there is greater reward for the Pesach sacrifice than for burying an abandoned body; nevertheless, the Torah commands that a body be buried without delay. Certainly, we on our own have no basis by which to decide to do one *mitzvah* rather than another.

◆§ שֶׁאֵין אַתָּה יוֹדֵעַ מַתַּן שְׂכָרָן שֶׁל מִצְוֹת — *for you do not know the reward given for the respective mitzvos*

The reason we do not know the reward for *mitzvos* is that reward awaits us in the World to Come, which we cannot comprehend from our perspective in this physical world.

God created the world so that people could come close to Him in the World to Come, by doing *mitzvos* in this world.[1] Ultimately, it is God's perspective which determines the value of a *mitzvah* and not our limited perception. The following *midrash*[2] illustrates that we do not share God's perspective on the whole of creation and hence we cannot assess the value of one kind of *mitzvah* in isolation.

> Rav Acha said: It is like a king who brought workers into his orchard and did not reveal to them the payment for tending each kind of tree. Had he revealed the pay scale, the workers would have tended to only the most profitable type of tree. The result would have been that part of the orchard would have been maintained and part would have been neglected. So it is that God did not reveal the reward for *mitzvos.*

◆§ שֶׁאֵין אַתָּה יוֹדֵעַ מַתַּן שְׂכָרָן שֶׁל מִצְוֹת — *for you do not know the reward given for the respective mitzvos*

The reward for a *mitzvah* is commensurate with its ability to bring a person close to God. It is entirely possible that a minor *mitzvah* brings a person closer to God than does a major one. There is no connection

---

1. Author's explanatory comment, based on Maharal's writings. This point is dealt with more fully in later chapters.
2. *Tanchuma, Eikev.*

between how close the *mitzvah* itself brings a person to God and how difficult or simple it is to do.

In addition to each *mitzvah*'s own ability to bring us close to God, there is reward for the effort exerted to perform a *mitzvah*. [1] We know that certain *mitzvos* carry extra reward because they entail exceptional effort or expense. This fact does not contradict the statement that "you do not know the reward," because the *mishnah* speaks only of the undisclosed reward for the *mitzvah* itself, and not of the reward for effort.

Negative *mitzvos* [2] do not have an inherent reward as do positive *mitzvos*. Their reward comes solely from the self-discipline and effort that their observance entails. [3]

It might appear that *mitzvos* such as acts of kindness, which bring reward in both this world and the World to Come, [4] have a double reward and are an exception to the statement that "you do not know the reward." This is not so, because the total reward in both this world and the next might not be greater than that of *mitzvos* whose reward is only in the World to Come.

Although we do not know how to calculate the reward for *mitzvos,* we do know that the reward for Torah study exceeds the reward for other *mitzvos.* [5] This is because Torah study brings us close to God more effectively than any other *mitzvah.*

---

§ וֶהֱוֵי מְחַשֵּׁב הֶפְסֵד מִצְוָה כְּנֶגֶד שְׂכָרָהּ — *Calculate the loss due to a mitzvah against its reward*

The loss due to fulfilling a positive commandment is the effort or expense required to fulfill it. The loss due to not transgressing a negative commandment is the pleasure it would have provided.

---

1. The greater the effort, adversity and outlay expended on a *mitzvah*, the greater its reward. See *infra,* Chapter 5, *mishnah* 26.

2. I.e., *mitzvos lo saaseh.* These are those *mitzvos* which are worded as things that are forbidden to do.

3. *Kiddushin* 39b. One is given reward for observing a negative commandment when opportunity and temptation are present and one disciplines his natural instincts.

4. *Peah,* Chapter 1, *mishnah* 1: "These are the precepts whose fruits a person enjoys in this world, but whose principal remains intact for him in the World to Come: honoring of father and mother, and acts of kindness. . . and bringing peace between man and his fellow."

5. *Ibid.:* "and the study of Torah is equivalent to them all."

2/ 1 Calculate the loss due to a mitzvah against its reward, and the reward of a sin against its cost. Consider

---

§ וּשְׂכַר עֲבֵרָה כְּנֶגֶד הֶפְסֵדָהּ — *and the reward of a sin against its cost*

The reward of a sin is the pleasure that the transgression offers; the cost is the lost reward which God would have bestowed for observing His commandment.

How can we weigh the reward against the loss, if we do not know the relative reward for *mitzvos*? The evaluation is easy. The loss due to a *mitzvah* is sustained in this world; it is only money, effort or the discomfort of self-discipline. Such a loss is far outweighed by the eternal reward of a *mitzvah* in the World to Come, which transcends any experience in this world, as the Rabbis said,[1]

> Better one hour of spiritual tranquillity in the World to Come than the entire life of this world.

The reward for fulfilling a positive commandment is immense, and exercising self-discipline in the face of temptation brings great reward for observing a negative commandment as well.

---

§ וֶהֱוֵי מְחַשֵּׁב הֶפְסֵד מִצְוָה כְּנֶגֶד שְׂכָרָהּ, וּשְׂכַר עֲבֵרָה כְּנֶגֶד הֶפְסֵדָהּ —
Calculate the loss due to a mitzvah against its reward,
and the reward of a sin against its cost.

This advice seems to advocate performing *mitzvos* for the sake of their reward, in contradiction of Antignos of Socho who said,[2] "Be not like servants who serve their master for the sake of receiving a reward!"

In reality, our *mishnah* does not consider reward to be the purpose behind observing *mitzvos*. It uses the fact that there is a reward as a practical stratagem, to deal with lethargy and temptation. Ideally, the motivation to observe *mitzvos* should clearly be the love of God.

Be as scrupulous . . . Calculate the loss . . .
Consider three things . . .

These three exhortations address the reasons for which people do not adequately observe the Torah: lack of motivation; concern for loss; and the temptation of pleasure. "Be scrupulous in performing a . . . *mitzvah*" addresses indifference to the chance to do a *mitzvah* because of a belief

---

1. *Infra*, Chapter 4, *mishnah* 22.
2. *Supra*, Chapter 1, *mishnah* 3.

בִּשְׁלֹשָׁה דְבָרִים, וְאֵין אַתָּה בָא לִידֵי עֲבֵרָה:
דַּע מַה לְמַעְלָה מִמְּךְ — עַיִן רוֹאָה, וְאֹזֶן
שׁוֹמַעַת וְכָל מַעֲשֶׂיךְ בְּסֵפֶר נִכְתָּבִים.

that the reward for doing the *mitzvah* is insignificant. "Calculate the loss of a *mitzvah* against its reward" addresses the willingness to let the opportunity to do a *mitzvah* pass because it is too difficult or expensive to fulfill. "Consider three things" enables one to control the passion aroused by an opportunity to sin.

◆§ הִסְתַּכֵּל בִּשְׁלֹשָׁה דְבָרִים, וְאֵין אַתָּה בָא לִידֵי עֲבֵרָה: דַּע מַה לְמַעְלָה מִמְּךְ — *Consider three things, and you will not come into the grip of sin: Know what is above you*

This is Rabbi's third item of advice to help us observe *mitzvos* properly. A person may prefer to have enjoyment now, and to forgo the future reward for resisting sin. He could even lose sight of the punishment that will derive from transgression. Constant awareness that God observes human deeds and remembers them all keeps one from the grasp of sin.

◆§ עַיִן רוֹאָה — *a watchful Eye*

The expression "a watchful Eye" means that God sees human action at the human level. The use of the singular "eye" rather than "eyes," indicates vision rather than actual eyes.

This statement rejects the notion that God does not know what transpires on earth.

◆§ וְאֹזֶן שׁוֹמַעַת — *an attentive Ear*

The image of "a watchful Eye" has already conveyed that God *knows* what we do. The additional metaphor of "an attentive Ear" conveys that God *cares* about what we do.

This statement rejects the idea that God does not concern Himself with human affairs.

◆§ וְכָל מַעֲשֶׂיךְ בְּסֵפֶר נִכְתָּבִים — *and all your deeds are recorded in a book.*

In the future, God will judge us on everything we have done. Our deeds

2/ 1   three things, and you will not come into the grip of sin:
Know what is above you — a watchful Eye, an atten-
tive Ear and all your deeds are recorded in a book.

---

are recorded, just as a storekeeper keeps an accounts book, and the total
is evaluated at the end.

Know what is above you — *a watchful Eye, an attentive
Ear and all your deeds are recorded in a book.*

These are three fundamentals of Jewish belief: God knows our actions, He is concerned about them, and He rewards and punishes. Awareness of these principles keeps us away from the grasp of transgression.

⊷§ וְכָל מַעֲשֶׂיךָ בְּסֵפֶר נִכְתָּבִים — *and all
your deeds are recorded in a book*

Actions are never forgotten; they leave a mark on the person, on his
environment and on other people.

This is the metaphor of "a book." The act of writing leaves a lasting
impression, and each letter joins with the others to tell an entire story.
So too, our deeds create an indelible history that accumulates and builds
an overall impression.

The "book" in this metaphor is not written by God; it is written by each
one of us. Each of our actions adds another brush stroke to our self-
portrait.[1]

Furthermore, our actions leave their mark on the world itself, contributing to its overall character. We can make the world a kind place and
worthy of its continued existence, or a place of injustice and evil. Each
individual is judged for the impact of his deeds on the character of the
world.

The phrase "and all your deeds are recorded in a book" refers to this
cumulative image of the world.[2] Moshe Rabbeinu used this metaphor
when he said,[3]

> " . . . and if not, erase me please from Your book which You have
> written."

---

1. Author's metaphor.
2. I.e., the "book" is the world itself. Human deeds make their mark on the world, and
they leave their mark on the person himself.
3. *Shemos* 32:32. He was saying, in effect, "Negate the impact of my life upon the
character of the world."

ב/ב

ב/ב [ב] רַבָּן גַּמְלִיאֵל, בְּנוֹ שֶׁל רַבִּי יְהוּדָה הַנָּשִׂיא, אוֹמֵר: יָפֶה תַלְמוּד תּוֹרָה עִם

Similarly, the Rabbis used this metaphor when they said:[1]

> Three books are opened on Rosh Hashanah, one of entirely wicked people, one of entirely righteous people and one of intermediate people.[2]

The righteous impart a different character to the world than do the wicked. Intermediate people confer still a different character on the world. These three images of the world are the "books" that are opened on Rosh Hashanah and this is the "Book" in which, the *mishnah* says, "all your deeds are recorded."

⋈§ הִסְתַּכֵּל בִּשְׁלֹשָׁה דְבָרִים — *Consider three things* §⋈

Rabbi Yehudah HaNasi says that keeping these three things in mind prevents us from coming within the grasp of sin. How can this advice possibly be of use? Presumably, anyone who is not watchful for the chance to do *mitzvos* and avoid sin will also not be careful to keep these three things constantly in mind.

The answer is that it is easier to follow this advice than it is to keep *mitzvos*. There is a natural drive to transgress, which we call the *yetzer hara*. It makes the burden of a positive *mitzvah* loom large and it magnifies the desire to transgress a negative commandment. Because it is not a *mitzvah* to remember the three things of this *mishnah*, there is no compelling desire to forget them, and with these things firmly in mind, the desire to transgress is minimal. For this reason, the *mishnah* states that one will not come within the "grasp" of sin, rather than saying that one will not sin.

⋈§ הִסְתַּכֵּל בִּשְׁלֹשָׁה דְבָרִים . . . דַּע מַה לְמַעְלָה מִמְּךָ — *Consider three things . . . Know what is above you* §⋈

The words, "Consider three things," teach us an important lesson about the purpose behind the unique human form.

---

1. *Rosh Hashanah* 16b.
2. Maharal, *Drush L'Shabbos Teshuvah*, "The human being himself is an account book in which everything is written. . . .As Rabbi said in *Avos*, Chapter 2: 'and all your deeds are recorded in a book.' This book is the person himself, for his merits and wrongdoings are registered in him."

Because God's presence is not visible in this world, it is easy for people to come to sin. God compensated for this physical blind spot with the spiritual ability to perceive and fear God. Our erect human posture permits us to easily gaze at the heavens. There we observe God's presence through the sun, the rain and other forces He directs, and we are less inclined to sin. The use of the Hebrew word *histakel* for "Consider three things" translates more literally as "Stare at three things and you will not come into the grip of sin." It suggests that we should use our upright physical stature to focus on God above, and not come within the grasp of sin.

Mishnah 2

Rabbi Gamliel's advice appropriately follows that of his father, Rabbi Yehudah HaNasi (Rabbi), in the previous *mishnah.* Rabbi's words encompassed good character attributes and the performance of *mitzvos,* which bring a person to the World to Come. He approached the subject in general terms, and his son now gives specific advice regarding proper social conduct in this world, which is preparatory to the Next World. Although the value of proper social conduct is less than that of *mitzvos,* it precedes *mitzvos* in this way: One must first conduct himself properly in society before acquiring Torah.[1] Hence, this *mishnah* establishes the practical foundation for the principles expressed in the first *mishnah.*

Torah study is good together with proper social conduct

The Hebrew *yafeh talmud Torah im derech eretz* implies that proper social conduct is primary and Torah study is subordinate. But surely Torah study is primary!

Rabban Gamliel does not mean to imply that proper social conduct is more important than Torah study. He means that spiritual matters must be observed in the correct sequence: Proper social conduct comes first and Torah comes afterwards. Proper social behavior must precede Torah study to provide the right environment for it. It is definitely not adequate to study Torah and to perform *mitzvos* without engaging in social norms such as working or good conduct.

This fact stems from the very nature of human development. Lesser intellectual skills, such as walking, develop first and only later do greater intellectual skills, such as reading, develop. Since intellectual growth

---

1. Based on *Vayikra Rabbah,* Section 9: "Proper social conduct, *derech eretz,* preceded the Torah by 26 generations."

ב/ב דֶּרֶךְ אֶרֶץ, שֶׁיְּגִיעַת שְׁנֵיהֶם מַשְׁכַּחַת עָוֹן. וְכָל תּוֹרָה שֶׁאֵין עִמָּהּ מְלָאכָה סוֹפָהּ בְּטֵלָה,

must be built on a physical foundation, we should first gain pragmatic social skills and then address our efforts to the intellectual endeavor of Torah study.

⊷§ שֶׁיְּגִיעַת שְׁנֵיהֶם מַשְׁכַּחַת עָוֹן — *for the exertion of them both makes sin forgotten*

One who is complete is remote from sin. The opposite is also true: Sin is synonymous with deficiency. The human being has both physical and spiritual components and both of these are subject to deficiency. Proper social conduct rounds out the practical side of life, while Torah study perfects the spiritual side. Through the pursuit of both together, we are complete in both aspects and hence remote from sin. If a person devotes his personal development entirely to practical matters, or entirely to Torah study without regard for his physical needs, he will remain undeveloped in the other major aspect, and that deficiency promotes the further deficiency of sin.

⊷§ שֶׁיְּגִיעַת שְׁנֵיהֶם — *for the exertion of them both*

Exertion is essential to avoiding sin, because sin is always found with repose.[1]

In this world of inevitable change, things improve until they are complete. At that point, the only change possible is for the worse.[2] To relax is to act as if one had achieved completeness, and that sets in motion the destructive forces that are personified as "Satan," or "the Evil Inclination" or "the Angel of Death."[3] In contrast, **exertion** implies that perfection has not yet been achieved. Since growth is the opposite of deterioration, the two do not coexist and the pursuit of personal growth will displace the degeneration that we call sin.[4]

---

1. Complacency invites deterioration, and we said in the previous paragraph that deficiency promotes the further deficiency of sin.
2. To illustrate from daily life: Deterioration is the inevitable next step for a bloom in its prime, or a ripe fruit or for a person in his prime.
3. *Bava Basra* 16a. These are different personifications of a single destructive force that acts to the detriment of human beings.
4. The thought is phrased very succinctly by the Vilna Gaon: "If a person does not continuously strive to rise higher and higher, he will inevitably descend lower and lower" (*Even Shleimah*, Chapter 4, number 9).

proper social conduct, for the exertion of them both makes sin forgotten. All Torah study that is not joined with work will cease in the end,

In summary, the Evil Inclination (*Yetzer Hara*) and the Satan, the personifications of desire and temptation to sin, are powerless against one who is still developing. By working at self-improvement, we demonstrate that we are not yet fully actualized, and that we are indeed prepared to grow further. That displaces the destructive desire for sin.

In contrast, one who is complacent acts as if he were already perfect, with no prospect of growth, and he will consequently degenerate through sin.

⊷§ שֶׁיְּגִיעַת שְׁנֵיהֶם מַשְׁכַּחַת עָוֹן — *for the exertion of them both makes sin forgotten*

The human being has a physical component and a spiritual component. Continuous effort in both areas is necessary to escape the desire for sin that permeates both arenas of life.

To explain this point in Kabbalistic terms: there are two fundamental types of destructive desire — the desire[1] for illicit physical gratification and the desire[2] for illicit spiritual fulfillment. The pursuit of worldly requirements and the pursuit of Torah are the antidotes for these desires. The pursuit of material needs displaces the desire for illicit physical satisfaction, while spiritual pursuits through Torah displace the desire for spurious spiritual gratification such as pride.[3]

⊷§ וְכָל תּוֹרָה שֶׁאֵין עִמָּהּ מְלָאכָה סוֹפָהּ בְּטֵלָה — *All Torah study that is not joined with work will cease in the end*

Work makes a person whole. Torah study that is not accompanied by work will "cease in the end" because the person himself is deficient, and anything that is deficient does not endure.

---

1. יצרא דערוה, *yitzra d'ervah.*
2. יצרא דעבודה זרה, *yitzra d'avodah zarah.*
3. Author's adaptation, based on Maharal's *Chidushei Aggados* to the statement in *Sotah 4b:* "Rabbi Yochanan said. . .everyone who has a haughty spirit is as though he worshiped idols."

ב/ב וְגוֹרֶרֶת עָוֹן. וְכָל הָעוֹסְקִים עִם הַצִּבּוּר יִהְיוּ
עוֹסְקִים עִמָּהֶם לְשֵׁם שָׁמַיִם, שֶׁזְּכוּת אֲבוֹתָם

וּבָל תּוֹרָה שֶׁאֵין עִמָּהּ מְלָאכָה . . . גּוֹרֶרֶת עָוֹן — *All Torah study that is not joined with work . . . leads to sin.*

The *mishnah* tells us that a person who does not work is susceptible to sin in general. Why would that be so? We would expect that a lack of work would cause only the sin of dishonesty, due to the need for money.

However, the *mishnah* reveals a fascinating principle: If a person does not work, he will find that various sins arise unexpectedly,[1] and this will be true even for a person who studies Torah.

In contrast, a person who is complete in body and soul, through the pursuit of both Torah study and work, will avert even sins which might normally have been expected.

וּבָל תּוֹרָה שֶׁאֵין עִמָּהּ מְלָאכָה . . . גּוֹרֶרֶת עָוֹן — *All Torah study that is not joined with work . . . leads to sin.*

In fact, there have been many Torah scholars who did not go to work![2] In some cases, they were engaged in trade, which is just as beneficial as work. In other cases, their soul was so enamored of Torah that the love itself sustained their Torah studies.

וְכָל הָעוֹסְקִים עִם הַצִּבּוּר יִהְיוּ עוֹסְקִים עִמָּהֶם לְשֵׁם שָׁמַיִם — *All who exert themselves for the community should exert themselves for the sake of Heaven*

Why are the two apparently different subjects of Torah study and of community work combined in the same *mishnah*? The similarity is that Torah and community are both general entities, in contrast to specific *mitzvos* of the Torah or individual members of the community.

A person who helps the community as a total entity is acting "for the sake of Heaven" because God concerns Himself especially with the community. In this light, the welfare of the community can be seen to be

---

1. The reason is that the lack of a necessary component brings in its wake still further deficiency, until one reaches the ultimate deficiency, sin.
2. Maharal considers "work" as *adding value* through manufacture or service, as opposed to "trade" which is just buying or selling. See Chapter 6, *Baraisa* 6 item 21.

a spiritual matter. Indeed, we are permitted to discuss affairs of communal welfare on Shabbos[1] for it is considered a religious matter.

However, a person whose community efforts are for personal self-aggrandizement is not engaged with the public and clearly is not acting "for the sake of Heaven." Even if his efforts are sincere, but directed towards particular individuals, his contribution is not at the special level of working on behalf of the overall community.

⧉ וְכָל הָעוֹסְקִים עִם הַצִּבּוּר — *All who exert themselves for the community*

Why does the *mishnah* combine the subject of community work with that of proper social conduct?

The *mishnah* informs us that although "proper social conduct" is generally just the groundwork for greater things such as Torah study, a person whose "proper social conduct" lies in providing for the needs of the community has a very substantial reward indeed.

⧉ שֶׁזְכוּת אֲבוֹתָם מְסַיִּעְתָּם — *for then the merit of their fathers aids them*

Their *fathers* refers to the forefathers, Avraham, Yitzchak and Yaakov.

The merit of *whose* fathers is aiding them? Since *father* means the forefathers, who are considered fathers to the nation in general, the phrase "*their* fathers" must refer to the nation of Israel's fathers.

To whom does the phrase "aids *them*" refer? It refers to the individuals helping the community. Hence, the complete statement means: "The merit of the nation's fathers helps community workers succeed in their task of helping the nation."

⧉ שֶׁזְכוּת אֲבוֹתָם מְסַיִּעְתָּם — *for then the merit of their fathers aids them*

An additional interpretation holds that the phrase *their* fathers does indeed refer to those individuals working for the community.

---

1. *Shabbos,* 150a: "They may designate charity funds to the poor on Shabbos." Discussions of a financial nature are generally prohibited on Shabbos.

ב/ג מְסַיַּעְתָּם, וְצִדְקָתָם עוֹמֶדֶת לָעַד. וְאַתֶּם, מַעֲלֶה אֲנִי עֲלֵיכֶם שָׂכָר הַרְבֵּה כְּאִלּוּ עֲשִׂיתֶם. [ג] הֱווּ זְהִירִין בָּרָשׁוּת, שֶׁאֵין מְקָרְבִין לוֹ לְאָדָם אֶלָּא לְצֹרֶךְ עַצְמָן; נִרְאִין כְּאוֹהֲבִין בְּשָׁעַת הֲנָאָתָן, וְאֵין עוֹמְדִין לוֹ לְאָדָם בִּשְׁעַת דָּחְקוֹ.

Although we said before that the forefathers are considered fathers only of the community and not of individuals, the *mishnah* tells us that an individual can personally acquire the special status of "community" by acting in the public welfare.[1] Therefore, the forefathers are considered *his* fathers, and their merit provides him with assistance, protection, and guidance.

◈§ וְצִדְקָתָם עוֹמֶדֶת לָעַד — *and their righteousness endures forever*

In this phrase, *whose* righteousness endures forever? It is not the righteousness of the community that "endures forever," for individual communities may come and go. Hence, "*their* righteousness" refers to the righteousness of the nation of Israel. The *mishnah* means that even if this specific community eventually moves or dwindles away, it is a part of the community of Israel that "endures forever." The implication for communal leaders is powerful, for they have tremendous merit that comes of benefiting an eternal nation and not just their specific community.

Those who work for the benefit of the community are participants in the merit which began with the forefathers[2] and which continues throughout all generations into the future. If the leaders of Israel understood these words with all their might, they would labor with the community for the sake of Heaven, and never for their own benefit.

◈§ מַעֲלֶה אֲנִי עֲלֵיכֶם שָׂכָר הַרְבֵּה כְּאִלּוּ עֲשִׂיתֶם — *I [God] will bestow upon you as great a reward as if you had accomplished it on your own*

The great merit of helping the community belongs to those who work with the community, despite the fact that the merit of the forefathers was

---

1. So close is their attachment to the community.
2. The forefathers initiated Torah-based civilization.

aids them and their righteousness endures forever. Nevertheless, as for you, I [God] will bestow upon you as great a reward as if you had accomplished it on your own.

3. Beware of rulers, for they befriend someone only for their own benefit; they act friendly when it benefits them, but they do not stand by someone in his time of need.

the enabling factor for their success. The needs of a community are many, and therefore the merit of addressing those needs is great.

Mishnah 3

This statement follows directly after the advice[1] that addresses "All who exert themselves for the community" because "rulers" are the antithesis of "community." They are distinct from the community, rather than being a part of it. Those in public office distance themselves from the community through their importance and prominence. Even when they seemingly attempt to lead the public as if they were concerned with community needs, it simply is not so.

וְאֵין עוֹמְדִין לוֹ לָאָדָם בִּשְׁעַת דָּחֳקוֹ — *but they do not stand by someone in his time of need*

If they do not stand by someone in his time of need, they certainly will not help someone who is not in need! When they do befriend someone it is only for their own advantage, not because they have any attachment to the people.

A warning to community leaders is implied by the juxtaposition of this *mishnah* and the preceding *mishnah,* "all who exert themselves for the community." Some leaders counsel the community in a way that is in conflict with its best interests, in an effort to please and ingratiate themselves to the authorities. They hope to gain personal benefit, but forget the message of this *mishnah*: The authorities act only to their own advantage. Therefore, not only will they fail to achieve their selfish purpose, but they will be punished for having misused their position to act against the community's interest.

---

1. *Supra, mishnah 2.*

[ד] הוּא הָיָה אוֹמֵר: עֲשֵׂה רְצוֹנוֹ כִּרְצוֹנֶךָ, כְּדֵי שֶׁיַּעֲשֶׂה רְצוֹנְךָ כִּרְצוֹנוֹ. בַּטֵּל רְצוֹנְךָ מִפְּנֵי רְצוֹנוֹ, כְּדֵי שֶׁיְּבַטֵּל רְצוֹן אֲחֵרִים מִפְּנֵי רְצוֹנֶךָ.

[ה] הִלֵּל אוֹמֵר: אַל תִּפְרוֹשׁ מִן הַצִּבּוּר; וְאַל תַּאֲמִין בְּעַצְמְךָ עַד יוֹם מוֹתְךָ; וְאַל תָּדִין אֶת חֲבֵרְךָ עַד שֶׁתַּגִּיעַ לִמְקוֹמוֹ;

Mishnah 4

---

§ כְּדֵי שֶׁיַּעֲשֶׂה רְצוֹנֶךָ — *so that He will treat your will* ⊱

This *mishnah* declares that it is within the power of a human being to direct God's full good will towards oneself.

---

§ כְּדֵי שֶׁיַּעֲשֶׂה רְצוֹנֶךָ כִּרְצוֹנוֹ — *so that He will treat your will as if it were His will* ⊱

Ultimately, a person needs only two things:
1) to acquire everything he needs but does not yet possess.
2) to ensure that he does not suffer at the hands of others.
   God provides these two needs in response to a person's love of God and fear of God, respectively.
1) Love of God with all our heart, which we express by doing God's will, is reciprocated by God's providing us with what we need.
   Since loving God completely is itself God's will, this merges God's will and our own will. It follows that God would fulfill our will as He would do His own will.
2) Fear of God brings protection against someone else's will being imposed upon us. Fear of God means abnegating our will to sin, in deference to the will of God, Who does not want sin. When a person desires to pursue a sinful act, but forgoes sinning because of his reverence for God, then his will becomes the same as God's will. As a result, God ensures that the will of others does not prevail against his will.
   In conclusion, one can improve all aspects of life through complete love and reverence for God, for this merges his own will and God's will until they are virtually one.

4. He used to say: Treat His will as if it were your own will, so that He will treat your will as if it were His will. Nullify your will before His will, so that He will nullify the will of others before your will.

5. Hillel says: Do not separate yourself from the community; do not believe in yourself until the day you die; do not judge your fellow until you have reached his place;

Mishnah 5

---

§⇒ הִלֵּל אוֹמֵר: אַל תִּפְרוֹשׁ מִן הַצִּבּוּר — *Hillel says: Do not separate yourself from the community*

It may be asked why this statement was not presented with Hillel's earlier statements.[1] It is also noteworthy that the statements within the *mishnah* appear to have nothing in common.

The sequence of this *mishnah* within the chapter is by subject matter, not by chronological order. It continues from the theme of community, exploring the contrast between the role of the community and the role of the individual. As we have seen, the community occupies a lofty position in the spiritual order of values. In contrast, an individual's significance is minimal and limited. Therefore, only a person who is part of the community can share in its lofty spiritual level in this world or the next. Hence, Hillel cautions against parting ways with the public.

---

§⇒ וְאַל תַּאֲמִין בְּעַצְמְךָ עַד יוֹם מוֹתְךָ — *do not believe in yourself until the day you die*

A community has stability, whereas an individual is changeable. Do not trust that you are righteous until the very day of your death, for a person can change at any moment.

The remainder of the *mishnah* examines different kinds of changeability that affect our lives.

---

§⇒ וְאַל תָּדִין אֶת חֲבֵרְךָ עַד שֶׁתַּגִּיעַ לִמְקוֹמוֹ — *do not judge your fellow until you have reached his place*

Since you, as an individual, can change, do not judge a person with

---

1. *Supra*, Chapter 1, *mishnayos* 12-14.

ב/ו וְאַל תֹּאמַר דָּבָר שֶׁאִי אֶפְשָׁר לִשְׁמוֹעַ שֶׁסּוֹפוֹ
לְהִשָּׁמַע; וְאַל תֹּאמַר, ,,לִכְשֶׁאֶפָּנֶה אֶשְׁנֶה,"
שֶׁמָּא לֹא תִפָּנֶה.

[ו] הוּא הָיָה אוֹמֵר: אֵין בּוּר יְרֵא חֵטְא, וְלֹא
עַם הָאָרֶץ חָסִיד; וְלֹא הַבַּיְשָׁן לָמֵד,

---

disdain. You might also have succumbed to the circumstances which caused that person to sin.

◈§ וְאַל תֹּאמַר דָּבָר שֶׁאִי אֶפְשָׁר לִשְׁמוֹעַ שֶׁסּוֹפוֹ לְהִשָּׁמַע — *do not make a statement that cannot be easily understood on the ground that it will be understood eventually*

Maharal understands the text to mean: "Do not say that something is inconceivable, for in the end it will happen."

One should not rationalize his life style by saying that there is no conceivable way that things can go wrong. For example, a rich person may believe, in the arrogance that accompanies success, that he can do whatever he wants and get away with it. He finds it inconceivable that a person with his wealth could ever lose his possessions. This *mishnah* warns that his good fortune can change no matter how unlikely that may appear to him, and his overconfidence is unfounded.

Hillel first warned us not to pass judgment without firsthand experience, because there may be some unusual circumstance that we do not know. He now goes a step further, and cautions us not to expect life to be free of change by even an inconceivable turn of events.

The next statement takes the progression yet a step further:

◈§ וְאַל תֹּאמַר, ,,לִכְשֶׁאֶפָּנֶה אֶשְׁנֶה", שֶׁמָּא לֹא תִפָּנֶה — *and do not say, "When I am free I will study," for perhaps you will not become free.*

A person cannot expect his life to be predictable for even an hour! One should not say, "I will study in an hour or two, when I will have time," thinking that life is stable enough to plan within such a short span. Even that assumption is incorrect. Life is so changeable that a situation that needs attention might arise even within the hour.

These four statements of Hillel identify the four causes of change in a person's life. These are: the instability inherent in human nature;

do not make a statement that cannot be easily understood on the ground that it will be understood eventually; and do not say, "When I am free I will study," for perhaps you will not become free.

6. He used to say: A boor cannot be fearful of sin; an unlearned person cannot be scrupulously pious; the bashful person cannot learn,

---

changing circumstances; developments which come about with time; and continual minor disruptions.

Mishnah 6

The terms "boor" and "unlearned person" emphasize different aspects of a person who is void of Torah and wisdom. The word "boor" emphasizes a lack of *knowledge*; it depicts a person who is intellectually barren. The term "unlearned person," *am haaretz,* emphasizes a lack of *wisdom*, which manifests itself through a lack of refinement in his conduct.

אֵין בּוּר יְרֵא חֵטְא — *A boor cannot be fearful of sin*

One who lacks Torah knowledge cannot acquire the fear of God.[1] The Rabbis say,[2]

> . . . if there is no wisdom there is no fear of Heaven.

> A person who does not have some intellectual inclination cannot develop the fear of God, because he cannot clearly perceive God's influence. People fear the king only when they are in his proximity. When they are far from the king, they are no longer as impressed by him and they no longer feel the same degree of fear.

> The boor is doomed to be remote from God and not fear Him properly, because closeness to God arises only through the intellect.

וְלֹא עַם הָאָרֶץ חָסִיד — *an unlearned person cannot be scrupulously pious*

The Hebrew term חָסִיד, *chasid,* a pious person, applies to a person of action. It denotes one who goes beyond the strict bounds of duty, to do more than the minimal requirement.

---

1. As will be presented *infra*, *mishnah* 14, the term יְרֵא חֵטְא, *yirei chait,* is associated with the purest form of intellect (*sechel*).
2. *Infra*, Chapter 3, *mishnah* 17.

True wisdom refines human action. As a result, if a person is fully given over to wisdom, he directs his deeds towards the good of all people, going beyond the strict call of duty. In contrast, the unlearned person does not direct his talents and skills towards goodness, for he lacks Torah wisdom,

In summary, a lack of Torah wisdom leaves one unable to acquire the fear of Heaven and disinclined to offer extra effort to help others.

וְלֹא הַבַּיְשָׁן לָמֵד, וְלֹא הַקַּפְּדָן מְלַמֵּד ‎§⊱ — *the bashful person cannot learn, and the quick, impatient person cannot teach*

Some explain this *mishnah* to mean that a shy person will not ask the questions necessary to fill the gaps in his knowledge; and that an impatient teacher makes the students afraid to ask such questions. That is a shallow explanation, which does not do justice to the profound truths behind the messages of the Rabbis.

Teacher-Student Relationship

This *mishnah* can be properly understood through the following principle: A teaching relationship can be effective only if the teacher, the student and the subject matter have something in common.

וְלֹא הַבַּיְשָׁן לָמֵד ‎§⊱ — *the bashful person cannot learn*

Torah is described as "fire."[1] It is the impassioned character of the nation of Israel that makes them especially attuned to the Torah and a student of Torah must also have a fiery character to be receptive to Torah.

Conversely, a shy personality, which is the opposite of fire, is not receptive to the fiery Torah because his spirit is not in harmony with the spirit of Torah.

וְלֹא הַקַּפְּדָן מְלַמֵּד ‎§⊱ — *and the quick, impatient person cannot teach*

As we said before, the student, the teacher and the subject must share qualities in common, if the student is to be receptive.

1. Yirmeyahu 23:29: "Is not My word like fire? says God." The metaphor of fire conveys intolerance for anything less than perfection." Devarim 33:2: "From His right hand went forth a fiery law for them (the people of Israel)."

and the quick, impatient person cannot teach; anyone excessively occupied in business cannot

---

People are both practical and intellectual. They can relate to the Torah, because it is likewise a mix of practical law and fiery intellect. However, if a teacher adds the fire of his impatience to the fire of Torah, there is too much fire. The studies become intolerable and the student cannot be receptive.

The metaphor of "fire" refers to being inflexible and intolerant of anything less than perfect truth.[1] A subject that is "fiery" appeals to an intelligent person's demand for precision and truth. A fiery teacher of the fiery Torah demands a thorough and precise grasp of a deep and exacting subject, and that combination is more than most students can bear.

⊷§ וְלֹא כָּל הַמַּרְבֶּה בִּסְחוֹרָה מַחְכִּים — *anyone excessively occupied in business cannot become a scholar*

This statement is included in the *mishnah,* because it is another example of a person whose character is not in harmony with the conceptual nature of Torah. We live in a physical world of interaction; but if one is to develop wisdom, he must foster the conceptual side of his personality. One who is too involved in trade — in buying, traveling and selling — has a much stronger attachment to the physical than to the conceptual. That person is unlikely to achieve great intellectual growth.

⊷§ כָּל הַמַּרְבֶּה בִּסְחוֹרָה — *anyone excessively occupied in business*

The warning of this *mishnah* is for those who just buy and sell, without adding value to the product. It does not apply to those who are artisans or otherwise improve the objects they sell. It does not apply even to those who buy and sell in moderation, according to their needs. We are, after all, physical human beings, and are only partly intellectual. However, one who is so occupied with trade that he is completely engrossed in the material side of life will not succeed in becoming a scholar.

Four Prescriptions for Spiritual Health

One of the ways that *Pirkei Avos* guides us to achieving spiritual growth is by helping us to understand ourselves. The people described in this *mishnah* are simply illustrations of disorders due to neglect of the

---

1. Author's explanation, based on commentary to Chapter 1, *mishnah* 14, *supra*.

ב/ז מַחְכִּים; וּבְמָקוֹם שֶׁאֵין אֲנָשִׁים, הִשְׁתַּדֵּל לִהְיוֹת אִישׁ.

[ז] אַף הוּא רָאָה גֻּלְגֹּלֶת אַחַת שֶׁצָּפָה עַל פְּנֵי הַמָּיִם. אָמַר לָהּ: „עַל דְּאַטֵפְתְּ אַטְפוּךְ,

four areas of our existence. We need a healthy intellect, spirit and body; and a healthy approach to material possessions.

The prescription for good spiritual health is easily recognized in each case, as we will now illustrate.

- The "intellect," *sechel,* is the most spiritual part of a person. The boor and the unlearned person manifest the symptoms of an undeveloped intellect. One who acts with reason can grasp the proper reverence for the Creator and will act with true piety. Therefore, one should strive to acquire wisdom.

- The "spirit," *nefesh,* animates the body; it is the origin of impatience and temper. Hillel illustrates this disorder by describing one whose anger interferes with teaching Torah. This is the second prescription: Do not be drawn excessively after emotions.

- One who is too shy is functioning as a placid "body." If we succumb to lethargy, instead of living our lives with spirited enthusiasm, it will interfere with Torah study. The third prescription is: Show some spirit! Do not be excessively drawn after physical characteristics of passivity and inertia.

- The "possessions" that sustain one in this world can distract a person from spiritual pursuits. The final prescription is: Do not be excessively drawn after money, but pursue a livelihood in moderation.

⥈§ וּבְמָקוֹם שֶׁאֵין אֲנָשִׁים, הִשְׁתַּדֵּל לִהְיוֹת אִישׁ — *and in a place where there are no people (to take charge), strive to be a person (who takes charge)*

This statement may appear unrelated to the rest of the *mishnah,* but in truth it completes the theme. The first part of the *mishnah* addressed aspects of a person, but this advice addresses the total human being.

If something must be done and there is no one else to do it, then be the person to do it. There is extra merit in doing the right thing if otherwise it will not be done at all.

become a scholar; and in a place where there are no people (to take charge), try to be a person (who takes charge).

7. He also saw a skull floating on the water. He said to it: "Because you drowned others, they drowned

---

◄§ וּבִמְקוֹם שֶׁאֵין אֲנָשִׁים — *in a place where there are no people (to take charge)*

However, if there is someone else who will do it equally well, and who is willing do it, you should let that person volunteer.

Mishnah 7

Hillel's words commence with "Because you drowned" and tell us that God metes out punishment in like kind for a transgression. This principle needs to be clarified, because we know that not every murderer is ultimately murdered, and we know that not everyone who has been drowned has drowned someone else.

The *mishnah* therefore added the image of a skull floating on water to put Hillel's words in context, as we will now explain.

◄§ אַף הוּא רָאָה גֻּלְגֹּלֶת אַחַת — *He also saw a skull*

Hillel actually saw a drowned body. The *mishnah* portrays the corpse as a "skull" to convey that the victim had been severed from the roots of life and left nothing behind: no reputation and no one to remember him. Had it been the corpse of someone who left a mark on the world, Hillel would not have concluded that it was the corpse of a murderer.

◄§ אָמַר לָהּ: ,,עַל דְּאַטֵּפְתְּ — *He said to it: "Because you drowned others*

Water that washes something away is itself washed away in the same process. This image describes the forces of retribution that the person himself had set in motion. He was destroyed by the backwash of the powerful destructive forces that he had unleashed against his victim. He must have destroyed his victim's reputation and eradicated any impact that the victim may have made on the world.

Hillel's remarks were made in the context of a person who deserved to have his life — past, present and future — destroyed. This observation

ב/ח וְסוֹף מְטַיְּפָיִךְ יְטוּפוּן.״

[ח] הוּא הָיָה אוֹמֵר: מַרְבֶּה בָשָׂר, מַרְבֶּה רִמָּה; מַרְבֶּה נְכָסִים, מַרְבֶּה דְאָגָה;

does not apply to the typical drowning victim, and it does not even apply to a murderer who takes only the victim's life, but does not eradicate his accomplishments.

Our history is filled with righteous, innocent and ordinary people who were brutally murdered. These people had not harmed anyone. The image of the disembodied skull was designed to exclude this kind of victim, because they in fact left the blessing of their memory and a legacy for future generations.

§ עַל דְּאֲטֵפְתְּ אַטְפוּךְ § — *''Because you drowned others they drowned you . . .*

The imagery in this *mishnah* is based on water, which in Hebrew has a plural form. Therefore Hillel says that *''they drowned you''* with reference to the metaphor of water.

§ וְסוֹף מְטַיְּפָיִךְ יְטוּפוּן § — *and those who drowned you will be drowned eventually.''*

Retribution for such a violent and extensive crime is quite likely to come, because the crime itself precipitates the punishment. Those murderers who do have natural and peaceful deaths will be ''drowned'' in the World to Come, which is yet a more severe form of being drowned.

Mishnah 8

There are two fundamental parts to a human being: the physical and the spiritual. The first part of the *mishnah* discusses five *physical* aspects of human life, while the latter part of the *mishnah* discusses five *spiritual* aspects of human life. The *mishnah* lists ten areas of life in total, ranging from the most physical to the most spiritual.

The number ten is the symbolic distance between earth and heaven; it is the span between the physical and the spiritual.[1] For example, the Ten Commandments, which span all of human life, are divided into

1. *Succah* 5a.

you; and those who drowned you will be drowned eventually."

8. He used to say: The more flesh, the more worms; the more possessions, the more worry;

---

five commandments that have a spiritual focus[1] and five that deal with the more physical side of life. Our *mishnah* reflects the same structure.

Physical things are limited in space and in time. Since they are of limited duration, they must deteriorate. This is the lesson of the first five items of our *mishnah:* Excess in physical matters sets the forces of deterioration in motion.

Spiritual activities are not limited by space or by time; rather, they are part of eternity. This is the lesson of the latter five items: The more one engages in spiritual activities, the more they elevate a person.

The physical elements of life are the foundation for all spiritual growth. A healthy body, essential possessions, one spouse and assistance with work in the home and in the field: This is the practical basis for spiritual success. The *mishnah* warns that *excess* in any of these areas is self-defeating.

---

§ מַרְבֶּה בָשָׂר, מַרְבֶּה רִמָּה — *The more flesh, the more worms* §

The references to *flesh* and to *worms* are only illustrations of a basic principle. "Flesh" represents any aspect of bodily indulgence. "Worms" is a symbol of physical deterioration, just as worms consume the flesh until it is no more. This image conveys the principle that bodily excess is a direct cause of bodily deterioration. The principle applies in life as well as in death.

---

§ מַרְבֶּה נְכָסִים, מַרְבֶּה דְאָגָה — *the more possessions, the more worry*

Possessions are a physical aspect of life, although they are not part of the body itself. The principle that physical excess directly causes negative consequences applies to assets as well. An increase of possessions brings with it an increase in the anxiety of losing them.

---

1. Honoring parents is included in these five, because it connected with honoring God, as elucidated in *Kiddushin* 30b.

מַרְבֶּה נָשִׁים, מַרְבֶּה כְשָׁפִים; מַרְבֶּה שְׁפָחוֹת, מַרְבֶּה זִמָּה; מַרְבֶּה עֲבָדִים, מַרְבֶּה גָזֵל. מַרְבֶּה תוֹרָה, מַרְבֶּה חַיִּים; מַרְבֶּה יְשִׁיבָה, מַרְבֶּה חָכְמָה; מַרְבֶּה עֵצָה, מַרְבֶּה תְבוּנָה; מַרְבֶּה צְדָקָה, מַרְבֶּה שָׁלוֹם.

---

§◄ מַרְבֶּה נָשִׁים, מַרְבֶּה כְשָׁפִים — *the more wives, the more witchcraft*

A man needs a wife to establish the home and the household. Although the Torah permits several wives, it is still an excess which eventually brings about problems. Historically, it was primarily women who practiced witchcraft because they excel in the prerequisite qualities of imagination and worldliness.

The warning of this *mishnah* is directed at the husband, not at the wives. Even if his wives are religious women, who would not practice witchcraft, a man who takes many wives is overly attracted to qualities that have the potential for mischief.

---

§◄ מַרְבֶּה שְׁפָחוֹת, מַרְבֶּה זִמָּה — *the more maidservants, the more lewdness*

These are maidservants who work in the house. The reference is to Canaanites, who by nature are inclined towards lewd behavior. Even if they are decent, the master demonstrates a leaning toward lewdness through an excess of female servants.

---

§◄ מַרְבֶּה עֲבָדִים, מַרְבֶּה גָזֵל — *the more menservants, the more thievery*

People refrain from theft because of their personal integrity. The menservants referred to here are Canaanites, who fundamentally lacked integrity and hence were inclined to steal.

Again, the *mishnah* implies criticism of the master, not of the servants. Sometimes they are driven to steal by the burdensome tasks their master sets for them. Lot's shepherds, for example, made their job easier by grazing his flocks on nearby private property rather then taking the time and effort to find unowned pastures.

---

§◄ מַרְבֶּה תוֹרָה, מַרְבֶּה חַיִּים — *[However] the more Torah, the more life*

Now the *mishnah* turns to the spiritual components of the human

2/ 8the more wives, the more witchcraft; the more maidservants, the more lewdness; the more menservants, the more thievery. [However] the more Torah, the more life; the more study the more wisdom; the more counsel, the more understanding; the more charity, the more peace.

---

being, which improve as they are increased.

Torah vitalizes the soul. It is through Torah that one comes close to God, the very source of life.

---

§⋙ מַרְבֶּה יְשִׁיבָה, מַרְבֶּה חָכְמָה — *the more study, the more wisdom*

The term "Torah" used in the first phrase refers to a solid knowledge of its laws and grasp of its commandments. The term "wisdom," in this phrase, refers to understanding the systems of Torah law. It is gained through extensive deliberation with colleagues.

The qualities listed in the *mishnah* are in order of increasing spiritual level. Wisdom, which deals with the principles of law, is a different and higher caliber of activity than the study of specific Torah laws.

---

§⋙ מַרְבֶּה עֵצָה, מַרְבֶּה תְבוּנָה — *the more counsel,*
the more understanding

The term "understanding" refers to depth of comprehension, by inferring one thing from another. It is at a higher spiritual plane than "wisdom."

The *mishnah* has covered three components of the soul:[1]

chachmah, binah and *da'as,* [2] i.e., wisdom, understanding and a thorough comprehension. One who increases any of these has acquired greater worth, unlike the first five items in the *mishnah,* for which increase is detrimental.

---

§⋙ מַרְבֶּה צְדָקָה, מַרְבֶּה שָׁלוֹם — *the more charity, the more peace*

Peace is achieved when we are free from interference and opposition. A lack of peace poses a barrier to Torah and to every one of life's pursuits and we therefore need peace to meet with success in life.

---

1. Hebrew: נְשָׁמָה, *neshamah.*

2. Torah is called *da'as,* as it says in the Haggadah of Pesach: כֻּלָּנוּ חֲכָמִים,כֻּלָּנוּ נְבוֹנִים כֻּלָּנוּ יוֹדְעִים אֶת הַתּוֹרָה.

ח /ב קָנָה שֵׁם טוֹב קָנָה לְעַצְמוֹ; קָנָה לוֹ דִבְרֵי תוֹרָה,
קָנָה לוֹ חַיֵּי הָעוֹלָם הַבָּא.

Securing peace requires that people do not harass each other, even within the bounds of law. Peace is abrogated when people press the law to its limit to get their own way, for such behavior creates contention. Conversely, peace is fostered when a person is so charitable that he is willing to forgo his legitimate rights.

True charity is peace itself, and is characterized by one's willingness to forgo money that is rightfully his, out of a sense of duty. The kind of charity where a person gives only out of the goodness of his heart does not bring peace. The heart that moves one to donate to charity will not necessarily move one to concede an argument, for he may only be willing to give up his rights when he feels like it, but will not succumb in the face of conflict.

It is the person who can act charitably when compelled, and not just out of good will, who can foster peace. Even when compelled to give charity, his sense of responsibility overrides his sense of autonomy and his right not to give. Clearly, this is the person who can bring peace into the world.

§◈ מַרְבֶּה צְדָקָה, מַרְבֶּה שָׁלוֹם — the more charity, the more peace

"The more charity" means that the more one is involved in charitable affairs, by insisting that others give to charity, "the more peace" he fosters. He cultivates an attitude that directs charity toward the recipient's needs, which brings peace, and away from the donor's ego, which brings strife.

§◈ קָנָה שֵׁם טוֹב — One who has gained a good reputation

The mishnah lists ten qualities, of which five are physical and five are spiritual.

Ten things can constitute a unified group, and the tenth embodies the essence of the entire group. For example, ten men constitute a quorum for prayer. The tenth is the prayer leader, through whom the other nine individuals coalesce into a group. Likewise, this mishnah has listed nine elements of a person. The tenth, his reputation, is the sum of the parts; it is the essence of the whole person.[1]

---

1. Author's explanatory paragraph. Compare infra, commentary to Chapter 3, mishnah 17 and Chapter 4, mishnah 13.

2/8 One who has gained a good reputation has gained it for his own benefit; one who has gained himself Torah knowledge has gained himself the life of the World to Come.

Similarly, the Ten Commandments (literally: statements) consist of nine commandments and the opening statement, "I am the Lord your God," which means "I am the root of everything." That is the principal statement of the group, to which the other nine are subordinate.

◆§ קָנָה שֵׁם טוֹב קָנָה לְעַצְמוֹ — *One who has gained a good reputation has gained it for his own benefit*

This tenth quality is the best of all the qualities listed, because it applies to the essence of the person, which is his reputation.[1]

◆§ קָנָה לוֹ דִבְרֵי תוֹרָה קָנָה לוֹ חַיֵּי הָעוֹלָם הַבָּא — *one who has gained himself Torah knowledge has gained himself the life of the World to Come.*

This is not an additional thought. It is a clarification of the earlier statement, that "the more Torah, the more life." In addition to adding to life in this world, Torah adds to eternal life. The statement was placed at the end of the *mishnah* in order to conclude with the loftiest of human goals.

Mishnah 9

The spirit, נֶפֶשׁ, is the part of a creature that wants and that instigates action to satisfy that want. For example, when an animal is hungry, its spirit is aroused; it hunts and eats. When it is satisfied, its spirit is at rest and the animal can curl up and sleep.

A human being has different levels of needs. We may consider three areas of needs and three parts of the spirit that sense and respond to each need.

- When a person is hungry, the lowest, animal type of spirit is aroused to forage and eat, and when his needs are satisfied, this spirit rests.
- When a person needs companionship, a higher level of spirit is aroused to communicate, and it rests when this need is satisfied.

---

1. The Hebrew for "reputation" literally means "name." In Hebrew, the name of something describes the very essence of the thing.

[ט] רַבָּן יוֹחָנָן בֶּן זַכַּאי קִבֵּל מֵהִלֵּל וּמִשַּׁמַּאי.
הוּא הָיָה אוֹמֵר: אִם לָמַדְתָּ תּוֹרָה הַרְבֵּה,
אַל תַּחֲזִיק טוֹבָה לְעַצְמְךָ, כִּי לְכָךְ נוֹצָרְתָּ.

[י] חֲמִשָּׁה תַלְמִידִים הָיוּ לוֹ לְרַבָּן יוֹחָנָן
בֶּן זַכַּאי, וְאֵלוּ הֵן: רַבִּי אֱלִיעֶזֶר בֶּן

• There is a spiritual need to grow in wisdom, and this arouses the highest level of the human spirit. A spiritual need cannot be satisfied with finite portions and there is no measure of what will fill the need. Therefore this highest level of the human soul, which seeks growth, can never rest.

◆§ — אִם לָמַדְתָּ תּוֹרָה הַרְבֵּה, אַל תַּחֲזִיק טוֹבָה לְעַצְמְךָ, כִּי לְכָךְ נוֹצָרְתָּ ◆§
If you have studied much Torah, do not take credit
for yourself, because that is what you were created to do.

Rabban Yochanan ben Zakkai tells us that an elevated human being finds learning Torah as basic a need as eating or drinking.

Besides man, all of creation was cast in a complete and finished state, and therefore remains stable. Mankind alone was created unfinished, and a human being's completion is achieved by his actualizing his potential. One can never reach such a state of perfection that it is time to rest, for human perfection is growth itself. The converse is also true: One who does not grow has no fulfillment.

The proper field for nurturing human growth is Torah.[1]

The highest human soul is the purely intellectual spirit, *sechel nivdal.* This is the spirit that moves people to intellectual development and expression. This spirit never reaches such a state of completeness in a Jew that he could be totally at rest. It can never be static, and constantly moves to actualize itself. Shabbos, for example, is a day of rest only from physical endeavors, but not from Torah, because we were created to toil in Torah.

Such continuous development and expression of the intellect is the essence of human existence. This is the meaning of the phrase,[2] "the day of death [is better than] the day of birth." At birth, one is not yet a complete creation; he has just started a lifetime of development. On the

---

1. *Sanhedrin* 99b: Rabbi Elazar said, "Mankind was created to toil."
2. *Koheles* 7:1.

9. Rabban Yochanan ben Zakkai received the tradition from Hillel and Shammai. He used to say: If you have studied much Torah, do not take credit for yourself, because that is what you were created to do.

10. Rabban Yochanan ben Zakkai had five [primary] disciples. They were: Rabbi Eliezer ben

---

day of death, however, one has achieved as much growth and fulfillment as he will ever achieve, and is now prepared to rest.

Relationship to the Previous Mishnah

The previous *mishnah* taught us that the material aspects of life, in moderation, are the foundation for spiritual growth. However, after physical needs are fulfilled, every excess leads to deterioration. It also taught us that the spiritual aspects of life can never be complete; they can only grow, and should be cultivated. Rabban Yochanan ben Zakkai's statement, "If you have studied much Torah, do not take credit for yourself, because that is what you were created to do," is a natural continuation.

Rabban Yochanan ben Zakkai is mentioned out of chronological order; he lived before Rabbi Yehudah HaNasi, whose words begin this chapter. By rights, Rabban Yochanan should have been listed in Chapter One, after Hillel and Shammai. One reason for placing his words in this chapter is that his statement is much longer and more detailed than the brief aphorisms of the first chapter.

Another reason is that the order of *mishnayos* in Chapter One was based on the chain of formal Torah transmission, which came to an end with Hillel and Shammai. Rabban Yochanan received his Torah knowledge from Shammai and Hillel, but he was not part of a chain of formal Torah transmission. This *mishnah* accords Rabban Yochanan the honor of the term "received," to spare him the humiliation of being the first generation not mentioned in the chain of Torah. He could not be mentioned in the first chapter because he "received" the Torah in a manner which was not up to the standards of those in the first chapter.

Mishnayos 10-14

The commentary treats *mishnayos* 10-14 as a unit and is presented after the translation of *mishnah* 14.

Maharal treats the five *mishnayos* of Rabban Yochanan ben Zakkai's students as a unit.

הֻרְקָנוֹס, רַבִּי יְהוֹשֻׁעַ בֶּן חֲנַנְיָא, רַבִּי יוֹסֵי הַכֹּהֵן,
רַבִּי שִׁמְעוֹן בֶּן נְתַנְאֵל, וְרַבִּי אֶלְעָזָר בֶּן עֲרָךְ.

[**יא**] הוּא הָיָה מוֹנֶה שְׁבָחָן: רַבִּי אֱלִיעֶזֶר בֶּן
הֻרְקָנוֹס, בּוֹר סוּד שֶׁאֵינוֹ מְאַבֵּד טִפָּה; רַבִּי
יְהוֹשֻׁעַ בֶּן חֲנַנְיָא, אַשְׁרֵי יוֹלַדְתּוֹ; רַבִּי יוֹסֵי הַכֹּהֵן,
חָסִיד; רַבִּי שִׁמְעוֹן בֶּן נְתַנְאֵל, יְרֵא חֵטְא; וְרַבִּי
אֶלְעָזָר בֶּן עֲרָךְ, כְּמַעְיָן הַמִּתְגַּבֵּר.

[**יב**] הוּא הָיָה אוֹמֵר: אִם יִהְיוּ כָל חַכְמֵי
יִשְׂרָאֵל בְּכַף מֹאזְנַיִם, וֶאֱלִיעֶזֶר בֶּן
הֻרְקָנוֹס בְּכַף שְׁנִיָּה, מַכְרִיעַ אֶת כֻּלָּם. אַבָּא
שָׁאוּל אוֹמֵר מִשְּׁמוֹ: אִם יִהְיוּ כָּל חַכְמֵי יִשְׂרָאֵל
בְּכַף מֹאזְנַיִם, וְרַבִּי אֱלִיעֶזֶר בֶּן הֻרְקָנוֹס אַף
עִמָּהֶם, וְרַבִּי אֶלְעָזָר בֶּן עֲרָךְ בְּכַף שְׁנִיָּה,
מַכְרִיעַ אֶת כֻּלָּם.

[**יג**] אָמַר לָהֶם: צְאוּ וּרְאוּ אֵיזוֹ הִיא
דֶרֶךְ טוֹבָה שֶׁיִּדְבַּק בָּהּ הָאָדָם.

He explains these *mishnayos* first at the literal level and then at a more
profound level, which takes us into the very structure of the human soul.
In *mishnah* 11, Rabban Yochanan ben Zakkai praises each student for a
particular outstanding quality. Maharal will show which specific element
of that student's soul is responsible for his outstanding quality, and how
it influences his choice of the "good path" that a person should adopt.
First we deal with the more literal level of explanation:

Mishnah 13

---

§ צְאוּ וּרְאוּ — *Go out and discern*

Rabban Yochanan ben Zakkai, as the *Rav* or Torah mentor, should have
taught his students which qualities are good, rather than ask for their opinion. Some things, however, must be learned by observation. It was precisely in his role as mentor that Rabban Yochanan sent out his students to

Hyrkanos, Rabbi Yehoshua ben Chanania, Rabbi Yose HaKohen, Rabbi Shimon ben Nesanel and Rabbi Elazar ben Arach.

11. He used to enumerate their praises: Rabbi Eliezer ben Hyrkanos is like a cemented cistern that loses not a drop; Rabbi Yehoshua ben Chanania, praiseworthy is she who bore him; Rabbi Yose HaKohen is a scrupulously pious person; Rabbi Shimon ben Nesanel fears sin; and Rabbi Elazar ben Arach is like a spring flowing stronger and stronger.

12. He used to say: If all the sages of Israel were on one pan of a balance-scale, and Eliezer ben Hyrkanos were on the other pan, he would outweigh them all. Abba Shaul said in his[1] name: If all the Sages of Israel, with even Rabbi Eliezer ben Hyrkanos among them, were on one pan of a balance-scale, and Rabbi Elazar ben Arach were on the other pan, he would outweigh them all.

13. He said to them: Go out and discern which is the good path to which a man should cling.

---

1. In Rabban Yochanan's name. Abba Shaul is not himself disagreeing with Rabban Yochanan ben Zakkai; rather, he is relating a different version of what Rabban Yochanan had said.

---

observe people and discern from them what is the best of all good qualities.

---

§ אֵיזוֹ הִיא דֶרֶךְ טוֹבָה שֶׁיִּדְבַּק בָּהּ הָאָדָם ₪ — *which is the good path to which a man should cling*

A person is considered as *clinging* to a positive personality trait only when such a trait has become entirely natural. We acquire new behavior only by practicing it until it has been ingrained as second nature.

---

§ אֵיזוֹ הִיא דֶרֶךְ טוֹבָה שֶׁיִּדְבַּק בָּהּ הָאָדָם ₪ — *which is the good path to which a man should cling.*

A way of life is considered "good" when it fulfills the purpose for which

רַבִּי אֱלִיעֶזֶר אוֹמֵר: עַיִן טוֹבָה. רַבִּי
יְהוֹשֻׁעַ אוֹמֵר: חָבֵר טוֹב. רַבִּי יוֹסֵי אוֹמֵר:
שָׁכֵן טוֹב. רַבִּי שִׁמְעוֹן אוֹמֵר: הָרוֹאֶה אֶת
הַנּוֹלָד. רַבִּי אֶלְעָזָר אוֹמֵר: לֵב טוֹב.

we were created. Goodness is cultivated in several areas of life, such as our personal growth through Torah, or our relationship with God through prayer. These *mishnayos* discuss goodness in our relationship with our fellow man. We seek to maximize opportunities for goodness, for in this context that is synonymous with being worthy of our very existence.

∗§ רַבִּי אֱלִיעֶזֶר אוֹמֵר: עַיִן טוֹבָה — *Rabbi Eliezer says: A good eye.* §∗

"A good eye" is the quality of being pleased with another's good fortune. Rabbi Eliezer proposes that this quality cultivates goodness most effectively because there are plentiful opportunities for us to practice it, and it takes no time at all to be happy for others' good fortune. Looking around, we can always find evidence of wealth, social position and other successes.

Rabbi Eliezer's colleagues felt that other personality traits offer even better opportunities to cultivate goodness. The difference of opinion as to which trait is best revolves around the balance of quantity and quality. For example, Rabbi Eliezer suggests that a kindly view of people's good fortune is best because the opportunity to make use of this trait is always available. In contrast, Rabbi Yehoshua favors the trait of being a good friend because it exercises a higher level of goodness, albeit with fewer opportunities to practice it.[1]

∗§ רַבִּי יְהוֹשֻׁעַ אוֹמֵר: חָבֵר טוֹב — *Rabbi Yehoshua says: A good friend.* §∗

A "good friend" is one who gives his friend advice.[2] Rabbi Yehoshua considers this practice superior to having "a good eye" because it engages more of our faculties. The quality of "a good eye" develops only the faculty of observation, whereas giving good advice also exercises

1. This paragraph is the author's summary of the following portion that follows.
2. Giving advice is only one example of being a good friend. However, the example was carefully chosen to illustrate a degree of goodness which takes more effort and occurs less frequently than "a good eye," and which is yet easier to practice than the opinions of lending and giving that follow.

2/ 13   Rabbi Eliezer says: A good eye. Rabbi Yehoshua says: A good friend. Rabbi Yose says: A good neighbor. Rabbi Shimon says: One who considers the outcome of a deed. Rabbi Elazar says: A good heart.

---

speech.[1] Since that entails concentration and effort, it is a more substantial quality than "a good eye," which is simply a benign attitude.

A good friend is pleased with his friend's good fortune and it is implicit that being "a good friend" encompasses the compassion that "a good eye" entails.

שָׁכֵן טוֹב :רַבִּי יוֹסֵי אוֹמֵר — *Rabbi Yose says: A good neighbor.*

Being a good neighbor is even better than being a good friend, because friendship can be maintained with mere speech, but good neighbors are good to each other in deeds. They lend things to each other and actively help one another. Good neighbors also fulfill the other good practices of giving helpful advice and sharing in the joy of each other's successes.

הָרוֹאֶה אֶת הַנּוֹלָד :רַבִּי שִׁמְעוֹן אוֹמֵר — *Rabbi Shimon says: One who considers the outcome of a deed.*

By the expression "one who considers the outcome of a deed," Rabbi Shimon recommends true *gemilas chasadim,* acts of kindness, such as lending money or other substantial kindness. One who sees consequences will not be reluctant to do kindness to others, as it says,[2]

Cast your bread upon the water, for you will find it after many days.

"One who considers the outcome of a deed" is aware that today's beneficiary may be tomorrow's benefactor and that recognition enables one to deal kindly with others.

Rabbi Shimon considers this a better quality than being "a good neighbor" because the good that neighbors do for each other, such as lending things on a short-term basis, is easier to do. The recipient benefits, but the object is promptly returned to the lender and he is is not deprived of its use.

---

1. The Kabbalistic explanation presented later will associate these opinions with different parts of the soul. Maharal is preparing us for that insight, by associating each opinion with a faculty such as sight or speech, for those faculties are themselves related to different parts of the soul.
2. *Koheles* 11:1.

אָמַר לָהֶם: רוֹאֶה אֲנִי אֶת דִּבְרֵי אֶלְעָזָר בֶּן עֲרָךְ מִדִּבְרֵיכֶם, שֶׁבִּכְלַל דְּבָרָיו דִּבְרֵיכֶם.

[יד] אָמַר לָהֶם: צְאוּ וּרְאוּ אֵיזוֹ הִיא דֶרֶךְ רָעָה שֶׁיִּתְרַחֵק מִמֶּנָּה הָאָדָם. רַבִּי אֱלִיעֶזֶר אוֹמֵר: עַיִן רָעָה. רַבִּי יְהוֹשֻׁעַ אוֹמֵר: חָבֵר רָע. רַבִּי יוֹסֵי אוֹמֵר: שָׁכֵן רָע. רַבִּי שִׁמְעוֹן אוֹמֵר: הַלֹּוֶה וְאֵינוֹ מְשַׁלֵּם;

ב/יד

◦§ רַבִּי אֶלְעָזָר אוֹמֵר: לֵב טוֹב §◦ — *Rabbi Elazar says: A good heart.*

A "good heart" means performing acts of kindness selflessly, without regard to the favor being returned. "A good heart" includes and surpasses all of the other good qualities.

Rabbi Elazar considers the selfless quality of "a good heart" to be superior to the pragmatic quality of doing a kindness that could be reciprocated. Indeed, some people might even refrain from doing a kindness because the recipient will not be able to reciprocate when they are in need of his help.

Although it is harder to perform a kindness that may not be reciprocated, a person who has "a good heart" will accept the possible loss and provide help to whomever may need it.

Mishnah 14

◦§ אֵיזוֹ הִיא דֶרֶךְ רָעָה שֶׁיִּתְרַחֵק מִמֶּנָּה הָאָדָם §◦ — *which is the evil path from which a man should distance himself.*

A person has *distanced* himself from a negative trait only if it has been entirely eradicated. As long as we practice that negative behavior or anything similar to it, even occasionally, it is still part of us.

◦§ רַבִּי אֱלִיעֶזֶר אוֹמֵר: עַיִן רָעָה §◦ — *Rabbi Eliezer says: An evil eye*

Be very careful not to view other people's good fortune begrudgingly, for the risk of malevolence is within the glance of an eye. This evil personality trait brings a person to jealousy, hatred and countless other transgressions.

2/14 He [Rabban Yochanan ben Zakkai] said to them: I prefer the words of Elazar ben Arach to your words, because your words are included in his words.

14. He said to them: Go out and discern which is the evil path from which a man should distance himself. Rabbi Eliezer says: An evil eye. Rabbi Yehoshua says: A wicked friend. Rabbi Yose says: A wicked neighbor. Rabbi Shimon says: One who borrows and does not repay;

◆§ רַבִּי יְהוֹשֻׁעַ אוֹמֵר: חָבֵר רָע — *Rabbi Yehoshua says: A wicked friend.*

This is the opposite of the good quality, "a good friend." A person with this character harms his fellow through deliberate bad advice. He certainly has an evil eye as well, begrudging his fellow's good fortune.

Each of Rabban Yochanan's students suggests a different character flaw to avoid. Each trait is progressively worse and each previous trait is encompassed in the succeeding ones.

◆§ רַבִּי יוֹסֵי אוֹמֵר: שָׁכֵן רָע — *Rabbi Yose says: A wicked neighbor.*

This person actively causes harm to his neighbor. Consequently, he would do harm through speech as the "wicked friend" does, and he certainly begrudges others their good fortune.

◆§ רַבִּי שִׁמְעוֹן אוֹמֵר: הַלֹּוֶה וְאֵינוֹ מְשַׁלֵּם — *Rabbi Shimon says: One who borrows and does not repay;*

This is a far worse quality, for such a person reciprocates a kindness with evil. He causes a financial loss to the person who helped him.

Although it is not immediately obvious, this advice is indeed the opposite of the good quality, "one who considers the outcome of a deed." One who borrows and does not repay is willing to perpetrate evil, even though this closes off an avenue of help that he may require at a later date. In addition, such a person will demonstrate the other evil traits: a "wicked neighbor," a "wicked friend" and an "evil eye."

ב/יד אֶחָד הַלּוֶה מִן הָאָדָם כְּלֹוֶה מִן הַמָּקוֹם,
שֶׁנֶּאֱמַר: „לוֶה רָשָׁע וְלֹא יְשַׁלֵּם, וְצַדִּיק חוֹנֵן
וְנוֹתֵן.״ רַבִּי אֶלְעָזָר אוֹמֵר: לֵב רָע. אָמַר לָהֶם:
רוֹאֶה אֲנִי אֶת דִּבְרֵי אֶלְעָזָר בֶּן עֲרָךְ
מִדִּבְרֵיכֶם, שֶׁבִּכְלַל דְּבָרָיו דִּבְרֵיכֶם.

∞ רַבִּי אֶלְעָזָר אוֹמֵר: לֵב רָע — *Rabbi Elazar says: A wicked heart.*

This evil personality trait is worse than all the others and it embraces all the others as well, as Rabban Yochanan ben Zakkai observes.[1]

A Kabbalistic Approach

The full explanation of this *mishnah* lies within the framework of the deeper, Kabbalistic wisdom of the Torah. Again, all the *mishnayos* that deal with Rabban Yochanan's disciples are treated as a unit.

The insights presented in Maharal's second approach will address the following questions:

- "Rabban Yochanan ben Zakkai had five disciples." As the leader of all of Torah society, he certainly had many, many more disciples. In what context does the *mishnah* state that he had only five disciples?

- Why was Yehoshua ben Chanania praised only with the expression: "praiseworthy is she who bore him"? Why was he not praised with a particular quality of character, as were the other students who were called pious or God fearing?

- Why are their praises mentioned in the *mishnah*? What difference could it make to us?

- He says that Eliezer ben Hyrkanos is better than all the Rabbis put together. Aside from the practical fact that Rabban Yochanan could not have known every Rabbi, such an evaluation would seem to be beyond human ability.

- Why is Rabbi Elazar ben Arach last in the list of praises? Rabbi Eliezer might be greater, but Rabbi Elazar, whom Abba Shaul considered the greatest of the five, should not be placed at the very end.

---

1. Maharal does not describe the behavior conveyed by the expression "an evil heart," but we might assume that it refers to a person who would perpetrate evil even without personal gain. That would be the opposite of the "good heart" who will do a kindness even if it entails personal loss.

2/ 14   one who borrows from man is like one who borrows from the Omnipresent, as it is said: "The wicked one borrows and does not repay, but the Righteous One is gracious and gives" (*Tehillim* 37:21). Rabbi Elazar says: A wicked heart. He [Rabban Yochanan ben Zakkai] said to them: I prefer the words of Elazar ben Arach to your words, for your words are included in his words.

Human Spiritual Anatomy

Textbooks of human anatomy illustrate the external limbs: the head, the arms and the legs. They also show parts that are visible only with the surgeon's knife: the heart, the lungs and the skeleton. However, there are spiritual parts of the human being that are not visible, such as intelligence, emotion and motivation. There are no pictures of these parts; how can we describe them?

The anatomy book shows not only the shapes of the bones, but how they fit together to form a functional skeleton. Is it possible to describe how elements of the soul fit together and work together?

This group of *mishnayos* is an "anatomy" lesson about the five elements of the soul. Each one of Rabban Yochanan's five students demonstrated particular strength in one of these five spiritual limbs and it is that strength which Rabban Yochanan praises. Furthermore, each student's advice reveals the role played by that part of the soul, and its relationship with other parts, as will be explained.

Five Parts of the Human Soul

The human being is sometimes considered simply as consisting of two components, the body and the soul. The following discussion takes a more detailed perspective and considers five components of the human soul.

The soul has two elements: the spirit, *nefesh,* and the intellect, *sechel.*

The spirit has some physical characteristics in that it responds to needs[1] and it links directly with the body.

The body and the soul are linked together. Maharal calls these links a נושא, *nosei*[2] but he does not provide names for the link between the

---

1. Purely spiritual entities do not react or change in response to anything else. Their characteristics are mutually exclusive of the characteristics of physical entities.

2. The element that Maharal calls a *nosei* is most precisely translated as "medium." If we use the metaphor of form imposed upon substance, then the substance is called the medium for form. That is the same relationship as the spiritual *nefesh* directing

body and the *nefesh* or for the link between the body and the *sechel*.

All of these parts spring from the heart, the root of all spiritual faculties.

In more detail, the five parts of the soul are:

- The *sechel*, spiritual intellect. This is entirely spiritual, with no physical characteristics. The intellect or *sechel* is the purest of the spiritual faculties. *Sechel* is the element wherein lie understanding and discerning. It is the *sechel* that grasps Torah concepts such as morality and inspires a person to perform *mitzvos*. *Sechel* is so spiritual that it is devoid of any physical characteristics.
- The *nefesh*, spirit. The *nefesh* is the element of will, and animates the body to action, but the linkage works in the other direction as well. For example, bodily needs such as hunger stimulate the *nefesh* to seek a response. It is spiritual, but with some physical characteristics.[1]
- The support, or link, joining the *nefesh* to our physical being. This support has certain physical characteristics.
- The support, or link, joining the *sechel* to our physical being. It has some physical characteristics, but it is very delicate and pure. It is more ethereal than the link between the spirit, *nefesh*, and the body. The latter might be compared to the wind directly moving the leaves of a tree, while the link between the *sechel* and the body might be compared to a magnet causing a compass needle to move, even though there is some distance separating the two.
- The *lev*,[2] heart. This is the source from which the four other faculties flow. It draws life from the realm of the Divine and distributes it to all parts of the personal soul. The physical and the spiritual meet in the heart. Through the heart, we draw upon both the spiritual realm and the physical realm. The religious person builds spiritual growth — wisdom and good deeds — on the physical foundations of reason and action. The irreligious person draws mainly from the physical inclination of the heart, to the exclusion of spiritual goals. In this way, the heart is the origin of both good and evil.

We may envision the soul's five elements in the structure as illustrated on the facing page:[3]

---

our physical actions. For simplicity we have sometimes translated *nosei* as "support," with the intention that substance supports form, and sometimes we have translated it as "link" implying the linkage of form imposed upon substance.

1. Will, sentience, memory and common sense are all faculties of the *nefesh*.
2. This does not necessarily refer to the physical heart.
3. All diagrams in this section are the author's attempt at a visual aid. With regard to the term "Support," please see footnote above, discussing the term *nosei*.

```
┌──────────────────────────────────────────────────────────┐
│                   FIVE PARTS OF NEFESH                    │
│                                                          │
│                                       שֵׂכֶל              │
│            נֶפֶשׁ                       Intellect          │
│            Spirit                                         │
│                                                          │
│          Support for                 Support for         │
│          Spirit                      Intellect           │
│                                                          │
│                        לֵב                               │
│                       Heart                              │
└──────────────────────────────────────────────────────────┘
```

Allusions to the structure of the soul appear in a variety of Scriptural and Rabbinic references. Consider these four examples.

- The Hebrew word for mankind is אָדָם, adam. The first letter, א (alef), is the beginning of the Hebrew alphabet and has the numerical value 1. It stands for the heart, the one part of the soul from whence the other parts originate and where they unite. The next letter, ד (daled), has the numerical value 4, and stands for the other four parts of the soul. The letter מ (mem) is the precise middle of the Hebrew alphabet, to demonstrate that half of these are more spiritual and half are more physical.
- The Rabbis said,[1] with reference to the moment of death,

   "One who is present as the soul exits is obligated to rend his clothes. What is [the departure of the soul] compared to? To a Torah scroll which is burned."

   One point of comparison is that the Torah has five books, just as the soul has five parts. The fifth book is *Devarim*, a summary of the Torah, and that corresponds to the heart, which encompasses all parts of the soul.

- The five parts of the soul are hinted at in the laws of *Arachim* which is a method of evaluating the monetary amount of a donation to the Temple. When one gives such a donation, he vows to give the *erech,* valuation of a specified individual. This value is based on the person's age and gender, as found in *Vayikra* 27:1-8. The "worth" of a youth is fixed at five shekels-weight of silver, and the "worth" of a man at fifty shekels, the "adult" version of five. The Torah deems five to be the base value because there are five components to the human soul.[2]

---

1. *Shabbos* 105b.

2. Uncharacteristically, Maharal references these components by their Kabbalistic terms: *nefesh, ruach, neshamah, yechidah* and *chayah. Ari'zal* reverses the order of *yechidah* and *chayah. Chayah, yechidah* and *neshamah* are components of what is more generally referred to as *neshamah.*

- Scripture portrays the soul through the image[1]

  "The lamp of God is the soul of man."

The metaphor calls to mind how a flame spreads and splits into different parts, some lower and some higher. The lower parts are closely attached to the wick while the higher parts are more distant, although still dependent upon the wick and oil. It is for this reason that a flame was chosen as the metaphor for the soul, half of which is closely linked to the body and half of which is more spiritual.

חֲמִשָּׁה תַלְמִידִים הָיוּ לוֹ לְרַבָּן יוֹחָנָן בֶּן זַכַּאי §• — *Rabban Yochanan ben Zakkai had five [primary] disciples.*

A person who is highly developed in one element of the soul will display a particular exemplary character trait as a result. Rabban Yochanan ben Zakkai observed that, of all his disciples, five manifested a unique outstanding character trait, epitomizing all five elements of the human soul. For this reason, the *mishnah* provides the apparently obvious detail that there are five disciples. The number five is specified to convey that these disciples together are the epitome of a full personification of the five parts of the soul.

הוּא הָיָה מוֹנֶה שְׁבָחָן §• — *He used to enumerate their praises*

The term "enumerate" is appropriate, rather than "tell," because their praises correspond exactly to the five parts of the human soul and because he listed them in the order of how each part joins with the next.

רַבִּי אֱלִיעֶזֶר בֶּן הָרְקָנוֹס, בּוֹר סוּד שֶׁאֵינוֹ מְאַבֵּד טִפָּה §• — *Rabbi Eliezer ben Hyrkanos is like a cemented cistern that loses not a drop*

His praise of Rabbi Eliezer's perfectly retentive memory is an allusion to the *nefesh*, נֶפֶשׁ. Memory is a faculty of the *nefesh;* indeed, it is the best of the *nefesh's* functions, because it is essential to acquiring wisdom.

The functions of the *nefesh,* such as motivation and memory, can be of physical origin, spiritual origin, or a degree of both. Because physical entities are subject to change, forgetting is indicative of a more physically based memory. Conversely, a purely spiritual entity is not subject to change, and so Rabbi Eliezer's perfect memory suggested that it was based in the purely spiritual *nefesh.* However, the proof that his special memory was of spiritual — and not physical

---

1. *Mishlei* 20:27.

— origin lay only in his fine qualities of character.

In summary, the *nefesh* receives and retains knowledge. Hence Rabbi Eliezer was praised as "a cemented cistern that loses not a drop" to convey that he observed and retained information without loss because his *nefesh* was free of physical influence.

﹠§ רַבִּי יְהוֹשֻׁעַ בֶּן חֲנַנְיָא, אַשְׁרֵי יוֹלַדְתּוֹ ﹠§ — *Rabbi Yehoshua ben Chanania, praiseworthy is she who bore him*

This expression refers to a "refined physical nature," as we will now explain.

Since our will to do something actually results in action, it is clear that the *nefesh* is ultimately linked to the body. In contrast to our coarse physical nature that is ready to act for its own gratification, this element may be understood as a refined physical nature that will submit to noble, selfless intentions.[1]

Rabbi Yehoshua's praise is phrased as "praiseworthy is she who bore him" because his exemplary quality is the refined physical nature which he inherited from his mother. Family characteristics are passed from parent to child and physical qualities are primarily derived from the mother. Therefore, Rabban Yochanan alluded to Rabbi Yehoshua's refined physical nature by pointing out that his special quality was inherited from his mother.

It is significant that Rabbi Eliezer and Rabbi Yehoshua, who are associated with one another throughout the entire Talmud, are likewise paired in this instance.

The paradigm behind Maharal's explanation has now been established, and can be summarized in the chart below.

FIVE DISCIPLES — FIVE PARTS OF NEFESH			
		שֵׂכֶל Intellect	Rabbi Shimon ben Nesanel
Rabbi Eliezer ben Hyrkanos	נֶפֶשׁ Spirit		
Rabbi Yehoshua ben Chanania	Support for Spirit	Support for Intellect	Rabbi Yose HaKohen
		לֵב Heart	
		Rabbi Elazar ben Arach	

---

1. Author's interpretation and explanation

❧ רַבִּי יוֹסֵי הַכֹּהֵן, חָסִיד — *Rabbi Yose HaKohen is a scrupulously pious person*

Rabbi Yose HaKohen is praised for being scrupulously pious, which means he goes beyond the demands of duty to help others.

Pious behavior gives expression to the *sechel.* Therefore, the praise of "pious" conveys that Rabbi Yose's special quality is the element that links the *sechel* to action. That link is yet more refined than the link between the *nefesh* and action; indeed, it would be purely spiritual,[1] except that it still must find expression through physical action. As the instrument of *sechel,* which is absolutely free of physical characteristics, Rabbi Yose displayed even more refinement than Rabbi Yehoshua.

It is fitting that the quality of piety was found in a Kohen (Priest), for it says,[2]

> "Let your *Tumim* and your *Urim*[3] be with your 'scrupulously pious' one."

❧ רַבִּי שִׁמְעוֹן בֶּן נְתַנְאֵל יְרֵא חֵטְא — *Rabbi Shimon ben Nesanel fears sin*

Rabban Yochanan praised Rabbi Shimon ben Nesanel as one who fears sin, alluding to his clear, fine and "pure intellect." A man distinguished by the high degree of insight and discernment that is the domain of *sechel* can come very close to God. As a result, he is greatly moved by God and fearful of Him, just as one who is near the king is very impressed and fearful of him.

Wisdom and the fear of Heaven are so inextricably bound together that one is not found without the other. This fact will be explained in the commentary to the *mishnah*,[4] "If there is no wisdom, there is no fear of God; if there is no fear of God, there is no wisdom." It also appears in the *mishnah*,[5] "a boor cannot be fearful of sin; an unlearned person cannot be scrupulously pious."

Nonetheless, Rabbi Shimon ben Nesanel was not a greater scholar than Rabbi Eliezer or Rabbi Elazar.[6] Rabbi Eliezer's scholarship embraced many areas of wisdom, due to his perfect retention, while Rabbi

---

1. As is the flow of goodness from God.
2. *Devarim* 33:8.
3. The *Urim* and *Tumim* were inscriptions of the Holy Name which were inserted into the breastplate (*choshen*) worn by the Kohen Gadol, High Priest.
4. *Infra,* Chapter 3, *mishnah* 21.
5. *Supra,* *mishnah* 6.
6. Rather, his scholarship was different in nature.

Elazar's talent was the ability to add, on his own, to the knowledge he acquired and to enhance it with insights. Rabbi Shimon had a different quality. He was distinguished by the clarity of his intellectual grasp, and that is a talent in its own right.

The praise of Rabbi Shimon follows naturally after that of Rabbi Yose, because Rabbi Yose personifies the element which supports (*nosei*) the intellect.

---

§• וְרַבִּי אֶלְעָזָר בֶּן עֲרָךְ כְּמַעְיָן הַמִּתְגַּבֵּר — *and Rabbi Elazar ben Arach is like a spring flowing stronger and stronger*

This is a reference to the heart, *lev,* the element from which all other qualities flow. Therefore, praising Rabbi Elazar as a "spring flowing stronger and stronger" implies that he embraces all the wisdom and laudable qualities of the other disciples as well.

The continuously flowing spring is an image of strength, of renewal and of continuous increase. Such a spring has a powerful source that causes it to continuously flourish. The spring is a metaphor for the spiritual source of intellect and of all the spiritual faculties that thrive and grow. Rabbi Elazar ben Arach was in complete possession of the root and the power-source of intellect. As a result, he continuously increased his wisdom, as a spring that flows forth and continuously increases the supply of water.

---

§• אִם יִהְיוּ כָּל חַכְמֵי יִשְׂרָאֵל בְּכַף מֹאזְנַיִם וֶאֱלִיעֶזֶר בֶּן הֻרְקָנוֹס בְּכַף שְׁנִיָּה, מַכְרִיעַ אֶת כֻּלָּם — *If all the sages of Israel were on one pan of a balance-scale and Eliezer ben Hyrkanos were on the other pan, he would outweigh them all.*

Rabbi Eliezer was not much different from other sages in his Torah knowledge. The reason Rabban Yochanan believed that Rabbi Eliezer would outweigh the others was that his power of retention was not a natural phenomenon. Rather, it was due to the unique strength of his *nefesh.* "He would outweigh them all" because a quality that transcends nature outweighs everything that operates in the natural way of the world.

---

§• אַבָּא שָׁאוּל אוֹמֵר מִשְּׁמוֹ . . . וְרַבִּי אֶלְעָזָר בֶּן עֲרָךְ בְּכַף שְׁנִיָּה, מַכְרִיעַ אֶת כֻּלָּם — *Abba Shaul said in his name . . . and Rabbi Elazar ben Arach were on the other pan, he would outweigh them all.*

Rabbi Elazar's wisdom was on a par with that of Rabbi Eliezer, and it likewise was not a natural phenomenon. However, their wisdom was unique in different ways. Rabbi Eliezer was a master of wisdom because of his perfect retention. Rabbi Elazar was a master of wisdom because he was a wellspring of creativity. He could deduce whatever he needed to know from that which he had already learned. Was it Rabbi Eliezer or Rabbi Elazar who possessed the more desirable quality? Is it better to know everything, backed by the authority of earlier rabbis? Or is it better to be able to determine the correct conclusion, even if you are not in possession of all the relevant information? The debate[1] is unresolved.

Mishnayos 10-14 in Greater Depth

At this point, we have identified the five parts of the soul and how Rabban Yochanan's disciples each exemplified one part and the faculties and personality traits associated with that part. We are now ready to consider Maharal's deeper explanation of this group of *mishnayos*.

Mishnayos 10-11

◆§ חֲמִשָּׁה תַלְמִידִים הָיוּ לוֹ לְרַבָּן יוֹחָנָן בֶּן זַכַּאי — *Rabban Yochanan ben Zakkai had five [primary] disciples.*

Rabban Yochanan ben Zakkai identified the praiseworthy quality exemplified by the soul of each disciple. He named five disciples because there are five parts to the soul.

Mishnah 13

◆§ אָמַר לָהֶם: צְאוּ וּרְאוּ אֵיזוֹ הִיא דֶרֶךְ טוֹבָה שֶׁיִּדְבַּק בָּהּ הָאָדָם — *He said to them: Go out and discern which is the good path to which a man should cling.*

Rabban Yochanan wanted to determine if the best quality of each disciple's personality was derived from his good spiritual nature. He asked each disciple to state his personal opinion of the best personality trait because everyone recognizes his own good qualities in other people and then praises them. From their answers, he would be able to determine if their behavior was inherently linked to their very souls, or whether it was an acquired behavior which did not have its roots in their very being.

Each of the five disciples identified a good quality of personality that corresponded to his own spiritual strength. The good behavior that they recommended is good at two levels. It is good as an exercise to

---

1. There is a difference of opinion as to whom Rabban Yochanan had said is the greater disciple. Abba Shaul maintains that Rabban Yochanan said it is Rabbi Elazar, and the unidentified first opinion maintains that Rabban Yochanan said it is Rabbi Eliezer.

strengthen that part of a person's soul. It is also good at the literal level as desirable social behavior.

Relationships between people in their social roles correspond directly to the relationships of the parts of the soul within the person himself. For example, Rabbi Eliezer recommends "a good eye." That advice includes an inner vision that perceives one's own wisdom and knowledge. It also encompasses directing one's insightful perception to appreciate and rejoice in other people's good fortune.

Rabban Yochanan proved that the outstanding goodness of each student's behavior was the direct consequence of his outstanding personal spiritual development.

Rabbi[1] Eliezer exemplifies the spirit, the *nefesh nivdal*. It is *nivdal*, devoid of physical characteristics. He said that the choice trait is "a good eye," because vision is considered *nivdal*. The eye perceives only the form of something, not the substance.[2] Vision is associated with conceptual perception, as one would say, "I see his point," or as Scripture says,[3] "my heart saw much wisdom and knowledge."

Rabbi Yehoshua exemplifies the element that supports the *nefesh* and joins with it. He said that the best trait is "a good friend." The Hebrew word for 'friend' is *chaver*. The root meaning of this word is "join," because friends are those who join together — *mis'chabrim*.

Rabbi Yehoshua is the fine, pure physical support to which the spirit is joined. At the level of personal spiritual development, his advice to be a "good friend" tells a person to refine and purify his nature. He means that we should refine our actions so that the physical aspect of the human being will be a suitable companion for the spiritual aspect.

A "good friend" directs his companion towards goodness, and such a person is completely "good." That is true at the literal level as well as the metaphysical level. Strong companionship is as important between friends as it is between the body and soul.

Rabbi Yose says: A good neighbor. Rabbi Yose represents the physical element that supports the element of intellect or *sechel*. *Sechel* is not actually connected to a person; it merely coexists with him. This matches Rabbi Yose's advice to be "a good neighbor," because a neighbor is a person whose residence is merely *adjacent*, as opposed to

---

1. Maharal's text of the *mishnah* did not have the title "Rabbi" prefixed to the names of the students in the *mishnayos* in which Rabban Yochanan describes them. He notes that the *mishnah* which reports their opinions *does* prefix the title "Rabbi," because their opinions carry the authority of their rabbinical roles.
2. Literally: Otherwise, how could the eye, which is small, behold the sky which is large?
3. *Koheles* 1:16.

a "friend" who *joins* with his companion. Just as a good neighbor reaches out to one who may be a stranger, Rabbi Yose personifies a physical link with the *sechel*, which has no physical attributes at all.

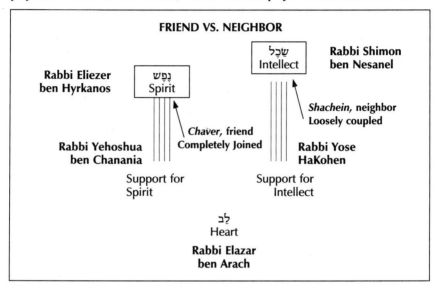

FRIEND VS. NEIGHBOR

Rabbi Yose is described as one who is scrupulously pious; that is, one who pursues goodness beyond the norm. Going beyond one's own sphere, to extend goodness to one who is not a close companion, is a personality trait of exceptional caliber.

This advice encourages a person to stretch beyond the comfortable norm. As advice for personal development, Rabbi Yose says that one should be a "good neighbor" to the *sechel* and reach out beyond one's grasp to pursue abstract conceptual insights.

At the practical, social level, he advises one to be a good neighbor even with people who are not close friends. A good neighbor is a completely good person at both levels of interpretation.

Rabbi Shimon says: One who considers the outcome of a deed. This advice exactly fits the intellect, *sechel,* which Rabbi Shimon personifies. *Sechel* is like a lamp that illuminates the darkness. *Sechel* is refined, clear and objective; it illuminates how things will transpire.[1]

Rabbi Elazar ben Arach says: A good heart. He exemplifies the heart, the root of one's physical and spiritual strengths. The heart is the seat of understanding and it is the source of life for all of the limbs. Therefore he says that being a good-hearted person is the way to pursue goodness, for both personal growth and within society. Rabbi Elazar's

---

1. Maharal continues: ". . .as one who sees by a lamp, which illuminates well and *has pure olive oil*, is able to perceive things at a distance."

outstanding spiritual quality and his view of the way to achieve goodness are perfectly aligned.

◆§ שֶׁבִּכְלַל דְּבָרָיו דִּבְרֵיכֶם — *for your words are included in his words*

He means that when the heart is good, then all of the physical and spiritual qualities that it comprises are also good.

Mishnah 14

◆§ צְאוּ וּרְאוּ אֵיזוֹ הִיא דֶּרֶךְ רָעָה שֶׁיִּתְרַחֵק מִמֶּנָּה הָאָדָם —
Go out and discern which is the evil path from which a man should distance himself.

Each one responded with the opposite of his opinion of the good way to embrace. The one who said "a good eye" says "a bad eye"; the one who said "a good friend" says "a bad friend" and so on. The exception is Rabbi Shimon ben Nesanel. He had stated that the good quality to adopt is to see the consequences of one's actions. We would expect him to say that the evil way is "One who does not consider the outcome of a deed." However, there is nothing evil about not seeing consequences. He therefore phrases it differently: "One who borrows and does not repay."

To understand why this is the opposite of "One who considers the outcome of a deed," we must understand Rabbi Shimon's special quality. He was sin fearing, a consequence of his pure and independent intellect. His is the spiritually highest quality, similar in nature to purely spiritual beings who are independent and do not accept anything from others. One who accepts a loan and does not repay it has taken from another and has relinquished his independence. One who is pure and self-sufficient will repay the loan, to extricate himself from being in possession of something received from someone else.[1]

---

1. Maharal addresses questions that arise from this explanation as follows:

Accepting a loan in the first place does not compromise one's independence, because people are social beings who interact and are interdependent. One who has a self-sufficient character, however, will be certain not to retain anything that is not his, because he stands on his own and does not enter into a "recipient" relationship with other people.

Theft is an even worse degree of receiving from others. Why didn't Rabbi Shimon declare "theft" as the worst quality to avoid, rather than not repaying a loan? The reason is that theft has another aspect to it; namely, taking things by force. The negative quality being described is the opposite of self-sufficiency and is adequately illustrated by not repaying a loan, which was given willingly. The use of force is an unrelated, additional sin.

[טו] הֵם אָמְרוּ שְׁלֹשָׁה דְבָרִים. רַבִּי אֱלִיעֶזֶר אוֹמֵר: יְהִי כְבוֹד חֲבֵרְךָ חָבִיב עָלֶיךָ כְּשֶׁלָּךְ, וְאַל תְּהִי נוֹחַ לִכְעוֹס; וְשׁוּב יוֹם אֶחָד לִפְנֵי מִיתָתָךְ.

⁕§ הַלֹּוֶה מִן הָאָדָם כְּלֹוֶה מִן הַמָּקוֹם — *one who borrows from man is like one who borrows from the Omnipresent*

In what way is borrowing from a person the same as borrowing from God? Scripture says,

"The earth is the Lord's and the fullness thereof."[1]

Everything on earth is God's, and He distributes it to the people as He sees fit. God permitted the temporary redistribution of wealth through this loan on the expectation that it would be repaid. Thus, borrowing from a person is equivalent to borrowing from God.

Mishnah 15

⁕§ הֵם אָמְרוּ שְׁלֹשָׁה דְבָרִים — *They each said three things.*

Why did each one of these Rabbis say precisely three things? And why did Rabbi Eliezer say six things, not three?

If words of *mussar* are to be effective and useful, they must be kept in mind at all times. A group of three related items is easy to remember because any one of the items calls to mind the other two.[2]

For this reason each rabbi chose three pieces of advice dealing with a single subject. Rabbi Eliezer used the same technique of presenting three related pieces of advice, but he did so for two subjects. He gave three pieces of practical advice that enhance relationships, and three more that round out the intellect.

---

1. *Tehillim* 24:1.
2. As suggested by this triangle:

Side **a** touches upon sides **b** and **c**; therefore, remembering **a** reminds one of the entire unit. The same is true for either of the other sides; each calls to mind the other two. Hence, remembering any one — a, b or c — can recall the entire picture.

More than three items are difficult to remember because they cannot all be immediately related to each other.

15. They each said three things.

Rabbi Eliezer says: (a) Let your fellow's honor be as dear to you as your own, and (b) do not anger easily; and (c) repent one day before your death.

---

§ רַבִּי אֱלִיעֶזֶר אוֹמֵר — *Rabbi Eliezer says* ₪

A person relates with his world in three dimensions.[1] One interacts with: (a) other people; (b) oneself, and (c) God.

Rabbi Eliezer has advice to enhance each of these relationships:

§ יְהִי כָבוֹד חֲבֵרְךָ חָבִיב עָלֶיךָ כְּשֶׁלָּךְ — *(a) Let your fellow's honor be as dear to you as your own* ₪

(a) Cherishing the honor of other people assures success in interpersonal relationships.

§ וְאַל תְּהִי נוֹחַ לִכְעוֹס — *and (b) do not anger easily* ₪

(b) Anger undermines the very fabric of a person. The Rabbis say,[2]

> Rabbi Yochanan said, "All kinds of *Gehinnom* dominate one who gets angry." Rabbah bar Rav Huna said, "Even the Divine Presence is not important to one who gets angry." Rabbi Yirmiah said, "He also forgets his Torah studies and increases in foolishness." Rav Nachman said, "It is certain that he has many sins."

The angry person forgets his Torah studies and becomes foolish and corrupt. What personal substance remains?

§ וְשׁוּב יוֹם אֶחָד לִפְנֵי מִיתָתְךָ — *and (c) repent one day before your death* ₪

(c) The Hebrew word for "repent" is *shuv* which denotes "return." This advice assures that one continually returns his focus toward God, day by day, until the moment of death when the soul returns to He Who gave it.

---

1. For more detail, see *Derech Chaim* to Chapter 1, *mishnah* 2.
2. *Nedarim* 22a.

וֶהֱוֵי מִתְחַמֵּם כְּנֶגֶד אוּרָן שֶׁל חֲכָמִים, וֶהֱוֵי זָהִיר בְּגַחַלְתָּן, שֶׁלֹּא תִכָּוֶה – שֶׁנְּשִׁיכָתָן נְשִׁיכַת שׁוּעָל, וַעֲקִיצָתָן עֲקִיצַת עַקְרָב, וּלְחִישָׁתָן לְחִישַׁת שָׂרָף, וְכָל דִּבְרֵיהֶם כְּגַחֲלֵי אֵשׁ.

This three-pronged advice rounds a person in all three human dimensions: social, personal and spiritual.

In addition, Rabbi Eliezer said three things with regard to perfecting the intellect. This is an entirely different topic, unrelated to the first three things.

◆§ וֶהֱוֵי מִתְחַמֵּם כְּנֶגֶד אוּרָן שֶׁל חֲכָמִים — *(a) Warm yourself by the fire of the sages*

---

a) This means: Cleave to Torah sages. The image of warming oneself by the fire conveys the idea of receiving benefit by simply being close to the benefactor.

◆§ וֶהֱוֵי זָהִיר בְּגַחַלְתָּן, שֶׁלֹּא תִכָּוֶה — *(b) but beware of their glowing coal, lest you be burnt*

(b) Be careful that closeness with the sages does not lead to a sense of familiarity that can result in offending them. The image of the glowing coal conveys the need for caution, to avoid getting burnt when coming close to the coals for warmth.

◆§ שֶׁנְּשִׁיכָתָן נְשִׁיכַת שׁוּעָל, וַעֲקִיצָתָן עֲקִיצַת עַקְרָב, וּלְחִישָׁתָן לְחִישַׁת שָׂרָף, וְכָל דִּבְרֵיהֶם כְּגַחֲלֵי אֵשׁ — *for their bite is the bite of a fox, their sting is the sting of a scorpion, their hiss is the hiss of a serpent*

These three metaphors correspond to three degrees of being "burnt" after offending the sages.

The most severe is "biting." The powerful intellect of a scholar does not act by bits and pieces, but with utter totality. Therefore, if his hatred is aroused it may well be compared to the vicious bite of a fox, who will bite completely through a limb.

A lesser offense, such as lack of due respect, may give rise to resentment rather than hatred. The image of a "sting" is less severe than a bite, although the sting of a scorpion is still quite dangerous.

2/ 15   (a) Warm yourself by the fire of the sages, (b) but beware of their glowing coal, lest you be burnt — for their bite is the bite of a fox, their sting is the sting of a scorpion, their hiss is the hiss of a serpent, and (c) all of their words are like fiery coals.

Finally, the scholar may feel only anger. This is portrayed by the "hiss of a serpent," just as an angry person may whisper to himself. The hissing of an aroused serpent is very likely a precursor to biting and similarly the anger of a scholar should be cause for concern that danger is imminent.

An alternative explanation is based on how dangerous each of these creatures is, and reverses the order of severity. The bite of a fox is not poisonous and is the response to the least degree of offense. The scorpion's sting is poisonous, corresponding to a greater degree of offense. The serpent's poison is the most deadly of all and can be drawn by a serious offense to the scholar's honor.

וְכָל דִּבְרֵיהֶם כְּגַחֲלֵי אֵשׁ §≈ — *and (c) all their words are like fiery coals*

(c) This is a reference to the fact that one who violates the enactments of the Rabbis is deserving of death.[1] The Talmud[2] adjures us to be even more careful with rabbinical enactments than we are with Torah laws. Whether the Torah requires us to do a *mitzvah* or to refrain from a sin, very few laws carry the death penalty. By contrast, every transgression of rabbinical law is liable to death at the hands of Heaven.[3]

Mishnah 16

Why do these three things remove a person from the world?

It is the goodness of things that justifies their ongoing existence. That is the meaning of the declaration, "and God saw that it was good," that

---

1. *Berachos* 4b. The death penalty for violating Rabbinical enactments is administered at the hands of Heaven, not by the courts.
2. *Eruvin* 21b.
3. Rashi *loc. cit.*: as it says (*Koheles* 10:8), "He who breaks down a wall will be bitten by a snake." The meaning is that deadly forces are unleashed by breaking through a safeguard. The enactments of the Rabbis are generally a safeguard to the laws of the Torah, and death is an inherent consequence of breaking the fence around the Torah.

[טז] רַבִּי יְהוֹשֻׁעַ אוֹמֵר: עַיִן הָרָע, וְיֵצֶר הָרָע, וְשִׂנְאַת הַבְּרִיּוֹת מוֹצִיאִין אֶת הָאָדָם מִן הָעוֹלָם.

[יז] רַבִּי יוֹסֵי אוֹמֵר: יְהִי מָמוֹן חֲבֵרְךָ חָבִיב עָלֶיךָ כְּשֶׁלָּךְ; וְהַתְקֵן עַצְמְךָ לִלְמוֹד תּוֹרָה, שֶׁאֵינָהּ יְרֻשָּׁה לָךְ; וְכָל מַעֲשֶׂיךָ יִהְיוּ לְשֵׁם שָׁמָיִם.

---

sealed each step of Creation. By the same token, the first tablets of the Ten Commandments did not contain the word "good," because they would ultimately be smashed.[1]

Conversely, evil is that which brings about extinction, and that which is evil must come to an end.

The things mentioned in this *mishnah* remove a person from the world because they are the three things that Scripture describes as evil.

• an evil eye — *ayin hara;* i.e., one who begrudges others' good fortune, as it says,[2] "Do not eat the bread of him who has an evil eye."

• the evil inclination, *yetzer hara,* as it says,[3] "for the desire of man's heart is evil from his youth."

• an evil heart — *lev ra,* as it says,[4] "nor shall they walk anymore after the stubbornness of their evil heart."

These three categories of evil are the very things of which Rabbi Yehoshua warns. An evil heart includes "hatred for people" because hatred is in the heart.[5] He did not use the Scriptural term, because most instances of "an evil heart," such as withholding charity, are not as serious as the other evils. Only "hatred for people" is so patently evil as to remove a person from the world.

This *mishnah* follows thematically from the previous *mishnah*. Rabbi Eliezer's *mussar* prevents us from forfeiting life in the World to Come, while Rabbi Yehoshua's advice prevents prematurely losing the life of this world.

---

1. Explained in Maharal's *"Tiferes Yisrael,"* near the end of Chapter 43.
2. *Mishlei* 23:6.
3. *Bereishis* 8:21.
4. *Yirmeyahu* 3:17.
5. *Vayikra* 19:17: "You shall not hate your brother in your heart."

16. Rabbi Yehoshua says: (a) An evil eye, (b) the evil inclination, and (c) hatred of other people remove a person from the world.

17. Rabbi Yose says: (a) Let your fellow's money be as dear to you as your own; (b) apply yourself to study Torah, for it is not yours by inheritance; and (c) let all of your deeds be for the sake of Heaven.

Mishnah 17

People live within the three dimensions of (a) social, (b) personal and (c) spiritual relationships. This *mishnah* provides guidance for improvement in all three areas.

⊷§ **יְהִי מָמוֹן חֲבֵרְךָ חָבִיב עָלֶיךָ כְּשֶׁלָּךְ** — *(a) Let your fellow's money be as dear to you as your own*

(a) This strengthens one's social relationships. Concern for another's money develops a person's relationship with other people.

⊷§ **וְהַתְקֵן עַצְמְךָ לִלְמוֹד תּוֹרָה** — *(b) apply yourself to study Torah*

(b) This advice perfects one's very being through Torah, as we have already explained.[1] It is Torah above all that elevates a person from a physical creature to a spiritual, intellectual being.

⊷§ **שֶׁאֵינָהּ יְרֻשָּׁה לָךְ** — *for it is not yours by inheritance*

The reason that Torah study requires application is precisely because it does not flow automatically from generation to generation, as does an inheritance.

⊷§ **וְכָל מַעֲשֶׂיךָ יִהְיוּ לְשֵׁם שָׁמַיִם** — *and (c) let all of your deeds be for the sake of Heaven*

(c) This addresses the spiritual relationship. A person can perfect his relationship with God to the point where he does everything with religious intention.

---

1. *Supra*, Chapter 1, *mishnah* 2.

בר1928ב/יח

ב/יח [יח] רַבִּי שִׁמְעוֹן אוֹמֵר: הֱוֵי זָהִיר בִּקְרִיאַת
שְׁמַע וּבִתְפִלָּה; וּכְשֶׁאַתָּה מִתְפַּלֵּל, אַל
תַּעַשׂ תְּפִלָּתְךָ קֶבַע, אֶלָּא רַחֲמִים וְתַחֲנוּנִים
לִפְנֵי הַמָּקוֹם, שֶׁנֶּאֱמַר: „כִּי חַנּוּן וְרַחוּם הוּא,
אֶרֶךְ אַפַּיִם, וְרַב חֶסֶד, וְנִחָם עַל הָרָעָה"; וְאַל
תְּהִי רָשָׁע בִּפְנֵי עַצְמֶךָ.

Mishnah 18

Avos 1:2 stated that the service of God is one of the pillars of the world. Therefore, this *mishnah,* which requires us to exercise care with the recital of Shema and with prayer, touches upon the very essence of human existence.

---

§ הֱוֵי זָהִיר בִּקְרִיאַת שְׁמַע וּבִתְפִלָּה — *(a) Be meticulous in reading the Shema and in prayer*

Reciting the Shema is an act of accepting the sovereignty of Heaven, and prayer is the principal service of God while we are without the holy Temple. These deserve meticulous observance, for through them we fulfill the very purpose for which we were created.

---

§ וּכְשֶׁאַתָּה מִתְפַּלֵּל, אַל תַּעַשׂ תְּפִלָּתְךָ קֶבַע — *when you pray, do not make your prayer a set routine*

We can learn the correct approach to prayer from the following excerpt from the Talmud:[1]

> What is meant by "a set routine"? Rabbi Yaakov bar Idi said in the name of Rabbi Oshaya: "Anyone whose prayer is like a burden to him." The Rabbis say, "Anyone who does not say it with a supplicating expression." Rabbah and Rav Yosef both say, "Anyone who cannot express something original in it." Rabbi Zeira said, "I can express something original in it, but I am afraid to actually do so, lest I get distracted."[2]

Prayer must be a supplication. It must be expressed in the way that we

---

1. *Berachos* 28b.
2. Prayer was recited by heart. Rashi, *loc. cit.,* explains that Rabbi Zeira is concerned that departing from the regular text of the prayer will cause him to err when continuing where he left off after expressing his personal thought.

18. Rabbi Shimon says: (a) Be meticulous in reading the Shema and in prayer; (b) when you pray, do not make your prayer a set routine, but rather [beg for] compassion and supplication before the Omnipresent, as it is said (*Yoel* 2:13): "For He is gracious and compassionate, slow to anger, abounding in kindness and relentful of punishment"; and (c) do not be a wicked person in private.

would plead for a favor from someone. Prayer that is just routine obligation is not properly considered the "service of God," for the following reason.

The phrase "service of God," *avodas Hashem,* means that we are His servants — indeed, His slaves. We cultivate that relationship by being aware that we need God and are totally dependent upon Him. We should realize that everything He does for us comes of His mercy and compassion, for He owes us nothing. If a person prays with the attitude that God ought to do his request, then he is not totally dependent upon Him and falls short of being His servant.

§⊷ אֶלָּא רַחֲמִים וְתַחֲנוּנִים — *but rather [beg for] compassion and supplication*

The essence of supplication is to humble oneself before God and to entreat of Him as a slave before his master. This is not possible by thought alone. It requires an action, for there is no comparison between one who humbles himself in his thoughts, and one who humbles himself through deeds. Therefore, prayer must entail some physical action, and for that reason we pray through speech, and not just in thought.

Since the substance of prayer is speech, the Rabbis of the cited passage required praying with language that expresses the supplicatory nature of the prayer.[1]

§⊷ וְאַל תְּהִי רָשָׁע בִּפְנֵי עַצְמֶךְ — *and (c) do not be a wicked person in private*

God will fulfill the petition of one who knows that he needs God and depends on Him completely. However, one who has gone outside the

1. Feelings alone do not fulfill the requirement of praying in a supplicatory manner.

ב/יט [יט] רַבִּי אֶלְעָזָר אוֹמֵר: הֱוֵי שָׁקוּד לִלְמוֹד
תּוֹרָה, וְדַע מַה שֶּׁתָּשִׁיב לְאֶפִּיקוֹרוֹס;
וְדַע לִפְנֵי מִי אַתָּה עָמֵל; וְנֶאֱמָן הוּא בַּעַל
מְלַאכְתְּךָ, שֶׁיְּשַׁלֶּם לְךָ שְׂכַר פְּעֻלָּתֶךָ.

bounds of proper behavior, even in private, might still not have his prayers answered.

The primary meaning of the term *rasha*, a wicked person, is one who is wicked to other people, as we find in the verse,[1]

And he said to the wicked one, "Why do you hit your fellow?"

The term *rasha* can also be applied in a more general sense to anyone who goes outside the bounds of propriety.

The *mishnah* enjoins us not to be wicked even in a degree that does not affect others, but is discerned only by oneself. Although such a person is not a *rasha* in the primary sense of the word, he still is in the general category of a *rasha*. Wickedness is so serious and so pernicious that even a minor degree of it is extremely destructive.

What is the connection between "do not be a wicked person" and the earlier two statements that address prayer? Prayer is the service of God, in place of the sacrificial service of the Temple, and Scripture says,[2]

The sacrifice of the wicked is an abomination to God, but the prayer of the upright is His delight.

The *mishnah* intends to say, "Even if you are a *rasha* privately, and no one else knows, still God knows and your prayer is not acceptable to Him."

The three statements of this *mishnah* share the single goal of improving our service of God by improving the quality of our prayer.

Mishnah 19

As noted before, mankind was created to live within three primary relationships, dealing with other people, with ourselves and with God. The previous *mishnah* discussed how we relate to God, by serving Him in prayer. This *mishnah* deals with how we attend to our personal growth.

---

1. *Shemos* 2:13.
2. *Mishlei* 15:8.

19. Rabbi Elazar says: (a) Be diligent in the study of Torah; (b) know what to answer a heretic; and (c) know before Whom you toil; and know that your Employer can be relied upon to pay you the wage of your labor.

---

§⊷ הֱוֵי שָׁקוּד לִלְמוֹד תּוֹרָה ⊷§ — *(a) Be diligent in the study of Torah*

Man was created to labor in Torah, as it says,[1] "man was born to toil." A person who takes Torah study casually, learning when he has time, falls short of his life's task which is to toil in Torah study. The *mishnah* therefore emphasizes that our task is to study with diligence.

§⊷ וְדַע מַה שֶׁתָּשִׁיב לְאַפִּיקוֹרוֹס ⊷§ — *(b) know what to answer a heretic*[2]

It is a *mitzvah* to study and to acquire the Torah, which is truth. To that end, we should eliminate false opinions so that truth can flourish, for when falsehood prevails it displaces truth. The *mishnah* exhorts us not to leave room for untruth to take hold and spread, but to know how to respond to a heretic.

This *mishnah* imposes a taxing burden on us, requiring us to labor energetically in the study of Torah, and to achieve a level of expertise that will let us answer a heretic. Therefore, it continues by saying:

§⊷ וְנֶאֱמָן הוּא בַּעַל מְלַאכְתְּךָ, שֶׁיְשַׁלֶּם לְךָ שְׂכַר פְּעֻלָּתֶךָ — *and know that your Employer can be relied upon to pay you the wage of your labor*

God will give you abundant reward for exerting effort in the pursuit of Torah.

Rabbi Elazar is not suggesting that we should learn Torah in order to get reward, for that would contradict Antignos of Socho who said[3] that one should not serve God to receive reward.

Rabbi Elazar's statement simply provides a strategy to counteract lethargy, for sometimes we are tempted to take the path which requires the least exertion.

---

1. *Iyov* 5:7.
2. Maharal appears to have had the text: "Be diligent in the study of Torah *in order to* answer a heretic."
3. *Supra*, 1:3.

Mishnayos 15-19: An Alternative Approach

Each of these Rabbis expressed their advice in three statements that address the three aspects of every human being:

- the physical component
- the spiritual component
- the total person.

Mishnah 15

⧫§ רַבִּי אֱלִיעֶזֶר אוֹמֵר: יְהִי כְבוֹד חֲבֵרְךָ חָבִיב עָלֶיךָ כְּשֶׁלָּךְ — *Rabbi Eliezer says: (a) Let your fellow's honor be as dear to you as your own*

This addresses the **total** human being, whose highest level is the conceptual, spiritual image of God. It is that aspect of the human being that befits the highest level of life, namely the eternal life of the World to Come. Honoring other people, who are the image of God, brings one to the World to Come,[1] just as embarrassing people causes one to forfeit the World to Come.[2]

⧫§ וְאַל תְּהִי נוֹחַ לִכְעוֹס — *and (b) do not anger easily*

This addresses the **soul**, because anger arises from the soul. Anger leads to sin, which causes one to lose the World to Come.

⧫§ וְשׁוּב יוֹם אֶחָד לִפְנֵי מִיתָתְךָ — *and (c) repent one day before your death*

This addresses the **physical** component. The opportunity for repentance arises from the ability to change, and that stems from the physical aspect of life.[3]

Mishnah 16

⧫§ רַבִּי יְהוֹשֻׁעַ אוֹמֵר: עַיִן הָרָע, וְיֵצֶר הָרָע, וְשִׂנְאַת הַבְּרִיּוֹת מוֹצִיאִין אֶת הָאָדָם מִן הָעוֹלָם — *Rabbi Yehoshua says: (a) An evil eye, (b) the evil inclination, and (c) hatred of other people remove a person from the world.*

---

1. *Berachos* 28b.
2. *Bava Metzia* 59b.
3. Physical things can change, whereas purely spiritual or conceptual things are not changeable. Therefore the ability to undo the negative effects of sin and to improve arises from the physical component of human existence.

The "evil eye" refers to the **spiritual** desire to destroy. "Evil inclination" refers to **physical** desires, foremost of which is the desire for forbidden sexual relations. Evil is, by definition, destructive and hence the pursuit of evil destroys one's worldly existence. The **total** person is destroyed by hatred of people, as he himself is a person.

Mishnah 17

§◆— רַבִּי יוֹסֵי אוֹמֵר: יְהִי מָמוֹן חֲבֵרְךָ חָבִיב עָלֶיךָ כְּשֶׁלָּךְ ◆§
Rabbi Yose says: (a) Let your fellow's money be as dear to you as your own

A person consists of body and soul, and of intellectual and material acquisitions. Obviously we must respect a person himself and the wisdom he has acquired,[1] but Rabbi Yose goes much further, saying that we must respect the **total** person, including his material possessions such as money.

§◆ וְהַתְקֵן עַצְמְךָ לִלְמוֹד תּוֹרָה, שֶׁאֵינָהּ יְרֻשָּׁה לָךְ ◆§ — *(b)* **apply yourself to study Torah, for it is not yours by inheritance**

This is advice to marshal all of one's strength to overcome the limitations of the **physical** component of one's being, which is not attuned to Torah. If a person would be entirely without a physical component, inherently he would be in possession of Torah.

§◆ וְכָל מַעֲשֶׂיךָ יִהְיוּ לְשֵׁם שָׁמָיִם ◆§ — *and (c)* **let all of your deeds be for the sake of Heaven**

This advice is addressed to the **soul**, which animates the body to action.

Mishnah 18

§◆ רַבִּי שִׁמְעוֹן אוֹמֵר: הֱוֵי זָהִיר בִּקְרִיאַת שְׁמַע וּבִתְפִלָּה ◆§ — *Rabbi Shimon* **says: (a) Be meticulous in reading the Shema and in prayer**

This addresses the **total** person, touching upon the very essence of human existence, for mankind was created to accept God's sovereignty

---

1. Author's explanation.

and to serve Him. This is specified in Scripture,[1]

> "Fear God and keep His commandments, for that is the whole of mankind," which the Rabbis explained[2] to mean: "All of mankind was created for this (i.e., fear and service of God)."

The physical aspect of human existence interferes with sharing God's presence. To encounter God in prayer, one must divest himself of physical matters. Removing oneself from the norm of physical existence is an onerous burden, to which one reacts defensively by approaching prayer as a set routine, and Rabbi Shimon counters this by saying:

וּכְשֶׁאַתָּה מִתְפַּלֵּל, אַל תַּעַשׂ תְּפִלָּתְךָ קֶבַע, אֶלָּא רַחֲמִים וְתַחֲנוּנִים §◆
לִפְנֵי הַמָּקוֹם — **(b) when you pray, do not make your
prayer a set routine, but rather [beg for] compassion
and supplication before the Omnipresent**

The code of Jewish law known as the *Tur* states,[3]

> "The pious and people of religious accomplishments used to seclude themselves to focus on their prayer; they were able to divest themselves of corporeal characteristics and to intensify the intellectual spirit until they came close to a state of prophecy."

A person whose prayer is supplication, to the degree that he cleaves to God, has removed the barrier of physical existence which separates God from mankind. Hence, the warning not to pray out of routine counteracts the physical aspect of mankind.

וְאַל תְּהִי רָשָׁע בִּפְנֵי עַצְמֶךָ §◆ — **and (c) do not be
a wicked person in private**

This statement addresses the soul, because wickedness lies within the soul, and it affects only the soul, not the physical faculties.

The Hebrew phrase *bifnei atzmecha,* which we have translated as "in private," could also be rendered as "do not be wicked *to yourself*," to physically mistreat yourself. The term *chasid* includes a pious person who bestows goodness on his own soul.[4] So the term *rasha* in this context may even apply to an otherwise good person who does evil to

---

1. *Koheles* 12:13.
2. *Berachos* 6b.
3. *Tur, Orach Chaim,* Number 98.
4. *Mishlei* 11:17: "The pious person does good to his own soul, but he that is cruel troubles his own flesh."

himself, by undertaking voluntarily fasts which are difficult for him to bear.[1]

רַבִּי אֶלְעָזָר אוֹמֵר: הֱוֵי שָׁקוּד לִלְמוֹד תּוֹרָה §❧ — *Rabbi Elazar says:*
(a) Be diligent in the study of Torah

This addresses a person in total, for mankind was created to labor in the Torah, as explained previously.

וְדַע מַה שֶּׁתָּשִׁיב לְאֶפִּיקוֹרוֹס §❧ — *(b) know what to answer a heretic*

This refers to heretical thoughts that arise in the thoughts of the soul. If one knows how to respond to a heretic, then heretical thoughts will not arise in his own heart.

וְדַע לִפְנֵי מִי אַתָּה עָמֵל; וְנֶאֱמָן הוּא בַּעַל מְלַאכְתְּךָ שֶׁיְשַׁלֶּם לְךָ שְׂכַר §❧
פְּעֻלָּתֶךָ — *and (c) know before Whom you toil; and know that your*
Employer can be relied upon to pay you the wage of your labor

---

This advice counteracts the temptations which arise from the physical component of existence. As explained previously, this statement is a practical device to stimulate a person out of the lethargy which entices one not to labor in Torah studies.

In summary, the five Rabbis have given three items of advice to remedy human shortcomings in each of the three components of human existence.

Mishnah 20

Rabbi Tarfon's message is that we must not permit ourselves to be distracted from Torah study. There is a great amount of work to do and if we waste time, we are delinquent. Sayings such as[2]

> "Whether one does much or one does little, as long as his heart is directed towards Heaven,"

and in the following *mishnah,*

> "you do not have to finish the labor,"

do not condone neglecting our studies. Everyone must study with the diligence needed to complete all of the Torah.

---

1. *Taanis* 11b.
2. *Berachos* 5b.

ב/
כ־כא

[כ] רַבִּי טַרְפוֹן אוֹמֵר: הַיּוֹם קָצֵר, וְהַמְּלָאכָה מְרֻבָּה, וְהַפּוֹעֲלִים עֲצֵלִים, וְהַשָּׂכָר הַרְבֵּה, וּבַעַל הַבַּיִת דּוֹחֵק.

[כא] הוּא הָיָה אוֹמֵר: לֹא עָלֶיךָ הַמְּלָאכָה לִגְמוֹר, וְלֹא אַתָּה בֶן חוֹרִין לְהִבָּטֵל מִמֶּנָּה. אִם לָמַדְתָּ תּוֹרָה הַרְבֵּה,

---

The different metaphors of this *mishnah* show, from every perspective, that we cannot afford to waste time. Consider the volume of material to cover; God's high expectations; the difficulty of the task; the limited ability of a human being; and the short time available. The inescapable conclusion is that there is not a moment to waste and that we must apply the maximum energy possible. We must make every effort to complete the task, and failure to do so constitutes negligence.

Statements such as "you are not required to complete the task" apply only to one who has made the maximum effort, and has accomplished all that he is personally capable of.

---

§ הַיּוֹם קָצֵר, וְהַמְּלָאכָה מְרֻבָּה — *The day is short, the task is abundant*

The Torah is conceptual, and therefore is unbounded in magnitude and time. As a result, "The day is short" because all the days since Creation would not be time enough to spend on Torah; and "the task is abundant" because finite mankind cannot embrace an infinite Torah.

---

§ וְהַפּוֹעֲלִים עֲצֵלִים . . . וּבַעַל הַבַּיִת דּוֹחֵק — *the laborers are lazy . . . and the Master of the house is insistent*

The "Master" for whom we are working is God, the All-powerful. From that perspective, He is extremely insistent, because nothing is laborious to Him. By contrast, human beings — like all physical things — have inertia that our *mishnah* describes as "the laborers are lazy."

This *mishnah* does not demand the impossible; a human being cannot be expected to be an angel, devoid of physical limitation. When God gave us the Torah, He challenged us to emulate spiritual beings within the limits of a physical being, by acting with energy and dedication.

20. Rabbi Tarfon says: The day is short, the task is abundant, the laborers are lazy, the wage is great, and the Master of the house is insistent.

21. He used to say: You are not required to complete the task, yet you are not free to withdraw from it. If you have studied much Torah,

---

To waste the limited resources that we do have is to sin flagrantly. How could anyone even think of wasting time and talent? Yet the majority of our eating and drinking[1] is wasteful, distracting us from studying Torah energetically. Rather, we must be as diligent and focused in our studies as if we intend to finish the Torah.

Mishnah 21

לֹא עָלֶיךָ הַמְּלָאכָה לִגְמוֹר</div> — *You are not required to complete the task*

Reward comes also from the very *mitzvah* itself, in addition to the effort of the *mitzvah*. One might believe, God forbid, that there is no reward for incomplete Torah study, just as an employer would not pay a builder for an unfinished house that is not usable, if there is no other worker to finish it. This *mishnah* refutes that notion. The Torah was given to us so that we may labor at it; it is not necessary to finish it to accomplish the purpose of our creation.

The fact that we receive reward even without knowing the entire Torah could lead to a different error. We might think that it is adequate to study Torah just once a day, in the same way that taking the *lulav* and *esrog* just once suffices for the entire day. Therefore the *mishnah* continues:

וְלֹא אַתָּה בֶן חוֹרִין לִהְבָּטֵל מִמֶּנָּה</div> — *yet you are not free to withdraw from it*

A human being must continually grow, for one cannot grow to his full potential in only one lifetime. To maintain continuous growth one must labor continuously at Torah, without halt.

---

1. How the variety of distractions has mushroomed in the 400 years since Maharal wrote these words!

נוֹתְנִים לְךָ שָׂכָר הַרְבֵּה; וְנֶאֱמָן הוּא בַּעַל
מְלַאכְתְּךָ, שֶׁיְשַׁלֵּם לְךָ שְׂכַר פְּעֻלָּתֶךָ, וְדַע
שֶׁמַּתַּן שְׂכָרָן שֶׁל צַדִּיקִים לֶעָתִיד לָבֹא.

❦ ❦ ❦

⋘§ אִם לָמַדְתָּ תּוֹרָה הַרְבֵּה, נוֹתְנִים לְךָ שָׂכָר הַרְבֵּה — *If you have studied much Torah, they will give you great reward*

This implies that the reward for Torah study is related to the quantity of study; but the following Talmudic passage appears to present a problem.

> Rabbi Elazar fell sick. Rabbi Yochanan went in to him and saw that Rabbi Elazar was crying. He said to him: Why are you crying? Is it because you did not learn enough Torah? We have learned: "Whether one does much or one does little, as long as his heart is directed towards Heaven."[1]

This passage implies that the rewards for learning much Torah and for learning a little Torah are the same. Yet our *mishnah* states that if you studied much Torah, then you receive great reward!

Our *mishnah* is referring to the effort expended on Torah study, not to the quantity of material that was learned. As we explained earlier,[2] part of the reward for a *mitzvah* comes from the effort applied to accomplish the *mitzvah*. Our *mishnah* means that the more effort spent studying, the more reward. If one studied intently for a year and learned much, while another studied intently for a year and learned little, the reward is the same for both.

⋘§ אִם לָמַדְתָּ תּוֹרָה הַרְבֵּה, נוֹתְנִים לְךָ שָׂכָר הַרְבֵּה — *If you have studied much Torah, they will give you great reward*

Since Torah is infinite, one never gets closer to completion. Therefore, one might think that there is reward for studying Torah, but that more study has no additional reward because it does not bring one closer to completion. To refute that idea, the *mishnah* says: If you have studied much Torah, they will give you great reward.

Studying Torah is not like building a house, which has no value unless it is complete. It is comparable to sowing seeds; every seed sown is a com-

---

1. *Berachos* 5b.
2. *Supra*, Chapter 2, *mishnah* 1.

they will give you great reward; and your Employer can be relied upon to pay you the wage of your labor, but be aware that the reward of the righteous will be given in the World to Come.

❈ ❈ ❈

pleted task, regardless of whether one finishes the entire field. The study of Torah is similar. The value lies in the effort, and every additional effort is a completed task. Therefore, the reward is commensurate with the effort.

❧ וְנֶאֱמָן הוּא בַּעַל מְלַאכְתְּךָ, שֶׁיְשַׁלֶּם לְךָ שְׂכַר פְּעֻלָּתֶךָ — *and your Employer can be relied upon to pay you the wage of your labor*

Payment is made when the task is complete. This is the basis of the view[1] that, in general, there is no reward for *mitzvos* in this world. Payment for *mitzvos* is bestowed after a person has finished his life's labors.

Torah law requires that a worker be paid without delay. One might expect that God would exemplify the Torah's value system of immediate compensation by rewarding people immediately for virtuous deeds. Such is not always the case, for God pays some people earlier and some people later. The precedent for delayed compensation can also be found in Torah law. A field laborer may undertake to be paid from the new crop of grain. In that case, payment is made immediately upon maturation of the new crop.

❧ וְדַע שֶׁמַתַּן שְׂכָרָן שֶׁל צַדִּיקִים לֶעָתִיד לָבֹא — *but be aware that the reward of the righteous will be given in the World to Come*

This limited world is not capable of providing the richness and intensity of the reward for virtuous deeds. Only the World to Come has the capacity to provide such reward adequately. For that reason we are like the laborer who is willing to wait for the new crop of grain to collect his reward. We undertake our task from the start with the understanding that God will provide our compensation in the World to Come and not in this world.

Those who are righteous might not receive reward for their good deeds in this world and those who do evil might not be punished immediately. The reason is that the principal place for penalty and reward is the World to Come.

------

1. *Kiddushin* 39b.

רַבִּי חֲנַנְיָא בֶּן עֲקַשְׁיָא אוֹמֵר: רָצָה הַקָּדוֹשׁ
בָּרוּךְ הוּא לְזַכּוֹת אֶת יִשְׂרָאֵל; לְפִיכָךְ
הִרְבָּה לָהֶם תּוֹרָה וּמִצְוֹת, שֶׁנֶּאֱמַר: „יהוה חָפֵץ
לְמַעַן צִדְקוֹ, יַגְדִּיל תּוֹרָה וְיַאְדִּיר."

Rabbi Chanania ben Akashia says: The Holy One,
Blessed is He, wished to confer merit upon Israel;
therefore He gave them Torah and *mitzvos* in
abundance, as it is said (*Yeshayahu* 42:21): "Hashem
desired, for the sake of His righteousness, that the
Torah be made great and glorious."

פרק שלישי ৬§
Chapter Three

כָּל יִשְׂרָאֵל יֵשׁ לָהֶם חֵלֶק לָעוֹלָם הַבָּא,
שֶׁנֶּאֱמַר: „וְעַמֵּךְ כֻּלָּם צַדִּיקִים; לְעוֹלָם
יִירְשׁוּ אָרֶץ; נֵצֶר מַטָּעַי, מַעֲשֵׂה יָדַי לְהִתְפָּאֵר."

All Israel has a share in the World to Come, as it is said (*Yeshayahu* 60:21): "And your people are all righteous; they shall inherit the land forever; they are the stem of My plantings, My handiwork, in which to take pride."

א/ג **עֲקַבְיָא** בֶּן מַהֲלַלְאֵל אוֹמֵר: הִסְתַּכֵּל בִּשְׁלֹשָׁה דְבָרִים וְאֵין אַתָּה בָא לִידֵי עֲבֵרָה: דַּע מֵאַיִן בָּאתָ, וּלְאָן אַתָּה הוֹלֵךְ,

Mishnah 1

Akavia ben Mahalalel lived in the generation after Shemayah and Avtalyon.[1] He is not mentioned in the first chapter because he was not part of the dedicated chain of Torah transmission; nor was he among the descendants of Hillel who are found in the remainder of Chapter One. Akavia's advice was deferred until this point because it is so fundamental and far reaching that it warranted to start a new chapter.

§ הִסְתַּכֵּל בִּשְׁלֹשָׁה דְבָרִים — *Consider three things*

The literal translation of *histakel b'shloshah devarim* is, "Stare at three things." Unlike animals, the human being was endowed with an upright anatomy and posture that enables him to see those three things: the source of the "putrid drop," the earth to which he will return, and the heavens. God created man in such a way that he might have these reminders constantly in front of him.

§ הִסְתַּכֵּל בִּשְׁלֹשָׁה דְבָרִים וְאֵין אַתָּה בָא לִידֵי עֲבֵרָה — *Consider three things and you will not come into the grip of sin*

Why are all three things necessary to keep a person from sin? Is it not adequate to remember that one has to account for his actions in front of God Himself, even if he does not consider his origin and destination? Furthermore, the fact that one comes from a putrid drop, or that he is going to a place of dust, is no reason to desist from sinning!

Akavia ben Mahalalel's advice addresses the root cause of sin. God placed in mankind a drive for sin, which is personified as the *yetzer hara*. A person may know that in the future he will have to account for his deeds in front of God Himself; nonetheless, when the *yetzer hara* is overwhelming, one sins without thinking about the future. To avoid transgression one must remove the power that the *yetzer hara* has over him, and thereby remove the very cause of sin.

The power of the *yetzer hara* arises from arrogance: All desire, jealousy and other causes of sin originate from a heart that swells with pride. The

1. *Supra,* Chapter 1, *Mishnah* 10-11.

1. Akavia ben Mahalalel says: Consider three things and you will not come into the grip of sin: Know whence you came, whither you go,

---

yetzer hara is the force that moves a person to act in a way that leads towards destruction. When a person thinks that he is on a very high level, then the *yetzer hara* is set in motion to knock down and destroy. However, if our spirit and heart are broken within us, and we do not consider ourselves important, then there is nothing for the *yetzer hara* to attack.

The Rabbis have alluded many times to the fact that the *yetzer hara* arises only from pride. In tractate *Nedarim*[1] we read,

> Shimon HaTzaddik said: In my life I ate only one sacrifice of a *nazir*.[2] Once a man who was a *nazir* came from the south. I saw that he had beautiful eyes and was good looking and his hair fell in curls. I said to him, "What is the reason you want to cut off your beautiful hair?" He said to me, "I was a shepherd for my father in my city. I went to fill water from the well and I stared at my reflection. My *yetzer* seized me and wanted to destroy me from the world.[3] I said to the reflection: Wicked one! Why are you proud in a world which is not yours, about one who is destined to be worms and maggots. By the Temple Service! I will shave you off for the sake of Heaven."
>
> I arose and kissed him on his head. I said to him, "My son, may there be more like you who take the nazirite vow in Israel!"

In summary, when the man saw his own beauty, the *yetzer hara* became strong and sought to destroy him, for the essence of the *yetzer hara* is that he seeks to destroy the edifice. He does not move against that which has been demolished, for there is nothing left to destroy. The *yetzer hara* would have nothing to pursue once the man freed himself of arrogance by shaving off his hair.

◆§ דַּע מֵאַיִן בָּאתָ, וּלְאָן אַתָּה הוֹלֵךְ — *Know whence you came, whither you go*

We now can explain why knowing "whence you came, whither you go" removes one from the grip of sin. The realization that one's existence

---

1. *Nedarim* 9b.

2. A *nazir* vows to abstain from wine and grapes for a fixed period of time. During that time the *nazir* may not cut his hair, nor come in contact with a corpse. At the end of the period, the *nazir's* head is shaved and the hair is burned. See *Bamidbar* 6:1-21.

3. Rashi, *loc. cit.* explains: My *yetzer hara* overpowered me. He sought to bring me to do evil acts, to destroy me from the world.

וְלִפְנֵי מִי אַתָּה עָתִיד לִתֵּן דִּין וְחֶשְׁבּוֹן. מֵאַיִן בָּאתָ? מִטִּפָּה סְרוּחָה. וּלְאָן אַתָּה הוֹלֵךְ? לִמְקוֹם עָפָר, רִמָּה וְתוֹלֵעָה. וְלִפְנֵי מִי אַתָּה עָתִיד לִתֵּן דִּין וְחֶשְׁבּוֹן? לִפְנֵי מֶלֶךְ מַלְכֵי הַמְּלָכִים, הַקָּדוֹשׁ בָּרוּךְ הוּא.

from beginning to end is very humble leaves little room for pride. Since the *yetzer hara* attacks only one who considers himself important, it has no influence over one who considers himself insignificant.

§ וְלִפְנֵי מִי אַתָּה עָתִיד לִתֵּן דִּין וְחֶשְׁבּוֹן — *and before Whom you will give judgment and reckoning*

One could come to sin even without temptation, if he felt that there is no judgment and no judge, God forbid! Why should he not sin? This possibility is countered by remembering that there is indeed a judgment.

The fact that one will have to face judgment is the third aspect of mankind's lowly existence. Not only is one's beginning and end very humble, but his existence itself is very humble. If one must account for every action for as long as he lives, it is better not to have been created![1]

Contemplating these reasons to feel humble might lead a person to feel worthless and to despair of ever achieving worth. There is a danger that the advice of this *mishnah* could have a negative effect, causing one to no longer care about what he does.

However, when approached with the proper attitude, this *mishnah* will not lead to discouragement and despair. Indeed, the opposite is true: It provides the motivation to acquire worth through fulfilling *mitzvos,* and thereby become a valued human being in a spiritual context.

The lowly physical nature of our existence can be invoked to plead with God not to be exacting in His judgment when we have sinned. However, it must not be used as an excuse to sin further. Rather, our humble physical existence should motivate us to acquire a high spiritual caliber, through *mitzvos.*

Some have questioned that the order of "judgment and reckoning" is

1. A reference to *Eruvin* 13a, "It is better for a person not to have been created." This opinion of the school of Hillel was accepted by majority vote after a 2 1/2-year debate. The point is that one's time and actions are not his own if he is scrutinized and accountable for everything. All one has as a result of being born is the risk of committing a sin.

3/ 1 and before Whom you will give judgment and reckoning. "Whence you came?" from a putrid drop; "wither you go?" to a place of dust, worms and maggots; "and before Whom you will give judgment and reckoning?" before the King Who reigns over kings, the Holy One, Blessed is He.

---

incorrect. The reckoning comes first and then the judgment. The answer is that the term *din* refers to the beginning of the trial, after which the reckoning is given. It does not refer to the final decision.

If one goes to a place of worms and maggots, how can he give a reckoning? The answer is that the judgment will take place in the future, in the era of resurrection.

❧ הִסְתַּכֵּל בִּשְׁלשָׁה דְבָרִים — *Consider three things*

A more profound explanation of the *mishnah* considers that mankind's existence is dependent on God. In this relationship, mankind is referred to as the dependent עָלוּל, *alul,* and God is the first cause עָלָה, *Illah.*

Sin is departure from God. The principle behind this *mishnah* is that one can escape the grip of sin as long as he sees that he is an *alul* whose existence depends on the *Illah,* God. He will realize that to leave God is to leave the source of his own existence. He will consider sin as a threat to his very being, not as a temptation, and that is the meaning of the phrase that he will not come even into the "grip" of sin.

A person's humble origin and humble end are evidence of his inherent insignificance. Significant existence comes only through one's relationship with God. Our relationship to God is based on the fact that, as an *alul,* we are accountable to God for his actions, and that, as the *Illah,* God scrutinizes our deeds as the basis for our future existence. One who acknowledges that he will face judgment and reckoning in the future acknowledges God as the Source of existence.

❧ הִסְתַּכֵּל בִּשְׁלשָׁה דְבָרִים — *Consider three things*

An entity consists of three parts: the beginning, the end and the substantive body. The three things listed in the *mishnah* demonstrate mankind's dependence on God with respect to all three parts. "Whence you came" and "whither you go" allude to our dependence on God for

145 / MAHARAL: PIRKEI AVOS

ג

ג/ב

[ב] רַבִּי חֲנִינָא, סְגַן הַכֹּהֲנִים, אוֹמֵר: הֱוֵי מִתְפַּלֵּל בִּשְׁלוֹמָהּ שֶׁל מַלְכוּת, שֶׁאִלְמָלֵא מוֹרָאָהּ, אִישׁ אֶת רֵעֵהוּ חַיִּים בְּלָעוֹ.

---

our origin and end. The substance of our life lies in between those two events. The fact that we will face judgment and reckoning for what we do with our life establishes our connection with the Source of life and removes us from the grip of sin.

This explanation of our *mishnah* is conveyed in the following *Midrash*:[1]

> Akavia ben Mahalalel says: Consider three things. Whence you came? from a putrid drop. Whither you go? to a place of dust, worms and maggots. Before Whom you will give judgment and reckoning? before the King of kings, the Holy One, Blessed is He.
>
> Rabbi Yehoshua ben Levi of Sachnin said: Akavia derives all three of these from a single word. "Remember your Creator, *borecha,* in the days of your youth."[2] There are three variations: *borecha,* (your Creator), *borcha* (your pit), *be'ercha* (your well). "Your well" refers to the putrid moisture; "your pit" refers to worms and maggots; "your Creator" refers to the King of kings, the Holy One, Blessed is He, before Whom you will give judgment and reckoning.

This *Midrash* points out that the Hebrew word for Creator conveys that the beginning of a person is nought, and his end is decay, and that the Creator is the Source of substance for the created.

In summary, when a person enters completely within the dominion of the Source of existence, he is freed from sin and from the drive to sin.

Mishnah 2

Introduction

Human creation was unique. When the other creatures were created, many of each kind were made, all at the same time. Adam, however, was created alone, and even the female did not yet have a separate existence.[3]

---

1. *Midrash Koheles Rabbah,* Chapter 12.
2. *Koheles* 12:1.
3. She was joined with him as one person; see *Eruvin* 18a.

פרקי אבות / 146

2. Rabbi Chanina, the deputy Kohen Gadol [High Priest], says: Pray for the welfare of the government because if people did not fear it, a person would swallow his fellow alive.

Why was this so? The Rabbis answer,[1]

> The first man was made alone for this reason: to teach that "if anyone destroys one human life, it is considered as if he destroyed an entire world"; and if anyone maintains one human life, it is considered as if he had maintained the entire world.
>
> . . . This tells the greatness of God. A mortal mints many coins from a single mold, and all are alike; but God forms everybody in the mold of the first man, yet no two people are identical. Therefore, each and every person is obligated to say: "The world was created for me."

The reason "if anyone destroys one human life, it is considered as if he destroyed an entire world" is not because the descendants of just one person can eventually populate the entire world. Such an interpretation would be problematic, implying that murder would be less serious if the victim was not capable of having children.

Rather, the explanation of this passage is as follows. The world was created with just one person, who served as king of the whole world. The role of king is to unify his subjects into a single community, and indeed Adam brought together all parts of creation for the sole purpose of serving God. Since God structured creation to need only a solitary human being, the existence of the entire world is fully justified for even one person. Therefore, if anyone sustains one person, it is as if he had sustained the entire world and if anyone destroys one person, it is as if he had destroyed the entire world.

🔸 שֶׁאִלְמָלֵא מוֹרָאָהּ, אִישׁ אֶת רֵעֵהוּ חַיִּים בְּלָעוֹ — *because if people did not fear it, a person would swallow his fellow alive*

The laws of nature were established at the time of creation.[2] Since Adam was created as the sole king, it is imbedded within nature that there be only one human being, who is king of the world.

---

1. See *Sanhedrin* 37a for the exact passage.
2. Author's explanatory comment, based on Maharal's commentary to *Avos* 5:8.

ג/ג [ג] רַבִּי חֲנִינָא בֶּן תְּרַדְיוֹן אוֹמֵר: שְׁנַיִם
שֶׁיּוֹשְׁבִין וְאֵין בֵּינֵיהֶם דִּבְרֵי תוֹרָה, הֲרֵי
זֶה מוֹשַׁב לֵצִים, שֶׁנֶּאֱמַר: ,,וּבְמוֹשַׁב לֵצִים לֹא
יָשָׁב." אֲבָל שְׁנַיִם שֶׁיּוֹשְׁבִין וְיֵשׁ בֵּינֵיהֶם דִּבְרֵי
תוֹרָה, שְׁכִינָה שְׁרוּיָה בֵינֵיהֶם, שֶׁנֶּאֱמַר: ,,אָז

The Rabbis said,[1]

> "God forms everybody in the mold of the first man, yet no two
> are identical."

We are all like Adam, in that we consider ourselves to be the solitary
king of the world. The conviction that "the whole world was created for
me"[2] has been inherited from the first man; it is inherent in our human
nature, and it is accurate. The result is an inescapable conflict: We are
autonomous, solitary individuals who have to share the world with other
people.

What drives people to kill other people? As we said, it is the nature of
creation that there be only one person as king of the world. Therefore,
there is a natural drive to return to the original state of being the only
person in the world. That drive is so strong that a person could devour
his neighbor alive until he alone remains.

The role of government is to bind the people into a unified nation. We
should pray for the welfare of the government, since only the fear of it
can bind individuals into a society and prevent each person from vying
to be the only one in the world.

Relationship of this Mishnah to the Preceding Mishnah

In the previous *mishnah* Akavia ben Mahalalel taught three things that
can counter the presence of pride. This *mishnah* continues that theme by
showing that human pride is so natural and runs so deep that it can be
a motive for murder.

This *mishnah* of Rabbi Chanina adjoins that of Akavia ben Mahalalel
who lived in the same period. The next *mishnah* is authored by Rabbi
Chanina ben Tradyon who lived in the generation following these two. In
general, when unrelated subjects are grouped together, it is because the
authors lived in or around the same era.

---

1. *Sanhedrin* 37a.
2. *Ibid.*

3. Rabbi Chanina ben Tradyon says: If two sit together and there are no words of Torah between them, it is a session of scorners, as it is said (*Tehillim* 1:1), "In the session of scorners he does not sit." But if two sit together and there are words of Torah between them, the Divine Presence rests between them, as it is said (*Malachi* 3:16): "Then

---

Mishnah 3

שְׁנַיִם שֶׁיּוֹשְׁבִין וְאֵין בֵּינֵיהֶם דִּבְרֵי תוֹרָה, הֲרֵי זֶה מוֹשַׁב לֵצִים §⊷
If two sit together and there are no words of Torah between them, it is a session of scorners

---

It is not clear why Rabbi Chanina understood the verse "In the session of scorners" to refer even to people who are simply not discussing Torah. After all, people can engage in idle chatter and discuss various frivolous matters that go on in the world, without necessarily scoffing.

"Scorners" refers to those engaged in jest and mockery, of no particular importance, an activity that most people find enjoyable. Rabbi Chanina says that carrying on inconsequential conversation is equally self-indulgent and empty.

Another reason that two who do not discuss Torah are considered a "session of scorners" is that they *ought* to be discussing Torah. Their preference for idle chatter is an insult to the Torah and certainly considered scoffing.

אֲבָל שְׁנַיִם שֶׁיּוֹשְׁבִין וְיֵשׁ בֵּינֵיהֶם דִּבְרֵי תוֹרָה . . . שֶׁאֲפִילוּ אֶחָד §⊷
שֶׁיּוֹשֵׁב וְעוֹסֵק בַּתּוֹרָה — *But if two sit together and there are words of Torah between them . . . if even one person sits and occupies himself with Torah*

True Torah study involves interaction and communication with another person. "Words of Torah" are found with two people because two people communicate with speech, but one person by himself only thinks. Even if he articulates the words, he is not truly talking but thinking out loud.

Therefore, our *mishnah* applies the expression "words of Torah" in the context of two people, and refers to the study of one person merely as

נִדְבְּרוּ יִרְאֵי יהוה אִישׁ אֶל רֵעֵהוּ, וַיַּקְשֵׁב יהוה וַיִּשְׁמָע, וַיִּכָּתֵב סֵפֶר זִכָּרוֹן לְפָנָיו, לְיִרְאֵי יהוה וּלְחֹשְׁבֵי שְׁמוֹ." אֵין לִי אֶלָּא שְׁנַיִם; מִנַּיִן שֶׁאֲפִילוּ אֶחָד שֶׁיּוֹשֵׁב וְעוֹסֵק בַּתּוֹרָה שֶׁהַקָּדוֹשׁ בָּרוּךְ הוּא קוֹבֵעַ לוֹ שָׂכָר? שֶׁנֶּאֱמַר: "יֵשֵׁב בָּדָד וְיִדֹּם, כִּי נָטַל עָלָיו."

'occupies himself with Torah," osek b'Torah. For this same reason the blessing we recite each morning upon the mitzvah of learning Torah is phrased la'asok b'divrei Torah, "to occupy ourselves with words of Torah," rather than lilmod Torah, "to study the Torah." Since the blessing applies to individual study, it mentions only occupation with the words of Torah, rather than Torah study.

---

§⇐ שְׁכִינָה שְׁרוּיָה בֵּינֵיהֶם — the Divine Presence rests between them

---

Why does the Divine Presence join those who study Torah? The following will answer that question and provide insight into the very essence of why Torah is such an effective vehicle to unite mankind with God.

As soon as the Torah was given to Israel, God commanded us to construct the Mishkan, the portable Temple, where the Divine Presence would reside[1] and which housed the Tablets of the Ten Commandments in its innermost chamber. The relationship between giving the Torah to Israel and building the Mishkan is portrayed in the following midrash:[2]

> This is a parable of a king who had an only daughter. A man came, sought her hand in marriage from the king and married her. He asked the king for permission to return to his native country with his bride. The king said to him: My daughter whom I gave to you in marriage is an only daughter. What can I do? I cannot separate from her because she is my only one. I cannot tell you not to take her, because she is your wife. Just do this one favor for me. Wherever you go, prepare one small room for me, so that I may dwell among you.
>
> So did God say to Israel: I have given you the Torah. I cannot

---

1. Shemos 25:8, "and you will make a Sanctuary for Me and I will dwell in your midst."
2. Midrash Rabbah, Shemos, Section 33.

those who fear God spoke to one another, and God listened and heard, and a book of remembrance was written before Him for those who fear God and give thought to His Name." From this verse we would know this only about two people; how do we know that if even one person sits and occupies himself with Torah that the Holy One, Blessed is He, determines a reward for him? For it is said (*Eichah* 3:28): "Let one sit in solitude and be still, for he will have received [a reward] for it."

---

separate from it; so wherever you go, make one house for Me that I may dwell among you.

The reason that the Divine Presence joins with two who study together is that God is inseparable from the Torah. Torah is a concept that follows cogently, and without alternative, from the truth of God's existence. The metaphor of Torah as the king's daughter conveys that Torah is a derivative of God Himself, just as the daughter was the flesh and blood of the king. Furthermore, as the daughter in the parable was an only daughter, so too is Torah the only truth; there is no alternative.

ـ8ـ — שֶׁהַקָּדוֹשׁ בָּרוּךְ הוּא קוֹבֵעַ לוֹ שָׂכָר שֶׁנֶּאֱמַר: ,, . . . כִּי נָטַל עָלָיו.'' — *that the Holy One, Blessed is He, determines a reward for him? For it is said: ". . . for he will have received [a reward] for it."*

The verse before the proof-verse is, "It is *good* for a man that he bear the yoke in his youth."[1] A person who lovingly occupies himself with Torah study accepts upon himself God's decrees. That is the essence of serving Him and service inherently brings remuneration.

ـ8ـ — שֶׁנֶּאֱמַר: ,,יֵשֵׁב בָּדָד וְיִדֹּם, כִּי נָטַל עָלָיו'' — *For it is said: "Let one sit in solitude and be still, for he will have received [a reward] for it."*

How do we know that this verse refers to Torah study?

The verse before the proof-verse is, "It is good for a man that he bear the yoke in his youth." The proof-verse, ". . .for he will have received [a

---

1. *Eichah* 3:27.

ג/ד

[ד] רַבִּי שִׁמְעוֹן אוֹמֵר: שְׁלֹשָׁה שֶׁאָכְלוּ עַל שֻׁלְחָן אֶחָד וְלֹא אָמְרוּ עָלָיו דִּבְרֵי תוֹרָה, כְּאִלּוּ אָכְלוּ מִזִּבְחֵי מֵתִים,

reward] for *it*," therefore refers to the yoke of Heaven,[1] which implies the obligation to perform *mitzvos*. How is it possible to "be still" and yet bear the yoke of God's *mitzvos*? The verse must refer to Torah study, which is one of God's decrees, yet its "labor" does not involve any discernible action.

Hence the *mishnah* concludes that a person who labors alone in Torah is the prime example of one who "has taken it (the yoke of Heaven} upon him" as "he sits in solitude and is still."

Another version of the *mishnah* reads: "how do we know that if even one person sits and learns, then Scripture considers him as if he had fulfilled the entire Torah?" This version is perfectly valid because the *mitzvos,* taken together, are the very substance of God's yoke.

Another text of the *mishnah* reads: "how do we know that if even one person sits and occupies himself with Torah the Divine Presence is with him and determines a reward for him?" According to this version, the Divine Presence is with even one person who studies, for such a person is His servant; he has accepted His yoke by effectively fulfilling the entire Torah.[2]

The Relationship of this Mishnah to the Preceding Mishnah

The preceding *mishnah* alerted us to the fact that one would swallow his fellow alive if not for fear of the government. This *mishnah* sheds light on that message. It tells us that one who is not involved with Torah is considered no better than a sarcastic buffoon, who has no substance and is therefore easily swallowed by his similarly worthless "fellow."[3] Conversely, the Divine Presence accompanies a person who engages in Torah study, and hence it would be very difficult for a worthless person to swallow him.

Mishnah 4

Everything that exists — the world and its contents — is entirely God's, as it says:[4] "The earth is God's and the fullness thereof." He gave

1. And not directly to Torah study.
2. According to this version also, he is considered as fulfilling the Torah, as stated in *Berachos* 6a.
3. I.e., an undisciplined person who will follow his passion to kill.
4. *Tehillim* 24:1.

4. Rabbi Shimon says: If three have eaten at one table and have not spoken words of Torah there, it is as if they have eaten of offerings to the dead,

the earth and its contents to mankind, as it says:[1] "The heavens are the heavens of God, He gave the earth to mankind." There are only these two categories: that which is God's and that which is now mankind's. Into which category does our daily sustenance fall?

Sustenance can come through either category. Normally, our livelihood is ours outright. Even though God provides it, He has given it to us as it says, "He gave the earth to mankind." However, some sustenance is His. It is in the category of "The heavens are the heavens of God," yet He shares it with mankind. A metaphor of the king's servants eating at the king's table best illustrates this latter type. The servants do not own the food; they simply are privileged to partake of the king's table.

◆§ **כְּאִלּוּ אָכְלוּ מִזִּבְחֵי מֵתִים** — *it is as if they have eaten of offerings to the dead*

It is the responsibility of a king to ensure sustenance for his nation. A king of flesh and blood provides only physical support; but the King on high, Who created the body and the soul, sustains both the body and the soul. As an historical example, when God began to rule over Israel during their stay in the desert, He gave them the manna and then He gave them the Torah.

The table at which people eat and discuss Torah is associated with God, for He sustains both the body and the soul of His subjects. A table where they eat but do not discuss Torah cannot be God's table, because then there is no nourishment for the soul, and the body without the soul is dead. As a result, that food is considered as "offerings to the dead."

◆§ **כְּאִלּוּ אָכְלוּ מִזִּבְחֵי מֵתִים** — *it is as if they have eaten of offerings to the dead*

"Offerings to the dead" means offerings to idols, and the essence of idol worship is removing oneself from God.[2] An altar for idol worship is

---

1. *Ibid.* 115:16.
2. We said earlier that sin in general is removing oneself from God. As Maharal defined *supra*, Chapter 2, *mishnah* 2, there are two categories of sin: spiritual and physical. Avoiding an opportunity to come close to God is the essence of the sin of idol worship.

ג/ד
שֶׁנֶּאֱמַר: „כִּי כָּל שֻׁלְחָנוֹת מָלְאוּ קִיא צוֹאָה,
בְּלִי מָקוֹם.״ אֲבָל שְׁלֹשָׁה שֶׁאָכְלוּ עַל שֻׁלְחָן
אֶחָד וְאָמְרוּ עָלָיו דִּבְרֵי תוֹרָה, כְּאִלּוּ אָכְלוּ
מִשֻּׁלְחָנוֹ שֶׁל מָקוֹם, שֶׁנֶּאֱמַר: „וַיְדַבֵּר אֵלַי,

also called a "table." In effect, these three people, instead of elevating
their table to be the King's table, have instead removed the table from
before God and taken it to the other side, to the realm of evil.

§ „כִּי כָּל שֻׁלְחָנוֹת מָלְאוּ קִיא צוֹאָה, בְּלִי מָקוֹם״ — *"For all tables
are full of vomit and filth, without place."*

The imagery of "vomit and filth, without place" needs explanation.
The accurate translation is "vomitous excrement without a place."
Vomitous excrement issues from a person because it is foreign, זָר, *zar*,
to his body. If it had belonged in the body, it would have remained there.
This is the concept behind the term for foreign worship, עֲבוֹדָה זָרָה,
avodah zarah, referring to the sacrifices for a foreign god, אֶל זָר, *el zar.*
The language of the proof-text conveys that these sacrifices are as
foreign to a person as vomitous excrement. Scripture does not refer to
idol worship as simply "excrement" because excrement is natural; it is
normal for everyone. "Vomitous excrement" depicts something unnatural, abnormal and absolutely foreign.

The expression "without place" also needs explanation. God created
a place for everything in the world; He gave everything a role to play
in the universal order of things. It is in this sense that the "offerings to
the dead" have no place and no role in the world. The verse uses the
image of "vomitous excrement" that is ejected from the stomach
because it is an unnatural foreign body that the stomach cannot tolerate.
Such are idolatrous sacrifices. The force of the expression "without
place" is that idolatrous sacrifices are foreign and strange; they have no
place and no use.

§ מָלְאוּ קִיא צוֹאָה, בְּלִי מָקוֹם — *are full of
vomit and filth, without place*

The term "full" is an expression of hyperbole. It conveys the extreme
loathsomeness and repulsiveness of idolatry.
We may understand this on a more philosophical plane as well. When

as it is said (*Yeshayahu* 28:8): "For all tables are full of vomit and filth, without place." But if three have eaten at one table and have spoken words of Torah there, it is as if they have eaten from God's table, as it is said (*Yechezkel* 41:22): "And he said to me,

---

is something "full"? When there is no place for any more. Since there is no place for idolatrous sacrifices in this world, a table is "full" of them in any amount. The tables are described as "full" and "without place" because there is never room for another idolatrous sacrifice.

In contrast, the Altar of God could never be described as "full," because sacrifices to God always have their place.

A further explanation of the expressions "full" and "without place" in the cited verse is based on the fact that God is frequently referred to as the Place (הַמָּקוֹם, *HaMakom*). That name indicates that He is the Place within which the entire world exists; He is the "Place" that includes all places. Offerings to other gods have no place because they are the antithesis of God, the Place within Which all existence occurs.

The *mishnah* refers to God as מָקוֹם, *Makom* (literally: Place), when it says that three who discuss Torah at the table have eaten from the שֻׁלְחָנוֹ שֶׁל מָקוֹם, *shulchano shel makom*. This contrasts with three who did *not* discuss Torah at the table, whose table is considered "full" (i.e., without place) of vomitous excrement because they have chosen to leave God's dominion. Their table is not literally full; rather, the point is that the food on their table has no place in God's world.

שְׁלֹשָׁה שֶׁאָכְלוּ . . . וְאָמְרוּ עָלָיו דִּבְרֵי תוֹרָה, כְּאִלּוּ אָכְלוּ מִשֻּׁלְחָנוֹ שֶׁל מָקוֹם — *if three have eaten . . . and have spoken words of Torah there, it is as if they have eaten from God's table*

Torah elevates a mundane table to be the table of the King. Torah is higher than the heavens and hence it is not in the category of "He gave the earth to mankind," but in the category of "The heavens are the heavens of God." Therefore, the table at which Torah is said is God's table and those present are privileged, as His servants, to partake of the King's table.

If the participants do not say Torah at the table, then the normal situation prevails: God gave them the food on the table so that they can take care of themselves.

The fact that a table can be considered the table of the King on high is conveyed by this saying of the Rabbis.[1]

Rabbi Avin HaLevi said, Everyone who partakes of a meal at which a Torah scholar is seated is as if he enjoys the splendor of the Divine Presence, for it says,[2] "and Aharon came, and all the elders of Israel, to eat bread with Moshe's father-in-law before God." Did they eat in front of God? Was it not actually Moshe in front of whom they ate? This teaches that one who partakes of a meal at which a Torah scholar is seated is as if he enjoys the splendor of the Divine Presence.

"The splendor of the Divine Presence" provides nourishment for the soul, as we find in the following saying of the Rabbis,[3]

The World to Come has neither eating nor drinking. . . Rather, the righteous sit with crowns on their heads and feast upon the splendor of the Divine Presence.

When a Torah scholar is present at a meal, the body receives nourishment from the food and the intellect receives nourishment from the splendor of the Divine presence that accompanies him.

⊷§ שְׁלֹשָׁה שֶׁאָכְלוּ עַל שֻׁלְחָן אֶחָד — *if three have eaten at one table*

It is immaterial whether the people sat at one table or at two tables. When they join together by discussing Torah, then all the tables are considered one — the table of the King.

It is fitting that the One King has one table. As we will see shortly, three (or more) people can unite as a group but two people cannot. Therefore, three people together can unite even different tables into "one table," whereas two people do not constitute "one table" even if they sit together.

Attributes of the Numbers Two And Three

The number three has the attribute of unity. The number two conveys plurality, since it has the quality of division and no attribute of unity. We

1. *Berachos* 64a.
2. *Shemos* 18:12.
3. *Berachos* 17a.

can see graphically why two remain a plural and will not unite, whereas three can unite as if they were one. If we place two lines together, such as this >, it is evident that they will not form one entity, because the lines cannot join together. By contrast, when three lines are placed together, they can unite to a closed, complete entity, such as this △.

The Hebrew word for two, שנים, *shenayim,* denotes plurality right in its very name, for it is the only digit that has the Hebrew plural ending מ"ם *mem.* Two connotes opposite extremes such as black and white, which have no connection. By contrast, it is impossible to have three things as opposites; indeed, when two things are opposites, such as black and white, a third intermediate thing, such as gray,[1] can link them together.

---

§⊷ זֶה הַשֻּׁלְחָן אֲשֶׁר לִפְנֵי ה' — *"This is the table that is before God."*

The proof-text, "This is the table that is before God" actually refers to the Altar, מִזְבֵּחַ, *mizbe'ach.* It teaches us that the Altar and a table are the identical concept and the Altar is God's table. An important attribute of the Altar, in both *halachah* and philosophy, is that it is one whole, and not divisible. By referring to the Altar as a "table," the passage teaches us that the table of human beings can equally be the table of the King. It needs only to be unified by three people who study together at that table.

The power of three people to join together as a unit is the principle behind a quorum of three for the special Invitation, *zimun,* to join in the Grace After Meals.

Mishnah 5

Life is fraught with danger. Robbery, physical illness and emotional distress are some of the dangers that threaten us. These are a natural part of God's creation, but He has also set up within His creation a system that provides protection. We may not know just how He keeps us from danger, but the *mishnah* does advise us of three things that put us outside that protection. Anyone who does not heed these things takes his life in his hands.

---

1. "Gray" has been used as a more natural example than the original text, which reads "red." The notion of "red" as the intermediate between white and black has precedent in Kabbalah. We may consider the rationale as follows. White is all colors; black is no color. Red is a strong color and hence lies between all (white) and no (black) colors.

ג/ה

בַּלַּיְלָה, וְהַמְהַלֵּךְ בַּדֶּרֶךְ יְחִידִי, וְהַמְפַנֶּה[1] לִבּוֹ
לְבַטָּלָה — הֲרֵי זֶה מִתְחַיֵּב בְּנַפְשׁוֹ.

---

1. This is the text on which Maharal's commentary is based. Alternative text: וּמְפַנֶּה.

◆§ הַנֵּעוֹר בַּלַּיְלָה — *One who is awake at night*

Night was created for only two purposes: sleeping and learning
Torah.[1] Although night is a time of danger, God provides protection for
a person who engages in one of these two activities.

If a person engages in any other activity, he has removed himself from
God's protective system. It should be noted, however, that earning a
living assures us the same protection as learning, because work is an
essential requirement of learning Torah, as the Rabbis said,[2]

> "All Torah study that is not joined with work will cease in the
> end."

Indeed, all productive activities, דֶּרֶךְ אֶרֶץ, *derech eretz*, are a *mitzvah*
and warrant God's protection from the inherent dangers of the night.

◆§ וְהַמְהַלֵּךְ בַּדֶּרֶךְ יְחִידִי — *or one who travels on the highway alone*

The highway runs at a distance from settlements such as cities or
villages and therefore is a place of danger. There is safety in being with
other people, and when a person is outside of a settlement, he is without
this natural protection.

◆§ וְהַמְהַלֵּךְ . . . יְחִידִי — *or one who travels . . . alone*

The *mishnah* cautions only against traveling alone. Two people
together are not as susceptible to harm, because God accompanies two
people more than He does one person. The reason is that the more
people resemble Him, the more God accompanies them and two people
together have more צֶלֶם אֱלֹקִים, (image of God) than does one person.

Indeed, three people have more *tzelem Elokim* than two people. This
fact sheds light on other *mishnayos*[3] that stated similarly how the
Divine Presence accompanies two who learn together more than it does

---

1. *Eruvin* 65a.
2. *Supra*, Chapter 2, *mishnah* 2.
3. *Supra*, 3:3 ; *infra*, 3:7.

is awake at night, or one who travels on the highway alone, or one[1] who turns his heart to idleness, has risked his life.

---

1. According to Maharal's text and explanation these are three separate situations. An alternative text: "*and* turns his heart to idleness" refers to the one who is awake or traveling alone. According to this version, there are two kinds of situations.

---

one person; and that it accompanies three who learn together more than it does two people.

וּמְפַנֶּה לִבּוֹ לְבַטָּלָה – הֲרֵי זֶה מִתְחַיֵּב בְּנַפְשׁוֹ — *or one who turns his heart to idleness, has risked his life*

Dangers are present at any time and at any place and it is only because of God's protection that we expect not to come to harm. The closer we are to God, the closer we are to His protection. Conversely, to the extent that a person rejects the opportunity to be close to God, he rejects living within His dominion, and he loses a degree of His protection.

Mishnah 6

This *mishnah* continues the theme, introduced earlier in the chapter, that Torah brings a person close to God. It is for that reason that a person who accepts the yoke of Torah is elevated to live life closer to the realm of the Creator, and less encumbered by the yokes of government and worldly needs.

The explanation of this *mishnah* starts with the fact that we can live life on several planes, each with its own set of rules, obligations and driving forces.

- On one plane, life revolves around the demands of nature; plowing, planting and other activities that are determined by agricultural or environmental considerations. On this level, mankind is subjugated to nature.
- There is the plane of life in which we live as members of civilized society. On this level life is constrained, not by nature, but by human will. This is the realm of government, which enacts legislation to govern social conduct. It determines what it wants people to do and what it does not want them to do, and then decrees laws on them. People are subjugated to this system by the king, through whom the system is enforced.
- The third plane is religion. God set up a system to regulate human affairs through the Torah that He gave. This system transcends the

[ו] רַבִּי נְחוּנְיָא בֶּן הַקָּנָה אוֹמֵר: כָּל הַמְקַבֵּל
עָלָיו עַל תּוֹרָה, מַעֲבִירִין מִמֶּנּוּ עַל
מַלְכוּת וְעַל דֶּרֶךְ אֶרֶץ. וְכָל הַפּוֹרֵק מִמֶּנּוּ עַל
תּוֹרָה, נוֹתְנִין עָלָיו עַל מַלְכוּת וְעַל דֶּרֶךְ אֶרֶץ.

[ז] רַבִּי חֲלַפְתָּא בֶּן דּוֹסָא אִישׁ כְּפַר חֲנַנְיָא

demands of nature and it transcends the arbitrary choices of government. In this system, people are subjugated to God.

One who accepts upon himself the yoke of Torah so completely that he is within God's system cannot, at the same time, fall entirely within the mundane systems of nature or government.

In Chapter 6 we will encounter the *baraisa*:[1]

> . . . for you can have no freer man than one who engages in the study of Torah. And anyone who engages in the study of Torah becomes elevated . . .

That *baraisa* tells us that one who engages in Torah study is elevated above the domination of the pragmatic systems determined by nature or by arbitrary will.

⧫§ מַעֲבִירִין מִמֶּנּוּ עַל מַלְכוּת וְעַל דֶּרֶךְ אֶרֶץ — *the yoke of government and the yoke of worldly responsibilities are removed from him*

The yoke of Torah frees one from the yokes of government and livelihood because the realm of *sechel,* intellect, transcends the world of pragmatism. It is true that a person cannot get by without a livelihood; indeed, he must work in order to occupy himself with Torah. However, when he shoulders the yoke of Torah, his income will result with less effort and his livelihood will not be a "yoke." Conversely, if he casts off the yoke of Torah, he will fall into the domain of the pragmatic world and its burdens.

The relationship of Torah, livelihood and government is symbolically embodied by certain elements of the holy Temple. The Sanctum (*Heichal*) symbolizes this world. The Table (*Shulchan*) was on the north[2] side of that room and the candelabrum (*Menorah*) was on the south side. The innermost chamber housed the Ark (*Aron*) which held

---

1. *Infra,* Chapter 6, *baraisa* 2.
2. The positions of north, south and innermost have Kabbalistic significance.

6. Rabbi Nechunia ben Hakanah says: If someone takes upon himself the yoke of Torah —
the yoke of government and the yoke of worldly
responsibilities are removed from him. But if
someone throws off the yoke of Torah from
himself — the yoke of government and the yoke
of worldly responsibilities are placed upon him.

7. Rabbi Chalafta ben Dosa of Kfar Chanania

---

the Tablets of the Ten Commandments.

- The monarchy is symbolized by the *Shulchan,* Table, which held the show-bread. The king is responsible for the economy, represented by the bread on the table.
- The *Menorah* represents nature. Its seven branches correspond to the seven days of Creation in which nature was set in motion.
- The Torah was in the innermost chamber of the Sanctum, קֹדֶשׁ קֳדָשִׁים, *Kodesh Kodashim,* the holiest of all holy places, which symbolizes the upper, spiritual world.

The yoke of government and the yoke of livelihood are opposite extremes, for government is an arbitrary human system, and livelihood, which comes through agriculture and nature, is imperative. So too, the *Shulchan* and the *Menorah* were on opposite sides of the *Heichal.*

The contrast between Torah and the other realms of life surfaces in this symbolism as well. Government and earning a livelihood are normal human affairs, whereas Torah is a spiritual occupation that transcends them both. Likewise, the Tablets of Law were kept in the innermost chamber, separate from and beyond the *Heichal* where the *Shulchan* and *Menorah* stood.

In summary, a person who is immersed in Torah is freed from the constraints and trivialities of secular life and is elevated to the highest plane that life offers.

Mishnah 7

Why does the *mishnah* discuss groups of various size that study together? If the Divine Presence rests with even one person, why bother to mention two, three, five and ten people?

Each of these numbers has a special distinction, which we will now explain.

The number ten is a complete group, because ten is the base of the

אוֹמֵר: עֲשָׂרָה שֶׁיּוֹשְׁבִין וְעוֹסְקִין בַּתּוֹרָה,
שְׁכִינָה שְׁרוּיָה בֵּינֵיהֶם, שֶׁנֶּאֱמַר: ,,אֱלֹהִים
נִצָּב בַּעֲדַת אֵל." וּמִנַּיִן אֲפִילוּ חֲמִשָּׁה?
שֶׁנֶּאֱמַר: ,,וַאֲגֻדָּתוֹ עַל אֶרֶץ יְסָדָה."

Torah's number system. Every number less than ten is a collection of
units, which can be added to. For example, adding to 3 gives 4; adding
to 4 gives 5, and so on. When the collection reaches ten, it is a complete
group that cannot be increased. Any increase, such as 11, just repeats
the digits over, starting at 1, without introducing any new qualities.

As a practical illustration, ten Jews are considered a community, in
the context of laws which revolve around God's holiness. The quorum for
public prayer is ten and adding to the quorum makes no qualitative
difference. That is the characteristic of a group as distinct from an
individual: Once it is complete, it cannot be further completed. It is
reasonable that God associates Himself with a quorum of ten, since He
Who is complete is found with that which is complete.

Each number mentioned in this *mishnah* has a unique characteristic,
as follows:

- **One** does not include anything else; hence, it is not relevant to
  counting.
- **Two** is the first number of counting, and is the first even number.
- **Three** is the first odd number.[1]
- **Five** is the first digit that comprises an odd number and an even
  number; i.e., 2 + 3.
- **Ten** constitutes a category, as opposed to individual members of
  that category.

Four is not mentioned in the *mishnah* because it has no characteristics
that have not already been demonstrated by the numbers up to three.

---

§— וּמִנַּיִן אֲפִילוּ חֲמִשָּׁה? שֶׁנֶּאֱמַר: ,,וַאֲגֻדָּתוֹ עַל אֶרֶץ יְסָדָה"
How do we know this even of five? For it is said:
"He has established His bundle upon earth."

How does this quotation refer to the number five? Five is the paradigm
of a bundle because it bundles everything together: an even number (i.e.,
2) and an odd number (i.e., 3).

---

1. Since Maharal does not consider 1 to be a cardinal number, 3 is the first odd
number.

says: If ten people sit together and engage in Torah study, the Divine Presence rests among them, as it is said (*Tehillim* 82:1): "God stands in the assembly of God." How do we know this even of five? For it is said (*Amos* 9:6): "He has established His bundle upon earth."

◦§ וּמִנַּיִן אֲפִילוּ חֲמִשָּׁה — *How do we know this even of five?*

Since the Divine Presence attends even one person who occupies himself with Torah, it would seem unnecessary to prove that the Divine Presence accompanies five people, three people and two people.

However, the *mishnah* wishes to tell us that it is better to study as a group of ten than as a group of five; that it is better as a group of five than a group of three; that it is better as three than with two; and that it is better with two than alone. Although the Divine Presence is found with even one person, It is more attached to two than to one. It is still more attached to three, still more to five, and attached still more to a group of ten.

God's Presence accompanies a human being by virtue of some point of similarity. We will now show how the progressively larger groups mentioned in this *mishnah* enjoy a stronger bond with God, because they are increasingly similar to Him.

◦§ וּמִנַּיִן אֲפִילוּ חֲמִשָּׁה — *How do we know this even of five?*

The number four represents division into individual elements, just as the four directions are completely separate and distinct from each other. The concept of a center is a fifth element with a special quality. The center is the common reference point that unifies and ties the four separate parts into a single entity. Therefore, the number five is the symbol of a significant group. The idea of separate items tied together by a fifth item is conveyed by the image of a bundle. The *mishnah* cites the verse "He has established His 'bundle' upon earth" as a reference to five people, because five contains the essential concept of a bundle, in that it unifies and ties the fragmented number four into a cohesive group.

A bundle unifies and embraces its components, and God is whole and embraces all. It is on this point of similarity that the Divine Presence

ג/ז וּמִנַּיִן אֲפִילוּ שְׁלֹשָׁה? שֶׁנֶּאֱמַר: ,,בְּקֶרֶב אֱלֹהִים
יִשְׁפֹּט.'' וּמִנַּיִן אֲפִילוּ שְׁנַיִם? שֶׁנֶּאֱמַר: ,,אָז נִדְבְּרוּ
יִרְאֵי יהוה אִישׁ אֶל רֵעֵהוּ וַיַּקְשֵׁב יהוה וַיִּשְׁמָע.''
וּמִנַּיִן אֲפִילוּ אֶחָד? שֶׁנֶּאֱמַר: ,,בְּכָל הַמָּקוֹם אֲשֶׁר
אַזְכִּיר אֶת שְׁמִי, אָבוֹא אֵלֶיךָ וּבֵרַכְתִּיךָ.''

accompanies a group of five people who occupy themselves with the Torah.[1]

⊷§ וּמִנַּיִן אֲפִילוּ שְׁלֹשָׁה — *How do we know this even of three?*

Similarly, the number three reflects a whole entity, as we explained in *mishnah* 4 above, "three who have eaten at one table." Whereas the number 2 conveys division and opposites, a third element can unify the opposites into a whole. For example, gray[2] is the in-between color that unites white and black. A group of three has a characteristic of wholeness that resonates with God's unity; however, it does not capture the concept as fully as five, which embraces four sides and unifies it into a whole entity.[3]

⊷§ וּמִנַּיִן אֲפִילוּ שְׁנַיִם — *How do we know this even of two?*

Two people interacting together bring a depth to Torah study that is not available to an individual. When two people study together they unite into a pair. The quality of two separate parts uniting is, to a modest degree, a quality of God's unity. For these reasons, His Presence is found more, in some degree, with two people than with one person.

⊷§ אָבוֹא אֵלֶיךָ וּבֵרַכְתִּיךָ — *I will come to you and bless you.*

God Comes to Us

All existence is the consequence of God. Our relationship with God is defined by the fact that He is the source of mankind's existence,

1. Not included in this adaptation is Maharal's discussion of the *Tosafos* to *Succah* 13a, discussing the term אֲגֻדָּה, *agudah,* based on this approach.
2. Literally: red. See *supra,* 3:4 page 157 note1.
3. Not included in this adaptation is Maharal's noteworthy analysis and explanation of a passage in *Berachos* 6a, which also deals with the subject of the Divine Presence coming to groups of different sizes.

How do we know this even of three? For it is said (*Tehillim* 82:1): "In the midst of judges He shall judge." How do we know this even of two? For it is said (*Malachi* 3:16): "Then those who fear God spoke to one another and God listened and heard." How do we know this even of one? For it is said (*Shemos* 20:21): "In every place where I will cause My Name to be mentioned, I will come to you and bless you."

Illah, and we are dependent, *alul*,[1] upon Him.

As the Source of human existence, God wants to be with those who are dependent upon Him. When there is a group of ten, which reflects His completeness, He brings His presence to them at His initiative. When the group is less than ten people, the group initiates the relationship by engaging in study and only then does the Divine Presence come, out of His love for His people, as the verse says, "I will come to you and bless you."

Mishnah 8

The previous *mishnah* made it clear that God and mankind are closely bound together, through Torah and through people joining together to serve Him. This *mishnah* extends that idea and tells us that we are bound together with God through our possessions as well.

An example of how we relate to God through our possessions is found in the requirement to recite a *berachah,* benediction, before eating. The Rabbis say[2]

> It is forbidden for a person to enjoy anything from this world without pronouncing a blessing; and anyone who does enjoy something from this world without pronouncing a blessing has made personal use of a sacred object.
>
> Rav Yehudah said in the name of Shmuel: Anyone who enjoys something from this world without pronouncing a blessing is as if he has made personal use of Heaven's sacred things, as it is written,[3] "The earth is God's and the fullness thereof."

---

1. These two Hebrew terms are found throughout Maharal's writings and are presented here for the benefit of those who wish to study Maharal in the original.
2. *Berachos* 35a.
3. *Tehillim* 24:1.

/ג

ח-ט

[ח] רַבִּי אֶלְעָזָר בֶּן יְהוּדָה אִישׁ בַּרְתּוֹתָא אוֹמֵר:
תֶּן לוֹ מִשֶּׁלּוֹ, שֶׁאַתָּה וְשֶׁלְּךָ שֶׁלּוֹ. וְכֵן בְּדָוִד
הוּא אוֹמֵר: „כִּי מִמְּךָ הַכֹּל, וּמִיָּדְךָ נָתַנּוּ לָךְ.‟
[ט] רַבִּי יַעֲקֹב אוֹמֵר: הַמְהַלֵּךְ בַּדֶּרֶךְ וְשׁוֹנֶה,

Rabbi Levi pointed out a paradox between verses. It is written,
"The earth is God's and the fullness thereof." It is also written,
"The heavens are the heavens of God, but He gave the earth to
mankind."[1] The solution is: The context of one verse pertains
before pronouncing the blessing; the context of the other verse
pertains after pronouncing the blessing.

Why is it considered a sacrilege to enjoy something without saying a
blessing?

God created everything for His glory, because all creation attests to
His greatness as Creator. Our only right to use His creation for our
enjoyment is that He bestows such blessings upon us. Indeed, when we
call Him "Blessed," we mean that He is the source of blessing for others.

By saying "Blessed are You" in the *berachah* over food, we recognize
that God created it and that our use of it is possible only because God
bestows goodness on us. Eating food without a *berachah* is a sacrilege
because its existence had implicitly expressed the glory of God as
Creator and Master. Conversely, by articulating a *berachah* we explicitly
declare His greatness and kindness and thereby enhance His glory when
enjoying His world.

◆§ תֶּן לוֹ מִשֶּׁלּוֹ, שֶׁאַתָּה וְשֶׁלְּךָ שֶׁלּוֹ — *Give Him from His Own,*
for you and your possession are His.

Since everything is God's, as it says,[2]

לַה׳ הָאָרֶץ וּמְלוֹאָהּ, "The earth is God's and the 'fullness' thereof"
and everything is His glory, as it says,[3]

מְלֹא כָל הָאָרֶץ כְּבוֹדוֹ, "The 'fullness' of the earth is His glory."[4]

Therefore, no one should be upset about giving to God, for it is His.

---

1. *Tehillim* 115:16.
2. *Ibid.* 24:1.
3. *Yeshayahu* 6:3.
4. Maharal's translation is different than the usual English translation, "The earth is
full of His glory."

פרקי אבות / 166

8. Rabbi Elazar ben Yehudah[1] of Bartosa says: Give Him from His Own, for you and your possessions are His. And so has David said (*Divrei HaYamim I* 29:14), "For everything is from You, and from Your Own we have given You."

9. Rabbi Yaakov says: One who walks on the road

---

1. Maharal's text includes "ben Yehudah"; most texts do not include it.

◦§ ''בִּי מִמְּךָ הַכֹּל, וּמִיָּדְךָ נָתַנּוּ לָךְ'' — *"For everything is from You, and from Your Own we have given You."*

This verse refers to the wealth that God bestowed upon the nation, with which they built the holy Temple.

We might have expected the verse to read "and from 'our own' have we given You." The fact that it says, "and from 'Your Own,'" underscores vividly the point of our *mishnah.* The subject of this verse says: "Wealth is not ours for even a moment. We consider it to still be in God's jurisdiction and not ours. Therefore, we have only given You of Your Own."

The Relationship of Mishnah 8 to Mishnah 7

The previous *mishnah* described in detail that God comes to be among people. This *mishnah* intends to avert any mistaken belief that He comes to us because He needs something from us. He needs nothing from us, because everything we have is His.

Mishnah 9

Mishnah 7 told us that God is present with an individual who studies Torah. *Mishnah 8* elaborated on the extent of the bond between God and mankind. This is the other side of the coin: One who breaks off from the Torah has broken away from He Who accompanies the Torah.

Imagine that someone is standing in front of a king and talking to him. This person's friend walks by and the person interrupts his conversation with the king to talk with his friend. This person has broken off from the king. He has demonstrated that he is no longer interested in being with him. That is clear opposition to the king and anyone who opposes the king is guilty of a capital offense.

The situation described in our *mishnah* is the very same. He has broken away from God's presence to enjoy the scenery and that is a perilous choice.

וּמַפְסִיק מִמִּשְׁנָתוֹ, וְאוֹמֵר: ,,מָה נָּאֶה אִילָן זֶה!
וּמַה נָּאֶה נִיר זֶה!" – מַעֲלֶה עָלָיו הַכָּתוּב
כְּאִלּוּ מִתְחַיֵּב בְּנַפְשׁוֹ.

[י] רַבִּי דוֹסְתָּאי בַּר יַנַּאי מִשּׁוּם רַבִּי מֵאִיר
אוֹמֵר: כָּל הַשּׁוֹכֵחַ דָּבָר אֶחָד מִמִּשְׁנָתוֹ,
מַעֲלֶה עָלָיו הַכָּתוּב כְּאִלּוּ מִתְחַיֵּב בְּנַפְשׁוֹ,

---

§ הַמְהַלֵּךְ בַּדֶּרֶךְ וְשׁוֹנֶה, וּמַפְסִיק . . . כְּאִלּוּ מִתְחַיֵּב בְּנַפְשׁוֹ — *One
who walks on the road while reviewing [a Torah lesson]
but interrupts . . . [is] as if he bears guilt for his soul.*

Another approach follows these logical steps:
- Full existence is found only with matters of *sechel,* intellect.
- Torah is *sechel,* and therefore Torah is referred to as "your life and the
length of your days."[1]
- Things that inherently belong together do not separate from each
other. For that reason, separating from something demonstrates
opposition to it.
- Therefore, one who separates from Torah opposes life, and one who
opposes life certainly places his life at risk.

---

§ ,,מָה נָּאֶה אִילָן זֶה! וּמַה נָּאֶה נִיר זֶה" — *"How beautiful
is this tree! How beautiful is this plowed field!"*

Trees are usually in a field, at a distance from the road and one has to
go over to the tree to properly admire it. We may have thought that only
such an excursion is called "separating from Torah," but admiring a field
by the roadside would not be as serious. Such is not the case: Even such
a minor interruption is a departure from Torah.

---

§ מַעֲלֶה עָלָיו הַכָּתוּב כְּאִלּוּ מִתְחַיֵּב בְּנַפְשׁוֹ — *Scripture
considers it as if he bears guilt for his soul.*

The *mishnah* refers to the verse,[2]

---

1. *Devarim* 30:20.
2. *Ibid.* 4:9. This verse is cited in the next *mishnah,* which also discusses separating
from Torah.

3/ 10 while reviewing [a Torah less] but interrupts his review, and exclaims: "How beautiful is this tree! How beautiful is this plowed field!" — Scripture considers it as if he bears guilt for his soul.

10. Rabbi Dostai bar Yannai says in the name of Rabbi Meir: Whoever forgets anything of his Torah learning, Scripture considers it as if he bears guilt for his soul, for it is said

But beware and guard your soul exceedingly lest you forget the things that your eyes have seen.

&8 **כְּאִלּוּ מִתְחַיֵּב בְּנַפְשׁוֹ** — *bears guilt for his soul*

This statement must be understood in context. Admiring the scenery is usually just an incidental interruption, and returning to his studies demonstrates that he did not intend to separate from Torah. The road he is walking on is outside of the city and hence he is exposed to harm befalling him in a moment.[1] Therefore, one can explain the *mishnah* as meaning that such incidental interruptions are a risk to life only in a dangerous situation such as traveling on the highway. If danger strikes, he will not have an opportunity to return to his Torah study.

In a normal situation, a brief distraction does not constitute "separating from the Torah," for we can be confident that he will soon return to his studies.

Mishnah 10

This *mishnah* continues on the subject of the seriousness of separating from Torah study, introduced in *mishnah* 9.

&8 **מַעֲלֶה עָלָיו הַכָּתוּב כְּאִלּוּ מִתְחַיֵּב בְּנַפְשׁוֹ** — *Scripture considers it as if he bears guilt for his soul.*

Things that are incompatible will separate when they are placed together. For example, water is incompatible with fire and will vaporize in the presence of fire. Since Torah is the substance of true life, one who separates from it reveals that he is antithetical to life.

---

1. As we saw in *mishnah* 5.

169 / MAHARAL: PIRKEI AVOS

שֶׁנֶּאֱמַר: ,,רַק הִשָּׁמֶר לְךָ וּשְׁמֹר נַפְשְׁךָ מְאֹד, פֶּן תִּשְׁכַּח אֶת הַדְּבָרִים אֲשֶׁר רָאוּ עֵינֶיךָ." יָכוֹל אֲפִילוּ תָּקְפָה עָלָיו מִשְׁנָתוֹ? תַּלְמוּד לוֹמַר: ,,וּפֶן יָסוּרוּ מִלְּבָבְךָ כֹּל יְמֵי חַיֶּיךָ." הָא אֵינוֹ מִתְחַיֵּב בְּנַפְשׁוֹ עַד שֶׁיֵּשֵׁב וִיסִירֵם מִלִּבּוֹ.

[יא] רַבִּי חֲנִינָא בֶּן דּוֹסָא אוֹמֵר: כֹּל שֶׁיִּרְאַת חֶטְאוֹ קוֹדֶמֶת לְחָכְמָתוֹ, חָכְמָתוֹ

---

§ יָכוֹל אֲפִילוּ תָּקְפָה עָלָיו מִשְׁנָתוֹ — *Does this apply even if [he forgot because] his studies were too difficult for him?*

If the studies are too difficult, he is not guilty. However, if he forgot because he did not review his studies, he is indeed guilty of: "Whoever forgets anything of his Torah learning."

---

§ אֵינוֹ מִתְחַיֵּב בְּנַפְשׁוֹ עַד שֶׁיֵּשֵׁב וִיסִירֵם מִלִּבּוֹ — *one does not bear guilt for his soul unless he sits [idly] and [through lack of concentration and review] removes them from his consciousness*

The proof-text "And lest they **be removed**," in the passive voice, implies that one is indeed guilty for passively allowing himself to forget.

Mishnah 11

This *mishnah* and the next continue the subject of forgetting one's Torah wisdom. They tell us that Torah studies stay with a person whose study is based on the fear of God and whose good deeds exceed his knowledge.

The phrase "fear of sin" is equivalent to the expression "fear of God." The fear referred to is the feeling that arises from the stark recognition that we are utterly dependent on God for our very existence.

---

§ כֹּל שֶׁיִּרְאַת חֶטְאוֹ קוֹדֶמֶת לְחָכְמָתוֹ, חָכְמָתוֹ מִתְקַיָּמֶת — *Anyone whose fear of sin precedes his wisdom, his wisdom will endure*

The *mishnah* refers to the wisdom of Torah. The Rabbis show how

3/11   (*Devarim* 4:9): "But beware and guard your soul exceedingly, lest you forget the things your eyes have seen."

Does this apply even if [he forgot because] his studies were too difficult for him? [This is not so, for] Scripture says (*Devarim* 4:9), "And lest they be removed from your heart all the days of your life." Thus, one does not bear guilt for his soul unless he sits [idly] and [through lack of concentration and review] removes them from his consciousness.

11. Rabbi Chanina ben Dosa says: Anyone whose fear of sin precedes his wisdom, his wisdom

---

wisdom depends on the fear of God:[1]

> Rava said: At the time when they bring a person in for judgment (in the World to Come) they say to him, "Did you deal faithfully? Did you set times for the study of Torah? Did you occupy yourself with having children? Did you look for salvation? Did you engage in depth in the analysis of wisdom? Did you understand one thing from another?"
>
> Even if each one counts, only if "the fear of God is his treasure"[2] does it count, and if not, it does not count. It can be explained by a parable of a man who sent someone on an errand, saying "Take the wheat up to the attic for me." He took it up. He said to him, "Did you mix some preservative in with it?" He said, "No." The first one said, "It would have been better if you had not taken it up."

The reason behind this is that Torah wisdom is spiritual, while we are physical beings, and hence it eludes our clear grasp. We need God to make our comprehension of Torah possible, and it will endure only if we recognize that dependence. This fact is conveyed by the verse,[3]

"The fear of God is the beginning of wisdom."

---

1. *Shabbos* 31a.
2. *Yeshayahu* 33:6.
3. *Tehillim* 111:10.

מִתְקַיֶּמֶת; וְכֹל שֶׁחָכְמָתוֹ קוֹדֶמֶת לְיִרְאַת
חֶטְאוֹ, אֵין חָכְמָתוֹ מִתְקַיֶּמֶת.

[יב] הוּא הָיָה אוֹמֵר: כֹּל שֶׁמַּעֲשָׂיו מְרֻבִּין
מֵחָכְמָתוֹ, חָכְמָתוֹ מִתְקַיֶּמֶת; וְכֹל
שֶׁחָכְמָתוֹ מְרֻבָּה מִמַּעֲשָׂיו, אֵין חָכְמָתוֹ
מִתְקַיֶּמֶת.

[יג] הוּא הָיָה אוֹמֵר: כֹּל שֶׁרוּחַ הַבְּרִיּוֹת נוֹחָה
הֵימֶנּוּ, רוּחַ הַמָּקוֹם נוֹחָה הֵימֶנּוּ; וְכֹל

---

§ **וְכֹל שֶׁחָכְמָתוֹ קוֹדֶמֶת לְיִרְאַת חֶטְאוֹ, אֵין חָכְמָתוֹ מִתְקַיֶּמֶת** —
but anyone whose wisdom precedes his fear of sin,
his wisdom will not endure

As a house is firmly established upon its foundation, so the fear of
God is the foundation upon which wisdom is firmly set. But if wisdom
comes before fear, it is like building a house without a foundation, and
such a building will not endure.

Mishnah 12

This *mishnah* continues the theme that wisdom must be built on a
foundation in order to endure.

What is wisdom, חָכְמָה, *chochmah*? Wisdom refers to objective
comprehension of the very essence of things. That knowledge and
understanding is not the person himself but an acquisition, just as a
person's house is *his,* but it is not *himself.*

Wisdom is a structure of concepts and relationships that we perceive
and experience, much as a building is a structure of bricks and mortar
that we can observe and live in. And like a building, it will fall apart if it
is not set on a proper foundation. Indeed, it may be compared more
precisely to a bridge[1] that has two foundations, one on each end.

Wisdom is the bridge that joins us to God. The fear[2] of sin establishes
a base of support on the side of the Creator, as we learned in *mishnah*
11:

---

1. Author's simile.
2. Fear of sin is equivalent to the expression "fear of God," and refers to the feeling
that comes from recognizing that our existence is absolutely dependent upon God.

3/
12-13

will endure; but anyone whose wisdom precedes his fear of sin, his wisdom will not endure.

12. He used to say: Anyone whose good deeds exceed his wisdom, his wisdom will endure; but anyone whose wisdom exceeds his good deeds, his wisdom will not endure.

13. He used to say: If the spirit of one's fellows is pleased with him, the spirit of the Omnipresent is pleased with him; but if the

Anyone whose fear of his sin precedes his wisdom, his wisdom will endure.

and our *mishnah* tells us that "good deeds" establish a base of support within the human soul.

◆§ מַעֲשָׂיו מְרֻבִּין מֵחָכְמָתוֹ — *Anyone whose good deeds exceed his wisdom, his wisdom will endure*

The "good deeds" referred to in this *mishnah* are *mitzvos*, actions that refine and purify the soul. When the soul has been adequately strengthened through *mitzvos*, it can bear the weight of wisdom. But wisdom that exceeds the capacity of the soul will not endure.

The Wisdom of the Nations

We know that there are people, in every nation, whose wisdom exceeds their good deeds, and yet their wisdom endures, contrary to this *mishnah.*

In their case, wisdom continues because they have an outstanding propensity towards wisdom[1] that prevails even without good deeds or the fear of sin. The *mishnah,* however, addresses people in general, and not exceptions.

Another approach to this question is to understand the term "wisdom" to mean the wisdom of Torah. Then the question does not even arise, because only the wisdom of Torah, which is Divine, requires a spiritual foundation. Secular wisdom does not lead to God, and hence does not need spiritual support.

1. *Niddah* 16b states that a person is born with a certain propensity for wisdom, just as he is born with a certain propensity for strength.

ג/יד שֶׁאֵין רוּחַ הַבְּרִיּוֹת נוֹחָה הֵימֶנּוּ, אֵין רוּחַ הַמָּקוֹם נוֹחָה הֵימֶנּוּ.

[יד] רַבִּי דוֹסָא בֶּן הָרְכִּינַס אוֹמֵר: שֵׁנָה שֶׁל שַׁחֲרִית, וְיֵין שֶׁל צָהֳרַיִם, וְשִׂיחַת הַיְלָדִים, וִישִׁיבַת בָּתֵּי כְנֵסִיּוֹת שֶׁל עַמֵּי הָאָרֶץ, מוֹצִיאִין אֶת הָאָדָם מִן הָעוֹלָם.

Mishnah 13

We learned in the preceding two *mishnayos* that God fulfills our search for wisdom in response to our fear of sin[1] and in response to our good deeds.[2] The reason is that God is so closely bound to people that He responds to our initiative. Our *mishnah* continues with yet another consequence of this connection between man and God: When people are pleased with someone, God favors him as well.

The reason that mankind is fully intertwined with God is that the human soul is derived from Him. This fact gives the prophets, in particular, the ability to interact with God, and it is the principle behind *Avos* 2:4,

> "Treat His will as if it were your own will, so that He will treat your will as if it were His will."

Mishnah 14

In *mishnah* 10 we learned that

> "Whoever who forgets anything of his Torah learning, Scripture considers it as if he bears guilt for his soul,"

even if he passively forgets by being idle. Our *mishnah* warns that even if he does not forget his studies, the hollow indulgences listed here will certainly **remove a person from the world** because they are an active departure from Torah, and Torah is life itself.

---

1. *Supra, mishnah* 11.
2. *Supra, mishnah* 12.

spirit of one's fellows is not pleased with him, the spirit of the Omnipresent is not pleased with him.

14. Rabbi Dosa ben Harkinas says: Late morning sleep, midday wine, children's chatter, and sitting in the meeting houses of the ignorant, remove a person from the world.

שֵׁנָה שֶׁל שַׁחֲרִית, וְיַיִן שֶׁל צָהֳרַיִם, וְשִׂיחַת הַיְלָדִים, וִישִׁיבַת בָּתֵּי כְנֵסִיּוֹת §⇨ שֶׁל עַמֵּי הָאָרֶץ — *Late morning* sleep, *midday* wine, *children's* chatter, *and sitting in* the meeting houses of the ignorant

There are four elements of human existence.

• The **physical** body
• the **spiritual** faculties
• and the **intellect** are facets of our individual existence. We also exist as members of **society.**

The four diversions of the *mishnah* undermine each of these elements, as follows.

• **Sleep** is a state of purely **physical** existence, because all spiritual components are dormant during sleep. Sleeping late is very sweet indeed, but it is also a taste of death.[1] Therefore, one who pursues sleep to such an inappropriate degree pursues non-existence and death, and leaves this world behind.
• **Midday wine** destroys the **spiritual** faculties. Wine gladdens the spirit. However, a person does not need cheering up until the end of the day, when the spirit is weary from work. A person is at his brightest at noon, and therefore wine drunk then is an excess that erodes his spirit.[2]
• **Children's chatter** undermines the **intellectual** part of existence. The conversation of elders is replete with wisdom. Conversely, children's talk is hollow banter and misinformation. It follows that such conversation removes a person from the world by effacing his wisdom.
• **Meeting houses of the ignorant** waste the fourth aspect of existence, which is **social** participation. The meeting houses of the ignorant are

---

1. *Berachos* 57b: "Sleep is one-sixtieth part of death."
2. A concept dealt with at length in the commentary to *Avos* 2:8.

[טו] רַבִּי אֶלְעָזָר הַמּוֹדָעִי אוֹמֵר: הַמְחַלֵּל אֶת הַקֳּדָשִׁים, וְהַמְבַזֶּה אֶת הַמּוֹעֲדוֹת, וְהַמַּלְבִּין פְּנֵי חֲבֵרוֹ בָּרַבִּים, וְהַמֵּפֵר בְּרִיתוֹ שֶׁל אַבְרָהָם אָבִינוּ, וְהַמְגַלֶּה פָנִים בַּתּוֹרָה שֶׁלֹּא כַהֲלָכָה — אַף עַל פִּי שֶׁיֵּשׁ בְּיָדוֹ תוֹרָה

---

the opposite of the synagogues of the learned, which are places of prayer and holiness. The ignorant gather for trivial purposes, for things without substance, and such a gathering does not contribute to the world's fabric. One who participates in these meetings is not engaged in the substance of life and hence is removed from the world.

שֶׁנָּה שֶׁל שַׁחֲרִית, וְיַיִן שֶׁל צָהֳרַיִם, וְשִׂיחַת הַיְלָדִים, וִישִׁיבַת בָּתֵּי כְנֵסִיּוֹת שֶׁל עַמֵּי הָאָרֶץ — *Late morning sleep, midday wine, children's chatter, and sitting in the meeting houses of the ignorant*

At a deeper level, we see that these activities undermine the nature of the Jewish nation that was instilled by the forefathers:

• **Late *morning* sleep** abrogates the morning prayer that our father **Avraham** instituted.

• ***Midday* wine** abrogates the noontime prayer that our father **Yitzchak** instituted.

• ***Children's* chatter,** which means engaging in the foolish talk found among children, is a misuse of the special blessing of children[1] that was **Yaakov's** privilege.

   Sitting in the *meeting houses* (כְּנֵסִיּוֹת, *kenaisiyos*) **of the ignorant** places him at a distance from the *community* (כְּנֶסֶת, *kenesses*) of Israel.

If a person violates any of these four elements from which Jewish life was formed, his own absence from life will surely follow.

Mishnah 15

The previous *mishnah* explained that the fitting retribution for people who direct all of their thought and purpose to the physical world is to be removed from that world.

This *mishnah* deals with people who have exactly the opposite fault. They value only the intellectual aspects of life and scorn the physical

---

1. *Bereishis* 33:5: "the **children whom God graciously gave** your servant (i.e., Yaakov)."

15. Rabbi Elazar the Moda'ite says: One who desecrates sacred things, who disgraces the Festivals, who humiliates his fellow in public, who nullifies the covenant of our forefather Avraham, or who perverts the Torah contrary to the *halachah* — though he may have Torah and

---

aspects. That attitude is appropriately requited by losing the purely non-physical life of the future world.

הַמְחַלֵּל אֶת הַקֳּדָשִׁים, וְהַמְבַזֶּה אֶת הַמּוֹעֲדוֹת 🙠 — *One who desecrates sacred things, who disgraces the Festivals*

The Hebrew term קֳדָשִׁים, *kodashim*, translated here in its more general sense of "sacred things," often refers specifically to sacrifices in the era of the Temple.

This person repudiates **sacrifices,** in his belief that God would not be associated with food or drink.

Since he is convinced that worldly enjoyment cannot bring religious success, he also treats the **Festivals** with disdain, for they are a time of worldly happiness through eating and drinking.

וְהַמַּלְבִּין פְּנֵי חֲבֵרוֹ בָּרַבִּים, וְהַמֵּפֵר בְּרִיתוֹ שֶׁל אַבְרָהָם אָבִינוּ 🙠 — *who humiliates his fellow in public, who nullifies the covenant of our forefather Avraham*

He considers people insignificant because they are physical beings. This leads him to **humiliate people** publicly, as is common among certain intellectuals, who belittle people at every opportunity.

In his single-minded pursuit of the intellectual, he **nullifies** the *bris* of Avraham's **covenant,** finding it disgraceful for the covenant with God to be attained through this appendage.

וְהַמְגַלֶּה פָנִים בַּתּוֹרָה שֶׁלֹּא כַהֲלָכָה 🙠 — *or who perverts the Torah contrary to the halachah*

When he finds that there are *mitzvos* in the **Torah** that require physical involvement, he explains them away in a manner that differs with halachic requirements.

וּמַעֲשִׂים טוֹבִים, אֵין לוֹ חֵלֶק לָעוֹלָם הַבָּא.

[טז] רַבִּי יִשְׁמָעֵאל אוֹמֵר: הֱוֵי קַל לְרֹאשׁ,

---

§ אֵין לוֹ חֵלֶק לָעוֹלָם הַבָּא — *he has no share in the World to Come*

Divine retribution fits the transgression by bringing about the oppo-site of the transgressor's intentions and wishes. This principle was illustrated in the previous *mishnah* which discussed pleasure-seekers who make this world their principal focus and defer spiritual matters in order to pursue physical pleasures. Their desire is thwarted through their punishment, for He removes them from this world, the object of their pursuit.

The same principle applies to the subject of our *mishnah*, who is the opposite of the hedonist. He considers this physical world to be worth-less and hence even good deeds are worthless in his eyes. He believes that the whole point of life is enlightenment and through it one reaches the World to Come, which is itself a realm of purely intellectual existence. Contrary to his beliefs, this person receives no portion in the World to Come.

The truth is that some worldly activities should indeed be avoided because they are trivial and indulgent. However, we acquire the spiritual World to Come by doing God's Will through *mitzvos,* even though they are physical acts. The reason is that this physical world is the corridor that leads to the World to Come.[1]

---

§ הַמְחַלֵּל אֶת הַקֳּדָשִׁים . . . אֵין לוֹ חֵלֶק לָעוֹלָם הַבָּא — *One who desecrates sacred things. . .he has no share in the World to Come.*

Another explanation is based on the observation that everything in our *mishnah* is called holy, קוֹדֶשׁ, *kodesh.* The holiness of the sacrifices, קֳדָשִׁים, *kodashim;* the Festivals;[2] the covenant, בְּרִית, *bris,* with God; and the Torah are obvious. As well, there is no higher level of holiness to be found in all creation than the human being, who was created in the "image of God," and therefore it is truly a desecration of holiness to humiliate a person in public.

It is befitting that a person who disgraces these holy things be deprived of the World to Come, for it is absolutely holy.

---

1. A reference to *Avos* 4:21.
2. Which are called "holy convocations" in *Vayikra* 23:4.

This World and the Next

This *mishnah* alludes to a Kabbalistic principle of creation and existence. God created two worlds: this world and the World to Come, and that fact is conveyed by His Name י־ה as found in the verse, "for with [the letters] י ה God fashioned the worlds."[1] The World to Come is represented by the letter י which symbolizes holiness and eternity,[2] while this world is represented with the letter ה.[3] The two letters, combined together as His Name, convey that He has infused this physical world with holiness and that it is associated with the World to Come.

The holiness implied by the letter י of His Name must be joined with this world, represented by the letter ה, which has the numerical value five. Therefore our *mishnah* lists five physical *mitzvos* that are holy and Divine, and tells us that if a person sins against them, then he has lost all connection with the י of His Name, which portrays the World to Come.

In simpler terms, God has placed us in a world which is a physical link to holiness in this life and a corridor to the holy World to Come. One who rejects the link to holiness in this world has no means to attain the Next World.

Mishnah 16

The order of the *mishnayos* primarily follows the chronological sequence of the authors. Rabbi Yishmael, the author of this *mishnah,* lived immediately after Rabbi Elazar the Moda'ite of the previous *mishnah,* and was contemporary with Rabbi Akiva of the next *mishnah.*

The *mishnayos* are also organized according to subject. Here we return to the thought introduced in *mishnah* 13,

"If the spirit of one's fellows is pleased with him."

By presenting three ways of acting with a pleasant demeanor.

Mishnah 15 stated that one who humiliates people in public loses his portion in the World to Come. Rabbi Yishmael provides a positive contrast by promoting respect for each individual, in a way that best fits the relationship with that person.

---

1. *Yeshayahu* 26:4.
2. This point is developed at length at the beginning of Chapter 5, *infra.*
3. Each Hebrew letter has a numerical value. The fifth letter is ה, the tenth is י.

וְנוֹחַ לַתְּשׁחֹרֶת וֶהֱוֵי מְקַבֵּל אֶת כָּל הָאָדָם
בְּשִׂמְחָה.

[יז] רַבִּי עֲקִיבָא אוֹמֵר: שְׂחוֹק וְקַלּוּת רֹאשׁ
מַרְגִּילִין אֶת הָאָדָם לְעֶרְוָה. מַסוֹרֶת

**הֱוֵי קַל לְרֹאשׁ, וְנוֹחַ לַתְּשׁחֹרֶת וֶהֱוֵי מְקַבֵּל אֶת כָּל הָאָדָם
בְּשִׂמְחָה** — *Be yielding to a superior, pleasant to
the young and receive every person cheerfully.*

The *mishnah* identifies correct behavior for dealing with three categories of people: those who are his *superiors,* those who are *junior* to him
and those who are his *peers.*

With his *superiors,* he should respond promptly to do as told. If he
makes a request of someone *younger,* he should do so pleasantly, not in
a way that is haughty or peremptory. The correct way to treat one's *peers*
respectfully is to greet them cheerfully.

וְנוֹחַ לַתְּשׁחֹרֶת — *pleasant to the young*

The translation of the Hebrew תְּשׁחֹרֶת *tishchores,* as "a young person"
follows Rambam. The more probable translation is "one in a position of
power," following Rashi and the Aruch. In that case, the *mishnah* deals
with the correct way to treat two kinds of superiors. One type is a person
who deserves to be in a leadership position, such as a Torah scholar. The
other type is someone who has reached a position of authority without
being worthy of it. Based on this interpretation, the *mishnah* would be
explained as follows.

הֱוֵי קַל לְרֹאשׁ — *Be yielding to a superior*

This refers to one who deserves to be a leader. Be swift to pursue the
wishes of this person and to build a close relationship with him.

וְנוֹחַ לַתְּשׁחֹרֶת — *pleasant to the young*

Rashi's translation would be "pleasant to the one in power" which
refers to one who is in command, but who is issuing orders by virtue of
his position, not his ability. Accept his orders graciously and do not
display reluctance to accept his authority.

pleasant to the young and receive every person cheerfully.

17. Rabbi Akiva says: Jest and levity accustom a person to immorality. The Massores

---

₅§ **וֶהֱוֵי מְקַבֵּל אֶת כָּל הָאָדָם בְּשִׂמְחָה** — *and receive every person cheerfully*

Treat all people cheerfully, even if they are not in a position of authority.

How does "receive every person cheerfully" differ from Shammai's advice[1] to "receive everyone with a cheerful face"?

Shammai's point is that if one does not greet another with a cheerful expression, he will feel unappreciated, and that will hurt his feelings. "Receive every person cheerfully" is more positive and substantial advice, intended to honor people.

Mishnah 17

₅§ **שְׂחוֹק וְקַלּוּת רֹאשׁ מַרְגִּילִין אֶת הָאָדָם לְעֶרְוָה** — *Jest and levity accustom a person to immorality.*

The Hebrew word for "jest" is שְׂחוֹק, *sechok,* and implies happiness to excess. There is a place for happiness, but the excesses implied by the word שְׂחוֹק, *sechok,* should be shunned. While the word denotes jest, it connotes lewdness because even innocent jest leads to lewdness.

Sexual intimacy is delicately referred to in the Torah as צְחוֹק, *tzechok,* which is a variant of the word שְׂחוֹק, *sechok.* The word is used in the context of both marital and immoral connections.

We find it in an immoral context, in Potiphar's wife's accusation against Yosef:[2]

"See, he has brought to us a Hebrew לְצַחֶק, *letzachek,* to mock us; he came in to lie with me and I called in a loud voice."

And it is also used to describe the purest and holiest of marital relationships:[3]

"and behold, Yitzchak was jesting, מְצַחֵק, *metzachek,* with his wife Rivkah."

---

1. *Supra,* 1:15.
2. *Bereishis* 39:14.
3. *Ibid.* 26:8.

ג/יז   סְיָג לַתּוֹרָה; מַעְשְׂרוֹת סְיָג לָעְשֶׁר; נְדָרִים סְיָג לַפְּרִישׁוּת; סְיָג לַחָכְמָה שְׁתִיקָה.

The same word is used in both contexts, because they are just different degrees of the same thing. "Jest and levity accustom a person to immorality" because the legitimate indulgence of jest leads to immoral indulgence.

Jest leads to sexual indulgence because the prerequisite for both activities is to feel remote from God's presence. When one is engaged with the Divine Presence, and fearful of his Creator Who is before him, he does not indulge in jest and levity.

All the more so is physical intimacy the opposite of spirituality, even within marriage, and when performed as an immoral act, it causes the Divine Presence to depart.

The Massores Is a Protective Fence for the Torah

In contrast to the indulgences discussed in the beginning of the *mishnah,* we now receive advice to achieve holiness and temperance. To this end, four fences are listed to protect the gains that a person makes as he goes through life.

Many people confuse *what they have* with *what they are.* We are only body and soul, as we are born. Otherwise, we are born naked of wisdom, naked of wealth and naked of good deeds, for these are things that must be acquired.

Because these things are only acquisitions and not the person himself, they can be lost just as they were gained and therefore they need a "fence" to protect them.

Wisdom, wealth and good deeds are almost part of us, but Torah knowledge is different. It is a much more remote and fragile acquisition because it is so abstract. Indeed, the Rabbis[1] say that Torah is as hard to acquire as pure gold, and it is lost as easily as glass is broken. Therefore, its fence is discussed first.

⚬§ מַסוֹרֶת סְיָג לַתּוֹרָה — *The* Massores *is a protective fence for the Torah*

The *Massores* refers to the traditional tally of how many words in the written Torah are written fully vocalized, and how many are written with deficient vocalization. It also includes mnemonic systems to remember details of the Oral Torah, such as who said which opinion, and the order

---

1. *Chagigah* 15a.

3/ 17 is a protective fence for the Torah; tithes are a protective fence for wealth; vows are a protective fence for abstinence; a protective fence for wisdom is silence.

in which various subjects are developed. The *Massores* protects the Torah from being forgotten and its system of mnemonics keeps the large amount of complex information at a person's fingertips.

Some commentaries explain the term *Massores* to refer to the Oral Law, because without it the meaning of the Written Torah would be lost. This explanation does not appear correct at all, because the Oral Law is an essential part of the Torah, and not just a protection.

מַעְשְׂרוֹת סְיָג לָעֹשֶׁר §⊷ — *tithes are a protective fence for wealth*

God commanded that we give a tenth of our wealth to Him, and when we give of our money to God, then a blessing flows from God to our wealth. Because the number ten is symbolic of holiness,[1] it is an appropriate quantity to dedicate to Him and a suitable vehicle through which He sustains our wealth.

This fact is intrinsically captured in the common root of the words עֹשֶׁר (*osher*, wealth) and עֲשֵׂר (*aser*, to tithe). Consequently, only מַעֲשֵׂר, *maaser*, is a fence for wealth and not other forms of charity.

נְדָרִים סְיָג לַפְּרִישׁוּת §⊷ — *vows are a protective fence for abstinence*

This refers to a vow to perform good deeds. Good deeds are an acquisition, unlike bad deeds which are natural to the person, as it says,[2]

"for the inclination of man's heart is evil from his youth."

If a person were to follow his nature, he would not do good deeds, but "vows" are a valuable aid to abstain from our inborn inclinations.

סְיָג לַחָכְמָה שְׁתִיקָה §⊷ — *a protective fence for wisdom is silence*

As we explained, wisdom is not an intrinsic part of us, but is acquired and can be lost. Silence helps us acquire wisdom and it helps us keep it.

As we explained in the commentary to 1:17, the faculty of speech is

---

1. As discussed in the commentary to 3:7 and to 5:1.
2. *Bereishis* 8:21.

183 / MAHARAL: PIRKEI AVOS

somewhat physical, which is the opposite of intellectual. Since opposites cannot exist simultaneously, one must suspend conceptual activity in order to talk. Hence, silence strengthens the intellect by enabling it to act effectively.

Mishnah 18

Mankind — the Image of God

Scripture says:[1]

> "And God created mankind in His own image; in the image of God He created him; male and female He created them."

This passage does not mean that God has an image or appearance, for He certainly does not. Rather, it refers to the fact that a physical image can represent the nature of something abstract. For example, a person could design a symbol, expressing that God is supreme King and none is above Him, by drawing an upright figure. That symbol, albeit in physical media, would not have to imply that He has a form. Similarly, mankind's upright stature symbolizes that God is King, without implying that He has a form.

Other living creatures are bent over, symbolizing their submission to a higher being; namely, mankind. Since God has no one over Him, the upright form that was given to mankind is fittingly described as an image of God.

We could use a straight line as a symbol of God's uprightness, to represent that He does not deviate from what is right, just as the straight line does not deviate from its direct path. In this way, man's straight posture represents God's uprightness. Man's eyes symbolize that God sees and cares about the world, and he has two eyes to express that there is a benevolent seeing for good and a harsh seeing for retribution. Indeed, we can discern God's nature by contemplating each aspect of the human form for its symbolic message, as conveyed in the verse,[2]

> "and from my flesh I will see God."

Not an Anthropomorphism

Many think that words denote physical entities. They then have a problem with verses that refer to "the eyes of God" or "the ears of God" and they are compelled to explain these phrases as borrowed expressions.

The truth is, Hebrew words do not denote physical entities, but the very essence of a thing. For example, the word "eyes" denotes vision. The "ears of God" denotes listening, and the "hand" refers to the utility

---

1. *Bereishis* 1:27.
2. *Iyov* 19:26.

of a hand, in any of its functions. Whether a thing is physical or not, these words never refer to the physical article but to its essential nature.

Similarly, the image of a thing is that by which it is recognized, and when the verse refers to man as the "image of God," it means that God is recognized through mankind. Therefore, the expression, "for He created man in the image of God" means that man is recognized as distinct and supreme in the physical world, just as God is distinct and supreme in the spiritual world.

It is for this reason that the Rabbis had no reluctance to formulate the blessing[1] "Who fashioned mankind in His image, in the image of His likeness," for these words have no physical implications, but convey only the concepts that we have discussed.

In summary, man's physical form is a symbol of God, for mankind is king of the creation beneath the sun, as God is King of all creation.

Limitations of Symbolism

The physical world is like clothing on the abstract, spiritual world. Clothes outline the wearer of those clothes according to the nature of the clothes, and not according to the true nature of the wearer. So is God perceived in this world according to the nature of this world, not according to His true essence.

It follows that a physical symbol of God's nature is possible only in the finite, physical world. On a purely conceptual level, there can be no accurate representation of God's nature. Therefore ordinary prophets symbolically saw God's nature in a prophetic vision of a man sitting on a throne,[2] but in Moshe's prophecy, which was through direct perception, it says,[3]

"And no man can see Me and live."

In other words, only certain aspects of God can be physically symbolized, but His true nature is not within conceptual grasp.

The Image of God — a Deeper Explanation

On a more profound level, the "image of God," צֶלֶם אֱלֹקִים, tzelem Elokim, refers to an intangible aura, rather than a physical shape. An example of this use of the word "image" is found in the verse,[4]

"Then Nevuchadnezzar was filled with fury and the image of his face changed."

---

1. One of the seven blessings of the marriage ceremony.
2. Yeshayahu 6:1.
3. Shemos 33:20.
4. Daniel 3:19.

ג/יח **[יח]** הוּא הָיָה אוֹמֵר: חָבִיב אָדָם, שֶׁנִּבְרָא בְצֶלֶם.
חִבָּה יְתֵרָה נוֹדַעַת לוֹ שֶׁנִּבְרָא בְצֶלֶם,

The physical shape of his face did not change; it was the expression of his face that changed. The events that befall a person can cause his face to be bright or dull, and it is this radiance that is referred to as the "image of God."

The "image of God," צֶלֶם אֱלֹקִים, is a spark that flows from God and infuses Divinity into each person. It is an aura, the radiance of life that lights a person's face, and the Rabbis referred to this aura when they said,[1]

> When Og, the (giant) king of Bashan, is dead, it is necessary to guard him against mice, but a one-day-old baby, who is alive, does not need to be guarded against mice.

This radiance is the very essence of existence. All existence comes from God, and therefore every created thing has it to some degree. In objects, we sense it as a certain intangible beauty, but in man it is so Godly that it is called צֶלֶם אֱלֹקִים, for nothing exists as fully as mankind, except for God.

Full existence is associated with autonomy. A person who is within the control of another does not have complete personal existence, because he lives partly within another's domain. Mankind was created with complete existence because God made him the king of the physical world, as it says:[2]

> "The heavens are the heavens of God, but He gave the earth to mankind."

For this reason, Scripture combines the idea of man being created in God's image, and the idea of man's mastery of the world, in a single verse:[3]

> "Let us make mankind in our image, in our likeness, and let them have dominion over the fish of the sea, and over the birds of the air and over the cattle and over all the earth."

Higher than the Angels

In the verse just cited, the phrase "in *our* image, in *our* likeness" is in the plural, referring to God and the angels, for angels also have the radiance of existence. However, the very next verse,

---

1. *Shabbos* 151b.
2. *Tehillim* 115:16.
3. *Bereishis* 1:26.

18. He used to say: Beloved is man, for he was created in God's image. It is indicative of greater love that it was made known to him that he was created in God's image,

---

"And God created the man in *His* own image," describes man's creation without reference to the angels, to tell us that he was created superior to the angels, and his existence can be compared only to God's.

Man's radiance is superior to that of angels because he is a physical being. A characteristic of physical things is that they change in response to external forces. For example, objects accept shape, and the body accepts the spirit, which animates it and gives it character. Similarly, our physical being is imprinted with the Divine spark of the "image of God."

Ironically, the non-physical existence of angels turns out to be a deficiency, because they cannot receive the Divine spark to the same degree as people can. In this world, the spiritual nature of angels is superior to the physical existence of human beings. In the World to Come, however, a person is likewise unfettered by the body, but he will retain God's spark of Divinity and will then be higher than the angels. The superiority of mankind relative to the angels came to a head when Yaakov wrestled with the angel,[1] in a struggle for supremacy in this world and the next.

חָבִיב אָדָם, שֶׁנִּבְרָא בְּצֶלֶם §⟨ — *Beloved is man, for he was created in God's image.*

Love develops between those who are similar. Since man has been created in God's image, there is a connection between God and mankind that culminates in Divine love.

חִבָּה יְתֵרָה נוֹדַעַת לוֹ שֶׁנִּבְרָא בְּצֶלֶם §⟨ — *It is indicative of a greater love that it was made known to him that he was created in God's image*

Articulating love forms a strong bond between two parties. Saying, "I love you," informs the other party that you seek his love. The *mishnah* calls this "a greater love" because God seeks the love of Israel in return.

God's love for mankind is revealed and active.

---

1. *Bereishis* 32:25-30.

שֶׁנֶּאֱמַר: ,,כִּי בְּצֶלֶם אֱלֹהִים עָשָׂה אֶת הָאָדָם.'' חֲבִיבִין יִשְׂרָאֵל, שֶׁנִּקְרְאוּ בָנִים לַמָּקוֹם. חִבָּה יְתֵרָה נוֹדַעַת לָהֶם שֶׁנִּקְרְאוּ בָנִים לַמָּקוֹם, שֶׁנֶּאֱמַר: ,,בָּנִים אַתֶּם לַיהוה אֱלֹהֵיכֶם.'' חֲבִיבִין יִשְׂרָאֵל, שֶׁנִּתַּן לָהֶם כְּלִי חֶמְדָּה. חִבָּה יְתֵרָה נוֹדַעַת לָהֶם, שֶׁנִּתַּן לָהֶם כְּלִי חֶמְדָּה שֶׁבּוֹ נִבְרָא הָעוֹלָם, שֶׁנֶּאֱמַר: ,,כִּי לֶקַח טוֹב נָתַתִּי לָכֶם, תּוֹרָתִי אַל תַּעֲזֹבוּ.''

⧫§ שֶׁנֶּאֱמַר: ,,כִּי בְּצֶלֶם אֱלֹהִים עָשָׂה אֶת הָאָדָם'' — *as it is said:*
"For in the image of God He made man."

The verse quoted by the *mishnah* reads in its entirety,[1]

"Whoever sheds man's blood, by man shall his blood be shed; for in the image of God He made man."

This verse expresses how precious and beloved human life is to God.

⧫§ שֶׁנֶּאֱמַר: ,,בָּנִים אַתֶּם לַיהוה אֱלֹהֵיכֶם'' — *as it is said:*
"You are children to Hashem your God."

The proof-text reads in its entirety,[2]

"You are children to *Hashem* your God; you shall not gash yourselves nor make any baldness between your eyes for the dead."

The relevant characteristics of a child are:

- The child is the parent's.
- A parent values the child for the child himself, and not for any utility he may provide.

The people of Israel are called "children" of God because they are His, and because they were created as an end in their own right, and not to serve some other purpose. Indeed, the world itself was created to serve His people and therefore only they are called "children." That is why His

---

1. *Bereishis* 9:6.
2. *Devarim* 14:1.

as it is said (*Bereishis* 9:6): "For in the image of God He made man." Beloved are the people Israel, for they are described as children of the Omnipresent. It is indicative of greater love that it was made known to them that they are described as children of the Omnipresent, as it is said (*Devarim* 14:1): "You are children to Hashem your God." Beloved are the people Israel, for a cherished utensil was given to them. It is indicative of greater love that it was made known to them for a cherished utensil was given to them, through which the world was created, as it is said (*Mishlei* 4:2): "For I have given you a good teaching; do not forsake my Torah."

---

love for Israel is like that of a father towards his son, and why we can have a complete bond with Him.

‎שֶׁנִּתַּן לָהֶם כְּלִי חֶמְדָּה‏ §⊷ — *for a cherished utensil was given to them*

The text in most editions of the *mishnah*[1] reads,

‎שֶׁנִּתַּן לָהֶם כְּלִי חֶמְדָּה, שֶׁבּוֹ נִבְרָא הָעוֹלָם‏ §⊷ — *a cherished utensil was givc to them, through which the world was created*

The gift He gave is the Torah and it is "a *cherished* utensil" because the world was created through it. Torah is the master plan, as devised by God, that dictates the workings of the universe.

This conceptual blueprint is also the tool of implementation, because the conceptual acts upon the corporeal. We know from experience that envisioning a result can make it happen. For example, if a person apprehensively crosses a stream over a narrow board, the thought of falling can cause him to actually fall.

All the more so can Torah, which embodies God's expectations, act upon creation.

---

1. The text of *Pirkei Avos* in most *siddurim* has minor variations from the text in the standard editions of the *Mishnah*.

[יט] הַכֹּל צָפוּי, וְהָרְשׁוּת נְתוּנָה. וּבְטוֹב

§⇐ שֶׁנִּבְרָא בְּצֶלֶם . . . שֶׁנִּקְרְאוּ בָּנִים לַמָּקוֹם . . . שֶׁנִּתַּן לָהֶם כְּלִי חֶמְדָּה §⇐ — *that he was created in God's image . . . for they are described as children of the Omnipresent . . . a cherished utensil was given to them*

Each of these three expressions of love corresponds to a different level of existence.

The greatness due to being made in the image of God comes in the context of mankind's mastery of the *physical* world.

Higher still is the gift of Torah, for that is the supreme wisdom of a higher, *spiritual* world.

The highest level of love is conveyed through the relationship of Israel as God's children. Through that relationship, Israel sets a crown upon the head of the *King of all kings,* as the Rabbis tell us:[1]

[An angel. . .] ties on a crown for his Master, made of the prayers of Israel.

That statement is a profound insight into our relationship as God's children that is found in the verse,[2]

"Children's children are the crown of grandparents . . ."

Mishnah 19

The previous *mishnah* disclosed the close, loving relationship between God and mankind, and this *mishnah* continues that theme.

§⇐ הַכֹּל צָפוּי — *Everything is seen,* §⇐

God directs His attention to every action that is performed for His sake. This is a natural consequence of the close bond with God that comes from mankind being the "image of God."[3]

§⇐ וְהָרְשׁוּת נְתוּנָה — *yet the freedom of choice is given.* §⇐

Freedom of choice is a direct consequence of the fact that mankind is made in the "image of God."

1. *Chagigah* 13b.
2. *Mishlei* 17:6.
3. Maharal explains further: There are degrees of existence. A person who is the "image of God" exists more fully than any other part of creation: His deeds are very significant. By contrast, the deeds of one who lives an empty existence are insignificant.

הַכֹּל צָפוּי, וְהָרְשׁוּת נְתוּנָה — *Everything is seen,
yet the freedom of choice is given.*

Even though God sees a person about to commit a transgression, He does not prevent him from transgressing. The Creator endowed human beings with the freedom to even violate His Will. This places mankind higher than angels, for angels do not have free choice but perform their appointed task without deviating from their mission.

Gan Eden — The Origin of Free Choice

The paradigm of the freedom to choose evil was established in *Gan Eden*. At first, man was so utterly tied to God's goodness that it was impossible, in practice, to choose to do evil. God sent the *nachash*, serpent, to pull Adam away from Him. He opened Adam's eyes to the opportunity for independence that lies in serving his own wishes and not God's. After he tasted the freedom of the Tree of Knowledge of good and evil, he was able to exercise free choice at every turn. He was truly "the image of God."

Man now longed for life, for knowledge brings about the connection with life. However, evil is self-destructive and it is impossible for man to do evil and to live indefinitely long. Therefore, access to the Tree of Life had to be cut off, and God expelled Adam from the Garden.

The Tree of Life in *Gan Eden* is the Torah, for Torah is the essence of life. "Eating" of the Tree of Life means assimilating Torah into the fabric of one's existence, so much so that it sustains his existence. God drove Adam from *Gan Eden* to keep him from eating of the Tree of Life. Outside the Garden, Adam would not have intimate access to the full depth of Torah.

By exercising his free choice, mankind now knew the ability to do both good and evil. Previously, only God Himself had known that latitude, and that is why free choice is associated with the "image of" God."

For generations, people have been surprised that Adam benefited from the sin of eating from the Tree of Knowledge. He became like God, knowing both good and evil. In truth, this was not to mankind's benefit: Man is better off not to be like God and not to have the ability to depart from his Creator to do evil.

◆§ הַכֹּל צָפוּי — *Everything is seen*

The *mishnah* uses the passive form צָפוּי, *tzafui* — "seen" — to emphasize that God observes both good and evil and He does not interfere with mankind's free choice.

Rambam understands the *mishnah* differently. He would translate צָפוּי as "foreseen." He considers the point of the *mishnah* to be that God knows everything, including the future, and yet mankind still has free choice at every moment. Maharal agrees with Rambam's belief in Divine prescience, but disagrees that our *mishnah* is discussing that point. If the intention of the *mishnah* were that God looks at the future, it would have used the Hebrew verb form צוֹפֶה, *tzofeh*.

The Enigma of Good, Evil and Free Choice

Free choice is uniquely human. The paradox of free choice is that God, Who is the ultimate of goodness, created a situation that allows evil.

God created the world to serve mankind, whom He endowed with free choice. If God intervened to prevent evil, He would undermine two basic principles of creation.

• If He withdrew a person's choice, that would undermine the Divine nature of mankind, which lies in free choice.

• If He interfered with a person's ability to succeed in doing evil, He would undermine the system of nature, which He created for the world to run by consistent and predictable rules.[1]

This thought is summarized in the following anecdote:[2]

> The philosophers asked the Rabbis in Rome, "If your God is displeased by idolatry, why does He not destroy it?" They answered, "If they worshiped [only] things that were of no use, He would destroy it. In fact, they [also] worship the sun and the moon and the stars; shall He destroy His world because of these fools?"[3]

---

1. God created the world to run according to the rules of nature, including mankind's free will. If God ran the world directly, without the rules of nature, He would have to support the execution of free will by actively participating in man's evil, and that contradicts his "goodness."

2. *Mishnah, Avodah Zarah* 54b.

3. The *mishnah* continues: The [philosophers] said to the [Rabbis], "If so, let Him destroy the things that the world can do without and leave the things that the world needs!" They replied to them, "If so, it would strengthen the belief of those who

with goodness, and everything depends on the majority of good deeds.

The answer, that He will not destroy His world, is sufficient as far as it goes, but it begs the further question: Why does He not destroy the idol worshipers themselves? The answer is: If he destroyed idol worshipers, people would no longer have free choice. What choice would a person have when faced with annihilation?

◄§ וּבְטוֹב הָעוֹלָם נָדוֹן — *The world is judged with goodness*

Good is defined as that which is worthy of creation and existence. God, in His goodness, allows evil, for to do otherwise would undermine His creations of nature and of human free choice. When we see that God does not thwart transgressors, we should not think that He approves of their evil. Rather, He gives an evildoer enough rope to hang himself.[1]

God punishes and eventually terminates evil. By the very definition of evil as the opposite of good, it does not have continuing existence. God, in His goodness, removes evil so that the world can continue to exist.

We must not misinterpret God's accommodation of evil. We might imagine that God permits sin because He seeks evil for the world. If He loves people so dearly, why does He not prevent evil? We might think that He judges the world, looking for an opportunity to condemn humanity!

The *mishnah* tells us not to make such an error. "The world is judged with goodness" means that God judges the world out of His quality of goodness. God judges the world, not to find opportunities for punishment, but to provide opportunities for goodness. In doing so He helps the world survive the evil that He permitted to occur. He brings punishments only to remove the evil and deal with its perpetrators.

Human beings, who do evil, do so out of their wickedness, but God brings constructive evil from His goodness.

In practice, we recognize that unhappy tidings are ultimately for our good by articulating the blessing ". . .the true Judge" with the same joy as we receive glad tidings with the blessing ". . .Who is good and does good."[2]

---

worship [the sun, moon and stars] for they would say that these are true gods, since they were not destroyed."

1. English vernacular for: "Feed a transgressor until he dies" (*Bava Kamma* 69a).
2. *Berachos* 54a.

וְהַכֹּל לְפִי רוֹב הַמַּעֲשֶׂה — and everything depends on the majority of good deeds

God does not assess a person deed by deed, but He assesses the person himself. One is considered a righteous person if he has acquired mainly merits. Alternatively, the majority of his actions could establish guilt. As a result, each sin carries an enormous risk, as the Rabbis said:[1]

> A person should consider himself as being half guilty and half worthy. If he does a single extra *mitzvah*, happy is he, for he swings the balance to an assessment of 'worthy.' If he does a single extra sin, woe to him, for he swings the balance to an assessment of "guilty."

This does *not* mean that God overlooks the sins of a person who on balance is righteous. It does not mean that one, who on balance is guilty, does not receive credit for the minority of good deeds that he did achieve. That is not the case. One is rewarded for each *mitzvah*, even if he did only one good deed in his entire life. Likewise, one is punished for each sin, even if he did only one transgression amid a life of goodness.

What, then, depends on "the majority of deeds"? The majority of deeds determines whether one is assessed as righteous or assessed as evil. One who is deemed righteous merits the World to Come; an evil person deserves to lose the World to Come. Nonetheless, the righteous person will be punished for his sins and the evil person will be rewarded for his good deeds.

An appropriate metaphor is a king, his friend and someone else whom he dislikes. The friend is always welcome. Even if he offends the king, the king assesses a penalty and the person continues to be his friend. By contrast, the person he dislikes might do the king a favor, which the king will reciprocate while remaining at odds with him. So it is with the righteous and the guilty. The righteous person, based on the majority of his deeds, is treated in a manner appropriate to a righteous person, but is penalized for the specific sins he committed. God treats an evil person as befits one who hates Him, but compensates him for the few *mitzvos* which he did.

The primary world is the World to Come; this world is secondary. It is proper for the primary nature of a person to be accommodated in the primary world; the secondary nature is properly dealt with in the

---

1. *Kiddushin* 40b.

secondary world. A person who is primarily righteous will receive his reward in the World to Come; his few sins are dealt with in this world. A person who is primarily evil will receive his punishment in the Next World, and his few good deeds, which are secondary, will be rewarded in this world.

This thought is expressed by the Rabbis as follows:[1]

> Rabbi Elazar the son of Rabbi Tzadok said, "To what are the righteous in this world compared? To a tree that stands en- tirely in a pure place except for a branch that overhangs an impure place. If that branch is cut off, then all of it is in a pure place. So does God bring afflictions upon the righteous in this world, in order that they will inherit the World to Come.
>
> "To what are the evil people in this world compared? To a tree that stands entirely in an impure place except for a branch that overhangs a pure place. If that branch is cut off, then all of it is in an impure place. So does God bring about good for them in this world, in order to drive them to inherit the lowest level of Gehinnom."

As we explained, the Rabbis compare the primary nature of a person to a tree and the secondary nature of a person to a mere branch. One's primary achievements are in the World to Come, which is the place of one's primary existence. Secondary behavior is dealt with in this world, for it is secondary to the World to Come.

It is also possible to explain this phrase of the mishnah as meaning:

עֵּ§ וְהַכֹּל לְפִי רוֹב הַמַּעֲשֶׂה — *and everything depends on the abundance of deeds*

Do not think that God has a standard reward for those deemed to be righteous, and that not every mitzvah is rewarded. Nor should you think that He has a standard punishment for those deemed to be guilty, and that not every sin is penalized. Rather, "everything depends on the abundance of deeds": Every mitzvah is rewarded and every sin is punished.

Mishnah 20

Rabbi Akiva told us in the previous mishnah that God judges the world in goodness. In this mishnah he elaborates on how God executes that judgment.

---

1. *Kiddushin* 40b.

[כ] הוּא הָיָה אוֹמֵר: הַכֹּל נָתוּן בָּעֵרָבוֹן,
וּמְצוּדָה פְרוּסָה עַל כָּל הַחַיִּים. הַחֲנוּת
פְּתוּחָה; וְהַחֶנְוָנִי מַקִּיף; וְהַפִּנְקָס פָּתוּחַ,
וְהַיָּד כּוֹתֶבֶת; וְכָל הָרוֹצֶה לִלְווֹת, יָבֹא
וְיִלְוֶה. וְהַגַּבָּאִים מַחֲזִירִין תָּדִיר, בְּכָל
יוֹם, וְנִפְרָעִין מִן הָאָדָם מִדַּעְתּוֹ וְשֶׁלֹּא
מִדַּעְתּוֹ. וְיֵשׁ לָהֶם עַל מַה שֶּׁיִּסְמְכוּ;

---

§ הַכֹּל נָתוּן בָּעֵרָבוֹן, וּמְצוּדָה פְרוּסָה עַל כָּל הַחַיִּים — *Everything is given on collateral, and a net is spread over all the living.*

The image of a "net" conveys that everything is within God's control, for His dominion and control embrace the entire world — inanimate creation as well as living creatures. The image of "collateral" conveys that He is in possession of our soul, and of the challenges and successes we encounter. The single message of these two images is that there is no escaping His judgment. He may assess penalties against our possessions or our person, or He may recall our very soul.

§ הַחֲנוּת פְּתוּחָה; וְהַחֶנְוָנִי מַקִּיף — *The shop is open; the Merchant extends credit*

This metaphor conveys that life is wide open for a person to do what he wants. There are no limits to what a person can achieve for good or for evil.

§ וְהַפִּנְקָס פָּתוּחַ, וְהַיָּד כּוֹתֶבֶת — *the ledger is open, and the hand writes*

Human action leaves its mark on the world. As we explained earlier,[1] mankind is the focus of creation and his actions paint a picture of the state of the world. The image of a ledger book expresses how our actions determine the worthiness, or the liability, of the world. It is our own hand that writes the ledger, for with each good deed we inscribe a credit and with each negative action we register a debt.

---

1. *Supra*, Chapter 2, *mishnah* 1.

20. He used to say: Everything is given on collateral, and a net is spread over all the living. The shop is open; the Merchant extends credit; the ledger is open, and the hand writes; and whoever wishes to borrow, let him come and borrow. The collectors make their rounds constantly, every day, and collect payment from the person whether he realizes it or not. They have proof to rely upon;

◆§ וְכָל הָרוֹצֶה לִלְוֹות, יָבֹא וְיִלְוֶה — *and whoever wishes to borrow, let him come and borrow*

God does not punish immediately. He allows a person to carry a liability for some time before ultimately settling the account.

◆§ וְהַגַּבָּאִים מַחֲזִירִין תָּדִיר, בְּכָל יוֹם — *The collectors make their rounds constantly*

God has all of creation available to Him to execute judgment against transgressors. The *mishnah* refers to any agent He chooses as a "collector."

◆§ וְנִפְרָעִין מִן הָאָדָם מִדַּעְתּוֹ וְשֶׁלֹּא מִדַּעְתּוֹ — *The collectors . . . collect payment . . . whether he realizes it or not*

The penalty for sin comes through afflictions. A righteous person pays **willingly**, accepting these afflictions with love, while others pay their debt against their will.

◆§ וְיֵשׁ לָהֶם עַל מַה שֶּׁיִּסְמֹכוּ — *They have proof to rely upon*

God set up nature in such a way that it would serve as the agency to administer penalties for sin. A person should not think that he can protect himself from the "collectors" just because they are natural causes. Rather, he must realize that God is the basis of those afflictions and there is no escape.

וְהַדִּין דִּין אֱמֶת; וְהַכֹּל מְתֻקָּן לִסְעוּדָה. ג/כא

[כא] רַבִּי אֶלְעָזָר בֶּן עֲזַרְיָה אוֹמֵר: אִם אֵין תּוֹרָה,
אֵין דֶּרֶךְ אֶרֶץ; אִם אֵין דֶּרֶךְ אֶרֶץ, אֵין תּוֹרָה.

◆§ וְהַדִּין דִּין אֱמֶת — *the judgment is a truthful judgment*

The judgment executed against a person is precisely fair, without
excess or diminution.

◆§ וְהַכֹּל מְתֻקָּן לִסְעוּדָה — *and everything is prepared*
for the [final festive] banquet

Rabbi Akiva has been describing this world, where mankind is at
liberty to sin and God then exacts a penalty. That kind of life leaves
much to be desired, falling far short of our sense of an ideal world.

In contrast, the World to Come is existence at perfection. Although we
cannot envision what that world will be like, we are given a glimpse of it
through the metaphor of a "banquet." There is no hunger at a banquet,
and hence that metaphor conveys that everything will be complete and
all needs will be satisfied.

The World to Come

Rav, a sixth-century Sage of the Talmud, would say:[1]

> In the World to Come there is no eating or drinking, no
> procreation, no business, no jealousy and hatred. Rather, the
> righteous sit with crowns upon their heads, and feast upon the
> splendor of the Divine Presence.

Existence in the World to Come will be complete, with no need to
sustain oneself through eating and drinking. There will be no need for
the fulfillment of bringing another generation into being. There will be
no point in doing business, because there will be no need to acquire
anything. Jealousy and hatred are spiritual deficiencies that will not
have a place in the World to Come.

The righteous are described as "sitting" because it is a place of
stability, where all are at rest. Only this world offers the possibility of
self-improvement. By the time we reach the World to Come, we will have
attained our full personal growth.

The image of a crown upon the head of the righteous expresses that

---

1. *Berachos* 17b.

the judgment is a truthful judgment; and everything is prepared for the [final festive] banquet.

21. Rabbi Elazar ben Azariah says: If there is no
Torah, there is no worldly occupation; if
there is no worldly occupation, there is no Torah.

---

there is no higher creature,[1] not even the angels. Only God has a higher existence.

Even in the World to Come, existence depends upon God. Just as *form* completes the existence of *substance*, so will God complete the existence of the righteous. "Splendor" refers to God's existence, because existence is always metaphorically associated with light.

In the expression "everything is prepared for the [final festive] *banquet*," our *mishnah* draws upon the same metaphor as "the righteous . . . *feast* upon the splendor of the Divine Presence."

Mishnah 21

In *mishnah* 17, Rabbi Akiva said that jest and levity bring a person to immorality because wrongdoing brings about further, similar wrongdoing. Rabbi Elazar ben Azariah now shows the positive side of that concept, by telling us that good deeds bring about similar good deeds. The *mishnayos* also follow the chronological sequence of the authors, since Rabbi Elazar ben Azariah was a generation younger than Rabbi Akiva.

---

§ — אִם אֵין תּוֹרָה, אֵין דֶּרֶךְ אֶרֶץ; אִם אֵין דֶּרֶךְ אֶרֶץ, אֵין תּוֹרָה —
If there is no Torah, there is no worldly occupation;
if there is no worldly occupation, there is no Torah.

Derech eretz, translated in the *mishnah* as "worldly occupation," refers to earning a living and to all aspects of participating within society. *Derech eretz* means living in a "natural" social system, as people did for the first 26 generations of history, from Creation until the giving of the Torah. However, human social systems cannot sustain themselves forever. Torah must eventually be incorporated into society for it to endure.

Something fully exists only when it has a purpose, and Torah crowns the social system with purpose.[2] This thought is conveyed by the following statement of the Rabbis,[3] noting that Scripture refers to the final

---

1. Just as the crown of a king is a symbol that no one is above the king. A crown is always a symbol of the highest level.
2. Author's elaboration.
3. *Shabbos* 88a.

day of Creation as "*the* sixth day," but calls the other days "*a* second day," "*a* third day" and so on. They conclude that the definite article alludes to a special sixth day: the sixth day of Sivan, when God gave the Torah to the Jewish nation. It was that "sixth day" which truly completed Creation.

> Why is there an extra [Hebrew letter] ה in the word הַשִּׁשִּׁי? It teaches us that God made a condition with the works of Creation. He said to them, "If Israel accepts the Torah[1] you will endure; but if they do not, I will return you to void and emptiness."

This homily demonstrates that Torah sustains nature by endowing it with worth. So too does Torah endow our personal daily lives with enduring spiritual worth, rounding out our "natural" social conduct with religious principles.

◆§ אִם אֵין תּוֹרָה, אֵין דֶּרֶךְ אֶרֶץ — *If there is no Torah, there is no worldly occupation*

Derech eretz and Torah go together, for each is necessary for success in the other. Success in Torah study and practice requires a firm base of *derech eretz* just as a building must have a foundation to endure. Conversely, *derech eretz* without Torah is as pointless as a foundation with no building. Social convention is the "natural" foundation upon which the Divine system of Torah rests. The two systems act together to provide us a system within which we can achieve our full human potential.

◆§ אִם אֵין דֶּרֶךְ אֶרֶץ, אֵין תּוֹרָה — *if there is no worldly occupation, there is no Torah*

One might ask: If there is no Torah without *derech eretz* and there is no *derech eretz* without Torah, how is it possible to achieve either one of them? If you can not have one without the other, there is no way to get started!

The answer is that "There is no Torah without *derech eretz*" means that Torah must be preceded by proper social conduct. *Derech eretz* comes chronologically before Torah in our personal lives, just as much of history preceded Torah.

---

1. Thousands of years later, at Mount Sinai, on the sixth of Sivan after the Exodus from Egypt.

If there is no wisdom, there is no fear of God; if there is no fear of God, there is no wisdom. If there is no knowledge, there is no understanding; if there is no understanding,

---

"There is no *derech eretz* without Torah" means that any *derech eretz* one has acquired will not endure indefinitely without Torah, just as the world's continuing existence is conditional upon Torah.

⇛§ **אִם אֵין חָכְמָה, אֵין יִרְאָה; אִם אֵין יִרְאָה, אֵין חָכְמָה —**
If there is no wisdom, there is no fear of God;
if there is no fear of God, there is no wisdom.

As Torah imbues practical daily life with lasting value, so does the fear of Heaven endow wisdom with true purpose. Rabbah used to say,[1]

> The purpose of wisdom is repentance and good deeds, so that a person should not study Torah and Mishnah and then rebel against his father or mother . . . or anyone greater than he is . . . as it says,[2] "The beginning of wisdom is the fear of God."

This passage confirms that wisdom is a step that leads up to the fear of God.

Only those who are close to a king are afraid of him, while those who are distant from the king do not feel that fear. So it is in our relationship with God. Only one who has acquired Torah wisdom is close enough to God to experience His fear.

Wisdom draws the fear of Heaven in its wake, and if fear of Heaven does not follow, we can be certain that it is not true wisdom.

⇛§ **אִם אֵין חָכְמָה . . . אִם אֵין דַּעַת . . . אִם אֵין בִּינָה** *— If there is no wisdom . . . If there is no knowledge . . . if there is no understanding*

חָכְמָה, בִּינָה וְדַעַת **— Wisdom, Understanding and Knowledge**

These terms are difficult to convey precisely in English, and deserve definition.

> חָכְמָה, *chochmah* — Knowledge and comprehension.
> בִּינָה, *binah* — Understanding: Deducing implications from what is already known, exercising creativity and initiative.

---

1. *Berachos* 17a.
2. *Tehillim* 111:10.

דַּעַת, *daas* — Translated in our *mishnah* as simply "knowledge," it is an expert, intimate knowledge of the very essence of things, including the characteristics that define something uniquely and distinguish it from similar things.

Rabbi Yose illustrated the difference between wisdom and understanding,[1]

What is the difference between a wise person and an understanding person? A wise person is like a wealthy man who is a currency expert. When he is brought coins to examine, he examines them. When he is not brought coins to examine, he sits unoccupied.

An understanding person is like one whose *trade* is to be a currency expert. When he is brought coins to examine, he examines them. When he is not brought coins to examine, he searches out coins on his own to examine.

A wise person learns and comprehends the material he is studying. A person of understanding, like the professional currency expert of the simile, searches out implications from other sources to add to his knowledge.

Scripture refers to these three qualities when it says,[2]

God founded the earth with **wisdom**; He established the heavens by **understanding**. By His **knowledge** the depths were broken up.

The association of "wisdom" with the earth implies that wisdom is close and accessible. "Understanding" is a more lofty and intellectual level and is therefore associated with the heavens. "Knowledge" appears in the context of breaking up the depths, for it is the ability to distinguish between similar things by discerning their essential characteristics. For this reason, the Rabbis established *havdalah*, which recognizes the distinction between Shabbos and weekdays, in the blessing of *Shemoneh Esrei*: "You grace man with *daas*."

§ אִם אֵין דַּעַת, אֵין בִּינָה — *If there is no knowledge, there is no understanding*

"Understanding" and "knowledge" go together. "Knowledge" is a

---

1. *Sifrei* to *Devarim* 1:13.
2. *Mishlei* 3:19-20.

---

stepping stone to the higher level of "understanding." Only after a person grasps the essence of a thing and its distinguishing attributes is he ready to proceed to "understanding."

For this reason, the blessing of *Shemoneh Esrei*:

> "You grace man with *daas*" places *daas*, the starting level, before *binah*. Furthermore, the blessing treats *daas* as a gift that God places before us, but treats *binah* as something that we need God to teach us, so to speak.

◆§ אִם אֵין בִּינָה, אֵין דַּעַת — *if there is no understanding, there is no knowledge*

If a person does not reach the level of "understanding," his "knowledge" is unfulfilled and insignificant.

◆§ אִם אֵין קֶמַח, אֵין תּוֹרָה; אִם אֵין תּוֹרָה, אֵין קֶמַח —
If there is no flour, there is no Torah; if there is no Torah, there is no flour.

Torah is frequently referred to, metaphorically, as bread. Just as bread is nourishment for the body, so Torah is nourishment for the soul. When we have both Torah and bread, we have our total sustenance.

The soul rests upon the body, and therefore **if there is no flour, there is no Torah.** The body finds its purpose in the soul and therefore **if there is no Torah, there is no** significance to the **flour** that sustains the body.

Why does the *mishnah* refer to flour instead of bread? Flour makes a more fitting parallel to Torah, because it is very fine. By contrast, bread is thick and an unsuitable parallel to Torah. Another reason is that bread is symbolic of the drive for sin, *yetzer hara,* and Torah is the antithesis of the *yetzer hara*.

Still another reason is that there *can* be Torah without bread, for a few days at least, because a person acquires bread daily and an absence of bread connotes a temporary problem. However, flour is acquired every few weeks and a shortage of flour implies that there will be no food for a long time. Therefore, if there is no flour he will have to leave his studies to earn a livelihood.

ג/כב

‏[כב] הוּא הָיָה אוֹמֵר: כֹּל שֶׁחָכְמָתוֹ מְרֻבָּה
מִמַּעֲשָׂיו, לְמָה הוּא דוֹמֶה? — לְאִילָן
שֶׁעֲנָפָיו מְרֻבִּין וְשָׁרָשָׁיו מוּעָטִין; וְהָרוּחַ
בָּאָה וְעוֹקַרְתּוֹ וְהוֹפַכְתּוֹ עַל פָּנָיו; שֶׁנֶּאֱמַר:

‏אם אֵין קֶמַח, אֵין תּוֹרָה — *If there is no flour, there is no Torah*

The *mishnah* lists first the more important of each pair. "If there is no Torah, there is no *derech eretz*. . .If there is no fear of God, there is no wisdom. . ." Why is the order reversed here, placing "flour" before "Torah"? The answer is that flour is different. It is a necessity that truly enables one to study Torah, and if there is no flour then there is no possibility of engaging in Torah study.

Mishnah 22

‏כֹּל שֶׁחָכְמָתוֹ מְרֻבָּה מִמַּעֲשָׂיו — *Anyone whose wisdom exceeds his good deeds*

Good deeds are physical actions,[1] and do not directly engage the intellect. For example, eating *matzah* or shaking a *lulav* is a physical activity, as are most *mitzvos*.

‏לְמָה הוּא דוֹמֶה? לְאִילָן שֶׁעֲנָפָיו מְרֻבִּין וְשָׁרָשָׁיו מוּעָטִין — *to what is he likened? — to a tree whose branches are numerous but whose roots are few*

Why is a tree a suitable metaphor for a human being?

A tree has two main parts: the roots, which support and nourish the tree, and the branches that grow continuously. A human being also has two parts: the physical body and the intellect that can grow and can spread up to the heavens and beyond. Interestingly, the physical part is the primary aspect of a person. Indeed, the Hebrew word for a human being is אָדָם, *adam,* which is derived from אֲדָמָה, *adamah,* meaning

---

1. This point is covered in the Maharal's Introduction, based on the verse in *Mishlei* (6:23): "For a lamp is the commandment and Torah is light." The verse associates *mitzvos* with a lamp, which is a physical device.

22. He used to say: Anyone whose wisdom exceeds his good deeds, to what is he likened? — to a tree whose branches are numerous but whose roots are few; then the wind comes and uproots it and turns it upside down; as it is said

---

"earth," because the essence of a human being is the earthly, physical aspect,[1] which supports growth.

Scripture itself uses this metaphor when it warns us not to destroy a fruit tree, even in the course of war. The verse says:[2]

> "You shall eat of it but you must not cut it down; is the tree of the field a man?"

Although the question "is the tree of the field a man. . .?" is rhetorical, there must be some point of similarity between a man and a tree or the comparison would be ludicrous. The point in common is that both people and trees are characterized by development and growth.

◆§ **דוֹמֶה . . . לְאִילָן** — *is likened . . . to a tree*

The physical performance of good deeds corresponds to the tree's strong roots, secured in the earth, while increasing wisdom is compared to the growth of the tree's branches.

◆§ **כֹּל שֶׁחָכְמָתוֹ מְרֻבָּה מִמַּעֲשָׂיו . . . דוֹמֶה . . . לְאִילָן שֶׁעֲנָפָיו מְרֻבִּין וְשָׁרָשָׁיו מוּעָטִין; וְהָרוּחַ בָּאָה וְעוֹקַרְתּוֹ וְהוֹפַכְתּוֹ עַל פָּנָיו;** — *Anyone whose wisdom exceeds his good deeds . . . is . . . likened . . . to a tree whose branches are numerous but whose roots are few; then the wind comes and uproots it*

The obvious difficulty is that this metaphor portrays intellectual achievement as a negative quality. It implies that we are better off with less intellectual development, because we will be unable to handle adversity if we learn a great deal of Torah! Does intellectual growth undermine the strength of character that comes from good deeds?

---

1. The point has been made previously that the essence of a human being is the body and the soul, components he possesses from birth. The metaphor of the tree reinforces the point that wisdom is not the essence of a human being, but rather develops later in life.

2. *Devarim* 20:19. The passage refers to conduct in warfare. It is permitted to attack the enemy soldiers, but not to destroy trees — a tree is not a soldier.

„וְהָיָה כְּעַרְעָר בָּעֲרָבָה, וְלֹא יִרְאֶה כִּי יָבוֹא
טוֹב, וְשָׁכַן חֲרֵרִים בַּמִּדְבָּר, אֶרֶץ מְלֵחָה וְלֹא
תֵשֵׁב.״ אֲבָל כֹּל שֶׁמַּעֲשָׂיו מְרֻבִּין מֵחָכְמָתוֹ,
לְמָה הוּא דוֹמֶה? — לְאִילָן שֶׁעֲנָפָיו מוּעָטִין
וְשָׁרָשָׁיו מְרֻבִּין, שֶׁאֲפִילוּ כָּל הָרוּחוֹת
שֶׁבָּעוֹלָם בָּאוֹת וְנוֹשְׁבוֹת בּוֹ, אֵין מְזִיזִין אוֹתוֹ
מִמְּקוֹמוֹ, שֶׁנֶּאֱמַר: „וְהָיָה כְּעֵץ שָׁתוּל עַל מַיִם,
וְעַל יוּבַל יְשַׁלַּח שָׁרָשָׁיו, וְלֹא יִרְאֶה כִּי יָבֹא
חֹם, וְהָיָה עָלֵהוּ רַעֲנָן, וּבִשְׁנַת בַּצֹּרֶת לֹא
יִדְאָג, וְלֹא יָמִישׁ מֵעֲשׂוֹת פֶּרִי.״

Yes. It is true that intellectual growth can be a negative, weakening influence. A tree's root system must be hardy enough to support its branch structure, and a person's intellectual attainment in Torah must be supported by an adequate base of practice.[1]

The burden of great theoretical knowledge can render a person unable to deal with adversity, if his root system of good deeds is shallow or incomplete. Intellectual growth can elevate a person to a higher level than he is prepared to live with. Good deeds bring one to the full comprehension of the wisdom behind those deeds, but Torah knowledge that exceeds one's practice of *mitzvos* is like poison. The Rabbis said,[2]

If a person is worthy, the Torah is a life-giving medicine for him. If he is not worthy, the Torah is a deadly poison for him.[3]

It must be noted that our *mishnah* does not imply that there is a limit

---

1. Based on Maharal's commentary to 4:13, this could be explained as follows. Adversity strikes at the physical plane of life, but the spiritual plane is immune to change. Therefore, stability must be achieved by strengthening the physical plane of human existence. That is accomplished by building a significant mass of good deeds, the momentum of which can carry a person through the storm.

When life becomes difficult, a well-developed intellectual prowess may make it too easy to rationalize inappropriate behavior to escape the winds of adversity. With a strong experience base of good deeds, we are unlikely to rationalize a course of action that would deny the validity of a lifetime of practice.

2. *Yoma* 72b.

3. A person who is committed to practicing Torah is granted an understanding of Torah; see 4:6. A person whose commitment to practice falls short of his Torah knowledge desecrates God's Name; see 4:5.

3/ 22 (*Yirmeyahu* 17:6): "And he shall be like an isolated tree in an arid land and shall not see when good comes; he shall dwell on parched soil in the wilderness, on a salted land, uninhabited." But one whose good deeds exceed his wisdom, to what is he likened? — to a tree whose branches are few but whose roots are numerous; even if all the winds in the world were to come and blow against it, they could not budge it from its place; as it is said (*ibid.* 17:8): "And he shall be like a tree planted by waters, toward the stream spreading its roots, and it shall not notice the heat's arrival, and its foliage shall be fresh; in the year of drought it shall not worry, nor shall it cease from yielding fruit."

---

to intellectual achievement. A tree whose root system is fully mature can support continuous growth of its branch structure for as long as the root system remains full and strong. This is true of a person as well, for once our practice of good deeds is fully established, we have no lack of ability to stand firm against adversity. At that point, we can develop our Torah knowledge continuously and still be able to cope with all of life's difficulties.

Mishnah 23

Our *mishnah* contrasts the wisdom of Torah with secular knowledge.

Mishnah 22 compared a person to a tree, for our wisdom is supported by good deeds, as a tree's branches are supported by its roots.

Clearly, that metaphor holds true as long as our wisdom and good deeds are a single unit, as are the roots and branches of a tree. But what type of wisdom is a single unit with good deeds? Is there any connection between secular wisdom and *mitzvos*?

Only the wisdom of Torah culminates in good deeds. The laws of the *mitzvos* are truly one unit with their practice, and hence performing good deeds enables us to comprehend the wisdom behind them.

◆§ קִנִּין — *The laws of bird-offerings*

These laws deal with the course of action to be taken in a situation of doubt. For example, a woman may have selected two doves for two

ג/כג [כג] רַבִּי אֶלְעָזָר בֶּן חִסְמָא אוֹמֵר: קִנִּין
וּפִתְחֵי נִדָּה — הֵן הֵן גּוּפֵי הֲלָכוֹת;
תְּקוּפוֹת וְגִמַּטְרִיָאוֹת פַּרְפְּרָאוֹת לַחָכְמָה.

❦ ❦ ❦

different kinds of bird-offerings, each of which has different sacrificial
rules. If one bird flies away or if other birds get mixed in with these birds,
she no longer knows which sacrificial procedure to apply to each bird.
Tractate *Kinnim*[1] deals with many such doubts that could arise with
bird-offerings, and specifies the correct course of action for each
situation.

⋙ **וּפִתְחֵי נִדָּה** — *and the laws regarding the*
beginning of menstrual periods —

A woman who has lost track of when her menstrual cycle began is in
doubt as to whether the blood flow is normal menstruation or an
abnormal condition called *zavah*. There are major differences regarding
the laws of these two conditions, and Torah law specifies how to deal
with doubts that arise from losing track of the dates.[2]

⋙ **תְּקוּפוֹת** — *astronomy*

This refers to the study of the motion of celestial bodies.

⋙ **וְגִמַּטְרִיָאוֹת** — *and mathematics*

This refers to the science of surveying and computations involving
fractions.
These two disciplines deal with hard facts that are observable and
measurable.

**The laws of bird-offerings and the laws regarding the beginning
of menstrual periods — these are the essential laws**

The *mishnah* illustrates the essence of Torah law with laws that deal
with doubtful situations, to dispel any notion that true wisdom deals only

---

1. *Kinnim,* Chapter 2.
2. Because of the complexity of these laws, it has been standard practice since the time
of the Talmud to apply the stricter considerations of *zavah* in all circumstances.

23. Rabbi Eliezer ben Chisma says: The laws of bird-offerings and the laws regarding the beginning of menstrual periods — these are the essential laws; astronomy and mathematics are like the seasonings of wisdom.

❧ ❧ ❧

with definite facts and with predictable situations. One might think that knowing how to deal with situations that arose out of carelessness or error is merely a practical necessity, and not an integral part of wisdom. Such is not the case! Torah wisdom can specify the correct course of action in the face of uncertain facts.

By contrast, even such precise sciences as astronomy and mathematics are of minor significance because they do not determine a correct course of action and good deeds.

Essential laws . . . versus . . . the seasonings of wisdom.

Torah law is the mainstay of society and of meaningful human endeavor. It is the "meat-and-potatoes" of the knowledge required to get through life successfully. Science is like seasonings that merely facilitate consumption of the main meal, because it does not contribute to proper moral or social conduct. Precise as these sciences may be, there is nothing in them that can help to sustain the soul or bring spiritual success.

❧ הֵן הֵן גּוּפֵי הֲלָכוֹת — *these are the essential laws*

The principal aspect of Torah is that it is the path to eternal life. The root of the name Torah, תּוֹרָה, means "to give direction," because Torah is the guide to the World to Come. Torah law is called *halachah,* הֲלָכָה, from the word הֲלִיכוֹת, *halichos,* meaning "paths."[1]

We need *halachah* to guide us to the World to Come, because the path leading there is extremely narrow. The World to Come was created with the letter י, *yud,* [2] the smallest of letters, and it takes a very straight and narrow path to make it to that endpoint.

Definitive *halachah* is a clear and positive system that leads straight to the World to Come. It is like a highway leading directly to the

---

1. *Megillah* 28b.
2. As discussed in detail in the commentary to 3:15, near the end, in the commentary to 5:1.

רַבִּי חֲנַנְיָא בֶּן עֲקַשְׁיָא אוֹמֵר: רָצָה הַקָּדוֹשׁ
בָּרוּךְ הוּא לְזַכּוֹת אֶת יִשְׂרָאֵל; לְפִיכָךְ
הִרְבָּה לָהֶם תּוֹרָה וּמִצְוֹת, שֶׁנֶּאֱמַר: ,,יהוה
חָפֵץ לְמַעַן צִדְקוֹ, יַגְדִּיל תּוֹרָה וְיַאְדִּיר.''

Rabbi Chanania ben Akashia says: The Holy One,
Blessed is He, wished to confer merit upon Israel;
therefore He gave them Torah and *mitzvos* in
abundance, as it is said (*Yeshayahu* 42:21): "Hashem
desired, for the sake of His righteousness, that the
Torah be made great and glorious."

---

destination, although one may be confronted with many possible paths
from which to choose.

This is another reason why the *mishnah* illustrates the essence of
halachah with laws that deal with complicated possibilities. *Halachah*
shows a clear and positive path to follow, in the face of the bewildering
number of paths that confront one who has lost track of her sacrifices or
her menstrual cycle. By contrast, astronomy and mathematics provide
no help in selecting among various courses of action and they certainly
provide no guidance towards the World to Come.

If people would only understand this message, they would not turn
aside from *halachah* to look into other books that the Sages detest.

פרק רביעי
Chapter Four

כָּל יִשְׂרָאֵל יֵשׁ לָהֶם חֵלֶק לָעוֹלָם הַבָּא,
שֶׁנֶּאֱמַר: ,,וְעַמֵּךְ כֻּלָּם צַדִּיקִים; לְעוֹלָם
יִירְשׁוּ אָרֶץ; נֵצֶר מַטָּעַי, מַעֲשֵׂה יָדַי לְהִתְפָּאֵר."

All Israel has a share in the World to Come, as it is said (*Yeshayahu* 60:21): "And your people are all righteous; they shall inherit the land forever; they are the stem of My plantings, My handiwork, in which to take pride."

א/ד

[א] בֶּן זוֹמָא אוֹמֵר: אֵיזֶהוּ חָכָם? הַלּוֹמֵד מִכָּל
אָדָם, שֶׁנֶּאֱמַר: "מִכָּל מְלַמְּדַי

Mishnah 1

◈§ בֶּן זוֹמָא אוֹמֵר — *Ben Zoma says* ◈§

Why does the *mishnah* not refer to the author by the title "Rabbi Shimon ben Zoma," as we would expect? The reason is that ben Zoma achieved renown while still young enough to be known by only his father's name, and the youthful designation persisted into adulthood. Rashi maintains that ben Zoma died at a young age, before being granted the title of respect — רַבִּי, *Rabbi* — that was conferred upon older scholars.

◈§ אֵיזֶהוּ חָכָם ... גִּבּוֹר ... עָשִׁיר ... מְכֻבָּד — *Who is wise ... strong ... rich ... honored?* ◈§

The common external measures of these qualities —academic success, physical prowess, assets and honors— do not reflect a person's true nature, just as the description of a house tells little about the person who lives inside. In contrast, ben Zoma's discussion of these qualities focuses on the very essence of a person.

What part of us is the essence and what part of us is acquired? Our essence is but body and soul, whereas possessions and even knowledge are acquired. Although a baby comes into this world with only body and soul, he is fully a human being. The baby is born naked: naked of possessions, knowledge and understanding. The possessions and knowledge that the child will eventually acquire are important, but they do not constitute his essence. Misfortune may claim his assets and senility may rob him of his knowledge; but he is a human being to the last breath.[1]

◈§ אֵיזֶהוּ חָכָם? הַלּוֹמֵד מִכָּל אָדָם — *Who is wise?* *He who learns from every person* ◈§

We might expect the answer to **"Who is wise?"** to be: "He who has learned much Torah." However, knowledge is just an acquisition. The true indication of a wise person is that he *searches* for knowledge. Ben Zoma tells us how to accurately appraise a person's soul and avoid being misled by external measures of success.

1. Author's amplification, based on Maharal's commentary to Chapter 3, *mishnah* 1.

1. Ben Zoma says: Who is wise? He who learns from every person, as it is said (*Tehillim* 119:99): "From all my teachers

---

הַלּוֹמֵד מִכָּל אָדָם *— He who learns from every person*

He who is wise by his very nature yearns for knowledge wherever he may find it. He can learn from anyone because desire for wisdom is in the very fabric of his being.

Is a successful student a product of his own abilities or of the teacher's skill? When two people are involved — the student and the teacher — we do not know if we are observing the wisdom of the student or the expertise of the teacher. When we observe that a student learns from every teacher he comes in contact with, it is perfectly clear that the student's success is the result of his own efforts.

הַלּוֹמֵד מִכָּל אָדָם *— He who learns from every person*

We explained before that knowledge is acquired; it is not the essence of a person. And yet, the loving pursuit of knowledge enriches the soul itself.

The analogy is an athlete who lifts weights to be strong. As he shoulders heavy weights, his muscles develop and strengthen. So too, the wise person desires the perfection that Torah wisdom can impart; as he internalizes knowledge, he strengthens and enriches his very being. Academic knowledge that does not lead to action does not stimulate personal growth, just as merely owning weights does not build a strong body.

In short, if you desire knowledge in the hope that it will mold you into a better person, then you are truly wise.[1]

מִכָּל מְלַמְּדַי הִשְׂכַּלְתִּי" *— as it is said:* *"From all my teachers I grew wise."*

How does this verse prove that a wise person seeks out wisdom? In earlier times one had only a few teachers throughout life.[2] The reason

---

1. Author's adaptation, based on Maharal's *Drush al HaMitzvos*, first paragraph. To paraphrase the original more closely: The relationship of knowledge to a person is like the relationship of form to substance. To yearn for Torah knowledge is to yearn for Torah to mold his personality and impart holiness to his character.

2. The proof-verse was composed by King David. Today, students have a different *rebbi* every year. In earlier times, one studied with his father and then went to study

הִשְׂכַּלְתִּי." אֵיזֶהוּ גִבּוֹר? הַכּוֹבֵשׁ אֶת יִצְרוֹ,
שֶׁנֶּאֱמַר: „טוֹב אֶרֶךְ אַפַּיִם מִגִּבּוֹר, וּמשֵׁל
בְּרוּחוֹ מִלֹּכֵד עִיר." אֵיזֶהוּ עָשִׁיר? הַשָּׂמֵחַ
בְּחֶלְקוֹ, שֶׁנֶּאֱמַר: „יְגִיעַ כַּפֶּיךָ כִּי תֹאכֵל,
אַשְׁרֶיךָ וְטוֹב לָךְ." „אַשְׁרֶיךָ" – בָּעוֹלָם הַזֶּה;

that a wise person has many teachers is that he searches for Torah from
everyone who has something to teach. His passion for Torah seeks Torah
at every turn.

In summary, the truly wise person yearns for knowledge in a way that
enhances his very being.

§ אֵיזֶהוּ גִבּוֹר? הַכּוֹבֵשׁ אֶת יִצְרוֹ — *Who is strong?*
He who subdues his personal inclination

The *mishnah* measures personal qualities, such as strength, in terms
of the person himself, and not in external terms. Capturing a city does
not prove that a person is strong: The city may have been weak, or
simply fated to fall. Conquering an adversary is only a relative measure
of strength and weakness. In contrast, conquering desire —the enemy
within— is an absolute measure of strength.

Furthermore, this *mishnah* praises only qualities of human distinction;
it has no interest in the brute strength that overwhelms an adversary.
Physical power is a distinguishing characteristic for animals, but the
measure of human strength is self-discipline, which is the power of the
intellect to direct the physical faculties according to what is right or
wrong.

§ אֵיזֶהוּ עָשִׁיר? הַשָּׂמֵחַ בְּחֶלְקוֹ — *Who is rich?*
He who is happy with his lot

It is true that one who is happy with his lot is wealthy, because he has
all he needs, but is this the only way to be wealthy? Even the Talmud[1]
recognizes that one who has hundreds of fields, vineyards and servants
is rich!

with more accomplished *rebbis*, only moving to a new *rebbi* when needed to match
his own Torah proficiency.
1. *Shabbos* 25b.

4/ 1 I grew wise." Who is strong? He who subdues his personal inclination, as it is said (*Mishlei* 16:32): "He who is slow to anger is better than the strong man, and a master of his passions is better than a conqueror of a city." Who is rich? He who is happy with his lot, as it is said (*Tehillim* 128:2): "When you eat of the labor of your hands, you are happy and all is well with you." "You are happy — in this world;

Ben Zoma describes the rich person whose wealth is not in the bank, but in his personality. He has amassed the benefits that one expects of wealth: He feels that he lacks nothing; he appreciates what he has; and he enjoys the tranquillity that comes from feeling secure and independent.

◄§ אֵיזֶהוּ עָשִׁיר? הַשָּׂמֵחַ בְּחֶלְקוֹ §► — *Who is rich? He who is happy with his lot*

The emphasis is on **his** lot. The *mishnah* does not mean simply "he who is happy with what he has," but "he who is happy with what he has worked for." The truly wealthy person has earned his portion. He has invested of his time, his toil, his very life. Thus, it is truly **his.**

◄§ ,,יְגִיעַ כַּפֶּיךָ כִּי תֹאכֵל, אַשְׁרֶיךָ וְטוֹב לָךְ'' §► — *"When you eat of the labor of your hands, you are happy and all is well with you."*

The Scriptural expression of "eating" connotes enjoyment and bene-fit. The expression means, "When you enjoy the results of your labor."

The Hebrew word for "happy," אַשְׁרֵי, *ashrei,* has connotations of being fulfilled and established.[1] The proof-verse does not explicitly mention wealth, but alludes to it by the self-sufficiency and stability that wealth can provide.

◄§ ,,אַשְׁרֶיךָ'' – בָּעוֹלָם הַזֶּה §► — *"You are happy"* — *in this world*

The self-sufficient personality enjoys this world more than a person who merely owns wealth, for two reasons: quantity and quality.

---

1. It shares the same Hebrew root as אִשּׁוּר, *ishur,* meaning "confirmation."

„וְטוֹב לָךְ" — לָעוֹלָם הַבָּא. אֵיזֶהוּ מְכֻבָּד?
הַמְכַבֵּד אֶת הַבְּרִיּוֹת, שֶׁנֶּאֱמַר: „כִּי מְכַבְּדַי
אֲכַבֵּד, וּבֹזַי יֵקַלּוּ."

In quantity, the happy person lacks nothing — he is happy. In contrast, the wealth of mere ownership is always lacking; even if one owns millions, his wealth is deficient compared to someone richer.

In quality, the work of one's own hands is more precious than incidental possessions.

§§ „וְטוֹב לָךְ" — לָעוֹלָם הַבָּא — *"and all is well with you"* — *in the World to Come*

Every righteous person will receive reward in the World to Come, whether or not he has the quality of "He who is happy with his lot." However, a person who depends on material wealth for happiness will not appreciate the highest degree of the World to Come, for it is a world that transcends material existence.

In contrast, a righteous person "who is happy with his lot" — whose satisfaction comes from within — can enjoy the highest level of the next world. Since he does not depend on material possessions for happiness, his personality is well suited for the spiritual life of the World to Come.

§§ אֵיזֶהוּ מְכֻבָּד? הַמְכַבֵּד אֶת הַבְּרִיּוֹת — *Who is honored? He who honors others*

Maharal understands this to mean: Who is *honorable?* He who honors others.

One who has enough honor to give others is honorable.

For that reason, Scripture refers to God as מֶלֶךְ הַכָּבוֹד, *Melech HaKavod,* [1] the King of Honor, because He confers honor upon those who revere Him, and one who confers honor upon others is called honorable.

Experience shows that some people who receive honor are not necessarily honorable. Once again, ben Zoma appraises human virtue directly, by the attribute of giving honor to others, rather than the

1. *Tehillim* 24:7. Commonly translated as "King of Glory," but the Hebrew word is the same: כָּבוֹד, *kavod.*

4/ 1   "and all is well with you" — in the World to Come. Who is honored? He who honors others, as it is said (*I Shmuel* 2:30): "For those who honor Me I will honor, and those who scorn Me shall be degraded."

---

external indication of receiving honor.

‎עֲשִׁיר‏ ‏. . . גִּבּוֹר‏ ‏. . . אֵיזֶהוּ חָכָם‏ — *Who is wise . . . strong . . . rich?*

These epithets are commonly used to talk about people in ways that really do not describe the individuals themselves. The prophet Yirmeyahu told us not to evaluate these aspects of people by external measures:[1]

> Thus says God: "Let not the wise man be praised for his wisdom, nor the mighty man be praised for his might; let not the rich man be praised for his riches."

Ben Zoma gives us relevant measures to evaluate these qualities.

Each of these qualities addresses a different human element. We noted earlier the essential and acquired aspects of human existence. The spirit is the human essence; knowledge is an intimate acquisition; and possessions are an important part of human life as well. The qualities of being **wise, strong** and **rich** correspond to the intellect, the spirit and possessions.

Yirmeyahu does not mention **honor,** because honor does not correspond to some other, fourth part of a person. Ben Zoma discusses **honor** because it is the garb that cloaks the whole person, who is the totality of intellect, spirit and possessions.[2]

Mishnah 2

In the previous *mishnah,* ben Zoma addressed four fundamental human qualities. In this *mishnah,* his contemporary ben Azzai rounds out the human personality by addressing the realm of action.

---

1. *Yirmeyahu* 9:22.
2. Wisdom: *Mishlei* 3:35, "The **wise** shall inherit **honor.**"
   Strength: *I Divrei Hayamim* 11:24, "and he had a name (i.e., **honor**) among the three **mighty** ones."
   Wealth: *Bereishis* 31:1, "and from that (**wealth**) which was our father's has he gotten all this **honor.**"

217 / MAHARAL: PIRKEI AVOS

ד / ד
ב-ג

[ב] בֶּן עַזַּאי אוֹמֵר: הֱוֵי רָץ לְמִצְוָה קַלָּה,
וּבוֹרֵחַ מִן הָעֲבֵרָה; שֶׁמִּצְוָה גוֹרֶרֶת
מִצְוָה, וַעֲבֵרָה גוֹרֶרֶת עֲבֵרָה, שֶׁשְּׂכַר מִצְוָה
מִצְוָה, וּשְׂכַר עֲבֵרָה עֲבֵרָה.
[ג] הוּא הָיָה אוֹמֵר: אַל תְּהִי בָז לְכָל אָדָם,

§ הֱוֵי רָץ לְמִצְוָה קַלָּה — Run to perform an easy mitzvah

If performing *mitzvos* is burdensome for someone, then he should run to do a *mitzvah* which is easy for him. That will lead him to do another *mitzvah,* because Torah is a single body, and where part of the body is, the rest will surely be found.

Ben Azzai did not tell us to flee from an *easy* sin, because all sins are easy and pleasurable.

§ שֶׁמִּצְוָה גוֹרֶרֶת מִצְוָה — one mitzvah leads to another mitzvah

The reason that doing one *mitzvah* leads to doing another *mitzvah* is that all *mitzvos* are a single entity; namely, the Torah. When Scripture says,[1] "For a lamp is the commandment and Torah is light," it does not mean that the Torah contains 613 *mitzvos* like a collection of many lamps. It means, rather, that the 613 *mitzvos* unite into a single, great flame, which is the one Torah.

Doing one *mitzvah* inherently begins another *mitzvah* because all *mitzvos* are one, indivisible unit. Transgressions likewise are one unit and hence one transgression inevitably draws in its wake another transgression.

§ שֶׁשְּׂכַר מִצְוָה מִצְוָה, וּשְׂכַר עֲבֵרָה עֲבֵרָה — the reward of a mitzvah is a mitzvah, and the reward of a sin is a sin

This statement does not intend to exclude the reward and retribution that awaits in the World to Come. Rather, it intends to point out that, additionally, **one mitzvah leads to another mitzvah.**

Reward for *mitzvos* and punishment for transgressions is an inherent consequence of the deed. It is not an arbitrary system of positive and negative behavioral reinforcement. Rather, it is like getting sick after

1. *Mishlei* 6:23.

2. Ben Azzai says: Run to perform an easy *mitzvah,* and flee from sin; for one *mitzvah* leads to another *mitzvah,* and one sin leads to another sin; for the reward of a *mitzvah* is a *mitzvah,* and the reward of a sin is a sin.

3. He used to say: Do not be scornful of any person

---

eating a poisonous substance.[1] Illness is not a motivational punishment, but a direct consequence of the effects of poison on the body. Likewise, a direct result of doing a *mitzvah* is that it brings to hand the opportunity to do another *mitzvah.*

In addition to the reward that comes one *mitzvah* at a time in this world, the accumulation of all the deeds of a lifetime, good or otherwise, will ultimately find their consequence, as a whole, in the World to Come.

◆§ שְׁשְׂכַר מִצְוָה מִצְוָה, וּשְׂכַר עֲבֵרָה עֲבֵרָה — *the* reward *of a mitzvah is a mitzvah, and the* reward *of a sin is a sin*

The **reward** is that we are given what we want. If a person wants to do *mitzvos,* he is given the opportunity to do additional *mitzvos.* If he wants to transgress, he is given the opportunity to do more transgressions. The unusual description of the consequence of sin as a "reward" is relative to the person himself: He wants to sin and he is 'rewarded' with more of what he wants.

Usually reward, or payment, comes at the completion of the job and remunerates the total effort. *The reward of a mitzvah* is different, for the opportunity to do another *mitzvah* is provided as each *mitzvah* is performed.

Mishnah 3

The previous *mishnah* made the point that the *mitzvos* are all one body: the Torah. Each *mitzvah* is unique and separate, and has its place in the total system of Torah. In this *mishnah,* we learn that each person and each thing similarly has its place within the totality of creation.

◆§ אַל תְּהִי בָז לְכָל אָדָם — *Do not be scornful of any person*

Do not think that any person is unimportant or unnecessary in the scheme of creation.

---

1. Author's illustration.

ד/ד וְאַל תְּהִי מַפְלִיג לְכָל דָּבָר, שֶׁאֵין לְךָ אָדָם
שֶׁאֵין לוֹ שָׁעָה וְאֵין לְךָ דָבָר שֶׁאֵין לוֹ מָקוֹם.
[ד] רַבִּי לְוִיטַס אִישׁ יַבְנֶה אוֹמֵר: מְאֹד מְאֹד
הֱוֵי שְׁפַל רוּחַ, שֶׁתִּקְוַת אֱנוֹשׁ רִמָּה.

─────────────────────────────

◈§ וְאַל תְּהִי מַפְלִיג לְכָל דָּבָר — *and do not be disdainful of anything*

Do not think that any created thing can be cast aside as not contributing to this world.

─────────────────────────────

◈§ שֶׁאֵין לְךָ אָדָם שֶׁאֵין לוֹ שָׁעָה — *for you have no person without his hour*

"Hour" refers to one's destiny in the unfolding of history. Each individual has a role in the totality of creation.

─────────────────────────────

◈§ וְאֵין לְךָ דָבָר שֶׁאֵין לוֹ מָקוֹם — *and no thing without its place*

"Hour" is used in reference to people, because individuals have a historical destiny. In contrast, "place" is used in the context of "things," because things have a "place" in creation.

Mishnah 4

This *mishnah* amplifies the *mussar* of ben Azzai, who said, "Do not be scornful of any person." One must be humble towards all, including a person who is of a lower station. Above all, a person must not use another as a foil for his own arrogance.

─────────────────────────────

◈§ מְאֹד מְאֹד הֱוֵי שְׁפַל רוּחַ — *Be exceedingly humble in spirit*

The only satisfactory degree of humility is total humility.

─────────────────────────────

◈§ שֶׁתִּקְוַת אֱנוֹשׁ רִמָּה — *for the anticipated end of mortal man is worms*

Does anyone aspire to worms? Surely the universal aspiration end is to be bound up with God for eternity!

When a person dies, the spirit is freed from its physical environment and the body joins the worms. Of course, we all achieve eternal *spiritual*

4/ 4 and do not be disdainful of anything, for you have no person without his hour and no thing without its place.

4. Rabbi Levitas of Yavneh says: Be exceedingly humble in spirit, for the anticipated end of mortal man is worms.

---

life. However, for the *body,* death is inevitable and there is no hope for anything better.

⋙ שֶׁתִּקְוַת אֱנוֹשׁ רִמָּה — *for the anticipated end of mortal* **man** *is worms*

Our *mishnah* uses the Hebrew word *enosh,* אֱנוֹשׁ, for "man," rather than the more common words *adam,* אָדָם, or *ish,* אִישׁ. Each of these words conveys a different aspect of mankind, and we will explain why the term *enosh* best fits the image of "worms."

The image of "worms" points to decaying flesh,[1] and conveys the loss and destruction of something significant.

The word *adam* is derived from the Hebrew *adamah,* אֲדָמָה, meaning earth. Earth itself does not decay, so the designation of man as *adam* does not fit with an image of decay.

The word *ish* conveys strength, as in the phrase[2] "A Man (*ish*) of war." Certainly, a term that emphasizes man's strength also does not fit with an image of "worms."

The word *enosh,* however, encompasses the connotations of both *adam* and *ish.* Indeed, even the numerical value of *enosh* is equal to the sum of the numerical values of *adam* and of *ish.* [3] In other words, *enosh* connotes strength that is cast into mortal substance. Hence the term *enosh* fits precisely with the image of "worms" and decay, which conveys the eventual separation of strength from its physical origin.

---

1. As noted, for example, *supra* Chapter 2, *mishnah* 8, "The more flesh, the more worms."

2. *Shemos* 15:3.

3. אֱנוֹשׁ = $1 + 50 + 6 + 300 = 357$
    אָדָם = $1 + 4 + 40 = 45$
    אִישׁ = $1 + 10 + 300 = 311$.

The sum of אָדָם + אִישׁ is only 356, not 357. It is accepted that numerologies can vary by 1 and remain valid. Alternatively, Maharal may be including the word itself in the equation, so that:

אֱנוֹשׁ = $357 + 1$ word $= 358$
אָדָם + אִישׁ = $356 + 2$ words $= 358$.

[ה] רַבִּי יוֹחָנָן בֶּן בְּרוֹקָא אוֹמֵר: כָּל הַמְחַלֵּל
שֵׁם שָׁמַיִם בְּסֵתֶר, נִפְרָעִין מִמֶּנּוּ בְּגָלוּי;
אֶחָד שׁוֹגֵג וְאֶחָד מֵזִיד בְּחִלּוּל הַשֵּׁם.

Mishnah 5

This *mishnah* follows in sequence from the previous admonitions that one not demean the honor due to others and not seek honor for oneself. Rabbi Yochanan ben Beroka continues this theme by warning a person to be concerned with honor of God as well as that of people.

The sin of *chillul haShem* is more serious than any other, because desecrating God's Name desecrates His honor. How could anyone be careful about honoring people and yet profane the honor of the Creator, Whose glory fills the world?

---

§ כָּל הַמְחַלֵּל שֵׁם שָׁמַיִם — *Whoever desecrates the Name of Heaven*

Desecration of God's Name, *chillul haShem,* refers to actions that cause people to feel that the world runs autonomously and without accountability, with neither a Judge nor judgment. The classic case of *chillul haShem* is a Torah scholar who sins,[1] for he knows his Master well and yet transgresses His will.

---

§ כָּל הַמְחַלֵּל שֵׁם שָׁמַיִם בְּסֵתֶר — *Whoever desecrates the Name of Heaven in secret*

Since *chillul haShem,* by definition, causes others to deny God's involvement with the world, how is it possible to desecrate His Name in secret? Who will see? Who will deny God's concern with sin?

One example would be ten Torah scholars assembled in a house, and one stole something. Everyone knows that a Torah scholar stole, but no one knows precisely who the culprit is. Although his identity is a secret at the time that he desecrates God's Name, by the time of his punishment events will unfold in a way that all will know who it was.

An alternative explanation of "Whoever desecrates the Name of Heaven in **secret**" is that a few people do know the details of what happened. The word **secret** is used to contrast with the eventual **public** knowledge of what he has done.

---

1. *Yoma* 86a.

5. Rabbi Yochanan ben Beroka says: Whoever desecrates the Name of Heaven in secret, they will exact punishment from him in public; unintentional or intentional, both are alike regarding desecration of the Name.

---

§ נִפְרָעִין מִמֶּנּוּ בְּגָלוּי — *they will exact punishment from him in public*

The punishment will be public so that people will see that God is involved with the world. God will bring events around in a way that people will know who desecrated His Name and will see that He exacts retribution. In the end, the culprit himself will be the vehicle by which God's honor is restored.

---

§ אֶחָד שׁוֹגֵג וְאֶחָד מֵזִיד — *unintentional or intentional, both are alike*

For most laws, the Torah draws a sharp distinction between deliberate and accidental transgressions. An accidental sin is still a sin, because a person must be careful not to transgress. In the end, however, the sin was done without intention or will and the Torah deals with it more leniently.

There are exceptions which do carry significant consequences for unintentional transgression:
- Unintentional murder is punishable by exile. Despite being accidental, there was a major consequence to his action.
- Unintentional damages must be repaid. Although unintentional, he caused damage to another.
- Unintentional desecration of God's Name is punished. Even if unintentional, he has desecrated His honor.

Whenever there is a discernible result, the Torah is not as lenient as it is with other accidental transgressions. Murder, damages and *chillul haShem* have substantial consequences and therefore the Torah takes a demanding stance for unintentional transgression.

---

§ אֶחָד שׁוֹגֵג וְאֶחָד מֵזִיד — *unintentional or intentional, both are alike*

The punishment for unintentional *chillul haShem* is not the same as if he had done it intentionally, for that would not be in keeping with the Divine quality of Justice. The *mishnah* means only that the culprit will be punished publicly whether the *chillul haShem* was intentional or not.

⏴§ אֶחָד שׁוֹגֵג וְאֶחָד מֵזִיד בְּחִלּוּל הַשֵּׁם — *unintentional or intentional, both are alike regarding desecration of the Name*

Chillul haShem has more stringencies than other laws, and these apply to all who desecrate His Name, unintentionally as well as intentionally.

- Other sins accumulate and are punished all at the same time, whereas *chillul haShem* draws retribution by itself, without waiting.
- *Chillul haShem* can tip the scales of evaluating whether or not a person is granted eternal life. If a person's sins and *mitzvos* are balanced, but one of the sins is *chillul haShem,* the overall assessment swings to the negative.

Why is the defamation of God's Name treated so much more seriously than other sins? Other sins do not affect God; rather they harm the person who commits them. By contrast, *chillul haShem* does affect God, by damaging people's perception of Him in the world. In one aspect, the damage caused by *chillul haShem* is more substantial than even murder. A murder victim, being mortal, would have died eventually, whereas God's honor is everlasting and would not have been eventually profaned.

⏴§ אֶחָד שׁוֹגֵג וְאֶחָד מֵזִיד בְּחִלּוּל הַשֵּׁם — *unintentional or intentional, both are alike regarding desecration of the Name*

Usually, unintentional transgressions are treated more leniently than intentional sins. The reason is that mistakes are the result of our physical limitations, which cause forgetfulness and distraction. Therefore, unintentional transgressions take place on a relatively unimportant plane of life, in the realm of mundane, incidental occurrences.

In contrast, *chillul haShem* touches upon the human perception of God at its very essence. Its consequences occur at the most important plane of life, in the spiritual realm where mankind and God meet. Therefore, the seriousness of the transgression, intentional or not, is inescapable.

In summary, leniency is usually appropriate for human foibles, and most sins hurt only the person committing the sin. *Chillul Hashem* is different on both counts, because it negatively impacts people's perception of God and that is not diminished just because it happened unintentionally.

The Extra Responsibility of a Rabbi

A Torah scholar exerts great influence on people's perception of God. He can cause God's Name to be degraded in people's eyes without committing an outright transgression. The Rabbis say:[1]

> How does desecration of God's Name occur?
>
> Rav said: For example, if I [2] do not pay the butcher immediately when I get meat, and the butcher is not one who collects his debts.
>
> Rabbi Yochanan said: For example, if I walk four cubits[3] without being engaged in Torah or without wearing *tefillin*. . . .
>
> Abaye said: As we have learned [that the verse,] "And you shall love the Lord your God"[4] [means] that the Name of Heaven shall be beloved [to others] through you.

Abaye informs us that a Torah scholar profanes God's Name if he does not act within social norms of courteous behavior. For example, he might not talk to people in a pleasant manner or deal politely with merchants, or act in good faith in his business transactions. People attribute his disappointing behavior to the fact that he is a Torah scholar, and as a result they deplore the fact that his father and his teachers taught him Torah. They conclude that a person is better off for not having studied.

Rabbinical Ordination

Maharal applies our *mishnah's* concern for *chillul Hashem* to the practice of ordaining *rabbis* who have not yet fully earned the title. A Torah scholar confronts a life-or-death situation. He can bring life by being the agency through which people come to love God, and he is also confronted with the deadly risk of defaming God's Name. For this reason, the title of "Rabbi" should not be conferred upon anyone whose conduct does not evoke the love of God.

Furthermore, ordaining an unworthy person confers the honor of Torah upon one who is not fit for it. That reflects so poorly on God's Name that it constitutes a violation of "You shall not take the Name of the Lord your God in vain."[5]

Also, ordaining people before they are worthy of the title contributes to the general loss of Torah from Israel. Sometimes these people ease off from intense Torah study, feeling that the title alone signifies that they have learned enough.

At one time the title of "Rabbi" was given readily, to confer honor

---

1. *Yoma* 86a.
2. Rav was the Torah leader of his generation.
3. About 8 feet.
4. *Devarim* 6:5.
5. *Shemos* 20:7.

ד/ו [ו] רַבִּי יִשְׁמָעֵאל בַּר רַבִּי יוֹסֵי אוֹמֵר: הַלּוֹמֵד
עַל מְנָת לְלַמֵּד מַסְפִּיקִין בְּיָדוֹ לִלְמוֹד
וּלְלַמֵּד; וְהַלּוֹמֵד עַל מְנָת לַעֲשׂוֹת מַסְפִּיקִין
בְּיָדוֹ לִלְמוֹד וּלְלַמֵּד, לִשְׁמוֹר וְלַעֲשׂוֹת.

---

upon those who study Torah, but today[1] this practice demeans the honor of Torah.

Our leaders must demonstrate concern for the honor of their Master and the honor of the Torah. These days,[2] only those individuals who are outstanding in Torah wisdom and maturity should be ordained. That would minimize the damage to God's honor, as people would not associate unbecoming behavior with a rabbi.

May He mercifully remove from us every obstacle and guide us in the path of uprightness and truth.

Mishnah 6

One whose intention is to teach or to observe is clearly dedicating his study to God,[3] and therefore God grants him the means to fulfill his intentions.

◆§ הַלּוֹמֵד עַל מְנָת לְלַמֵּד מַסְפִּיקִין בְּיָדוֹ לִלְמוֹד וּלְלַמֵּד — *One who studies Torah in order to teach is given the means to study and to teach*

Why does one who studies with the intention to teach or to practice have his intentions fulfilled?[4]

Torah is the essence of existence, and hence every attempt to imbue this world with the theory and practice of Torah enhances the world's existence. The Creator helps these efforts succeed because they contribute to His creation.

The following paragraph of background will help us approach this idea on a more profound level.

Physical life is an inferior existence; it is limited, fragmented and moribund. Conceptual things are the opposite, and have a superior existence. They are unlimited by space or time and need never come to

---

1. See previous note.
2. Maharal wrote this in the late 1500s.
3. As opposed to a general interest in study or wishing to obtain the title of "Rabbi."
4. This section has been liberally paraphrased. Students of Maharal may wish to consult the original before drawing general conclusions about Maharal's principles as expressed here.

6. Rabbi Yishmael bar Rabbi Yose says: One who studies Torah in order to teach is given the means to study and to teach; and one who studies in order to practice is given the means to study and to teach, to observe and to practice.

an end. Another quality of conceptual things is that they can infuse their superior existence into the physical, just as shape enhances substance.

Torah[1] is on a completely conceptual plane and therefore does not automatically appear in this physical world. However, when mundane life cries out for the conceptual, to enrich its existence, Torah responds enthusiastically, always at the ready to share and impart its superior existence.

As a metaphor,[2] consider the power that drives air to join with wood to make a fire. Despite the great power waiting to be unleashed, the fire needs to be initiated by lighting the wood or there will be no flame at all. So too does Torah have great creative power to unify, elevate and actualize the world. When a person tries to bring Torah teachings and observance into the world he lights the fire, so to speak, and unleashes the power of Torah.

Thought brings about practical results.[3] It is Torah itself that empowers thought to be self-fulfilling; a person need simply "light the fire."

§◆ מַסְפִּיקִין בְּיָדוֹ לִלְמוֹד וּלְלַמֵּד — *is given the means to study and to teach*

Since success in teaching depends upon success in learning, God grants him both.

§◆ וְהַלּוֹמֵד עַל מְנָת לַעֲשׂוֹת מַסְפִּיקִין בְּיָדוֹ לִלְמוֹד וּלְלַמֵּד, לִשְׁמוֹר וְלַעֲשׂוֹת — *and one who studies in order to practice is given the means to study and to teach, to observe and to practice*

One who *studies* Torah in order to *teach* is given only the means to *study* and to *teach*, but he is not given special Divine assistance to

---

1. i.e., the system of Torah principles.

2. Author's metaphor.

3. *Supra*, commentary to 3:18, "the conceptual acts upon the corporeal. We know from experience that envisioning a result can make it happen. For example, if a person apprehensively crosses a stream over a narrow board, the thought of falling can cause him to actually fall. All the more so can Torah, which embodies God's expectations, act upon creation."

[ז] רַבִּי צָדוֹק אוֹמֵר: אַל תִּפְרוֹשׁ מִן
הַצִּבּוּר; וְאַל תַּעַשׂ עַצְמְךָ כְּעוֹרְכֵי
הַדַּיָּנִין; וְאַל תַּעֲשֶׂהָ עֲטָרָה לְהִתְגַּדֵּל בָּהּ,
וְלֹא קַרְדֹּם לַחְפֹּר בָּהּ. וְכָךְ הָיָה הִלֵּל
אוֹמֵר: וְדָאִשְׁתַּמֵּשׁ בְּתָגָא חֲלָף. הָא לָמַדְתָּ

practice Torah. The reason is that intentions bring about their own fulfillment, and only a far-reaching intention brings about far-reaching results. The intention to *practice* Torah is so far-reaching that it encompasses learning in the depth and breadth needed to succeed in learning and teaching as well as doing.

In summary, Torah is so conceptual that it is far removed from this physical world. However, the world needs Torah for its existence[1] and therefore Heaven assists people in their efforts to bring Torah into the world.[2]

Mishnah 7

Maharal's text of this *mishnah* does not include "Do not separate yourself from the community" or "do not act as a lawyer." It begins with "Do not make the Torah a crown for self-glorification," as is the text in most editions of *mishnayos*. That version flows smoothly from the previous *mishnah,* which states that sincere Torah study brings about multiple benefits. In contrast, Rabbi Zadok now warns that one who exploits Torah study for personal benefit shortens his life.

§ וְעַל תַּעֲשֶׂה . . . וְלֹא קַרְדֹּם לַחְפֹּר בָּהּ — *do not make the Torah . . . nor a spade with which to dig*

A previous *mishnah*[3] stated: "If there is no Torah, there is no flour," meaning that Torah brings livelihood. One might then conclude that it is permissible, and in keeping with that *mishnah,* to earn money from Torah scholarship.

---

1. As explained *supra,* Chapter 1, *mishnayos* 1 and 2, that the world's existence flows from Torah.

2. Mankind is thus a partner in Creation, because he acts as a catalyst to bring existence into the world by linking it with Torah. That message is found in Chapter 1, *mishnayos* 1, 2 and 18; Chapter 5, *mishnayos* 1-18; and many other places in Maharal.

3. *Supra,* 3:21.

7. Rabbi Zadok says: Do not separate yourself from the community; [when serving as a judge) do not act as a lawyer; do not make the Torah a crown for self-glorification, nor a spade with which to dig. So too Hillel used to say: He who exploits the crown [of Torah for personal benefit] shall fade away. From this you derive

---

Such is not the case! Our income is determined by Divine decree and we use that income to buy "flour." The statement, "If there is no Torah, there is no flour," means that Torah study is a major factor to evoke a positive Divine decree for sustenance. It does not mean that we may profit directly from our Torah studies.

⊷§ וְאַל תַּעֲשֶׂה עֲטָרָה לְהִתְגַּדֶּל בָּה — *do not make the Torah a crown for self-glorification*

One might think that only something so crass as making money from Torah scholarship demeans the Torah, whereas gaining honor from Torah expands the honor given to Torah and might be permissible. The *mishnah* corrects such a view, and says: "Do not make the Torah a crown for self-glorification."

⊷§ וּדְאִשְׁתַּמֵּשׁ בְּתָגָא חֲלָף — *He who exploits the crown [of Torah for personal benefit] shall fade away.*

The king's crown symbolizes that the king is incomparably different from the rest of the nation; he is without peer. Similarly, the image of "the crown of Torah" conveys that Torah is incomparably different from this world. If a person, who is only a subject of the king, places the crown upon his own head, he will surely be put to death. Likewise, one who benefits from a sacred article brings about his own death.[1]

The philosophical basis for this is that Torah is Divine wisdom; it is conceptual with no physical[2] characteristics. Therefore, any attempt to merge our physical lives with Torah, which has no physical qualities, must result in undermining our physical existence.

One may well ask, then, if the union of Torah with physical life is

---

1. Through Divine agency.

2. For example, physical entities exist in time and occupy space.

ד/ז כָּל הַנֶּהֱנֶה מִדִּבְרֵי תוֹרָה נוֹטֵל חַיָּיו מִן
הָעוֹלָם.

destructive, how can Torah coexist with mankind? The answer is that
Torah is only *associated* with mankind. The two are connected like two
ropes that are knotted together, and not as if the strands of Torah are
interwoven with the strands of human life. Since Torah is not an integral
part of the substance of human life, the relationship between Torah and
human life is sustainable and positive.

By contrast, one who uses Torah for personal gain and enjoyment has
integrally merged material things with holiness. Of that relationship with
Torah, Hillel says: "He who exploits the crown [of Torah for personal
benefit] shall fade away."

◆§ חֲלָף — *shall fade away*

Although חֲלָף, *chalaf*, has been translated here as "shall fade away,"
the Hebrew connotes a swift action. Anything that is holy and intangible
is independent of time and can change in a single moment.

◆§ וּדְאִשְׁתַּמֵּשׁ בְּתָגָא — *He who exploits the crown [of Torah for personal benefit]*

Studying Torah for self-aggrandizement is still better than not
studying at all, for we have learned[1] "One who does not study Torah is
worthy of death." Furthermore, one who is initially motivated by
personal gain may eventually mature to study out of sincere, religious
motivation.

◆§ וּדְאִשְׁתַּמֵּשׁ בְּתָגָא — *He who exploits the crown [of Torah for personal benefit]*

"Exploiting" Torah includes: studying for personal honor; studying to
gain financial support; or receiving special benefit from one's reputation
as a Torah scholar.

It is permissible to accept a gift or financial support that has been
tendered to strengthen and honor Torah. But if the recipient studies in
order to obtain such gifts, he transgresses this *mishnah*.

1. *Supra,* 1:13.

The following incident illustrates the degree to which a Torah scholar should avoid using his reputation for personal gain,[1]

> It happened that Rabbi (Yehudah HaNasi) opened his storehouse in the years of famine. Rabbi Yonasan ben Amram came and said to him: "My master! Support me." He responded back: "Have you studied Scripture or *Mishnah*?"
>
> He said, "No." He said: "In that case, how can I justify supporting you?"
>
> He said: "Support me as a dog or a raven." He gave to him.

After some time, Rabbi Yehudah HaNasi said: "Woe to me, that I supported an ignoramus from my possessions." His students said to him: "Rabbi! Perhaps it was Rabbi Yonasan ben Amram, who does not wish to benefit from the honor of his Torah." Despite the urgency of receiving support during a famine, R' Yonasan ben Amram actually denied his Torah scholarship to ensure that it would not bring him preferential treatment.

◆§ כָּל הַנֶּהֱנָה מִדִּבְרֵי תוֹרָה — *whoever seeks personal benefit from the words of Torah*

A rabbi's stipend is not considered as benefiting from the words of Torah. It is compensation for not being able to pursue other avenues of employment, because he must constantly be available for teaching. Similarly, an endowment to permit a Torah scholar to marry one's daughter without interrupting his studies is only compensation for not working, so that he may study. For this same reason, remuneration is permissible for any appointment to community office.

The community is obligated to provide a respectable level of support for the rabbi, because he cannot go work elsewhere. On the other hand, rabbis should accept a minimum, so that people will not think negatively of Torah scholars receiving public support. The rabbi's salary should reflect the right balance of the community's respect for Torah and the rabbi's reluctance to accept community funds. Otherwise, the Torah's honor may be degraded.[2]

---

1. *Bava Basra* 8a.
2. Maharal, writing 400 years ago, concludes with the fascinating statement that this discussion has little application anymore, because there are so few true Torah scholars left.

[ח] רַבִּי יוֹסֵי אוֹמֵר: כָּל הַמְכַבֵּד אֶת הַתּוֹרָה גוּפוֹ מְכֻבָּד עַל הַבְּרִיּוֹת; וְכָל הַמְחַלֵּל אֶת הַתּוֹרָה גוּפוֹ מְחֻלָּל עַל הַבְּרִיּוֹת.

[ט] רַבִּי יִשְׁמָעֵאל בְּנוֹ אוֹמֵר: הַחוֹשֵׂךְ עַצְמוֹ מִן הַדִּין פּוֹרֵק מִמֶּנּוּ אֵיבָה, וְגָזֵל וּשְׁבוּעַת שָׁוְא;

Mishnah 8

The previous *mishnah* discusses one who disgraces the Torah by using it for personal aggrandizement. This *mishnah* expands that theme by explaining that one who disgraces the Torah will be disgraced and one who honors the Torah will be honored.

כָּל הַמְכַבֵּד אֶת הַתּוֹרָה — *Whoever honors the Torah*

Rashi explains that one can honor Torah by ensuring that a Torah scroll is placed only in a place which is holy, and not on a bench where people sit. It is also not respectful to place one Torah scroll on top of another Torah scroll.

How much more so does one honor the Torah by honoring those who study Torah, as the Rabbis said,[1]

> "How foolish are people who stand up [to honor] a Torah scroll, but do not stand up [in honor of] a great rabbi."

כָּל הַמְכַבֵּד אֶת הַתּוֹרָה גוּפוֹ מְכֻבָּד עַל הַבְּרִיּוֹת — *Whoever honors the Torah is himself honored by people*

Torah is the essence of honor itself. By giving honor to the Torah, one establishes an affiliation with Torah and shares in the honor it receives.

This explanation might imply that one who chases after honor will achieve his goal, because he truly wishes to establish a connection with honor. In truth, honor flees from someone who tries to chase after it, because the pursuit of *receiving* honor does not establish a connection with honor.

כָּל הַמְכַבֵּד אֶת הַתּוֹרָה — *Whoever honors the Torah*

It is interesting to note that *studying* Torah does not in itself result in being honored. Torah study establishes an association with a different

---

1. *Makkos* 22b.

8. Rabbi Yose says: Whoever honors the Torah is himself honored by people; and whoever disgraces the Torah is himself disgraced by people.

9. Rabbi Yishmael his son says: One who withdraws from judgment removes from himself hatred, robbery and [the responsibility for] an unnecessary oath;

---

aspect of Torah, not with the aspect of Torah as the essence of honor. Only the connection formed by *honoring* Torah associates a person with its honor.

Mishnah 9

This *mishnah* continues the discussion of those who disgrace the Torah and those who honor it.

∽§ הַחוֹשֵׂךְ עַצְמוֹ מִן הַדִּין — *One who withdraws from judgment*

There is always a considerable risk of error in rendering a decision of Torah law. One who acknowledges that Torah is too deep for him to grasp fully, and declines to render legal judgment, treats Torah with its due honor.

Torah is beyond the full grasp of even the greatest people ever to have lived. King David was expert in the law and spirit of Torah. He composed psalms of incomparable substance and inspiration. Yet even a man of such talent and accomplishment called himself a stranger within the dominion of Torah and said,[1]

> "I am a stranger in the land; do not hide Your commandments from me."

We are all strangers to the world of Torah. We, who inhabit an ephemeral world, are aliens to the eternal world of Torah. We visit that world through our studies, but can never feel at home.

Such respect for the depth of Torah is clearly missing in one who can not wait to render his decision and issue judgment.

∽§ הַחוֹשֵׂךְ עַצְמוֹ מִן הַדִּין פּוֹרֵק מִמֶּנּוּ אֵיבָה, וְגָזֵל וּשְׁבוּעַת שָׁוְא — *One who withdraws from judgment removes from himself hatred, robbery and [the responsibility for] an unnecessary oath*

The point of litigation is frequently to restore property to its rightful

---

1. *Tehillim* 119:19.

ד/י וְהַגַּס לִבּוֹ בְּהוֹרָאָה שׁוֹטֶה, רָשָׁע וְגַס רוּחַ.

[י] הוּא הָיָה אוֹמֵר: אַל תְּהִי דָן יְחִידִי,
שֶׁאֵין דָּן יְחִידִי אֶלָּא אֶחָד; וְאַל תֹּאמַר,

---

owner. An incorrect judgment places the goods in the wrong hands and
hence is equivalent to theft. In particular, if the court enforces the
erroneous judgment by force, that is outright **robbery.** The victim of
such an erroneous judgment will surely come to **hate** the judge. A judge
is not permitted to administer **an unnecessary oath.** If he does, and the
defendant swears falsely, then the judge shares in the guilt of that oath.

One may wish to fill the role of judge because justice is one of the
three pillars upon which the world stands, as the Rabbis said,[1]

> The world endures on three things — **justice, truth** and **peace.**

But he must be careful, in his pursuit of the pillar of justice, not to
demolish all three pillars!

Errors on the part of a judge can embroil him in "hatred, robbery and
[the responsibility for] an unnecessary oath" and thus jeopardize the
three pillars upon which the world stands:

- **hatred** is the opposite of *peace*
- **robbery** is the opposite of *justice*
- and an improper **oath** is the opposite of *truth.*

⊷§ הַחוֹשֵׂךְ עַצְמוֹ מִן הַדִּין — *One who withdraws from judgment*

Rashi explains that a judge should withdraw from judgment by
negotiating a settlement.

Maharal disagrees, and explains the *mishnah* as meaning that one
should not act as judge if a more competent judge is available. However,
if he is the most capable person, then he performs a *mitzvah* by judging
the case.

⊷§ וְהַגַּס לִבּוֹ בְּהוֹרָאָה — *while one who is too self-confident
in handing down legal decisions*

One who feels quite comfortable with issuing halachic decisions acts
as if he is fully familiar with Torah; as if it is something that is neither

---

1. *Supra*, Chapter 1, *mishnah* 18.

while one who is too self-confident in handing down legal decisions is a fool, wicked and arrogant of spirit.

10. He used to say: Do not act as judge alone, for none judges alone except One; and do not say,

---

deep nor complex. That attitude belittles the Torah, which in fact is so deep and subtle that no one can fully comprehend it.

וְהַגֵּס לִבּוֹ בְּהוֹרָאָה שׁוֹטֶה, רָשָׁע וְגַס רוּחַ — *while one who is too self-confident in handing down legal decisions is a fool, wicked and arrogant of spirit*

It is a sign of wisdom to take all the time necessary before issuing a pronouncement. Conversely, a person who hurries to issue judgment displays a definite sign of **foolishness.** He is also **wicked,** because he shows no concern for possibly making an error in his ruling. He is obviously **arrogant,** for why else would he enter into the effort and difficulty that judgment entails, if not to display by his swift decision how great he is and how clear Torah is to him?

Mishnah 10

This *mishnah* continues on the subject of not being overly self confident in handing down legal decisions. A judge who undertakes to hear cases alone is a further example of arrogance.

שֶׁאֵין דָּן יְחִידִי אֶלָּא אֶחָד — *none judges alone except One*

The Torah demands a fully impartial system of justice; judges and witnesses must be separate from the litigants. It is the demand of the judicial process for detachment and disinterest that disqualifies witnesses who are related to the litigants. Even though Moshe's testimony about his brother Aharon would be impeccably accurate and reliable, it must be disqualified because the process demands detachment.[1]

The minimum number of judges is three, for the following reason. The judicial process requires judges to be so detached from the litigants that there is no potential for a personal relationship. Because people are alike, there is an inherent tendency for people to join in groups of two[2]

---

1. This sentence is based on Maharal's *Netzach Yisrael,* Chapter 57.
2. *Koheles* 4:9: "Two are better than one."

ד/יא   ,,קַבְּלוּ דַעְתִּי,'' שֶׁהֵן רַשָּׁאִין, וְלֹא אָתָּה.

[יא] רַבִּי יוֹנָתָן אוֹמֵר: כָּל הַמְקַיֵּם אֶת

---

or three.[1] However, a group of three does not have a tendency to join with a fourth. Therefore, a body of three judges is sufficient to ensure their detachment from the litigants.[2]

שֶׁאֵין דָּן יְחִידִי אֶלָּא אֶחָד — *none judges alone except One* ◆§

The *mishnah* uncharacteristically refers to God as "One," to draw our attention to the point of judicial detachment just discussed. He can judge alone and still maintain the demands of judicial process, because in His Oneness He is certainly distinct and separate from people.

An expert judge, authorized by the Supreme Court, is technically permitted to hear cases alone.[3] Even so, it is a pious practice to follow the advice of this *mishnah* and not to judge alone, as the Rabbis said,[4]

"One who wishes to be pious should fulfill the words of *Avos.*"

וְאַל תֹּאמַר, ,,קַבְּלוּ דַעְתִּי,'' שֶׁהֵן רַשָּׁאִין, וְלֹא אָתָּה — *and do not say,* "Accept my view," for they are permitted to, but not you ◆§

"They are permitted to," refers to the litigants. They are permitted to accept the judges' reasoning and they are permitted to reject it, as long as they comply with the judgment. On his part, the judge does not have the right to insist that they accept his reasoning, only the decision.

If a litigant feels that the decision favors one party, the judge cannot demand **"Accept my view"** but should explain the sources and logic on which the judgment is based.

וְעַל תֹּאמַר, ,,קַבְּלוּ דַעְתִּי,'' שֶׁהֵן רַשָּׁאִין, וְלֹא אָתָּה — *and do not say,* "Accept my view," for they are permitted to, but not you ◆§

Another approach is to apply this statement in a general context, in any situation where people do not want to accept one's advice. To try to

---

1. *Koheles* verse 12: "and a three-ply cord is not easily severed."
2. For example, a body of three judges will not be prone to favoring one of the litigants.
3. *Sanhedrin* 5a.
4. *Bava Kamma* 30a.

11   "Accept my view," for they are permitted to, but
          not you.

          11. Rabbi Yonasan says: Whoever fulfills the

---

force one's opinion on others is not acceptable from either a social or a
religious point of view.[1]

Mishnah 11

The words in brackets have been added to the standard translation of
the *mishnah* to bring it into conformance with Maharal's interpretation
and commentary.

Our *mishnah* means: "One who substantiates the primacy of Torah
through the self-sacrifices that come with poverty will eventually
substantiate the primacy of Torah through the self-sacrifices that come
with wealth."

Maharal understands the terms of the *mishnah* as follows:

- "Whoever **fulfills** מְקַיֵּם (*mekayaim*) **the [study of] Torah. . .**" means
  that he demonstrates and substantiates the primacy of Torah, by
  studying Torah from the midst of oppressive conditions.

- "**despite** poverty" means that poverty itself is responsible for
  demonstrating the primacy of Torah. One who actively places
  Torah foremost in his life, through the continual self-sacrifices
  imposed by poverty, establishes that Torah is the primary focus in
  his life.

- "will ultimately fulfill it in **wealth**" means a moderate degree of
  wealth, adequate to provide for his needs. His business affairs make
  demands on his time, yet his portfolio of assets is not so large that it
  demands his full attention.

- "**will ultimately fulfill it in** wealth" means that his wealth is responsible for fulfilling Torah study. Like the poor person, the
  wealthy man also establishes the primacy of Torah through self-
  sacrifice. His steadfast devotion to Torah study, as he withstands
  the distractions of managing his wealth, gives special meaning to
  his studies. Torah study as a leisurely pastime, made possible by
  not having to go to work, does not substantiate the primacy of
  Torah.

---

1. Although in this interpretation the statement is not addressed to judges, it is
presented in the same *mishnah* as "Do not act as judge alone" because the point of
the *mishnah* is that we should not force our personal view on others.

237 / MAHARAL: PIRKEI AVOS

ד/יא   הַתּוֹרָה מֵעֹנִי סוֹפוֹ לְקַיְּמָהּ מֵעֹשֶׁר; וְכָל הַמְבַטֵּל
אֶת הַתּוֹרָה מֵעֹשֶׁר סוֹפוֹ לְבַטְּלָהּ מֵעֹנִי.

───

⤙ **כָּל הַמְקַיֵּם אֶת הַתּוֹרָה מֵעֹנִי סוֹפוֹ לְקַיְּמָהּ מֵעֹשֶׁר** — *Whoever fulfills the [study of] Torah despite poverty will ultimately fulfill it in wealth*

The principle behind this *mishnah* is that there is a normal order of things that prevails over time. There can be short-term deviations from that system, but nature tends to restore things to run within the norm.

The normal order of things is that wealth enables a person to study more Torah, because he does not have to spend too much time earning a living. The opposite is also normal: Poverty interferes with a person's Torah studies.

A poor person, who nonetheless finds the time to pursue Torah study, runs counter to the norm, and in the long run, nature must prevail. Since he will not compromise his Torah studies, then he will eventually be enabled to study Torah with an adequate income, as is normal.

───

⤙ **וְכָל הַמְבַטֵּל אֶת הַתּוֹרָה מֵעֹשֶׁר** — *but whoever neglects the [study of] Torah because of wealth*

The *mishnah* wishes to emphasize that his wealth has *caused* him to neglect his Torah study. It is quite normal for people to be wealthy and not study Torah. However, it is not normal for a comfortable degree of wealth to be the *cause* of neglecting Torah.

Torah and wealth belong together. They go hand in hand, as Scripture says of Torah,[1] "in her left hand are riches and honor." It violates the natural order of things when wealth, which is a companion of Torah, becomes the very cause of neglecting Torah.

───

⤙ **סוֹפוֹ לְבַטְּלָהּ מֵעֹנִי** — *will ultimately neglect it in poverty*

If one neglects Torah study *because of* wealth, the natural order will eventually be restored and the normal reason for neglecting Torah will prevail; namely, he will neglect Torah because of poverty.

───

1. *Mishlei* 3:16.

4/ 11 [study of] Torah despite poverty will ultimately fulfill it in wealth; but whoever neglects the [study of] Torah because of wealth will ultimately neglect it in poverty.

---

§⊷ **כָּל הַמְקַיֵּם אֶת הַתּוֹרָה מֵעֹנִי סוֹפוֹ לְקַיְּמָהּ מֵעשֶׁר** — *Whoever fulfills the [study of] Torah despite poverty will ultimately fulfill it in wealth*

This statement is just one of many factors that determine whether or not one will be wealthy. There have been many people, such as Rabbi Chanina ben Dosa, who dedicated themselves to Torah study out of abject poverty, and who never became wealthy. Sometimes, wealth is more of a curse than a blessing, and sometimes poverty may be more of a blessing than a curse.

Those who are entirely righteous as well as great Torah scholars can fall under a different rule than the one expressed in our *mishnah.* The *midrash,* commenting on the verse,[1] "Length of days is in her right hand; in her left hand are riches and honor," says,[2]

> The Torah said to God: It is written: "in her left hand are riches and honor." Why are my children poor?
>
> God replied [with the verse]:[3] "That I may cause those who love me to inherit substance, יֵשׁ, *yeish* [in the Next World]." Why are they poor in this world? In order that they not occupy themselves with other things and come to forget the words of Torah.

The need to manage wealth in any degree presents distractions. Those who are completely righteous are better off without those distractions.

Poverty in this life can contribute to an exceptionally substantial existence in the eternal life. God creates *ex nihilo,* יֵשׁ מֵאַיִן (*yeish mei'ayin*). Exceptional spiritual substance יֵשׁ, *yeish,* in the next world can be created out of material absence אַיִן, *ayin,* in this world.

Another reason that one who studies Torah out of poverty might never be wealthy is that some people are simply destined to be poor.

Each person faces a set of challenges that are intended to refine his personality.[4] If a person has been placed on earth to be honed to

---

1. *Mishlei* 3:16.
2. *Yalkut Mishlei,* number 934.
3. *Mishlei* 8:21.
4. Author's explanation of why certain things are predestined.

ד/יב **[יב]** רַבִּי מֵאִיר אוֹמֵר: הֱוֵי מְמַעֵט בְּעֵסֶק וַעֲסֹק בַּתּוֹרָה. וֶהֱוֵי שְׁפַל רוּחַ בִּפְנֵי כָל אָדָם. וְאִם בָּטַלְתָּ מִן הַתּוֹרָה, יֶשׁ לְךָ בְּטֵלִים הַרְבֵּה כְּנֶגְדֶּךָ;

perfection by the grindstone of poverty, he will remain poor even if he dedicates himself to Torah study. Our *mishnah,* which says he will become wealthy, refers only to people whose destiny has a normal latitude for wealth or poverty.

Mishnah 12

This *mishnah* follows naturally from the previous one. It discusses how one who turns away from the demands of business to pursue Torah study substantiates the primacy of Torah.

●§ הֱוֵי מְמַעֵט בְּעֵסֶק וַעֲסֹק בַּתּוֹרָה — *Reduce your business activities and engage in Torah study.*

The point of this *mishnah* is missed if one merely avoids work due to laziness or disinterest. The *mishnah* means that even one who loves his work should reduce his business activities in order to study Torah. In that way he demonstrates that Torah comes ahead of material needs, when Torah and business compete for his time and energy.

A human being has both physical and spiritual aspects. One who directs his efforts away from the material side of life and towards Torah elevates himself to the spiritual plane of life. The Rabbis said,[1]

> Reish Lakish said: How do we know that the words of Torah endure only in one who kills himself for it? Because it says,[2] "This is the Torah: When a man dies in a tent . . ."

"Tent" is understood as an image for the *bais hamidrash;* the house of study. The expression "kills himself" means that he removes his involvement with the material side of life, so that he may elevate himself to the spiritual, intellectual plane of Torah.

●§ וֶהֱוֵי שְׁפַל רוּחַ — *Be humble of spirit*

This phrase appears to be unrelated to the statements about Torah study that surround it. Humility is mentioned at this point because it also

---

1. *Berachos* 63b.
2. *Bamidbar* 19:14.

12. Rabbi Meir says: Reduce your business activities and engage in Torah study. Be humble of spirit before every person. If you neglect the [study of] Torah, you will have many causes of neglect;

---

elevates one to the spiritual and intellectual plane on which Torah resides, as we will now explain.[1]

An arrogant person assesses himself as being great, and by evaluating his greatness he places a limit on himself. Being limited is a physical attribute that does not apply to a conceptual and spiritual entity such as Torah. As a result, the arrogant person has a quality that is incompatible with Torah. Therefore the Rabbis said,[2]

Why are the words of Torah compared to water, in the verse[3] "Everyone that thirsts, come to water"? To tell you that just as water leaves a high place and goes to a low place, so too the words of Torah remain only in one whose character is humble.

Water spreads out in all directions, for it has no inherent constraints or limits. It is unlike a solid object that extends only as far as its size and no farther. Water flows away from heights because a high place is constrained to occupy only its own spot, whereas water spreads without limit until it is in a low place that also extends without limit. So too does Torah, which is conceptual and unbounded, leave an arrogant person who has placed a boundary on himself by evaluating his own greatness. It flows to a low place; namely, to humble people, of simple spirit, who do not limit themselves but consider themselves as nothing. "Nothing" has no bounds.

Moshe Rabbeinu deserved his unparalleled Torah achievements only because he had more humility than anyone on the face of the earth.

וְאִם בָּטַלְתָּ מִן הַתּוֹרָה — *If you neglect the [study of] Torah*

Maharal's commentary indicates the translation:

וְאִם בָּטַלְתָּ מִן הַתּוֹרָה, יֶשׁ לָךְ בְּטֵלִים הַרְבֵּה כְּנֶגְדֶּךְ — *If you are diverted from the [study of] Torah, there are many things that will divert you [further from goodness]*

We are created incomplete, and that which is incomplete tends to

---

1. This explanation is from Maharal's *Nesiv HaTorah,* Chapter 2.
2. *Taanis* 7a.
3. *Yeshayahu* 55:1.

וְאִם עָמַלְתָּ בַּתּוֹרָה, יֶשׁ לוֹ שָׂכָר הַרְבֵּה לִתֶּן לָךְ.

[יג] רַבִּי אֱלִיעֶזֶר בֶּן יַעֲקֹב אוֹמֵר: הָעוֹשֶׂה מִצְוָה אַחַת קוֹנֶה לוֹ פְּרַקְלִיט אֶחָד,

deteriorate further.[1] Only through Torah can we be complete. Without Torah, a person moves ever further away from goodness and well-being and becomes more susceptible to being a victim of thieves, war, or natural dangers.

ומ — וְאִם עָמַלְתָּ בַּתּוֹרָה, יֶשׁ לוֹ שָׂכָר הַרְבֵּה לִתֶּן לָךְ — *but if you labor in the Torah, God has ample reward to give you*

Even a small accomplishment in Torah study constitutes enormous progress, because Torah study is all encompassing. It touches upon every important element of life, and each point of Torah is a general principle that applies to countless specific situations.

Mishnah 13

Mishnah 12 taught that Torah study is a broad engagement with far-reaching results, in contrast to the very specific effects of doing a *mitzvah,* as this *mishnah* now describes. The Rabbis highlighted this difference when they said,[2]

> These are the precepts whose fruits a person enjoys in this world, but whose principal remains intact for him in the World to Come: honoring of father and mother, acts of kindness, early attendance at the house of study morning and evening, hospitality to guests, visiting the sick, providing for a bride, escorting the dead, absorption in prayer, bringing peace between man and his fellow, and **the study of Torah is equivalent to them all.**

Nine things are enumerated and Torah study brings the total to ten, a number that represents the fusion of separate parts into a complete entity.[3] The Rabbis are telling us that one who does a single *mitzvah*

---

1. For example, a piece of paper with a small tear will rip easily; a fruit which has been pierced will spoil quickly.

2. *Peah,* Chapter 1, *mishnah* 1.

3. See *supra,* Chapter 2, *mishnah* 8. Ten is a complete unit, embracing and consolidating all of the constituent parts into a single entity. The tenth embodies the essence of the entire group; it is the sum of the parts. For example, ten men constitute a quorum for prayer. The tenth is the prayer leader, through whom the other nine individuals coalesce into a group.

but if you labor in the Torah, God has ample reward to give you.

13. Rabbi Eliezer ben Yaakov says: He who fulfills even a single mitzvah gains himself a single advocate,

---

receives reward for doing but one thing; while the reward for Torah study reflects its broadly encompassing consequences. If doing a *mitzvah* is like giving an apple to a hungry person, then studying Torah is like planting an apple tree.[1]

‎אָחָד פְּרַקְלִיט לוֹ קוֹנֶה אַחַת מִצְוָה הָעוֹשֶׂה‎ — *He who fulfills even a single mitzvah gains himself a single advocate*

An "advocate" may be thought of as a lobbyist at the king's court. The image of an advocate emphasizes the difference between the effects of Torah study and the effects of performing a *mitzvah*. The "advocate" can put in a good word for a person, but his effectiveness can be canceled by a negative report from someone else. So it is with a *mitzvah*. While a *mitzvah* improves one's relationship with God, that can be nullified by the accusations attested to by a sin. In contrast, the labor of Torah study so effectively establishes a relationship with God that it is not described as producing an advocate, or even many advocates. The relationship between the study of Torah and its reward cannot be described by mere numbers.

The Rabbis[2] see this message conveyed in the verse,[3]

"For a lamp is the commandment and Torah is light."

Scripture associates a *mitzvah* with a lamp and Torah with light. Just as a lamp can be extinguished, the glow of a *mitzvah* can be "extinguished" by a transgression. However, as light itself cannot be extinguished, Torah is not extinguished by a transgression.

Therefore, when the previous *mishnah* describes the reward that comes "if you labor in the Torah," it does not make reference to an "advocate," but says rather, "God has ample reward to give you."

---

1. Author's analogy.
2. This paragraph is Maharal's summary and explanation of a passage from *Sotah* 21a.
3. *Mishlei* 6:23.

ד/יג וְהָעוֹבֵר עֲבֵרָה אַחַת קוֹנֶה לוֹ קַטֵּיגוֹר אֶחָד. תְּשׁוּבָה וּמַעֲשִׂים טוֹבִים כִּתְרִיס בִּפְנֵי הַפֻּרְעָנוּת.

⧫§ הָעוֹשֶׂה מִצְוָה אַחַת קוֹנֶה לוֹ פְּרַקְלִיט אֶחָד — *He who fulfills even a single mitzvah gains himself a single advocate*

An advocate enters into the king's chambers to give a good reference for a person, while the person himself remains outside. So too, the goodness of the *mitzvah* presents itself directly to God, while it could not be expected that a human being would enter directly into God's close Presence.

⧫§ וְהָעוֹבֵר עֲבֵרָה אַחַת קוֹנֶה לוֹ קַטֵּיגוֹר אֶחָד — *and he who commits even a single transgression gains himself a single accuser*

An "accuser" operates in a different manner than an "advocate." The accuser does not enter into the king's inner chamber, as a *confidant* may. So too, evil never comes close to God's Presence, but accuses the transgressor from a distance.

⧫§ כִּתְרִיס בִּפְנֵי הַפֻּרְעָנוּת — *are like a shield against retribution*

A primary characteristic of physical entities is that they are susceptible to change. As a result, they are affected by external forces and are subject to deterioration. So it is that a person who lives on a very physical plane is exposed to forces of destruction.

⧫§ תְּשׁוּבָה — *Repentance*

A person has a body and a soul and consequently we inhabit both physical and spiritual realms. The fact is, the less spiritual one is, the more he lives within the realm of physical characteristics.[1]

Transgression stems primarily from the physical level of human existence.[2] Therefore, while a person is preoccupied with the physical aspects of life, he inhabits the realm where he is most likely to be affected by both sin and adversity.

---

1. See "Author's Introduction," section on "Maharal's Philosophy," subheading "Form and Substance."

2. If not for the physical aspect, we would be like angels, without transgression.

and he who commits even a single transgression gains himself a single accuser. Repentance and good deeds are like a shield against retribution.

In contrast, spiritual entities are stable and impervious to external influence. Since repentance is the removal of transgression, it moves us from the physical plane of life towards the spiritual plane, where the winds of catastrophe can blow past without effect.

ּ וּמַעֲשִׂים טוֹבִים — and good deeds

Good deeds are Godly; they are so spiritual that they do not have any of the characteristics of our physical nature.

ּ כִּתְרִיס בִּפְנֵי הַפֻּרְעָנוּת — are like a shield against retribution

---

Both repentance and good deeds propel a person to a spiritual level that does not react to physical adversity. The image of a **shield** conveys the ability to withstand destructive forces without yielding.

ּ כִּתְרִיס — are like a shield

A shield is an external protection, held at some distance from the person himself. It is an apt image for repentance and good deeds, which link a person with a level of spirituality that is beyond the human being himself.

A shield does not prevent the blows from falling, but merely deflects them. Likewise, repentance and good deeds do not prevent the blows of adversity from coming, but rather deflect their destructive power, leaving us unscathed.

It goes without saying that Torah study also shields against adversity, and at least as effectively as repentance and good deeds.

ּ תְּשׁוּבָה וּמַעֲשִׂים טוֹבִים כִּתְרִיס בִּפְנֵי הַפֻּרְעָנוּת — Repentance and good deeds are like a shield against retribution.

This statement would appear to be contradicted by the Rabbinical dictum,[1]

If one transgressed a Biblical prohibition and repented, [the

---

1. *Yoma* 86a.

[יד] רַבִּי יוֹחָנָן הַסַּנְדְּלָר אוֹמֵר: כָּל כְּנֵסִיָּה
שֶׁהִיא לְשֵׁם שָׁמַיִם סוֹפָהּ לְהִתְקַיֵּם,
וְשֶׁאֵינָהּ לְשֵׁם שָׁמַיִם אֵין סוֹפָהּ לְהִתְקַיֵּם.

effect of] repentance is not complete until after afflictions cleanse [the transgression].

If so, repentance is not a shield, for afflictions will still come upon him!

That case is different, for it discusses afflictions that come as a direct result of one's own sins. Repentance and good deeds do not protect against punishments that come to directly cleanse a person's sins. A transgression is like having a wound in one's flesh. A shield does not protect against a wound; it protects only against an external force. Repentance and good deeds protect one from the harsh blows that are a normal part of life. They are effective even against punishments that come because one's sins in general have left him exposed to misfortune. For these, repentance and good deeds act as a shield by placing one on the spiritual plane of life, while afflictions occur on the physical plane.

Mishnah 14

An assembly of Israel acting for the sake of Heaven will endure, because God is with it and maintains it. This thought is conveyed by the Rabbis,[1]

> When Israel agrees on a single plan down on earth, God's great Name is praised on high, as it says,[2] "And He was King in Yeshurun." When was that? "when the heads of the nation were gathered together."

The king rules over the community overall. When God succeeds in uniting Israel, and they agree on a single plan, His Name is praised for He is the King Who rules over all the nation together. The passage cited continues,

> Rabbi Shimon ben Yochai says: The allegory is that of a man who brought two boats and tied them to anchors and metal bars and steadied them and built a palace upon them. As long as the boats are tied, the palace stands; if the boats are not tied, the palace will not stand.

---

1. *Sifrei* to *Devarim* 33:5.
2. *Devarim* 33:5.

14. Rabbi Yochanan the Sandler says: Every assembly that is dedicated to the sake of Heaven will endure to the end, but one that is not for the sake of Heaven will not endure to the end.

So it is with Israel. When they are bound together, the kingdom of God is upon them and the royal palace endures. If parts of Israel separate from each other then His kingdom does not endure, so to speak, because He does not have a nation over which He can reign.

This fact is alluded to by the very name Israel, יִשְׂרָאֵל. The Name of God, אֵ־ל, is part of Israel, to demonstrate that whenever they are a unified assembly, God is with them.

§ כָּל כְּנֵסִיָּה שֶׁהִיא לְשֵׁם שָׁמַיִם סוֹפָה לְהִתְקַיֵּם — *Every assembly that is dedicated to the sake of Heaven will endure to the end*

It is appropriate that every assembly dedicated to Him should itself be supported by Him.

§ וְשֶׁאֵינָה לְשֵׁם שָׁמַיִם אֵין סוֹפָה לְהִתְקַיֵּם — *but one that is not for the sake of Heaven will not endure to the end*

The assembly will not endure because dissension and separation will come between them. People are separate individuals, and an assembly is quite unsuitable for them. Individuals can form a lasting, united assembly only if God unites and binds the community,[1] in His role as King. If the assembly is not directed for the sake of Heaven, then they do not have the unifying effect of His Presence, and they lapse into natural human divisiveness.

Therefore it was most apt that the *mishnah* chose the word כְּנֵסִיָּה, *keneisiyah,* to express "assembly," because the final two letters are a Name of God.

Mishnah 15

The previous *mishnah* discussed a cohesive assembly of unified individuals, while this *mishnah* looks at the relationships that unify individuals such as students, friends and teachers.

---

1. See *supra,* Chapter 3 *mishnah* 2. Effective, stable government likewise provides the role of king in unifying individuals into a nation.

[טו] רַבִּי אֶלְעָזָר בֶּן שַׁמּוּעַ אוֹמֵר: יְהִי כְבוֹד תַּלְמִידְךָ חָבִיב עָלֶיךָ כְּשֶׁלָּךְ; וּכְבוֹד חֲבֵרְךָ כְּמוֹרָא רַבָּךְ; וּמוֹרָא רַבָּךְ כְּמוֹרָא שָׁמָיִם.

[טז] רַבִּי יְהוּדָה אוֹמֵר: הֱוֵי זָהִיר בְּתַלְמוּד, שֶׁשִּׁגְגַת תַּלְמוּד עוֹלָה זָדוֹן.

וּכְבוֹד חֲבֵרְךָ כְּמוֹרָא רַבָּךְ — *the honor of your colleague as the reverence for your teacher*

How can the *mishnah* suggest that the **honor** due to a friend should be the same as the **reverence** due to one's *Rav* (Torah teacher)? These concepts are so completely different that they cannot be compared!

The *mishnah* means that a person must be as careful with his friend's honor as he is careful with his respect for his *Rav*. He would never degrade the reverence due to his teacher. His friend's honor must be equally precious to him: He must never do anything that would undermine or degrade his friend's honor.

וּמוֹרָא רַבָּךְ כְּמוֹרָא שָׁמָיִם — *and the reverence for your teacher as the reverence of Heaven*

The **teacher** of Torah referred to, for whom one must have reverence comparable to that of Heaven, is only a Rav from whom one has learned most of his Talmudic studies, as will be defined in the next *mishnah*.

Mishnah 16

Talmud is the explanation of the principles and rules governing the cases presented in the Oral Law, which is called *Mishnah*.

שֶׁשִּׁגְגַת תַּלְמוּד — *for a careless misinterpretation in Talmud*

If one is not careful with his Talmudic studies, and makes an erroneous assumption about the principle behind the *Mishnah,* he will derive from it an incorrect ruling.

עוֹלָה זָדוֹן — *is considered tantamount to willful transgression*

Why should an error in Talmud be considered as deliberate? And why

15. Rabbi Elazar ben Shamua says: Let the honor of your student be as dear to you as your own; the honor of your colleague as the reverence for your teacher; and the reverence for your teacher as the reverence of Heaven.

16. Rabbi Yehudah says: Be meticulous in Talmud, for a careless misinterpretation in Talmud is considered tantamount to willful transgression.

---

does Rabbi Yehudah require such care for Talmud only, and not for the *Mishnah* itself?

This may be understood through an allegory of one who walks in the dark. As he goes along, he accidentally kicks things and breaks them. This breakage is completely accidental, because it was dark. Suppose, however, that he has a lamp in his hand and nonetheless he continues to break things as he walks because he does not bother to look where he's going. In that case, the breakage would certainly be considered deliberate.

The Talmud is pure reason: It is the light by which we see the rest of Torah. Studying Scripture and *Mishnah* without the light of Talmud is like walking in the dark, and errors truly are accidental. When the light of Talmud is available but not carefully used, errors must be treated as dereliction, not as an accident.

Rabbi Yehudah's words are directed at Torah scholars, as the Rabbis said,[1]

Rabbi Yehudah bar Ilai[2] expounded: What is this that is written:[3] "and tell My people their willful transgression and the house of Yaakov their accidental sins"?

"My people" refers to Torah scholars. "Their willful transgression" means that all of their sins are considered willful transgressions, even if done accidentally.

"The house of Yaakov" refers to ordinary people. "Their accidental sins" means that all of their sins are considered accidental, even if they are due to deliberate negligence.

The point of this passage is clear from the allegory of the person

---

1. *Bava Metzia,* 33b.
2. This is the very Rabbi Yehudah who is the author of our *mishnah.*
3. *Yeshayahu* 58:1.

ד/יז

[יז] רַבִּי שִׁמְעוֹן אוֹמֵר: שְׁלשָׁה כְתָרִים הֵם —
כֶּתֶר תּוֹרָה, וְכֶתֶר כְּהֻנָּה, וְכֶתֶר מַלְכוּת;

walking in the dark. A Torah scholar has the lamp of reason to guide his steps, while the simple person remains in the dark. For him, even negligence is treated the same as an accident, as it is written:[1] "The sage's eyes are in his head, but the fool walks in darkness."

What links the previous *mishnah* and this one? The previous *mishnah* said that the reverence for one's Torah teacher should be like the reverence for Heaven. However, such reverence is due only to the teacher from whom he learned the majority of his Talmud,[2] and this *mishnah* demonstrates why the study of Talmud is of paramount importance.

Mishnah 17

Life flows from God at all levels: personal, national and global. The world is firmly rooted in His existence, and sustenance and blessing flow from Heaven to earth through agencies embodied by **Torah, priesthood** and **kingship.**

As the king's crown symbolizes monarchy, so the metaphor of the three crowns conveys the highest point of the institutions they represent.[3]

§⨼ שְׁלשָׁה כְתָרִים הֵם — כֶּתֶר תּוֹרָה, וְכֶתֶר כְּהֻנָּה, וְכֶתֶר מַלְכוּת —
There are three crowns — the crown of Torah, the crown of priesthood and the crown of kingship

These three crowns represent the three pillars of national and individual existence.[4]

At the national level, the crowns belong to the three institutions of leadership: the rabbinical court[5] embodies Torah; the High Priest exem-

---

1. *Koheles* 2: 14.

2. Maharal bases this definition of "teacher" — as being the one from whom he learned most of his Talmud — on *Bava Metzia* 33a:

"If one has to choose between restoring his father's lost article and his teacher's lost article, the teacher's article comes first. Rabbi Meir says: The 'teacher' referred to is the teacher who taught him wisdom, not the teacher who taught him Scripture or *Mishnah*. Rabbi Yehudah says: [and only if] the majority of his studies are from him."

The bracketed words represent Maharal's explanation of the passage. Rashi explains the passage in a somewhat different way.

3. Author's introductory comments, based on Maharal's writings.

4. A reference to Chapter 1, *mishnah* 2, *supra*: "The world depends on three things — on Torah study, on the service [of God] and on kind deeds." See commentary *ad loc.*

5. Author's amplification.

plifies the priesthood; and the king, of course, personifies the monarchy.

At the personal level, the crowns correspond to the three parts of the individual: the intellect, the spirit and the body.

- **Torah** corresponds to the **intellect,** *sechel.*
- As the **king** is the driving force behind the nation, so the **spirit,** *nefesh,* is the driving force that animates a person.
- **Priesthood** corresponds to the physical **body.** The sanctity of priesthood is inseparable from the physical body, for priesthood derives solely from parentage. The sanctity of the priest is in his very flesh and bones, and physical deformity can disqualify him from serving the priestly function.

These elements have an order of priority. Intellect, *sechel,* is the highest level, followed by the spirit, *nefesh,* and then the body. National roles follow the same hierarchy: The Torah scholar is the most indispensable of national assets, followed by the king and then the High Priest, as the Rabbis say,[1]

> [If a Torah scholar, the king and the High Priest are in captivity and not all can be saved, then] a Torah scholar takes precedence over a king of Israel, for if a Torah scholar dies there is none like him, whereas if a king dies, all Israel are eligible for kingship. A king takes precedence over a High Priest.

This analysis sheds light on the law that a priest should not be selected as king. The priest, at the national level, corresponds to the body at the individual level. The king corresponds to the spirit. The spirit and the body are as mutually exclusive, *nivdal,* as are form and substance; the two coexist but they can never coalesce. So it is inappropriate for the role of priest and the role of king to be fulfilled by one individual.

Intellect, *sechel,* is not an integral part of the human being, but just closely associated with a person.[2] Hence, Torah scholarship

---

1. *Horayos* 13a.

2. *Supra,* commentary to 4:1: "What part of us is the essence and what part of us is acquired? Our essence is but body and soul, whereas possessions and even knowledge are acquired. Although a baby comes into this world with only body and soul, he is fully a human being. . . The possessions and knowledge that the child will eventually acquire are important, but they do not constitute his essence. Misfortune may claim his assets and senility may rob him of his knowledge; but he remains a human being to the last breath."

does not nullify the roles of the priest or the king, but enhances them.

In summary, the crown of priesthood belongs with the descendants of Aharon, and the crown of kingship belongs with the descendants of David. The crown of Torah, however, is available for all who wish to claim it.

⊷§ שְׁלֹשָׁה כְתָרִים הֵם — *There are three crowns* —

This discussion leads to a reason that the *mishnah* counts three crowns but lists four. The three crowns correspond to the three parts of a person. The crown of a good name corresponds to the essence of a person, which comprises all parts together. The crown of a good name, being the sum of the parts, is not counted as a separate crown, distinct from the three component parts. The three tangible crowns and the one abstract crown cannot be added together, any more than one would enumerate four parts of a tree: fruit, leaves, branches, and the tree as a concept!

⊷§ שְׁלֹשָׁה כְתָרִים . . . תּוֹרָה . . . כְּהֻנָּה . . . מַלְכוּת; וְכֶתֶר שֵׁם טוֹב עוֹלֶה עַל גַּבֵּיהֶן — *There are three crowns* — . . . *Torah,* . . . *priesthood and* . . . *kingship; but the crown of a good name surpasses them all.*

In the Sanctum, *Heichal,* of the Temple were three sacred articles, each adorned by a "crown" of gold work surrounding the upper border. These three crowns symbolize the three crowns enumerated in our *mishnah.* [1]

The crown upon the Ark containing the Ten Commandments corresponds to the crown of **Torah.** The crown upon the incense Altar corresponds to the crown of the **priesthood,** for serving at the Altar is a priestly privilege. The crown upon the Table, which carries the show-bread, corresponds to the crown of **kingship,** because it is the role and responsibility of the king to ensure the sustenance of the nation.

What sacred article represents the crown of a **good reputation?** One answer given is that it is the *Menorah,* the seven-lamp candelabrum of the Sanctum. A good reputation is earned by one whose life shines with the light of an exemplary fulfillment of *mitzvos.* The *Menorah* represents this crown within the Scriptural metaphor,[2] "For

---

1. *Yoma* 72b.
2. *Mishlei* 6:23.

a lamp is the commandment and Torah is light."

Just as the crown of a good reputation rises above the other three crowns, so the *Menorah* literally towered over the other three crowned vessels.[1] However the *Menorah* did not, in fact, have a crown encircling the top of the lamps. One reason is that the crown must be at the highest point of the object, just as a king's crown rests on top of his head. In the case of the *Menorah,* the flames rise above the lamps, and therefore a crown could not have been at the highest point of the *Menorah.*

⏤§ וְכֶתֶר שֵׁם טוֹב עוֹלֶה עַל גַּבֵּיהֶן §⏤ — *but the crown of a good name surpasses them all*

A second reason that the *Menorah* did not have a crown is that the crown of a good name so surpasses the other crowns that it defies physical representation.

⏤§ וְכֶתֶר שֵׁם טוֹב עוֹלֶה עַל גַּבֵּיהֶן §⏤ — *but the crown of a good name surpasses them all*

The crown of a good reputation is fundamentally different from the other three crowns. While the first three crowns reside respectively with the Torah scholar, the priest and the king, a good reputation resides not with the person who has earned it, but rather with the people who hold that good opinion. In fact, the person may not even be aware of the reputation he has earned.

The crown of a good name surpasses the other crowns, for priesthood, kingship and even Torah are contained within the nation, but a good reputation can span across the world.

We now understand more clearly why the *mishnah* counts three crowns, but lists four crowns in all. The three that it enumerates together have physical counterparts in the Temple and are recognizable in the person himself, by his Torah wisdom, his priestly duties or his royal authority. These three intrinsic crowns cannot be numerically added to the extrinsic crown of a good reputation, because they are so very different in nature.

---

1. The *Menorah* was almost six feet tall. The Table and Ark were half that height, and the Altar was less than four feet high.

ד/יח   **[יח]** רַבִּי נְהוֹרַאי אוֹמֵר: הֱוֵי גוֹלֶה לִמְקוֹם
תוֹרָה, וְאַל תֹּאמַר שֶׁהִיא תָבוֹא אַחֲרֶיךָ,
שֶׁחֲבֵרֶיךָ יְקַיְּמוּהָ בְּיָדֶךָ; וְאֶל בִּינָתְךָ אַל תִּשָּׁעֵן."

The Crown of Torah

Mishnah 16 extolled the importance of Talmud over the importance of *Mishnah* and Scripture. *Mishnah* 17 was placed after that statement because the "crown of Torah" refers primarily to the study of Talmud, rather than Scripture or *Mishnah*.

Mishnah 18

Rabbi Nehorai was not the author's name, but rather a title of admiration. Some say that his real name was Rabbi Elazar ben Arach and some say it was Rabbi Nechemiah. The name "Nehorai" is derived from the Aramaic word for light, and was deserved because he enlightened the eyes of the Rabbis in Torah law.[1]

According to the opinion that Rabbi Nehorai is actually Rabbi Nechemiah, this *mishnah* is placed in chronological order within the chapter. Rabbi Nechemiah was contemporary with Rabbi Shimon and Rabbi Yehudah, whose opinions are presented in the preceding *mishnayos*.

§ הֱוֵי גוֹלֶה לִמְקוֹם תּוֹרָה, וְאַל תֹּאמַר שֶׁהִיא תָבוֹא אַחֲרֶיךָ —
Exile yourself to a place of Torah,
and do not assume that it will come after you

The only way to acquire Torah is to pursue it. Torah knowledge, in its full depth, is elusive, for it transcends human qualities and abilities. It goes without saying that Torah will not come on its own.

§ וְאַל תֹּאמַר שֶׁהִיא תָבוֹא אַחֲרֶיךָ — *and do not*
assume that it will come after you

Some things in life may indeed come after you. Wealth, for instance, comes by Divine decree. Since God has decreed wealth for a person, it truly will pursue him, as events unfold in such a way that the decree can come to fruition. For example, he could simply find a valuable object and become wealthy without effort.

---

1. *Shabbos* 147b.

18. Rabbi Nehorai says: Exile yourself to a place of Torah, and do not assume that it will come after you, for it is your colleagues who will cause it to remain with you; "and do not rely on your own understanding" (*Mishlei 3:5*).

Torah is different. Torah can be acquired only through personal effort. As the Rabbis said,[1]

> If a person says, "I labored but I did not succeed" do not believe it. [If one says,] "I succeeded without labor" do not believe it. [If one says,] "I labored and I succeeded," believe it. These words apply to Torah, but business succeeds by Divine assistance.

שֶׁחֲבֵרֶיךָ יְקַיְּמוּהָ בְּיָדֶךְ ﬩ — *for it is your colleagues who will cause it to remain with you*

This expression explains why you should not say that **"it will come after you."** Do not think that you can study on your own and rely on your colleagues, who did study in a place of Torah, to clarify points of uncertainty for you.

Furthermore, we must go to the teacher in keeping with the principle that "it will not come after you." If we rely on our colleagues, who may indeed come to us, we will not have established the proper context for Torah study.

According to this explanation, it is not necessary to exile oneself to another city if there is a Torah teacher, *Rav*, in his own city. The point is that he must go to the *Rav* and not expect the *Rav* to come to him.

וְאֶל בִּינָתְךָ אַל תִּשָּׁעֵן ﬩ — *"and do not rely on your own understanding."*

Continuing along this line of explanation, this phrase means that Torah must be learned from a *Rav*. The wisdom of Torah is beyond anyone's ability to discover on the strength of his own unaided understanding.

A Second Approach

An alternative explanation of the *mishnah* is based on an incident related by the Rabbis,[2]

---

1. *Megillah* 6b.
2. *Shabbos* 147b.

Rabbi Chelbo said, [indulgence in the pleasures of] the wine of Perugisa, and the [bathing] water of Diomsis, cut off the Ten Tribes from Israel. Rabbi Elazar ben Arach visited there (Perugisa and Diomsis) and was drawn after them (i.e., the wine and bathing water). His Torah learning was uprooted from him. When he returned, he got up to read from the scroll of the Torah. He should have read,[1] "הַחֹדֶשׁ הַזֶּה לָכֶם, hachodesh hazeh lachem," "This month is for you [the beginning of months]." He said [instead], "הַחֶרֶשׁ הָיָה לִבָּם, hachoresh hayah libam,"[2] "Their heart[3] was clay." The Rabbis prayed for him and his Torah learning returned.

That is what we learned in the mishnah, "Rabbi Nehorai says: Exile yourself to a place of Torah, and do not assume that it will come after you, for it is your colleagues who will cause it to remain with you; and do not rely on your own understanding."

We learned: His name was not Rabbi Nehorai but Rabbi Nechemiah; and some say, his name was Rabbi Elazar ben Arach. Why then was he called Rabbi Nehorai? Because he enlightened the eyes of the Rabbis in Torah Law.

The wine and water were indulgences in worldly pleasures. One who lives in a place that is devoid of Torah will be drawn after such pleasures and his Torah will leave him, as happened even to the great Rabbi Elazar ben Arach. From this incident we see that the importance of going to a place of Torah is not just to learn from a Rabbi, but to live in an environment that is imbued with Torah. We may now explain our mishnah as follows.

---

§⊷ הֱוֵי גוֹלֶה לִמְקוֹם תּוֹרָה — *Exile yourself to a place of Torah*

Go to a place where the environment is infused with Torah and where you will not be drawn after worldly matters.

---

1. *Shemos* 12:2.
2. An error of the middle letter of each word.
3. See *supra,* commentary to Chapter 2, *mishnah* 10-14, chart titled "Five Disciples — Five Parts of Nefesh." Each of Rabban Yochanan's five outstanding disciples represented a different part of the soul, and Rabbi Elazar ben Arach represented the heart (noted in the commentary of Maharsha to *Shabbos* 147b).

Maharal *ibid.* points out that a primary characteristic of the heart is that it is in the center. Perhaps it was for this reason that Rabbi Elazar ben Arach erred in the middle letter of each word.

19. Rabbi Yannai says: It is not in our power [to explain] either the tranquillity of the wicked

וְאַל תֹּאמַר שֶׁהִיא תָבוֹא אַחֲרֶיךְ ﻌ — **and do not assume that it will come after you**

Torah will not follow one who indulges in life's pleasures.

וְאַל תֹּאמַר . . . שֶׁחֲבֵרֶיךְ יְקַיְּמוּהָ בְּיָדֶךְ ﻌ — **and do not assume . . . it is your colleagues who will cause it to remain with you**

Do not think that studying with your colleagues will protect you from forgetting your studies.

וְאֶל בִּינָתְךָ אַל תִּשָּׁעֵן ﻌ — **"and do not rely on your own understanding."**

One cannot rely on his own intellectual strength to keep him away from ephemeral physical pleasures. We are physical beings and hence we will be drawn after worldly matters unless we are in an environment that is saturated with Torah.

Mishnah 19

We cannot grasp the reason that there are wicked people who enjoy tranquillity and there are righteous people who suffer afflictions. This was one of the mysteries that Moshe Rabbeinu prayed to comprehend. According to Rabbi Meir[1] this request was denied, for God said,

"I will be gracious to whom I will be gracious and I will show mercy on whom I will show mercy."[2]

This means: "I will be gracious to whom I will be gracious. . ." — even if it is not deserved. "And I will show mercy on whom I will show mercy" — even if it is not deserved.

אֵין בְּיָדֵינוּ לֹא מִשַּׁלְוַת הָרְשָׁעִים ﻌ — **It is not in our power [to explain] either the tranquillity of the wicked**

The Rabbis said,[3]

"I will be gracious to whom I will be gracious."[4]

1. *Berachos* 7a.
2. *Shemos* 33:19.
3. *Midrash Rabbah, Shemos,* Section 45.
4. *Shemos* 33:19.

ד/כ   הָרְשָׁעִים וְאַף לֹא מִיסוּרֵי הַצַּדִּיקִים.
[כ] רַבִּי מַתְיָא בֶּן חָרָשׁ אוֹמֵר: הֱוֵי מַקְדִּים

At the time [that He said these words to Moshe] God showed him all the storehouses of reward that are prepared for the righteous. [Moshe] said, "Whose storehouse is this?" and [God] said, "That belongs to those who observe the commandments."

"Whose storehouse is this?" "That belongs to those who raise orphans."

So it went with each and every storehouse. Finally, he saw a large storehouse. He said, "Whose storehouse is this?" [God] said, "To one who has, I give of his own reward; to one who has not, I grant for free and give to him from this." As it says, "I will be gracious to whom I will be gracious," [and this means,] to the one to whom I wish to be gracious.

What message lies in this allegory? Why should the storehouse of undeserved bounty be larger than the storehouses of earned reward?

The first storehouses were not large, because the reward for *mitzvos* is finite and there are rather few people who perform *mitzvos* or who raise orphans. The last storehouse was large, because the undeserved goodness that God dispenses is unrelated to the deeds of the recipients. Indeed, the storehouse of unearned goodness is limitless, for it comes from God's unbounded goodness.

This is the reason that we cannot understand the good life that evil people may enjoy. Their undeserved comfort flows from God's perspective of how the world should run, and God's perspective eludes the grasp of human comprehension.

וְאַף לֹא מִיסוּרֵי הַצַּדִּיקִים ❧ — *or the suffering of the righteous*

The righteous who are not perfect suffer afflictions so that they may achieve atonement in this world and enjoy unmitigated reward in the next world. That fact is well within our grasp. The point we cannot comprehend is that afflictions that are not due to transgression beset the righteous. The righteous can suffer even when they do not accept the opportunity for increased reward that these afflictions provide.

לֹא מִשַּׁלְוַת הָרְשָׁעִים וְאַף לֹא מִיסוּרֵי הַצַּדִּיקִים ❧ — *either the tranquillity of the wicked or the suffering of the righteous*

The practical significance of this *mishnah* lies in being aware that the

58 / פרקי אבות

20. Rabbi Masya ben Charash says: Initiate a

---

wicked may have undeserved comfort and the righteous may have unexplainable suffering. If we see a wicked person enjoying the good life, we should not conclude that his deeds are meritorious and that we should emulate his conduct. Similarly, if we see a righteous person who is devastated despite his righteousness, we must not conclude that his deeds were not righteous.

The truth is that a righteous person can be cut down in the midst of his righteousness and a wicked person may be granted to continue in his evil ways.

---

§◄ אֵין בְּיָדֵינוּ — *It is not in our power [to explain]*

The words "to explain" are not present in the Hebrew, but have been added to convey the first explanation.

Alternatively, the *mishnah* could be translated as: "It is not in our power [to do anything about] the tranquillity of the wicked or the suffering of the righteous."

As well, the expression could mean "It is not in our power [to know what good deed is responsible for] the tranquillity of the wicked or [what transgression is responsible for] the suffering of the righteous."

This *mishnah* follows upon the *mishnah* of "Exile yourself to a place of Torah" to help us accept that a righteous person might suffer a difficult life away from home, in order to learn Torah, while a transgressor enjoys himself in the comfort of his own home. Such anomalies are not within our grasp of comprehension nor within our range of control.

Mishnah 20

This *mishnah* gives us guidance in three areas of social relationships: the role of leader; the role of subordinate; and the role within which we interact with peers.

---

§◄ הֱוֵי מַקְדִּים בִּשְׁלוֹם כָּל אָדָם — *Initiate a greeting to every person*

The appropriate personality trait to be called upon when dealing with peers is *anavah*, עֲנָוָה.[1] The English word "humility" does not do justice

---

1. Author's introductory paragraph.

ד/כ בִּשְׁלוֹם כָּל אָדָם, וֶהֱוֵי זָנָב לָאֲרָיוֹת; וְאַל תְּהִי
רֹאשׁ לְשׁוּעָלִים.

to this concept. *Anavah* means that one considers other people important, while not assessing his own importance.[1] It is a trait that is
fundamental to the pursuit of peace.[2]

It is an act of *anavah* to initiate a greeting to another person, and it
demonstrates that he considers others to be important.

We should not wait for the other person to extend greetings to which
we will then respond, because it treats him as an inferior. Ordinary
people should be important enough to us that we wish to encourage their
friendship, and it goes without saying that we should not avoid their
friendship!

Those who are the first to extend greetings are, by nature, people who
seek harmonious relationships. Conversely, those who only respond to
others' greetings do not demonstrate a genuine concern for social
harmony.

⋙ וֶהֱוֵי זָנָב לָאֲרָיוֹת; וְאַל תְּהִי רֹאשׁ לְשׁוּעָלִים — *and be
a tail to lions; and do not be a head to foxes*

These are two separate points. We should choose to be subordinate to
great people, and we should not choose to be the head of knaves.

One might be just the "tail" — the least of all limbs — but he is, after
all, part of a lion. Likewise, the glory of being the "head" is lost when we
consider that it is just the head of a fox.

Relationship of this Mishnah to the Preceding Mishnah

This *mishnah* follows upon the previous statement that we cannot
grasp the comfort of the wicked or the suffering of the righteous. The
adjacency of these two *mishnayos* emphasizes that it is truly necessary
to initiate greetings to everyone, whether they be good or evil.

A good person, of course, deserves to be greeted first. However,
you should also extend greetings to a transgressor, for he does not
consider himself to be wicked and he will misinterpret the lack of
greeting as a lack of respect for people in general. He will erroneously

---

1. The English word "humility" actually denotes the opposite. It conveys a negative
evaluation of oneself, rather than the positive evaluation of others implied by
"*anavah.*"

2. As noted *supra,* in the commentary to 1:12.

---

conclude that you are willing to treat people in a degrading manner.

The traditional Hebrew greeting is to wish him peace, and there is nothing wrong with bestowing that blessing upon an evil person. Although their soul will not have peace after death, the previous *mishnah* made it clear that in this world, at least, the wicked may enjoy peace.

Mishnah 21

This *mishnah* is about the ultimate human destiny. The Rabbis knew from the prophets that there is a World to Come. This fact was faithfully handed down from the prophets, generation after generation, until it reached the Rabbis. Even among other nations, no one doubted or disputed this fact. Indeed, a person who is sufficiently wise, discerning and perceptive could discover it on his own.

It is logically cogent that the world should be perfect because it is the product of the perfect God. Yet we see that the present world is imperfect: Its inhabitants are in continual need of food and drink; they die, and procreation is needed to keep the world inhabited. Clearly, this world does not reflect its Creator, Who lives forever and has none of these needs. Therefore, we must conclude that this is not the only world that God created and there will be another world that does reflect God's perfection.

Do not think that there is a spiritual world that reflects His perfection but people are not part of it. The fact is, we are the sole purpose for creating the world

Rather, the present world was created only to prepare for the World to Come, for that is the primary Creation and properly reflects the perfection of the Creator.

Journey Through Eternity

It will be helpful to present Maharal's view of the stages of life through which we are destined to proceed, to establish the basis of his commentary to the *mishnah* and many others that address the World to Come.

Our journey through eternity commences with a living seed that comes of flesh and blood and which grows to be a flesh and blood human being. We live a life of thought, study, belief, emotion, desire, experience, needs, choices and actions. But all that is born of flesh and blood must pass away, and in the instant before we depart this world, God assesses our life and decrees the next phase of several phases yet

[כא] רַבִּי יַעֲקֹב אוֹמֵר: הָעוֹלָם הַזֶּה דּוֹמֶה
לִפְרוֹזְדוֹר בִּפְנֵי הָעוֹלָם הַבָּא; הַתְקֵן
עַצְמְךָ בַּפְּרוֹזְדוֹר כְּדֵי שֶׁתִּכָּנֵס לַטְּרַקְלִין.

---

to come. The average person — such as you or I — will enter a pleasant
phase of existence the Rabbis entitle *Gan Eden,* although this will likely
be preceded by a distressing remedial phase the Rabbis term *Gehinnom.*

On earth, history will continue to unfold, through successive prosperity and calamity, until the advent of *Mashiach.* He will destroy our
archenemy Amalek, restore the Jews to the Land of Israel, and rebuild
the Holy Temple. According to Maharal, that life on earth, after the era
of *Mashiach,* proceeds without those who have already departed this
world and who occupy a different realm.

A time will come when those who have departed will be restored to life
in a new body. Not born of ephemeral flesh and blood, but formed from
the earth as was the first man, Adam, we too will have the potential to
live forever. This phase of life, *techias hameisim,* תְּחִיַּת הַמֵּתִים, launches
the era termed the World to Come, and therefore there is no route to the
World to Come for those who do not merit resurrection.[1]

There are levels of the World to Come, ranging from the elementary
existence of *techias hameisim,* to a very long, good life, to truly eternal,
non-physical[2] existence. The World to Come can be a pleasant, happy
tranquil experience, or it can be endlessly intolerable. After we are
restored to life, God will conduct the ultimate judgment, דִּין וְחֶשְׁבּוֹן.
Those who merit will proceed to long life, while others will proceed to
endless shame, and all will depend on the beliefs, choices and actions
taken in this world.

The era of the World to Come follows the resurrection of the dead, and
therefore there is no route to the World to Come for those who do not
merit resurrection.[3]

God will judge the resurrected. Some will enjoy the World to Come
and some will suffer eternal shame. The World to Come is whole in every
aspect,[4] and it is therefore the place where *mitzvos* are rewarded.

---

1. Author's summary of Maharal's view of the sequence of death, return to life,
judgment, reward and punishment, and eternal life in the World to Come.

2. The nature of the transition from the bodily existence of תְּחִיַּת הַמֵּתִים to non-
physical eternity is not described.

3. Such as those who deny the resurrection of the dead of the Divine origin of Torah.
See *Sanhedrin* 90a.

4. Something is whole if it lacks nothing; i.e., there are no needs to be satisfied.

21. Rabbi Yaakov says: This world is like a lobby before the World to Come; prepare yourself in the lobby so that you may enter the banquet hall.

‏הָעוֹלָם הַזֶּה דוֹמֶה לִפְרוֹזְדוֹר בִּפְנֵי הָעוֹלָם הַבָּא ‏§⸗ — *This world is like a lobby before the World to Come*

Just as a lobby is but an adjunct to the banquet hall, so this world is but an adjunct to the World to Come.

Why did God bother to make this world, when He could have made just the World to Come?

Creation is a paradox. It must reflect the characteristics of its perfect and eternal Creator. Yet, as a creation it must have a beginning and therefore be finite, with all the limitations, incompleteness and instability that implies. The resolution of the paradox is that the conflicting characteristics do not appear at the same time. The world comes into being from nothingness as a finite world and is followed by the perfect World to Come. It may be compared to a baby, who is born out of no prior existence, small and immature. Throughout life he grows and develops until he ultimately actualizes his potential. So too, Creation came into being as this finite, developing world and is ultimately followed by the wholeness of the World to Come.

Still, why is it necessary for us to die and then return to life? Could we not just continuously advance until we reach our ultimate level?

The answer is that the ultimate level cannot reached by a continuous progression from one's finite origin. The finite characteristics of that which has come from non-existence into existence must be totally cast off. A person, who comes from a drop of semen, cannot achieve the highest level of existence while he is still finite flesh and blood. Physical nature must be first shed through death and then one can live in an eternal world.[1]

‏הַתְקֵן עַצְמְךָ בִּפְרוֹזְדוֹר כְּדֵי שֶׁתִּכָּנֵס לַטְרַקְלִין ‏§⸗ — *prepare yourself in the lobby so that you may enter the banquet hall*

As the lobby is the beginning of the banquet hall, so this world is the beginning of the World to Come. The world must progress from the

---

1. Maharal makes the point elsewhere that we do not know how people return to life in the future, but when we will see it we will consider it a very natural process; much more so than the process of pregnancy and birth.

ד/כב **[כב]** הוּא הָיָה אוֹמֵר: יָפָה שָׁעָה אַחַת
בִּתְשׁוּבָה וּמַעֲשִׂים טוֹבִים בָּעוֹלָם הַזֶּה
מִכָּל חַיֵּי הָעוֹלָם הַבָּא; וְיָפָה שָׁעָה אַחַת שֶׁל
קוֹרַת רוּחַ בָּעוֹלָם הַבָּא מִכָּל חַיֵּי הָעוֹלָם הַזֶּה.

physical nature that comes from having an origin to the wholeness that is implied by eternal existence.

The physical characteristics that come of having a beginning allow change and hence preparation. That is why this world is the opportunity to prepare for the next world. Since the World to Come is a place of stability and durability, it is too late to make preparations there.

In summary, only this world offers the opportunity to prepare for eternity.

Mishnah 22

⊷§ **יָפָה שָׁעָה אַחַת בִּתְשׁוּבָה וּמַעֲשִׂים טוֹבִים בָּעוֹלָם הַזֶּה** — *Better one hour of repentance and good deeds in this world*

Repentance is possible only in this world, which the previous *mishnah* referred to as the "lobby" in front of the "banquet hall." This is our only chance to prepare for the World to Come, as the "banquet hall" was made only for dining, and not for preparing.

Why is it that we can improve and develop, through repentance and good deeds in this world, while there is neither improvement nor growth in the World to Come? The answer lies in the nature of physical existence:

• A physical entity can change and indeed constantly changes.
• Since a physical entity can change, it is always in a state of potential, ready to take on some different form. It is never fully actualized.
• Conversely, things that are *nivdal*, not physical, do not change.

⊷§ **יָפָה . . . בִּתְשׁוּבָה . . . בָּעוֹלָם הַזֶּה מִכָּל חַיֵּי הָעוֹלָם הַבָּא** — *Better . . . repentance . . . in this world than the entire life of the World to Come*

Repentance is the change from evil to good and hence it is possible only in this physical world, for change is possible only while a person is in a physical state. In the World to Come, which does not have physical properties, repentance is not possible because change is not possible.

22. He used to say: Better one hour of repentance and good deeds in this world than the entire life of the World to Come; and better one hour of spiritual tranquillity in the World to Come than the entire life of this world.

⚜ יָפָה . . . מַעֲשִׂים טוֹבִים בָּעוֹלָם הַזֶּה מִכֹּל חַיֵּי הָעוֹלָם הַבָּא ⚜ — *Better . . . good deeds in this world than the entire life of the World to Come*

Likewise, the personality growth that comes of performing good deeds can develop only in this physical world. It is here that we grow to whatever level we achieve and we remain at that level forever in the ultimate, *nivdal*, world.

⚜ יָפָה . . . בָּעוֹלָם הַזֶּה . . . הָעוֹלָם הַבָּא . . . וְיָפָה . . . בָּעוֹלָם הַבָּא . . . הָעוֹלָם הַזֶּה — *Better . . . in this world than the . . . World to Come; and better . . . in the World to Come than . . . this world.*

This world is better than the next world in one way, and the next world is better in a different way. This world is better, because it offers the possibility of spiritual growth through repentance and good deeds, which are not possible in the next world. The next world is superior because its tranquillity of existence is not possible in this world.

⚜ יָפָה שָׁעָה אַחַת בִּתְשׁוּבָה וּמַעֲשִׂים טוֹבִים בָּעוֹלָם הַזֶּה מִכֹּל חַיֵּי הָעוֹלָם הַבָּא — *Better one hour of repentance and good deeds in this world than the entire life of the World to Come*

How can this *mishnah* compare such totally dissimilar things as good deeds and quality of life?

The answer is very profound. The salient feature of life in the World to Come is one's proximity to God. However, there is an opportunity to be even closer to God in this world, through repentance and good deeds, for the following reason. One who sets his sights on a destination and moves towards it is considered as being at one with it, for it engages his interest and action. While we engage in good deeds or repentance, our attention and energy are directed towards God and we are united with Him. When we are no longer engaged in the activity,

ד/כג ‎[כג]‎ רַבִּי שִׁמְעוֹן בֶּן אֶלְעָזָר אוֹמֵר: אַל תְּרַצֶּה אֶת חֲבֵרְךָ בִּשְׁעַת כַּעְסוֹ; וְאַל תְּנַחֲמֵהוּ בְּשָׁעָה שֶׁמֵּתוֹ מֻטָּל לְפָנָיו; וְאַל תִּשְׁאַל לוֹ בִּשְׁעַת נִדְרוֹ;

that special closeness goes away until the next time we engage in a *mitzvah*. However, in the World to Come where there is no action or change, one's proximity to God is only that which he achieved in his lifetime and never more.

⊷§ יָפָה שָׁעָה אַחַת בִּתְשׁוּבָה וּמַעֲשִׂים טוֹבִים בָּעוֹלָם הַזֶּה מִכֹּל חַיֵּי עוֹלָם הַבָּא — *Better one hour of repentance and good deeds in this world than the entire life of the World to Come*

The *mishnah* does not mean that this world can surpass the World to Come in enjoyment, for that is not true at all. It means only that the ability to elevate ourselves through repentance and good deeds in this world is better than the static quality of existence in the World to Come. **One hour** of this life is compared to the **entire** eternal life, because it takes but a short time to elevate ourselves through *mitzvos* in this world. In contrast, our level will not improve in the entire life of the World to Come.

⊷§ קוֹרַת רוּחַ בָּעוֹלָם הַבָּא — *spiritual tranquillity in the World to Come*

The Hebrew term רוּחַ denotes rest and hence reveals to us the essential nature of the World to Come as a place of rest.

The soul can suffer anxiety or it can be at ease. As we noted before, everything in this world is in a state of flux, while the soul can be at rest in the next world.

Relationship of this Mishnah and the Preceding Mishnayos

We can summarize these four *mishnayos*, which discuss this world in relation to the World to Come as follows.

The suffering of righteous people is their opportunity to earn a better portion in the World to Come,[1] for this world is the place to prepare for the next world,[2] through repentance and good deeds.[3]

---

1. *Mishnah* 19: "It is not in our power [to explain]. . .the suffering of the righteous."
2. *Mishnah* 21: "This world is like a lobby before the World to Come."
3. *Mishnah* 22.

23. Rabbi Shimon ben Elazar says: Do not appease your fellow in the time of his anger; do not console him while his dead lies before him; do not question him about his vow at the time he makes it;

Do not envy the tremendous success that the wicked may enjoy in this world,[1] for that worldly success is like being "a head to foxes," a position which no one should seek. It is better to be the least of the righteous,[2] for they will merit tranquillity in the World to Come that cannot be experienced in this world.[3]

Mishnah 23

Sometimes a person tries to improve a situation but makes things worse than they were. The four cases of our *mishnah* illustrate a single principle. Not only is it futile to try to ease the unhappiness of a person whose emotions are still building, but those very efforts will extend and intensify his unhappiness.

⊷§ אַל תְּרַצֶּה אֶת חֲבֵרְךָ בִּשְׁעַת כַּעֲסוֹ §⊷ — *Do not appease your fellow in the time of his anger*

Trying to appease a person while his anger is increasing adds to his anger.

⊷§ וְאַל תְּנַחֲמֵהוּ בְּשָׁעָה שֶׁמֵּתוֹ מֻטָּל לְפָנָיו §⊷ — *do not console him while his dead lies before him*

Attempts to comfort a person who is in anguish and intense mourning only increase and intensify his mourning.

⊷§ וְאַל תִּשְׁאַל לוֹ בִּשְׁעַת נִדְרוֹ §⊷ — *do not question him about his vow at the time he makes it*

According to this translation of תִּשְׁאַל, *tishal,* the *mishnah* refers to questioning one who takes a vow as to exactly what he means to include in it.

---

1. *Mishnah 19:* "It is not in our power [to explain]. . .the tranquillity of the wicked."
2. *Mishnah 20:* "and be a tail to lions; and do not be a head to foxes."
3. *Mishnah 22.*

וְאַל תִּשְׁתַּדֵּל לִרְאוֹתוֹ בִּשְׁעַת קַלְקָלָתוֹ.

[כד] שְׁמוּאֵל הַקָּטָן אוֹמֵר: „בִּנְפֹל אוֹיִבְךָ אַל תִּשְׂמָח, וּבִכָּשְׁלוֹ אַל יָגֵל לִבֶּךָ. פֶּן יִרְאֶה יהוה וְרַע בְּעֵינָיו, וְהֵשִׁיב מֵעָלָיו אַפּוֹ."

Any doubt as to what is included in a vow makes it difficult to live up to it. Questions about the vow are a well-intentioned attempt to clear up any uncertainties and hence make it easier to fulfill the vow. However, as the person taking the vow is asked, "Do you mean to include this? Do you mean to include that?" he will include more and more things as he goes along. In the end, the good intention to make the vow easier to fulfill will actually make it more difficult.

However, the word תִּשְׁאַל more likely refers to the process by which a Rabbi can annul a vow retroactively. The translation would then be: **"do not [attempt to]** *annul* **his vow at the time he makes it."**

The annulment process includes asking the person whether he regrets undertaking the vow and if he would like the Rabbi to annul it. To ask a person who has just made a vow whether he regrets making it will likely cause him to reinforce his commitment and to undertake additional vows.

§— וְאַל תִּשְׁתַּדֵּל לִרְאוֹתוֹ בִּשְׁעַת קַלְקָלָתוֹ — *and do not attempt to see him at the time of his degradation*

This refers to a well-intentioned wish to see how his friend is doing after suffering some disgrace. The result will be that he causes his friend further anguish. One who has suffered ruin finds company a burden, for they observe him in a degraded state that has made him different from other people, and being different is itself a source of discomfort.

This *mishnah* is based on the following rule of human nature. If someone's emotions are still mounting, and we attempt to oppose them, his emotional state will intensify in reaction to our efforts.

Mishnah 24

Shmuel HaKattan says: "When your enemy falls be not glad, and when he stumbles let your heart not be joyous. Lest Hashem see and it displease Him, and He will turn His wrath from him [to you]" (*Mishlei* 24:17-18).

4/24 and do not attempt to see him at the time of his degradation.

24. Shmuel HaKattan says: "When your enemy falls be not glad, and when he stumbles let your heart not be joyous. Lest Hashem see and it displease Him, and He will turn His wrath from him [to you]" (*Mishlei* 24:17-18).

Shmuel HaKattan was a student of Rabban Gamliel and lived about two generations before the Rabbis of the preceding *mishnayos*. His advice should have been placed earlier in *Pirkei Avos,* but was inserted at this point to shed light on the preceding *mishnayos*.

We learned in *mishnah* 22 that the unique quality of this world is the ability it affords us to repent. One might begrudge the wicked an opportunity to repent, invoking the verse,[1] "when the wicked perish there is jubilation." Shmuel HaKattan informs us that it is forbidden to rejoice at anyone's ruin, unless it is the retribution of a capital offense by the court. Even then, we rejoice only because God's honor is restored by eradicating evil. God Himself, however, never rejoices in destruction, because one of the beautiful aspects of this world is the opportunity for even a transgressor to improve by repenting.

If your enemy's downfall is not a direct retribution for sin, it is forbidden to rejoice even if he is a transgressor.

---

§ וְהֵשִׁיב מֵעָלָיו אַפּוֹ — *and He will turn His wrath from him [to you]*

One who rejoices at another's misfortune deserves to incur God's wrath, as it says,[2] "one who is glad at calamity shall not go unpunished." The reason is that a person who does not want evil does not want it even for his enemy. However, one who "is glad at calamity" is happy about an evil occurrence, and will get one — for himself.

Mishnah 25

Elisha ben Avuya says: One who studies Torah as a child, to what can he be likened? - to ink written on fresh paper. And one who studies Torah as an old man, to what can he be likened? - to ink written on smudged paper.

---

1. *Mishlei* 11:10.
2. *Mishlei* 17:5.

[כה] אֱלִישָׁע בֶּן אֲבוּיָה אוֹמֵר: הַלּוֹמֵד יֶלֶד,
לְמָה הוּא דוֹמֶה? — לִדְיוֹ כְתוּבָה עַל
נְיָר חָדָשׁ. וְהַלּוֹמֵד זָקֵן, לְמָה הוּא דוֹמֶה? —
לִדְיוֹ כְתוּבָה עַל נְיָר מָחוּק.

[כו] רַבִּי יוֹסֵי בַּר יְהוּדָה אִישׁ כְּפַר הַבַּבְלִי
אוֹמֵר: הַלּוֹמֵד מִן הַקְּטַנִּים, לְמָה הוּא
דוֹמֶה? — לְאוֹכֵל עֲנָבִים קֵהוֹת וְשׁוֹתֶה יַיִן

Why is the metaphor of writing with ink on paper appropriate to human memory? The faculty of memory receives an image of things to the point where they are engraved upon the memory like writing on a sheet of paper. When the memory is clean and clear of extraneous matters, then the image is registered with clear definition, and is difficult to remove.

When a person gets old, the faculty of memory has extraneous matters that interfere with clearly registering the image and hence it is easily removed.

⋖§ הַלּוֹמֵד יֶלֶד . . . וְהַלּוֹמֵד זָקֵן — *One who studies Torah as a child . . . and one who studies Torah as an old man*

Maharal's text read: "One who teaches Torah to a child. . ." and "One who teaches Torah to an old man. . ." That text begs the question: Why is the act of teaching not represented in the *mishnah's* metaphor as *writing* with ink on fresh paper, rather than being compared to the ink and paper itself? The answer is that a teacher does not impress information on a student's memory. Rather, the student himself must take in the studies. It may be likened to one who points to a painting hanging on the wall. Although the second person receives the picture in his mind, it would not be accurate to say that the first person impressed the image on the second person's memory. It would be inaccurate to describe the teacher as writing on the paper, for the student himself must absorb the information.

Mishnah 26

The previous *mishnah* contrasted teaching the young and teaching the old.[1] This *mishnah* contrasts learning from the young and learning from the old.

---

1. According to Maharal's text of the previous *mishnah,* which reads: "One who teaches Torah to a child. . ." and "One who teaches Torah to an old man. . ."

4/
25-26

25. Elisha ben Avuyah says: One who studies Torah as a child, to what can he be likened? — to ink written on fresh paper. And one who studies Torah as an old man, to what can he be likened? — to ink written on smudged paper.

26. Rabbi Yose bar Yehudah of Kfar HaBavli says: One who learns Torah from the young, to what can he be likened? — to one who eats unripe grapes or drinks unfermented wine

---

לְאוֹכֵל עֲנָבִים קֵהוֹת וְשׁוֹתֶה יַיִן מִגִּתּוֹ § — *to one who eats unripe grapes or drinks unfermented wine from his vat*

Why does the *mishnah* use two metaphors, grapes and wine, to convey its message? These two metaphors correspond to the two kinds of knowledge: revealed and hidden. Grapes are a metaphor for revealed knowledge, while wine is a metaphor for hidden knowledge. Whereas grapes are visible, thick and readily grasped, wine lies within the grape, hidden from sight. It needs to be extracted, and it is thin and fine.

The hidden nature of wine makes it a perfect metaphor for the secrets of the Torah. Indeed, the numerical value of the word for "wine" יַיִן, *yayin,* is the same as the numerical value of the word for "secret," סוֹד, *sod.* [1]

לְאוֹכֵל עֲנָבִים קֵהוֹת . . . לְאוֹכֵל עֲנָבִים בְּשׁוּלוֹת § — *to one who eats unripe grapes. . .to one who eats ripe grapes*

In ripe grapes, the strength and flavor have been fully actualized and exist apart from the pulp of the grape. In unripe grapes, the potential for full growth and flavor still lies within the pulp. Similarly, the intellect of a child is still embedded within his body. It has not yet been independently actualized, and a youth's knowledge is not distinct from his experience.[2] As a person ages and the body weakens, the intellect develops until it is distinct from the personal being. For this reason, the Rabbis said,[3]

the understanding of elderly Torah scholars becomes increasingly clear with age.

---

1. יין = 10 + 10 + 50 = 70; סוד = 60 + 6 + 4 = 70
2. Literally: from his imagination.
3. *Kinnim,* Chapter 3, *mishnah* 6.

מִגִּתּוֹ. וְהַלּוֹמֵד מִן הַזְּקֵנִים, לְמָה הוּא דּוֹמֶה? **ד/כז**
— לְאוֹכֵל עֲנָבִים בְּשׁוּלוֹת וְשׁוֹתֶה יַיִן יָשָׁן.

[כז] רַבִּי מֵאִיר אוֹמֵר: אַל תִּסְתַּכֵּל בַּקַּנְקַן,
אֶלָּא בְּמַה שֶׁיֶּשׁ בּוֹ; יֵשׁ קַנְקַן חָדָשׁ מָלֵא
יָשָׁן, וְיָשָׁן שֶׁאֲפִילוּ חָדָשׁ אֵין בּוֹ.

---

§ וְשׁוֹתֶה יַיִן מִגִּתּוֹ . . . וְשׁוֹתֶה יַיִן יָשָׁן *§ — or drinks unfermented wine from his vat . . . or drinks aged wine*

The image of **unfermented wine from his vat** conveys that the wine is mixed with dregs and embedded in murkiness. **Aged wine** is a fitting metaphor for mature comprehension, because the dregs have completely settled and it is now clear and pure.

---

§ וְשׁוֹתֶה יַיִן מִגִּתּוֹ *§ — or drinks unfermented wine from his vat*

The metaphor of drinking wine is used to highlight another difference between youth and age. The image of wine fermenting in the vat corresponds to the excitement of youth. Young people boil over with excitement, mixing ideas together, like freshly fermenting wine that bubbles up, stirring up the dregs. They do not have the composure that comes with age and allows one to distill and clarify his thoughts.

Mishnah 27

The simple meaning of this *mishnah* is that we should not assume that a man of imposing appearance is wise. However, that message is so obvious that it hardly needs stating.

One might think that our *mishnah* wishes to qualify the previous *mishnah*, [1] for there are indeed some young people whom God has granted true wisdom and there are many old people who are devoid of wisdom. However, it is difficult to suggest that such a simple point would merit inclusion in a *mishnah*. Actually, the *mishnah* is making a much stronger point than those two interpretations bring out; namely, that the *only* significant variation among people is their knowledge and opinions.

---

1. "One who learns Torah from the young. . .can. . .be likened. . . to one who eats unripe grapes."

from his vat. But one who learns Torah from the old, to what can he be likened? — to one who eats ripe grapes or drinks aged wine.

27. Rabbi Meir says: Do not look at the vessel, but what is in it; there is a new vessel filled with old wine and an old vessel that does not even contain new wine.

אַל תִּסְתַּכֵּל בַּקַּנְקַן — *Do not look at the vessel*

Physical appearance *cannot* be a reliable indication of a person's knowledge, because the variation in people's physical appearance is insignificant compared to the variation in people's knowledge, wisdom and opinions.

אֶלָּא בְּמַה שֶׁיֶּשׁ בּוֹ — *but what is in it*

What truly distinguishes us from each other is that we each have a unique viewpoint and understanding. The fact that people have different opinions is as natural as looking different, but much more significant. The Rabbis say,[1]

> One who sees a throng of [600,000] Israelites says, [the blessing of] "Blessed is He Who discerns secrets," for [He discerns] the opinion of each, which is as different from the other as the face of each is different from the other.

From this we see that individuals are distinguished by the diversity of knowledge and viewpoint. Therefore, we should select a teacher based only on inner merit.

יֵשׁ קַנְקַן חָדָשׁ מָלֵא יָשָׁן — *there is a new vessel filled with old wine*

The *mishnah* could have started at this point, but it wanted to emphasize, with the opening phrase "Do not look at the vessel," that there is no point whatsoever in looking, for people are distinguished only by inner qualities. Physical appearance is not a suitable test to distinguish people, for that difference might be nothing more than the difference of youth and age.

---

1. *Berachos* 58a.

ד/כח **[כח]** רַבִּי אֶלְעָזָר הַקַּפָּר אוֹמֵר: הַקִּנְאָה,
וְהַתַּאֲוָה וְהַכָּבוֹד מוֹצִיאִין אֶת הָאָדָם
מִן הָעוֹלָם.

This *mishnah* does not take issue with *mishnah* 26, which said that "Torah from the young . . . can . . . be likened . . . to one who eats unripe grapes." Both rabbis agree that God has endowed many young people with wisdom and that many old people have not acquired wisdom. The point of the previous *mishnah* is that everyone's wisdom grows and matures with age, and therefore, though there are superior grapes and inferior grapes, all grapes are better when they are ripe.

In summary, the significant feature that distinguishes people is neither age nor appearance, but knowledge and opinion.

Mishnah 28

Prodigies, described in the previous *mishnah* as a "new vessel filled with old wine," often display juvenile behavior such as pursuing honor or being jealous of others. This *mishnah* follows to warn about such behavior.

The Soul

The human soul consists of three major faculties: the physical, the spiritual and the intellectual. The Rabbis call these, respectively: רוּחַ, נֶפֶשׁ, נְשָׁמָה, *ruach, nefesh* and *neshamah*.[1]

• The physical part of the soul, *ruach,* maintains the bodily functions such as the digestive system, the reproductive system and their physical desires.
• The spirit, *nefesh,* is responsible for will, motivation and for such emotions as resentment, jealousy and hatred.
• Intellect, *neshamah,* embraces perception such as the five senses; rational thought, imagination, memory, and understanding.
 The three faculties enable a person to survive and to thrive, but they can cause harm when exercised to excess. For example:
• The desire to eat keeps a person well nourished, but in the excess it is gluttony and unhealthy.
• The will motivates us to acquire wealth and to protect our possessions, but jealousy can drive people to fraud or theft.

---

1. Maharal's commentary to Chapter 2, *mishnah* 10-14, identifies five components of the soul in a more detailed analysis than that presented here.

28. Rabbi Elazar HaKappar says: Jealousy, lust and glory remove a man from the world.

- Human intellect deserves respect, but the pursuit of honor and glory has ruined men and civilizations.[1]

We can safely accommodate a normal range of activity for each faculty, but a way of life that exceeds those boundaries is dangerous. If one deviates from the normal range of all three faculties, there is no sphere of existence left for him and he will depart this world prematurely.

הַקִּנְאָה וְהַתַּאֲוָה וְהַכָּבוֹד מוֹצִיאִין אֶת הָאָדָם מִן הָעוֹלָם — *Jealousy, lust and glory remove a man from the world.*

These three excesses that threaten our existence correspond to the three elements of the soul, as follows.

Jealousy is an excess of the spiritual element called *nefesh.* The spirit is responsible for will, motivation and emotion, but jealousy exceeds its legitimate sphere of engagement — why should one be moved by another's possessions? Therefore, jealousy causes deterioration of the *nefesh.*

Lust is an excess of the spiritual element called *ruach,* which is responsible for physical drives. When one's appetite for physical gratification exceeds what the body actually needs, the body is subjected to excesses that are unhealthy.

Glory belongs to the intellectual element of the soul.[2] Everyone deserves glory for all were created in the image of God. However, the excessive pursuit of glory can destroy the intellectual element of the soul.

הַקִּנְאָה, וְהַתַּאֲוָה, וְהַכָּבוֹד מוֹצִיאִין אֶת הָאָדָם מִן הָעוֹלָם — *Jealousy, lust and glory remove a man from the world.*

These three things removed the first man from the world. The tree from which he ate appealed to these very traits, dragging him from the

---

1. Author's explanatory paragraph.
2. The proof is that the Torah requires us to honor those who have acquired the wisdom that comes with years, as it says [*Vayikra* 19:32], "In the presence of an old person shall you rise and you shall honor the presence of an elder." "An elder" is one who has acquired the wisdom of an elder, regardless of age [*Kiddushin* 32b].

domain of healthy spiritual existence to death.[1] Scripture says,[2]

> "And the woman saw that the tree was *good for food* and that it was a *delight to the eyes* and the tree was *desirable to make one wise.*"

- "The tree was *good for food*" refers to the faculty of *ruach,* which ensures that the body is provided with its physical needs.
- "It was a *delight to the eyes*" refers to the *nefesh*, for sight stimulates emotional response.[3]
- "The tree was *desirable to make one wise*" refers to the intellectual faculty of the *neshamah.*

Had the tree appealed to only one or two of the spiritual faculties, the remaining ones would have maintained him. In fact, the attacks on all three dimensions of the soul prevailed against his life.[4]

הַקִּנְאָה, וְהַתַּאֲוָה וְהַכָּבוֹד ❧ — *Jealousy, lust and glory*

Each of Adam's sons, Kayin, Hevel and Sheis, manifested a different element of the soul.

To their detriment, Kayin and Hevel each inherited one of their father's excessive traits. Kayin inherited his father's excess of the *nefesh,* and therefore he was **jealous** of Hevel. Indeed, the very name קַיִן shares the grammatical root of his primary characteristic, קִנְאָה, *jealousy.* Hevel inherited his father's excess of *ruach,* and had a strong appreciation of ephemeral worldly delicacies, which is the trait of **lust.** His name Hevel, הֶבֶל, has the same meaning as the word in the Scriptural phrase,[5] הֶבֶל הַיֹּפִי, "beauty is *vain.*"

Sheis, the third son, did not inherit Adam's excess of the intellectual faculty, because only the more physical traits can be passed on.[6] Therefore, he was born without blemish in the intellectual faculty of the soul.[7]

---

1. Maharal does not distinguish, in this discussion, between Chavah and Adam.
2. *Bereishis* 3:6.
3. Vision — the ability to identify objects and to discern one object from another — is an intellectual faculty of the *neshamah.* Maharal intends the word "sight" as one of the five senses and the emotional response to them, which is the domain of the *nefesh.*
4. See *Derech Chaim* in its entirety for a discussion of which part of the soul was the primary to succumb to temptation. The Rabbis in *Sanhedrin* 70b express different views by suggesting different foods that the tree of knowledge may have consisted of.
5. *Mishlei* 31:30.
6. Because the parent is primarily physical, as indicated by the name Adam, אָדָם from the same Hebrew root as אֲדָמָה, meaning earth.
7. Sheis was the ancestor of the Jewish nation.

His exemplary character was the result of Divine assistance, and not of heredity, as his mother Chavah stated:[1] "for God has appointed other progeny to me, instead of Hevel whom Kayin slew."

הַקִּנְאָה, וְהַתַּאֲוָה וְהַכָּבוֹד §⊷ — *Jealousy, lust and glory*

In a variation of the previous explanation, the human being may be seen as a composite of the body, the soul and the image of God that adorns mankind.

Jealousy is associated with the spirit, and **lust** is associated with the body. **Glory** is associated with the image of God[2] in which mankind was created, for that image deserves honor.

הַקִּנְאָה, וְהַתַּאֲוָה וְהַכָּבוֹד מוֹצִיאִין אֶת הָאָדָם מִן הָעוֹלָם §⊷ — *Jealousy, lust and glory remove a man from the world.*

In Chapter 2, *mishnah* 16 above, we learned,

> Rabbi Yehoshua says: (a) An evil eye, (b) the evil inclination, and (c) hatred of other people remove a person from the world.

Rabbi Yehoshua's list of traits that remove a person from the world stem from the same origin as those named by Rabbi Elazar HaKappar in our *mishnah.*

An "evil eye," which begrudges another's good fortune, originates from the *nefesh,* as does **jealousy.**

- The inclination for evil [יֵצֶר הָרַע, *yetzer hara*] originates from the physical appetite of *ruach,* as does **"lust."**
- "Hatred of other people" is a sin against the image of God in which mankind was created, while **glory** means excessive pursuit of glory for his own "image of God."

Why does Rabbi Yehoshua list different traits than does Rabbi Elazar HaKappar? Rabbi Yehoshua maintains that being removed from the world can result only from *destructive* traits: an evil eye, evil inclination and hatred of other people. Rabbi Elazar HaKappar maintains that even beneficial faculties, such as appetite, will and intellect can cause premature departure from this world when taken to excesses of jealousy, lust and the pursuit of glory.

---

1. *Bereishis* 4:25.
2. As discussed in detail in the commentary to 3:18, *supra.*

[כט] הוּא[1] הָיָה אוֹמֵר: הַיִּלּוֹדִים לָמוּת;
וְהַמֵּתִים לִחְיוֹת; וְהַחַיִּים לִדּוֹן – לֵידַע,
לְהוֹדִיעַ וּלְהִוָּדַע שֶׁהוּא אֵל, הוּא הַיּוֹצֵר, הוּא

Mishnah 29

The previous *mishnah* discussed the risk of premature departure from this world as a result of physical, emotional and intellectual excesses. This *mishnah* reminds us that timely death is part of the natural order, even for those who stay within the bounds of spiritual propriety.

◆§ הַיִּלּוֹדִים לָמוּת — *Those born will die*

Those born of a mortal father and mother must themselves be mortal. When the dead return to life, it will be quite possible to live forever, for that life will not come from a father and mother, but directly from God. In this world, however, people are born and must die.

◆§ וְהַמֵּתִים לִחְיוֹת — *the dead will live again*

The Hebrew word for a dead person, מֵת, *meis,* [2] denotes one who lacks the life that he used to have. A dead person has not vanished; death is just a state where the life one had before is yet to be restored. Just as it is inevitable that those who are born will die, so is it inevitable for the deceased, מֵת, to be restored to life.

◆§ וְהַחַיִּים לִדּוֹן — *the living will be judged*

People receive Divine decree and judgment by virtue of being alive. Judgment is the link between living people and the living God.

The closer one is to God, the closer one is to receiving judgment. As an example, Rosh Hashanah is the time of judgment because God comes close to the world on those days. However, the dead, for their part, are not close to God[3] and hence only **the living** will be

---

1. Rabbi Elazar HaKappar.
2. Maharal: Scripture uses the word מֵת by itself only in reference to a dead person. The word is never used, without a clear antecedent, to refer to a dead animal, for an animal is dead forever.
3. Maharal: Although the righteous are close to God even in death, "beneath the throne of glory," that is because the righteous, even in death, are considered living.

29. He used to say: Those born will die; the dead will live again; the living will be judged — in order that they know, teach and make aware that He is God, He is the Fashioner, He

---

judged.[1] **The living** refers to both those who are alive now and those who will be living after the dead return to life.

◆§ וְהַחַיִּים לְדוֹן — *the living will be judged*

The Hebrew expression for the verb "to judge" also means to provide people with their needs,[2] for that involves judging what is good for them. In that context, people are judged at every moment as to whether they deserve to receive what they need. This form of judging comes without the closeness inherent in the usual kind of judgment and hence is not reserved for the time of God's closeness on Rosh Hashanah.

◆§ וּלְהוֹדַע שֶׁהוּא אֵל — *in order that they know. . . that He is God*

Everything is in God's hand: He creates and removes; He gives life and brings death and restores life. Through judgment, He controls everything.

◆§ לֵידַע, לְהוֹדִיעַ וּלְהַוָּדַע — *that they know, teach and make aware*

Why does the *mishnah* use three different expressions to convey the idea that people should know of God's supremacy? Maharal offers a variety of interpretations.

• **Know** implies knowing for oneself. **Teach** means informing several others. **Make aware** means to publicize the matter to all. Hence, the three expressions emphasize how widely known it is that **He is God. . .**
• The three expressions of knowledge can be seen as referring to three levels of conviction.

---

1. Our *mishnah* says that the living are judged, implying that the dead are not judged. This appears to be contradicted by *Eduyos* Chapter 2, *mishnah* 10, which states that the **judgment** of the wicked in *Gehinnom* lasts for 12 months. Maharal answers that the judgment occurs at the time of his death, not when death has removed him from God. It is the punishment itself that lasts 12 months.
2. *Melachim I*, 8:59: "that He might maintain the cause (מִשְׁפָּט) of His servant and the cause of His people Israel." Maharal equates מִשְׁפָּט and דִין.

הַבּוֹרֵא, הוּא הַמֵּבִין, הוּא הַדַּיָּן, הוּא
הָעֵד, הוּא בַּעַל דִּין, הוּא עָתִיד לָדוּן. בָּרוּךְ
הוּא, שֶׁאֵין לְפָנָיו לֹא עַוְלָה, וְלֹא שִׁכְחָה,
וְלֹא מַשּׂוֹא פָנִים וְלֹא מִקַּח שֹׁחַד,

— Some statements are merely possible.[1]
— There is knowledge that is just less than certain.[2]
— There is cogent truth.[3]

The use of three expressions — **know, teach** and **make aware** —
conveys that the fact of God's total dominion is the highest level of
logically compelling truth.

• The thrice-repeated expression may be considered a literary device for
emphasis of the point that God is the Master of all, whether people
wish it to be so or not.

◄§ שֶׁהוּא אֵל — *that He is God*

The name of God employed by the *mishnah* is אֵל. This name conveys
that God is the origin, for א is the first letter of the Hebrew alphabet, and
ל begins the second half of the alphabet.[4] In other words, God is the
origin of the higher world and of the lower world. God guides everything
from its beginning to its conclusion.

◄§ הוּא הַבּוֹרֵא, הוּא הַמֵּבִין — *He is the Fashioner, He is the Creator*

The Hebrew word for "Fashioner" is יוֹצֵר *yotzer,* from the same root as
צוּרָה, *tzurah,* meaning physical form: He endowed everything in the
world with its physical form. The word Creator, בּוֹרֵא, *borei,* refers to the
creation of a Divine, non-physical, form such as the expression that
shines from the human face, and is distinct from facial features. For this
reason, the verb "form" is used for most of the Scriptural account of

---

1. Even if it *is* true, that is just incidental, since there is no theoretically compelling
reason for it to be so.

2. For example, one may believe with substantial confidence that a certain person
has hands. This is still not a certainty, for some people do not have hands.

3. For example, knowledge that a person who is walking is alive.

4. When the Hebrew alphabet is written using only the 22 basic letters, then it is
divided א-כ (1-11), ל-ת (12-22). When the additional ending letters ך,ם,ן,ף,ץ are added,
the total becomes 27 letters and מ (*mem*) is the middle letter.

is the Creator, He is the Discerner, He is the Judge, He is the Witness, He is the Plaintiff, He will judge. Blessed is He, before Whom there is no iniquity, no forgetfulness, no favoritism and no acceptance of bribery,

---

Creation. The verb "create" was used only for creations with a spiritual aspect, such as people, and the Heavens and the Earth.[1]

The next section of the *mishnah* refers to the mandatory elements of the judicial process as defined by the Torah: a defendant, a witness, a judge and a plaintiff.

✍§ הוּא הָעֵד — *He is the Witness*

A witness does not simply provide information to the judge. Even if the judge has knowledge of all details of the case, the process of judgment according to the Torah is valid only if a witness articulates his testimony to the judge. That process demands that testimony be objective and firm, so that the judge deals with manifest fact.

✍§ הוּא בַּעַל דִּין — *He is the Plaintiff*

A trial is held only if a plaintiff makes a claim against another party. God acts in the role of plaintiff against the one who has sinned against Him.

✍§ הוּא הַדַּיָּן . . . הוּא עָתִיד לָדוּן — *He is the Judge . . . He will judge*

Just as He is the Judge now, God will always act in the role of judge.

✍§ שֶׁאֵין לְפָנָיו לֹא עַוְלָה, וְלֹא שִׁכְחָה, וְלֹא מַשּׂוֹא פָנִים וְלֹא מִקַּח שֹׁחַד — *before Whom there is no iniquity, no forgetfulness, no favoritism and no acceptance of bribery*

The *mishnah* now expands upon the metaphor of God in the role of judge. The four qualities listed in the *mishnah* corresponds to the

---

1. An exception is the great fish called *tanninim* which were "created" (*Bereishis* 1:21) rather than "formed," and for this reason the Rabbis say that this fish will be present even in the future world.

four qualities of judges listed in Scripture,[1]

> And you will provide out of all the nation (1) men of valor, (2) God fearing, (3) men of truth, (4) hating unjust gain.

(1) *Men of valor* means that they are energetic to save the oppressed from their oppressors. The corresponding Divine quality is that there is **no forgetfulness,** for God is energetic in remembering.

(2) *God fearing* means that they fear only God, and not men. Even if the defendant is the king, a judge must not show consideration for his position. The corresponding Divine quality is that there is **no favoritism.**

(3) *Men of truth* means that they love truth. They will render a judgment only if they are certain it is correct, for judgment based on mere opinion is unacceptable. The corresponding Divine quality is that there is **no iniquity** by drawing a false conclusion.

(4) *Hating unjust gain* is not acceptable for a judge. When the outcome of a judgment might result in a financial benefit for the judge, one who loves money will not be able to investigate the case to its truthful conclusion. The parallel Divine quality is that there is **no acceptance of bribery.**

&§ שֶׁאֵין לְפָנָיו . . . לֹא מִקַּח שֹׁחַד §— *before Whom there is. . . no acceptance of bribery*

How could the *mishnah* make such an obvious and trivial statement? What could we bribe Him with?

However, people honor Him and that is a form of bribery. The *mishnah* informs us that honoring God is not like giving Him something extra, because God created everything for His honor, including us and we are already His.

&§ שֶׁהַכֹּל שֶׁלוֹ §— *for everything is His*

The *mishnah* says that we cannot bribe God because everything is His. Can that imply that God's judgment would be affected by a bribe if we did have something to give?

To understand the message of this *mishnah,* we must realize that a bribe is not simply a business deal in which one offers to buy a favorable

---

1. *Shemos* 18:21.

judgment.[1] A bribe abrogates the requirement that judge and litigant be
utterly separate and independent. It is not just that the suspicion of a
biased conclusion is raised, but that an essential element of judicial
process is missing once there is an association between the judge and
the defendant. This fact is embodied in the Hebrew word for bribe, שׁוֹחַד,
shochad. The word may be considered as the contraction of the words
שֶׁהוּא אֶחָד, shehu echad = he is one; i.e., the judge becomes one with the
litigant and the clear segregation of judge and the one judged is
breached.

Therefore, the mishnah's concern with "bribing" God is not that a bribe
could affect God's decision. The concern is that a bribe, if it were
possible, would undermine the requirements of judicial process and
therefore prevent God from judging us.

Rambam explains **"no acceptance of bribery"** to mean that God's
judgment is not affected by the fact that a person has done many mitzvos. He explains the mishnah to mean that no matter how many mitzvos
one has to his credit, one is punished for each transgression and rewarded for every mitzvah, because mitzvos and sins do not cancel each other.

Rambam's assertion is a correct statement. However, it cannot be the
intention of our mishnah, which says that the reason God does not
accept bribery is that everything is His, whereas the fact that mitzvos do
not sway God's judgment is not because "everything is His."

◦§ וְלֹא מִקַּח שׁוֹחַד — no acceptance of bribery §◦

God does not accept bribes from the guilty, but there is one form of
"bribe" that He does accept from the righteous. The Rabbis say,[2]

> King David said to God: Master of the universe! You wrote in
> Your Torah, "You shall not accept a bribe," but You accept a
> bribe as it says,[3] "He takes a bribe from the bosom of a wicked
> person."
>
> God said to Israel: My children, as long as the gates of
> repentance are open, repent. For I take a bribe in this world, but

---

1. Author's introductory remarks.
2. Midrash Socher Tov, 17.
3. Mishlei 17:23.

יַבְטִיחֲךָ יִצְרְךָ שֶׁהַשְׁאוֹל בֵּית מָנוֹס לָךְ —
שֶׁעַל כָּרְחֲךָ אַתָּה נוֹצָר; וְעַל כָּרְחֲךָ אַתָּה
נוֹלָד; וְעַל כָּרְחֲךָ אַתָּה חַי; וְעַל כָּרְחֲךָ אַתָּה
מֵת, וְעַל כָּרְחֲךָ אַתָּה עָתִיד לִתֵּן דִּין וְחֶשְׁבּוֹן
לִפְנֵי מֶלֶךְ מַלְכֵי הַמְּלָכִים, הַקָּדוֹשׁ בָּרוּךְ הוּא.

❀ ❀ ❀

רַבִּי חֲנַנְיָא בֶּן עֲקַשְׁיָא אוֹמֵר: רָצָה הַקָּדוֹשׁ
בָּרוּךְ הוּא לְזַכּוֹת אֶת יִשְׂרָאֵל, לְפִיכָךְ
הִרְבָּה לָהֶם תּוֹרָה וּמִצְוֹת, שֶׁנֶּאֱמַר: ,,יהוה חָפֵץ
לְמַעַן צִדְקוֹ, יַגְדִּיל תּוֹרָה וְיַאְדִּיר.''

---

when I sit in judgment in the World to Come, I do not take a bribe.

God takes the "bribe" of repentance and good deeds. This is the one thing that He wants, and hence it is fittingly referred to in the allegory as a "bribe."

If a person has fewer good deeds than bad, he is classified as wicked and his trial is serious indeed. By performing good deeds he becomes predominantly worthy but his sins will still be judged. The most effective act is repentance, which eradicates the sin entirely.

Repentance and good deeds are definitely a bribe by the definition that applies to human courts, for they cause a person to be at one with God. Furthermore, repentance and good deeds can entirely abrogate judgment, for they render innocent a person who was previously guilty.

שֶׁהַכֹּל שֶׁלּוֹ — *for everything is His*

This is not only the reason that He does not accept bribes, but it is the reason for everything up to this point. He can be the Judge of all the world because it is His; He is the witness and the plaintiff because everything is His. He would not do iniquity with His own things and He forgets nothing because nothing of His own is hidden from Him. He does

your evil inclination promise you that the grave will be an escape for you — for against your will you were created; against your will you were born; against your will you live; against your will you die, and against your will you are destined to give an account before the King Who rules over kings, the Holy One, Blessed is He.

❧ ❧ ❧

Rabbi Chanania ben Akashia says: The Holy One, Blessed is He, wished to confer merit upon Israel; therefore He gave them Torah and *mitzvos* in abundance, as it is said (*Yeshayahu* 42:21): "Hashem desired, for the sake of His righteousness, that the Torah be made great and glorious."

---

not show favoritism even to kings; no one impresses the One Who owns him. And certainly, bribery is not possible with He Who already owns everything.

---

§► וְאַל יַבְטִיחֲךָ יִצְרְךָ שֶׁהַשְּׁאוֹל בֵּית מָנוֹס לָךְ — *And let not your evil inclination promise you that the grave will be an escape for you*

As we said, God judges only the living, not the dead. One might erroneously imagine that only the righteous will come to life, to receive their reward, and that the wicked will escape judgment by not returning to life. Therefore the *mishnah* says,

---

§► וְעַל כָּרְחֲךָ אַתָּה מֵת, וְעַל כָּרְחֲךָ אַתָּה עָתִיד לִתֵּן דִּין וְחֶשְׁבּוֹן לִפְנֵי מֶלֶךְ מַלְכֵי הַמְּלָכִים, הַקָּדוֹשׁ בָּרוּךְ הוּא — *against your will you die, and against your will you are destined to give an account before the King Who rules over kings, the Holy One, Blessed is He*

Coming back to life is not within a person's control. It is up to God alone, for He is everything and everything is His.

פרק חמישי ◈
Chapter Five

כָּל יִשְׂרָאֵל יֵשׁ לָהֶם חֵלֶק לְעוֹלָם הַבָּא,
שֶׁנֶּאֱמַר: ,,וְעַמֵּךְ כֻּלָּם צַדִּיקִים; לְעוֹלָם
יִירְשׁוּ אָרֶץ; נֵצֶר מַטָּעַי, מַעֲשֵׂה יָדַי, לְהִתְפָּאֵר."

All Israel has a share in the World to Come, as it
is said (*Yeshayahu* 60:21): "And your people
are all righteous; they shall inherit the land
forever; they are the stem of My plantings, My
handiwork, in which to take pride."

Author's Introduction to Chapter 5

The Messages of Numbers

The Hebrew language is unique, because Hebrew words describe not only an object but its very essence. For example, the Hebrew word for "eye" means both the anatomical eye and the essence of vision.[1] Similarly, the numbers quoted in the *mishnayos* of this chapter have a deeper meaning which transcends mere quantity.

The root concept conveyed by a number may also be conveyed by its corresponding letter. For example, the **number** 4 symbolizes the physical attribute of occupying space in the four directions. The 4th **letter** of the alphabet, ד, consists of a horizontal bar and a vertical bar, indicating length and width which define the expanse of four directions.

Another example is the number 10. This number embodies the concept of holiness, which is *nivdal*: non-physical, requiring no space. Accordingly, the 10th letter of the alphabet is *yud,* י, a mere dot that occupies a minimum of space.

Presented here is a brief summary of the symbolic message for each number from 1 to 10, culled from Maharal's writings.

One

- One conveys "completeness." Since 1 is not divisible, it has no parts and it is intrinsically whole.
- One may imply "unique."
- One may be used to describe that something is "foremost," to which all else is a mere adjunct.

Two

- Two implies proliferation. No number so completely conveys proliferation as the number two (Hebrew: שְׁנַיִם), for it is the only number that has the plural ending מ״ם, *mem.* Hence, two implies bountifulness and blessing. Similarly the higher orders of 2 (ב), namely 20 (כ) and 200 (ר), also imply increase. These are the letters of בְּכֹר, *bechor,* meaning the firstborn who gets a double portion, and the letters of בֶּרֶךְ, the root of בְּרָכָה, *berachah,* meaning blessing.
- Two, even together, are not a unified entity. Unlike other numbers, 2 cannot be whole, just as two parts > cannot link together to complete a closed, unified figure. Every other number *can* be whole: 1 is inherently whole and we will explain how numbers 3 and higher can bond into a whole entity.
- Two hints at "dispute." It takes two to argue.

---

1. *Supra,* Maharal's commentary to 2:1, "Know what is above you — a watchful Eye."

Three

- Three connotes a complete unit, by embracing an item, its opposite, and the middle ground between those two. To illustrate, three parts △ make a complete form by joining the end with the beginning. Numbers higher than three are also able to close and be whole.

Four

- Four indicates "place," because a "place" extends in the four directions.
- The number four symbolizes diversity, as the four directions are independent of each other and have no part in common.

Five

- Five portrays the five "directions" of this world, for there is a spiritual dimension in addition to the four directions of physical expanse. The fifth dimension is the spiritual core of existence; it focuses the four diverse sides into a single entity, by infusing the world with purpose. Hence, the "fifth" dimension is the intangible spiritual element of life. The fifth letter of the Hebrew alphabet is ה. Its *shape* conveys the 5 dimensions of this world, for it is composed of the symbol of four directions, ד, beside the minuscule י which connotes spirituality. The *pronunciation* of ה is just breath, as appropriate to its connotation of spirituality. It is only aspirated, without need of articulation by the throat, mouth, or lips.

Six

- Six connotes being "one" in the sense of being whole and all encompassing, rather than being part of something else. The concept is illustrated by the six sides of an object (right, left, front, back, top and bottom) that fully encompass it. For example, the number six befits the Jewish nation, which is "one" nation and not "one of" many nations.[1]

Seven

- Seven represents the complete world of nature. God took seven days to complete the world. There were six days of physical creation and the seventh day saw wholeness and stability, which are attributes of holiness.
- The seventh part is the spiritual heart of an otherwise physical entity. It is *kadosh,* holy, like the spirit that gives life to the body. For example, the seventh day is *Shabbos,* the spiritual heart of the week. *Tishrei,* the month in which Rosh Hashanah, Yom Kippur and Succos are celebrated, is the seventh month of the year, and it is clearly the spiritual center of the year.

---

1. The Jews numbered 600,000, from the time of leaving Egypt through the era of living in the desert.

- Seven indicates order. Every physical thing exists along six directions, consisting of opposite pairs: top and bottom; front and back; and the right and left sides. The center is the seventh element; it joins the opposites together and unites the extremes into a whole. The center serves as a reference point to the six directions, providing symmetry and order to the sides. In particular, seven represents the unification of the physical and non-physical.
- Seven can connote complete multiplicity, as in the verse (*Devarim* 28:7), "they shall come out against you in one way and flee before you in seven ways."

Eight

- Eight is associated with that which transcends nature. The reason is that eight is above seven, which is the symbol of nature in its most complete state. For example, the *mitzvah* of *bris milah* (ritual circumcision), which elevates the human body beyond physical nature, is conducted on the eighth day after birth.

Nine

- Nine is the epitome of "many." The reason is that nine is the highest digit. Ten is a complete group and nine is the highest number of individuals before they merge into a group.

Ten

- Ten is associated with holiness, *kedushah*.
- Ten conveys the idea of many consolidated into one. For example, ten or more people assembled for prayer form a single group.
- Ten is a complete group. No matter how many more people join a prayer quorum, it remains one quorum. We see from this example that ten is so complete that adding to it does not make a qualitative change.
- Ten represents the maximum degree of differentiation. The reason is that there are only 10 unique numbers: the 9 digits and a group of ten. For example, 1 is different from 2; and 2 is different from three, and so on up to ten. After ten, the digits just repeat, such as 11.
  Because 10 is the symbol of the difference between least and most, we find that 10 is symbolic of the distance between earth and heaven.
- Ten symbolizes the full range of possibilities and it symbolizes being at the highest of all possible levels.
  For example, *mishnah* 1 of this chapter tells us that the world was created through ten declarations of Creation ("Let there be light," etc.). The number carries a significant part of the *mishnah*'s message, because ten statements cover all possible aspects of Creation. It follows

that the world is complete and at such a high level that it is linked to the Divine Presence. It is no accident that these qualities of completeness, consolidation and holiness are all symbolized by the number 10.

In summary, the literature of Torah, whether Scriptural or rabbinic, relies upon numerical associations to express ideas much as the English language uses color to express "feeling blue" or being "in the pink." The contemporary Hebrew idiom no longer employs these numerical associations, and Maharal has rendered a valuable contribution by identifying this literary device as it occurs and explaining each instance.

Mishnah 1

With ten utterances the world was created. What does this come to teach us? Indeed, could it not have been created with one utterance? This was to exact payment from the wicked who destroy the world that was created with ten utterances, and to bestow goodly reward upon the righteous who sustain the world that was created by ten utterances.

Author's Introduction to Mishnah 1

Summary

In his commentary to this *mishnah,* Maharal provides intriguing insights on the relationship of the Creator and His Creation. The commentary addresses the anomaly that He, Who is One and Holy in the highest degree, can associate with this mundane world of multiplicity.

How do these conflicting qualities coexist? Heaven and earth meet as Divine influence consolidates and unifies the finite, individual parts of physical creation. Where exactly do they meet? In mankind, for we are both spiritual and physical and we can unify Creation by directing all of Its components to God's service.

Ten — Symbol of Holiness

The following illustrate the sanctity that is associated with the number ten:
- The Divine Presence comes to a group of ten people gathered for joint study or prayer.
- The Ten Commandments.
- The creation of the World to Come is hinted at in Scripture through the letter *yud,* which is the tenth letter of the Hebrew alphabet.[1]

The number ten expresses the following properties of holiness:

---

1. *Bereishis* 2:7: "And the Lord God fashioned, וַיִּיצֶר, *vayeitzer,* man." Rashi: Two fashionings. A fashioning in this world and a fashioning for [the era of] the resurrection of the dead.

[א] בַּעֲשָׂרָה מַאֲמָרוֹת נִבְרָא הָעוֹלָם. וּמַה תַּלְמוּד לוֹמַר? וַהֲלֹא בְמַאֲמָר אֶחָד יָכוֹל לְהִבָּרְאוֹת?

- Holiness is a total, encompassing principle; it is not specific items.
- It is complete, whole and not divisible.
- Holiness exerts a unifying influence, since it is a quality of the one God.

Ten represents a group, as distinct from the individual members of that group. For example, no matter how many people assemble for prayer, the quorum has been completed with ten people. Hence, the number ten also conveys completeness, which is an attribute of holiness.

When nine are joined with a tenth, they merge into a unit. One of the ten focuses the group and consolidates the parts into a whole. For example, a quorum appoints one person as prayer leader, to address God on behalf of the group. Another example is the first of the Ten Commandments, "I am the Lord your God," for this statement summarizes and focuses the other nine.

One and Many

The concepts of *one* and *many* are mutually exclusive. Something that is *one* is not more than one, nor is it divisible into parts.

Numbers between 2 and 9 have the attribute of being many. Nine, in particular, emphasizes being many because it is the highest number that still falls short of the unity found in a group of 10.

Things are either one, or many. Since God is unique in His Oneness, it follows that Creation must have the ability to be many. On the other hand, we would expect God's Creation to mirror His Oneness in the same way, and that presents an anomaly. How can God's Oneness be discerned in a complex universe?

The answer is that God's Oneness is the origin of the fact that the diverse elements of Creation are linked together into a coherent system.

§⊱ בַּעֲשָׂרָה מַאֲמָרוֹת נִבְרָא הָעוֹלָם — *With ten utterances the world was created.*

These "utterances" are God's statements for Creation, from "And God said, Let there be light"[1] to "And God said, Behold I have given you

---

1. *Bereishis* 1:3.

1. With ten utterances the world was created. What does this come to teach us? Indeed, could it not have been created with one utterance?

---

every herb. . .and every tree."[1] There are, in fact, only nine such utterances by which the different parts of Creation were brought into being. The tenth utterance is "the Lord created the heavens and the earth."[2] It is not introduced with the words "And the Lord said" because it is an all-embracing declaration of Creation. That tenth statement is the single Divine command that brought about the world through the nine detailed statements. It blended the nine fragments of Creation into a harmonious whole that embraces and reflects God's holiness.

וַהֲלֹא בְּמַאֲמָר אֶחָד יָכוֹל לְהִבָּרְאוֹת §№ — *Indeed, could it not have been created with one utterance?*

The *mishnah,* at first glance, seems to say that the world could have been created with one utterance, but was created with ten so that the wicked would get more punishment and the righteous would get more reward. However, that interpretation is not tenable, for the following reasons.
- Imagine that a wealthy person insists on paying $1 million for a house that costs $100,000 to build, so that anyone who burns his house down would owe him $1 million. How much does someone who burns down the house really owe? In fact, he has to pay only the $100,000 it should have cost to build the house.

    Similarly, does one deserve more reward or punishment because God chose to create the world with ten utterances, if He could have created it with one utterance?
- The *mishnah* does not ask, "Why did God create the world with 10 utterances?" It asks simply, "What does this come to teach us?"
- God does not create with labor or exertion. What difference would it make if He created the world with ten utterances or with one?

    The *mishnah* should be understood as follows:

    What can be learned from the fact that the world was created with ten utterances? We learn that the world was created with sanctity, for the number ten is the symbol of sanctity. Ten resonates with the glory of God's presence. God truly enhanced the world's importance by creating

---

1. *Bereishis* 1:29.
2. *Bereishis* 1:1

it with ten statements and demonstrating that He imbued the world with holiness. A world without sanctity would indeed have been created with only one utterance.

Holiness in a Material World

The fact that physical Creation is imbued with holiness is hinted at by the verse,[1] "for with [the letters] י־ה God fashioned the worlds." With these two letters He created this world and the World to Come.

The letter yud, י, is the instrument through which He created the World to Come. It is a place of holiness and the Divine Presence, appropriately symbolized by the tenth letter, yud. [2]

God created *this* world through the letter hei, ה. We will now see how that letter is a picture of the material world joined with spiritual presence. Physical things occupy space, and the spatial expanse of length and width is represented by the vertical and horizontal bars of the letter ד. Moreover, the exalted level of sanctity represented by the letter י clings to this world, as illustrated by the letter ה, which is a ד with a י in it.

The י turns the ד into a ה without touching it. In the same way, holiness is present in this world, but does not merge with it. Physical and spiritual qualities always remain distinct because their attributes are mutually exclusive.[3]

Since God is One, the world He created will in some way reflect God's unity. On the other hand, the material world is very different from God and therefore it must have the ability to have multiple, separate components. How can the world combine the spiritual quality of God's unity and the physical quality of multiple components? The spiritual presence harmonizes the diverse components,[4] as a tree trunk embraces many branches as a single tree.

---

1. *Yeshayahu* 26:4.

2. See Author's Introduction to Chapter 5.

3. Physical entities occupy space; exist in time; they change and deteriorate; and tend to proliferate. Spiritual entities occupy neither space nor time; they do not change, but are a source of influence; they are not divisible and tend to unify other things.

4. That God's influence can unify diverse and even opposing things is a recurring theme of Maharal. It will be found again in this chapter, in *mishnah* 20, to explain that God supports opposing Torah opinions if both are the result of a sincere, religiously motivated, pursuit of truth.

5/ 1 This was to exact payment from the wicked who destroy the world that was created with ten utterances,

---

‎אֶלָּא לְהִפָּרַע מִן הָרְשָׁעִים — *to exact payment from the wicked*

As we said before, this does not mean that God created the world in such a way as to increase the punishment of the wicked. A similar expression is found in the next *mishnah*, [1]

> "There were ten generations from Adam to Noach — to show the degree of His patience."

This does not mean that God made ten generations in order to show His patience! It means that we may infer His patience from the fact that He tolerated ten recalcitrant generations from Adam to Noach.

Similarly, our *mishnah* means that we can infer that the world must be important from the fact that it was created with ten utterances. Those who destroy such an important world will be punished and those who maintain it will be rewarded.

‎לְהִפָּרַע מִן הָרְשָׁעִים שֶׁמְּאַבְּדִין אֶת הָעוֹלָם שֶׁנִּבְרָא בַּעֲשָׂרָה מַאֲמָרוֹת, — *to exact payment from the wicked who destroy the world that was created with ten utterances*

The wicked would not merely be punished less if the world had been created with only one utterance. They would not have been punished at all.

To understand this better, consider someone who kills. If he kills an animal, there is no punishment. If he kills a human being, he deserves the death penalty. The difference is that human beings have within them the image of God.

The message behind the ten statements of Creation is that the world is infused with a lofty spiritual quality, just as a person is infused with a soul. As a result, there are significant consequences for destroying or for maintaining a world that has within it a Divine element. If the world were a purely physical entity — a spiritual vacuum — then it would have been created with only a single statement, and there would be no reward or punishment.

---

1. *Avos* 5:2.

ה/ב

וְלִתֵּן שָׂכָר טוֹב לַצַּדִּיקִים שֶׁמְּקַיְּמִין אֶת
הָעוֹלָם שֶׁנִּבְרָא בַּעֲשָׂרָה מַאֲמָרוֹת.

[ב] עֲשָׂרָה דוֹרוֹת מֵאָדָם וְעַד נֹחַ – לְהוֹדִיעַ
כַּמָּה אֶרֶךְ אַפַּיִם לְפָנָיו; שֶׁכָּל הַדּוֹרוֹת
הָיוּ מַכְעִיסִין וּבָאִין, עַד שֶׁהֵבִיא עֲלֵיהֶם אֶת
מֵי הַמַּבּוּל.

⊷ **לְהִפָּרַע מִן הָרְשָׁעִים שֶׁמְּאַבְּדִין אֶת הָעוֹלָם שֶׁנִּבְרָא בַּעֲשָׂרָה**
מַאֲמָרוֹת — *to exact payment from the wicked who*
destroy the world that was created with ten utterances

Some question: Is it a worse crime to steal ten dollars than to steal one
dollar? We can build on the previous explanation to answer that it is
worse to steal the king's crown than it is to steal a dollar. Indeed, if not
for God's Presence in the world, nothing would be considered important
enough to be a crime.

⊷ **הָרְשָׁעִים שֶׁמְּאַבְּדִין אֶת הָעוֹלָם שֶׁנִּבְרָא בַּעֲשָׂרָה מַאֲמָרוֹת** — *the wicked*
who destroy the world that was created with ten utterances

How do the wicked destroy the world?

God maintains the world's existence because of its value in bringing
mankind close to Him through the *mitzvos*. [1] Without *mitzvos*, mankind
would be insignificant — indeed, the first man was given seven commandments on the day of his creation.[2] In the time of Noach these
commandments were not obeyed and the world lost its justification for
existence. Scripture relates:[3] "And He destroyed every living thing
which was upon the face of the earth, whether man or animals or
creeping things or birds of the heaven."

The Rabbis say[4] about that verse,

> Although man sinned, did the animals sin? It was taught in the
> name of Rabbi Yehoshua ben Karcha: It can be explained with a
> parable of a man who made a wedding canopy for his son and

---

1. See *supra*, commentary to 1:2, section titled "Historical Illustration."
2. Maharal disagrees with Rambam's view that Adam received only six *mitzvos*.
3. *Bereishis* 7:23.
4. *Sanhedrin* 108a.

5/ 2 and to bestow goodly reward upon the righteous who sustain the world that was created by ten utterances.

2. There were ten generations from Adam to Noach — to show the degree of His patience; for all those generations angered Him increasingly, until He brought upon them the waters of the Flood.

---

prepared all manner of feast. After some days his son died. He arose and tore down the wedding canopy, saying, "Did I make this other than for my son? Now that he is dead, for what do I need a wedding canopy?" So did God say, "Did I create animals other than for man? Now that man has sinned, for what do I need animals?"

The wicked destroy the world by transgressing the Torah and the righteous maintain the world by fulfilling the *mitzvos*.

It is true that the entire world may not be destroyed through the acts of the wicked, if the deeds of the righteous adequately maintain the world. However, as we said above,[1] the world was created for each individual, and therefore each person is accountable for what he does with his world.

לְהִפָּרַע מִן הָרְשָׁעִים . . . וְלִתֵּן שָׂכָר טוֹב לַצַּדִּיקִים — *This was to exact payment from the wicked . . . and to bestow goodly reward upon the righteous*

The wicked must **pay** for their damage, but the righteous are not "paid" for their good deeds. To say that God "pays" the righteous would not be respectful in this context, for the Creator has no debts to His Creation; everything is His. Therefore, God **bestows** reward out of His good Will, as a kindness and not as due payment. We find this distinction in the verse,[2]

Who keeps the covenant and kindness with those who love Him. . .and repays to their face those who hate Him.

Justice *obligates* repaying evil, while kindness **bestows** reward.

Mishnah 2

Mishnah 2 and *mishnah* 3 will be explained together, as they form a unit.

---

1. Commentary to 3:2, *supra.*
2. *Devarim* 7:9-10.

297 / MAHARAL: PIRKEI AVOS

Mishnah 3

Numbers used in rabbinical homiletics have meaning well beyond quantity, as summarized in the author's introduction to this chapter. In particular, the many *mishnayos* of this chapter that specify ten things intend that number to convey that the maximum of possibilities have been embodied.[1] For example, in *mishnah* 1, the 10 utterances, with which the world was created, covered all possible aspects of Creation.

⊷§ עֲשָׂרָה דוֹרוֹת מֵאָדָם וְעַד נֹחַ — *There were ten generations from Adam to Noach*

Scripture traces the ten generations of Adam's descendants to express that the maximum opportunity for mankind to repent was provided. God waited ten generations to see if one of them would be righteous, but there was no change, and He brought the Flood to exact payment of the wicked.

⊷§ עֲשָׂרָה דוֹרוֹת מִנֹּחַ וְעַד אַבְרָהָם — *There were ten generations from Noach to Avraham*

God again tolerated ten generations of evil, until it was certain that people would not change, but this time He demonstrated another aspect of patience. He did not destroy the world for lack of ten righteous people, as He did in the time of Noach. Rather, He showed an additional degree of patience, by deeming the unprecedented righteousness of Avraham alone as having the balance to forestall destruction of the wicked.

Human Development — The First 2,000 Years[2]

A person functions at three levels. The highest level is צֶלֶם, *tzelem*, a reference to mankind's "image of God," an aspect of which is the

---

1. The numbers from 1 to 10 are unique, but after 10 the same digits are used over again as, for example, in the number 11. Hence, ten of something is a symbol of the maximum of possibilities.

2. Author's introductory comments, based on other parts of Maharal's *Derech Chaim* as well as his commentary to this *mishnah*.

---

independent spirit of individual existence. The middle level is צוּרָה, *tzurah,* which literally means form. It is the aspect of personality that seeks to impose form and structure on things, on oneself and on others. The level called חוֹמֶר, *chomer,* is the physical, pragmatic plane of existence. The qualities of *tzelem* and *tzurah* are, of course, more spiritual and intellectual whereas *chomer* is totally physical.

The human being is a union of the spiritual and the physical. Some people function at a more spiritual level, and others at a more pragmatic level. The three eras of history — from Adam to Noach, from Noach to Avraham, and from Avraham on — are each characterized by the predominant level at which people functioned.

• Adam, the first human being, was created in "the image of God," *tzelem Elohim*. However, we learned in *Avos* 3:22 that,

> Anyone whose wisdom exceeds his good deeds, to what is he likened? — to a tree whose branches are numerous but whose roots are few; then the wind comes and uproots it and turns it upside down.

The lofty spiritual and intellectual qualities of *tzelem* dominated the personality of Adam's descendants for ten generations. However, since they did not build a firm foundation of good deeds, they went off the proper path and angered God by engaging in theft and immorality.

• The intermediate plane, *tzurah,* form, was prominent for the ten generations commencing with Noach. *Tzurah* is more physically directed than *tzelem,* and Noach did engage in agriculture, but those generations still did not cultivate personal growth through good deeds and they rebelled against God.

• The final stage of human development came with Avraham, who integrated *chomer,* the physical side of human existence, with the spiritual planes of *tzurah* and *tzelem*. Avraham established the roots that would keep the human "tree" strong, stable and able to flourish. For that reason, he was the first to have the *mitzvah* of circumcision, a *mitzvah* that is realized within the body itself. His name itself has the numerical value[1] of 248, corresponding to the traditionally accepted number of limbs in the human body.

---

1. אברהם = 1 + 2 + 200 + 5 + 40 = 248.

ה/ד שֶׁכָּל הַדּוֹרוֹת הָיוּ מַכְעִיסִין וּבָאִין, עַד שֶׁבָּא
אַבְרָהָם אָבִינוּ וְקִבֵּל שְׂכַר כֻּלָּם.
[ד] עֲשָׂרָה נִסְיוֹנוֹת נִתְנַסָּה אַבְרָהָם אָבִינוּ,
וְעָמַד בְּכֻלָּם – לְהוֹדִיעַ כַּמָּה חִבָּתוֹ שֶׁל
אַבְרָהָם אָבִינוּ.

The integration of *tzelem, tzurah* and *chomer* — Divine spirit, expression and good deeds — took 2,000 years to complete. The Rabbis[1] call that developmental period of history the era of תוֹהוּ, *tohu,* void. In this sense, Avraham marked the culmination of human development and the beginning of religion as we know it, founded upon the practice of *mitzvos*.

Avraham marked the end of the era of void and the beginning of the era of Torah practice and principles.

Mishnah 2: There were ten generations from Adam to Noach.
Mishnah 3: There were ten generations from Noach to Avraham.

The ten generations from Adam to Noach include both Adam and Noach, but the ten generations from Noach to Avraham do not include Noach. Why are these "ten generations" calculated differently?

Adam shone with *tzelem,* the "image of God," and Noach began the era of dominant *tzurah,* human expression. These are two ends of a spiritual spectrum and therefore Adam and Noach are included in the same span of ten generations. In contrast, Avraham initiated a new focus, founded on dedicating the physical plane to the service of God. Since the physical and the spiritual are qualitatively different, Avraham and Noach would not be listed in the same grouping of the generations.

⊷§ עַד שֶׁבָּא אַבְרָהָם אָבִינוּ וְקִבֵּל שְׂכַר כֻּלָּם — *until our forefather Avraham came and received the reward of them all*

Avraham, by himself, embodied sufficient righteousness to protect an unrepentant world from destruction. He harnessed the volatile spiritual qualities of the preceding generations to the physical realm of life, and created a lasting paradigm for righteousness.

---

1. *Avodah Zarah* 9a: "The world is 6,000 years [duration.] Two thousand years of void, two thousand years of Torah and two thousand years of Messiah."

for all those generations angered Him increasingly, until our forefather Avraham came and received the reward of them all.

4. Our forefather Avraham was tested with ten trials, and he withstood them all — to show the degree of our forefather Avraham's love for God.

Although the early generations were closer to the lofty origin of God's Creation, that unbridled spiritual vigor was itself the cause of their undoing.

Mishnah 4

As explained in the preceding *mishnah,* the number 10 signifies all possible facets of something. To say that God tested Avraham with ten tests is to say that He tested him in all possible ways to actualize his full potential.

עֲשָׂרָה נִסְיוֹנוֹת נִתְנַסָּה אַבְרָהָם אָבִינוּ §◄ — *Our forefather Avraham was tested with ten trials*

Why did God need to test Avraham? He knew what Avraham was like without conducting a test!

God wants a good person's righteousness to be actively apparent. He tests good people so that their righteous response will serve as a role model for the rest of humanity. God endowed Avraham with many good qualities so that, through his righteous reputation, he would serve as mentor to the entire world.

There are different kinds of knowledge. We may know something objectively based on factual observation; or we may speculate on what might happen if a situation were to arise. God wanted the world to know of Avraham's righteousness through solid evidence, not by charitable assumptions.

After Avraham demonstrated his willingness to sacrifice his only son in submission to God's command, the angel of God says,[1] "now I know that you fear God."

Did God not know until now that Avraham was God fearing? Rashi[2] cites the Midrash as to what it was that God finally knew:

---

1. *Bereishis* 22:12.
2. *Ad loc.*

"Now I know how to answer the Satan and the nations that are amazed at the love I have for you. I have a chance to reply, now that they see how you fear God."

God had granted Avraham wealth and conferred upon him eminence as king of his followers. The nations were critical of his success: What did God see in this man that could be worthy of such support? Why were they being displaced from prominence? God now had objective, cogent and visible proof of Avraham's righteousness. He answered their criticisms and reproved their behavior by comparing it to Avraham's.

נִתְנַסָּה אַבְרָהָם אָבִינוּ §— Our forefather Avraham was tested

Why does God test people?

God is the light of existence. When mankind has turned its back on God and left Him, it is lost in the ensuing dark, but a righteous person can serve as a light to illuminate the path to teshuvah. God challenges a righteous person with trials, to bring out their inner light, to shine as a beacon by which others will see a higher purpose in life and start on their journey back.

Why does God test some people and not others?

The Rabbis use the metaphor of an artisan who strikes upon vases to draw attention to his wares. So might God strike upon His righteous followers to draw attention to them as people who have succeeded in life's mission. The merchant will chime upon the best quality merchandise and only upon those vases that will withstand being hit. So God chooses to strike the righteous in times when He wishes to draw the world's attention to His wares. He too is careful to strike only those who can withstand the blow and not those who will be shattered by it.

נְסַנָּסָה אַבְרָהָם אָבִינוּ §— Our forefather Avraham was tested

All of the forefathers were tested. The tests demonstrated that the forefathers were not ordinary people who responded in the natural way. For example, Avraham would have failed the test if he had done the natural thing and refused to sacrifice his only son. Rather, the forefathers transcended human nature in their service of God and earned the highest of spiritual levels.

---

§⊷ עֲשָׂרָה נִסְיוֹנוֹת — *with ten trials*

We noted before that the number ten conveys holiness. As Avraham rose to meet the superhuman challenge of the ten trials, he rose above nature to the level of Godliness.

The ten trials are identified in *Pirkei D'Rabbi Eliezer:*

1) When Nimrod, the king who opposed Avraham's teachings of the One God, sought to kill him, he hid underground for 13 years.
2) Nimrod finally threw him into a furnace of fire in Ur Casdim.
3) He was exiled from his birthplace.
4) God brought a famine in his time.
5) His wife Sarah was taken to Pharaoh's palace.
6) The kings abducted his nephew Lot.
7) God revealed to him the oppression of his descendants by later governments, who would rule over them.
8) He was commanded to circumcise himself and his son.
9) God told him to drive his son Yishmael out of the house, along with Yishmael's mother Hagar.
10) God commanded him to sacrifice his son Yitzchak.

Mishnah 5

---

§⊷ עֲשָׂרָה נִסִּים נַעֲשׂוּ לַאֲבוֹתֵינוּ בְּמִצְרַיִם — *Ten miracles were performed for our ancestors in Egypt*

The **ten miracles** are the ten plagues that God brought on behalf of the children of Israel, when He took them out of Egypt.

Rambam considers the **ten miracles** to be the fact that the Jews were saved from the ten plagues. The plagues afflicted the land of Egypt but miraculously bypassed the Jews. For example, if a Jew and an Egyptian were together during the plague of darkness, the Egyptian would experience darkness and the Jew would have light.

---

§⊷ עֲשָׂרָה נִסִּים נַעֲשׂוּ לַאֲבוֹתֵינוּ בְּמִצְרַיִם — *Ten miracles were performed for our ancestors in Egypt*

The number 10 signifies the inclusion of all possible aspects of something. Each miracle in Egypt was different from the others in a way

ה/ה וַעֲשָׂרָה עַל הַיָּם. עֶשֶׂר מַכּוֹת הֵבִיא הַקָּדוֹשׁ בָּרוּךְ הוּא עַל הַמִּצְרִים בְּמִצְרַיִם וְעֶשֶׂר עַל הַיָּם.

that would show how God directs yet another part of nature. *Mishnah 1* points out that the world was created with ten statements, to convey that every aspect of existence was included. Similarly, there were ten miracles to convey that every aspect of nature is directed by God.

---

§ וַעֲשָׂרָה עַל הַיָּם — *and ten at the Sea*

Why was it necessary to do miracles at the sea after the miracles done in Egypt?

God performed miracles to take us as His people and to be our God, as it says in the Ten Commandments,[1] "I am the Lord your God Who took you out from the land of Egypt." He saved us from two different kinds of opposition: opposition from people and opposition from nature.

Each kind of opposition is harder to deal with in one way and easier to deal with in another. People are harder to deal with because they have intelligence. They are creative, resourceful and unpredictable. They are easier because they can change their mind and cease their opposition. Nature is easier to deal with because it is stable and predictable, but it is harder because it is not subject to change.

God saved us from both kinds of opposition. He saved us from Pharaoh and the Egyptian people through the ten miracles in Egypt. He rescued us from nature through the ten miracles that saved Israel from the Sea that blocked their escape.

There is another reason that it was necessary to do miracles at the Sea after the miracles done in Egypt. The miracles in Egypt delivered them only from individual Egyptians who could have blocked their exit. However, even after escaping, they would have remained slaves of the Egyptian nation.[2] It was the miracles at the Sea that overthrew Egypt as a nation, not as individuals, and completely severed the bondage to Egypt.

Ten Plagues — Ten Tests

The Rabbis say[3] that God brought ten plagues on the Egyptians in the merit of Avraham who withstood ten tests. How are the ten tests and ten plagues connected to each other?

---

1. *Shemos* 20:2.
2. A runaway slave remains a slave.
3. *Avos D' Rabbi Nassan*, 33:2.

Avraham passed the tests by taking control of his own natural inclinations, as one might ride upon an animal. As a result, God abrogated nature to save the children of Avraham, who had abrogated his nature in the service of God.

Avraham — Father of Civilization

In *mishnah* 1, we noted that the physical Creation can embrace a very high spiritual element. The world was created that way to serve as a vehicle for mankind to come close to God. Before Avraham, a few individuals were on the right track, but humanity as a whole was lost in the darkness. Avraham seized the spiritual potential of life and restored spiritual focus to the center of practical life.

Unlike any before him, Avraham brought about the service of God at the level of an entire society. In other words, he participated in the creation of the world by fulfilling the purpose of Creation in a substantial and a sustainable way. He was truly the father of worthy civilization. The Rabbis make this point in commenting on the change of his name from Avram to Avraham,[1]

> At first he was father of Aram and eventually he became father of the entire world.

Ramban points out that events in Jewish history echoed events in Avraham's life. For example, King Nimrod persecuted Avraham and threw him into a furnace. God rescued him and took him out of Ur Casdim. Later in history, the Egyptians threw Jewish children into the river. God rescued the nation and took them out of Egypt.

Avraham, Yitzchak and Yaakov — Fathers of Jewish History

Avraham was the first of the forefathers, and it was his life from which the pattern for early Jewish history was cut. The life of Yitzchak, middle of the forefathers, was the model for the middle portion of history. Yaakov was the last forefather; and his life corresponds to the last era of Jewish history.

- Avraham's early life was filled with difficulty, as he was persecuted by Nimrod for his religious teachings. After God saved him, he enjoyed

---

1. *Berachos* 13a.

a life of blessing and prosperity. Likewise, the Jewish nation suffered oppression in Egypt in its formative years, but after God saved them they enjoyed blessings in the early part of their history.

• Yitzchak's life started in comfort and blessing but at the end he could no longer see; he was the archetype of suffering. The Jewish nation also passed from a period of comfort to a period of suffering in exile. Their eyes have also been darkened from the oppression of the nations.

• Yaakov spent most of his life in suffering due to a succession of difficult situations,[1] but ended his days at ease, after being reunited with his son Yosef. The last phase of Jewish history likewise embodies seemingly endless years of suffering in exile, but eventually there will be respite and the final years will be good ones.

There really is no end to Jewish history, for life will enter a phase of eternal spirituality. Yaakov's life reflects that as well, in the words of the Rabbis[2] who said that our father Yaakov did not die. As Yaakov now enjoys eternal, spiritual, life, so in the final phase of Jewish history the eternal people will have eternal goodness.

In addition Avraham, Yitzchak and Yaakov correspond to the three Temples.

• The First Temple stood in the merit of Avraham. The ten miracles of the Temple, listed *infra* in *mishnah* 7, occurred only in the First Temple, in the merit of the ten trials of Avraham. Furthermore, Avraham referred to the Temple site as a mountain,[3] hinting that the Temple would be destroyed and that the site would revert to be just a mountain.

• The Second Temple stood by the merit of Yitzchak. He referred to the Temple site as a field,[4] hinting that the Temple would be destroyed and plowed into a field.

• The Third Temple will stand through the merit of Yaakov. He referred to the Temple site as a house,[5] indicating that the final Temple will forever continue to fulfill its function as a house of prayer.

---

1. Fleeing from Eisav; years with deceitful Lavan; and years of mourning for Yosef.

2. *Taanis* 5a.

3. *Bereishis* 22:14: "God will appear on the mountain."

4. *Bereishis* 24:63. "And Yitzchak went out to meditate [i.e., pray] in the field."

5. *Bereishis* 28:17: "...and he [Yaakov] said, '...this is no other than the house of God.' "

Mishnah 6

The ten trials consist of paired groups, as the ten fingers consist of five fingers on one hand and five corresponding fingers on the other hand. Similarly, the Ten Commandments were laid out as five commandments on each of two stone tablets.

The ten trials were:[1]

- Two at the Red Sea: (1)Before escaping through the Red Sea, they said, "Were there no graves in Egypt that you took us to die in the Wilderness?"[2] (2)They were afraid to come out of the split sea because they thought that the Egyptians would be waiting for them on the other side. The fear lasted until they saw the dead Egyptians on the shore.[3]

- Two for lack of water: (3) At Marah they had no water to drink and "the people murmured against Moshe."[4] (4) At Refidim they had no water and "the nation contended with Moshe."[5]

- Two about manna: (5) They were told not to gather it on Shabbos and some people did go out to gather manna on Shabbos.[6] (6) They were told not to leave any manna over until the next day and some people did leave over until the next day.[7]

- Two complaints that were answered with quail: (7) "Would we had died by the hand of God in the land of Egypt, as we sat by the pot of meat, when we ate bread to satiety,"[8] in response to which God gave them quail and manna. (8) They complained a second time about the lack of meat, and insisted that Moshe give them some.[9]

- Two that displayed their lack of faith in God: (9) They acted as if there were gods other than God and made the golden calf.[10] (10) They doubted God's ability to displace the inhabitants of Canaan. They believed the spies, saying: "Why has God brought us to this land, to fall by the sword."[11]

---

1. See *Arachin* 15a.
2. *Shemos* 14:11.
3. *Ibid.* v. 30-31.
4. *Shemos* 15:24.
5. *Shemos* 17:2.
6. *Shemos* 16:27.
7. *Ibid.*, v. 20.
8. *Shemos* 16:3.
9. *Bamidbar* 11:13.
10. *Shemos* Chapter 32.
11. *Bamidbar* 14:3.

[ו] עֲשָׂרָה נִסְיוֹנוֹת נִסּוּ אֲבוֹתֵינוּ אֶת הַקָּדוֹשׁ בָּרוּךְ הוּא בַּמִּדְבָּר, שֶׁנֶּאֱמַר: „וַיְנַסּוּ אֹתִי זֶה עֶשֶׂר פְּעָמִים, וְלֹא שָׁמְעוּ בְּקוֹלִי.‟

[ז] עֲשָׂרָה נִסִּים נַעֲשׂוּ לַאֲבוֹתֵינוּ בְּבֵית הַמִּקְדָּשׁ: לֹא הִפִּילָה אִשָּׁה מֵרֵיחַ בְּשַׂר הַקֹּדֶשׁ;

◆§ עֲשָׂרָה נִסְיוֹנוֹת נִסּוּ אֲבוֹתֵינוּ אֶת הַקָּדוֹשׁ בָּרוּךְ הוּא — *With ten trials did our ancestors test the Holy One, Blessed is He*

The translations of נִסָּיוֹן as **trial** and נִסּוּ as **test** does not fit well with the context of the *mishnah*, for making the golden calf was an outright sin, not a test or trial.

A better approach to the word נִסָּיוֹן is to understand it as coming from the word, נֵס, *neis*, meaning "not within nature." The nation acted towards God in a way that was unnatural; their behavior was unimaginable.

This is also the best way to understand the word נִסְיוֹנוֹת in *mishnah* 4, above: Ten times was Avraham required to act in a way that broke through nature and elevated him above nature.

We can now explain why our *mishnah* would mention something this negative about the Jewish nation. It follows the *mishnah* that tells us how Avraham rose above nature. It was the merit of Avraham's ten נִסְיוֹנוֹת, *nisyonos,* acts that transcended human nature, that protected his descendants when they provoked God with ten נִסְיוֹנוֹת, acts that broke natural standards of behavior.

◆§ עֲשָׂרָה נִסְיוֹנוֹת נִסּוּ אֲבוֹתֵינוּ אֶת הַקָּדוֹשׁ בָּרוּךְ הוּא — *With ten trials did our ancestors test the Holy One, Blessed is He*

However, the usual translation of נִסְיוֹנוֹת as **trials** can be retained. The *mishnah* would then mean that our ancestors tested God to see if He would be flexible or inflexible. Would He allow them to have gods like the other nations? Would He be sensitive to their fears and desires?

When understood in this way, the ten trials were a deliberate conspiracy; they were an experiment to determine God's response. The people's intention was evil; they wanted to know what they could get away with. God's response was swift and clear. Although God does not

6. With ten trials did our ancestors test the Holy One, Blessed is He, in the Wilderness, as it is said (*Bamidbar* 14:22): "They have tested Me these ten times and did not heed My voice."

7. Ten miracles were performed for our ancestors in the Holy Temple: No woman miscarried because of the aroma of the sacrificial meat;

---

immediately reprove an individual who sins,[1] He did respond to the nation, so that they would understand the limits that He demanded of them.

When we translate נְסִיוֹנוֹת as **trials,** we can explain that the *mishnah* mentions the sins of Israel because those trials increased God's glory. The ten experiments proved to them that all the ways of God are upright and in no way accommodate wrongdoing.

Mishnah 7

Development and deterioration are inseparable in normal life, as things come and go. The Temple, however, was unique, and it provided protection from loss. These ten miracles convey the degree to which the Temple and its environs were immune from loss, decay or deterioration. They are listed in order from the most severe and obvious of losses, through lesser degrees of damage, deterioration or scarcity.

∽§ לֹא הִפִּילָה אִשָּׁה — *No woman miscarried*

Miscarriage is a major loss, for it is the loss of a human fetus.

The other losses that were spared in the Temple were more likely, but much less serious, until the final item, lack of space is just a discomfort without actual injury.

A Kabbalistic Approach

It is well known that Maharal couches the ideas of the esoteric and arcane system of *Kabbalah* in general language, without explicit recourse to its nomenclature and methodology. Rare and outstanding exceptions are found in this *mishnah,* the next and in *mishnah* 18. In his

---

1. As noted in the commentary to *Avos* 3:19, *supra.*

וְלֹא הִסְרִיחַ בְּשַׂר הַקֹּדֶשׁ מֵעוֹלָם; וְלֹא נִרְאָה
זְבוּב בְּבֵית הַמִּטְבְּחַיִם; וְלֹא אֵירַע קֶרִי לְכֹהֵן
גָּדוֹל בְּיוֹם הַכִּפּוּרִים; וְלֹא כָבוּ הַגְּשָׁמִים אֵשׁ
שֶׁל עֲצֵי הַמַּעֲרָכָה; וְלֹא נִצְּחָה הָרוּחַ אֶת
עַמּוּד הֶעָשָׁן; וְלֹא נִמְצָא פְסוּל בָּעֹמֶר, וּבִשְׁתֵּי
הַלֶּחֶם, וּבְלֶחֶם הַפָּנִים; עוֹמְדִים צְפוּפִים,
וּמִשְׁתַּחֲוִים רְוָחִים; וְלֹא הִזִּיק נָחָשׁ וְעַקְרָב
בִּירוּשָׁלַיִם מֵעוֹלָם; וְלֹא אָמַר אָדָם לַחֲבֵרוֹ:
„צַר לִי הַמָּקוֹם שֶׁאָלִין בִּירוּשָׁלָיִם."

---

commentary to this *mishnah*, Maharal associates each of the ten miracles in the Temple with each of the ten *Sefiros.*

In keeping with the advice of *Gedolei Torah,* the author has omitted such discussions from this English-language adaptation. However, readers with the appropriate background will find the original *Derech Chaim* to be of substantial interest.

Mishnah 8

Rambam[1] makes the following points:

- God does not alter the laws of nature that He put in motion at the time of Creation.
- God's will does not change.
- Therefore, these miracles had to be built into Creation from the first, ready to unfold later.

When these miracles occurred at the appropriate time, later in history, they happened as the result of the original Creation. Therefore, the occurrence of miracles does not imply a change of God's will or a mutation of the laws of nature.

Of this, Maharal writes:

Rambam explains this *mishnah* in a way that the Rabbis never intended. His words are without basis or foundation.

He questions Rambam's explanation as follows:

- Why were the miracles listed in this *mishnah* created on Shabbos eve, whereas other miracles were prepared on the appropriate day of

---

1. *Maimonides.*

the sacrificial meat never became putrid; no fly was seen in the place where the meat was butchered; no seminal emission occurred to the High Priest on Yom Kippur; the rains did not extinguish the fire on the Altar-pyre; the wind did not disperse the vertical column of smoke from the Altar; no disqualification was found in the Omer, or in the Two Loaves, or in the Showbread; the people stood crowded together, yet prostrated themselves in ample space; neither serpent nor scorpion ever caused injury in Jerusalem; nor did any man say to his fellow, "The space is insufficient for me to stay overnight in Jerusalem."

Creation? For example, when God created the seas, on the second day of Creation, He gave water the ability to split when the Jews would need to cross the Red Sea.

Rambam's explanation does not address why it was necessary to create the "mouth of the earth," which would in the future swallow Korach, at twilight of Shabbos eve. He should have given the earth the ability to form a mouth on the day that earth was created.

- If God does not change His will to bring about miracles, why does He change His will about other events? To say that everything is preordained from the six days of Creation is to reject the verse:[1]

> "And God relented of the evil He had thought to do to His people."

Maharal deals with the constancy of nature as follows.

It is true that God made the laws of nature immutable. He does not change the laws of nature, for that would undermine His Creation. However, God did not place the world under the sole control of nature. Rather, He tied this world to the spiritual world so that He can change it without changing the laws of nature.

In the following section, Maharal asserts that the *mishnah* should not be explained according to philosophy, which the Rabbis never espoused, but according to *Kabbalah,* on which all their words are built.

---

1. *Shemos* 32:14. God had intended to destroy the nation of Israel as a result of the sin of the golden calf, but relented after Moshe's prayers.

ה/ח

עֲשָׂרָה דְבָרִים נִבְרְאוּ בְּעֶרֶב שַׁבָּת [ח]
בֵּין הַשְּׁמָשׁוֹת. וְאֵלוּ הֵן: פִּי הָאָרֶץ,,

Philosophy vs. Kabbalah

The philosophers believe that God's will and His knowledge are His essence. It follows that, if God were to change His will then His essence would be changed, and therefore they say that God does not change His will.

How far these words are from common sense! If they would be true, what need was there for the nation of Israel to pray at the time of the splitting of the Red Sea? If the splitting of the Sea was built into nature, then it would have to split. If it was not built into the nature of the Sea, then it could not split.

Rambam addresses such problems by saying that God's prior knowledge does not compel future events to happen. He says that we cannot understand how that can be, because His knowledge is Himself and just as we cannot understand His essence, we cannot understand His knowledge.

In this way he avoids all the problems that arise from saying that God knows everything in advance of its occurrence.

All of these statements are compelled by the theory that knowledge is His essence, for then a change in His knowledge would be a change in Himself. This theory does not appeal to common sense and it is not found in the words of the Rabbis. Knowledge is not His essence. It is one of God's actions, as we find in Scripture[1] when the Jews were enslaved:

> And God heard their groaning, and God remembered His covenant with Avraham, with Yitzchak and with Yaakov. And God looked upon the children of Israel **and God knew.**

Neither the *Zohar* nor the books of the Kabbalists say that His essence is intellect. Instead, the Rabbis compare God to the soul. The soul grasps knowledge, but knowledge is not the essence of the soul. Consider a situation where God knows that a person is righteous, but the person then becomes wicked and God knows that he is wicked. That is not a change in knowledge; it is a change in the person, the object of the knowledge. Saying that God knows is just a description of Him, like other descriptions.

Furthermore, the philosophers say that, because we cannot know His essence, it is impossible to assign any description to Him other than by

---

1. *Shemos* 2:24-25.

negatives.[1] Some people have come to think that this opinion is in the Torah and they panic if someone expresses a different opinion. After they see the merit of the Kabbalistic approach, they try to say that the difference on this point is just semantic. However, the truth is that the two systems are diametric opposites.

Proofs that God cannot be described are just empty words. God is the Source of this world's existence and its Creator. Is this not a direct description, to say that He is the Creator, or that He is the Master of the world. The world itself describes God!

The Kabbalists have ascribed to God the minimum set of unique descriptions and call them by the general term *Sefiros*. The *Sefiros* include Wisdom and Understanding, which are knowledge. The *Sefiros* are a description of God's qualities; they are not His essence.

Hence, the statement that God's knowledge is His essence contradicts all of *Kabbalah*. Indeed, the assertion itself, that God's essence is knowledge, places a boundary on Him.

God knows; but the knowledge is not Him. If a thing changes, the knowledge of the thing changes, but He does not change.

Maharal's explanation of the *mishnah* now follows.

עֲשָׂרָה דְבָרִים נִבְרְאוּ בְּעֶרֶב שַׁבָּת, בֵּין הַשְּׁמָשׁוֹת — *Ten things were created on Sabbath eve, at twilight.*

Why were the Rabbis compelled to say that ten things were created at twilight of Shabbos eve? That time was special, and it was specially suited to these ten things.

The day concludes at sunset and the next day begins at night. Twilight is the intervening period, the time of transition from one day to the next. The twilight periods of the days preceding the first Shabbos had been part of the six days of Creation. This twilight was different. It was the transition from a day of creating nature to a day of sanctity when there was no creation. The day of rest had not yet arrived and therefore there had to be creation. However, the six days of creating nature were over and therefore the things created had to be beyond nature.

Time was marching towards the holiness of Shabbos; therefore this twilight was a time of elevated sanctity, albeit less than that of Shabbos

1. I.e., what He is not, such as: He is not finite; He is not physical.

וּפִי הַבְּאֵר; פִּי הָאָתוֹן; וְהַקֶּשֶׁת; וְהַמָּן;
וְהַמַּטֶּה; וְהַשָּׁמִיר; הַכְּתָב; וְהַמִּכְתָּב;
וְהַלּוּחוֹת. וְיֵשׁ אוֹמְרִים אַף הַמַּזִּיקִין, וּקְבוּרָתוֹ
שֶׁל מֹשֶׁה, וְאֵילוֹ שֶׁל אַבְרָהָם אָבִינוּ. וְיֵשׁ
אוֹמְרִים אַף צְבַת, בִּצְבַת עֲשׂוּיָה.

---

itself. That sanctity is reflected by the number ten, which is symbolic of
holiness as explained in the Introduction to this chapter.

---

§ וְיֵשׁ אוֹמְרִים אַף . . . — *Some say also . . .*

Maharal compares our *mishnah* with similar Talmudic texts and
concludes that there are three opinions that add to the list of things
created at twilight of the first Shabbos. The correct text, in his view, is:
וְיֵשׁ אוֹמְרִים אַף אֵילוֹ שֶׁל יִצְחָק וְקִבְרוֹ שֶׁל מֹשֶׁה. וְיֵשׁ אוֹמְרִים אַף הַמַּזִּיקִין. וְיֵשׁ אוֹמְרִים אַף
צְבַת, בִּצְבַת עֲשׂוּיָה, *Some say also the **ram of Yitzchak and Moshe's grave**.
And some say also **destructive spirits**. And some say also **tongs, which
are made with tongs**.*
    Within the interval of twilight there are three periods: the beginning,
the middle and the end. In addition, there is also the final moment at
which the day changes.[1] All the opinions expressed in our *mishnah*
agree that the first ten things listed in the *mishnah* were created during
that final moment. Each opinion introduced by the words "some say also"
then adds to the opinions before it, and is not meant as an alternative.
    Each of the three additional opinions corresponds to one of the three
periods of twilight:

• The opinion that Yitzchak's ram and Moshe's grave were created at
  twilight refers to the last part of twilight, which is furthest from the six
  days of creating nature and closest to the holy Shabbos.
• The opinion that includes destructive spirits maintains that they were
  created during the middle part of twilight which is still closer to nature.
• The opinion that includes tongs maintains they were created at the
  beginning of twilight, right after sunset, for fabricating tongs is not far
  at all from everyday life. Indeed, tongs can be made with a mold; it is
  not necessary to use other tongs.[2]

---

1. *Shabbos* 34b lists two of the opinions as to how long twilight extends and the
opinion of Rabbi Yose that the final transition is but a moment.
2. *Pesachim* 54a.

the mouth of the well; the mouth of the donkey; the rainbow [which was God's sign to Noah that there would be no future floods]; the manna; the staff; the shamir worm; the script; the inscription; and the Tablets. Some say also destructive spirits, Moshe's grave, and the ram of our fore-father Avraham. And some say also tongs, which are made with tongs.

---

§§ **עֲשָׂרָה דְבָרִים נִבְרְאוּ בְּעֶרֶב שַׁבָּת, בֵּין הַשְּׁמָשׁוֹת** — *Ten things were created on Sabbath eve, at twilight.*

These were created at the final instant that joined Shabbos to the preceding days. It would be problematic to say that these things were created in an instant if they were physical, because physical things cannot appear instantly, but are subject to time. However, the thing that was created was the supranatural root from which the physical object would derive later in history. Since the aspect that was created at twilight was non-physical, it did not require any duration of time.

---

§§ **וּפִי הַבְּאֵר** — *the mouth of the well*

Rashi explains[1] this as the well that accompanied the nation of Israel through the desert, in the merit of Miriam. He describes it as a rock that accompanied them wherever they went. However, it is unlikely that he means the rock traveled by rolling along, because that would imply the rock provided water even though it was not attached to the ground. If that were so, the Rabbis would surely have mentioned it as a miracle in its own right. Rather, the miracle is called "the **mouth** of the well" because God created a mouth from where water would rise up from the well and spout, wherever they camped.

---

§§ **הַכְּתָב; וְהַמִּכְתָּב** — *the script; the inscription*

Script refers to the form of each letter. **Inscription** refers to the actual writing. They were decreed at twilight on Shabbos eve so that the script

---

1. *Ibid.*

[ט] שִׁבְעָה דְבָרִים בְּגֹלֶם, וְשִׁבְעָה בְּחָכָם. חָכָם אֵינוֹ מְדַבֵּר לִפְנֵי מִי שֶׁגָּדוֹל מִמֶּנּוּ בְּחָכְמָה וּבְמִנְיָן; וְאֵינוֹ נִכְנָס לְתוֹךְ

used for the Tablets of the Ten Commandments and for Torah scrolls should be of Divine origin and not man made.

◆§ אֵילוֹ שֶׁל יִצְחָק[1] — *the ram of Yitzchak*[1]

It is unlikely that the ram lived from the six days of Creation until Avraham, an interval of about 2,000 years. The *mishnah* means that God decreed the creation of the ram at twilight and that truly is its creation.

◆§ וְיֵשׁ אוֹמְרִים אַף צְבָת — *And some say also tongs*

God did not make tongs at twilight of the eve of the first Shabbos, but rather He decreed their existence. In other words, He decreed that mankind would have the inspiration to invent tongs, so that the world would have the benefit of the art of forging metal.

◆§ עֲשָׂרָה דְבָרִים נִבְרְאוּ בְּעֶרֶב שַׁבָּת בֵּין הַשְּׁמָשׁוֹת — *Ten things were created on Sabbath eve, at twilight*

This *mishnah* was not placed in chronological order, after *mishnah* 1, which discussed Creation. Rather, it was placed last in the list of 'tens' because it discusses creations that are not part of the natural order but are above nature.[2]

Mishnah 9

This *mishnah* describes the conduct of wise people.

The essence of wisdom is order and structure. What are the properties of ordered structure?

• Each element is distinguished from the other elements.

---

1. See commentary above.

2. Maharal concludes the *mishnah* as he started it, with a rejection of the philosopher's interpretation of the *mishnah* as an attempt to rationalize miracles within nature.

9. Seven traits characterize a dullard and seven a wise one. A wise person does not begin speaking before one who is greater than he in wisdom or in years; he does not interrupt

---

- Each element's proper place is identified according to some ordering criteria.
- The elements are linked to each other.

  All of these properties are functions of the *sechel,* intellect.

  The actions of a wise person are evaluated and orderly, and hence each of the seven traits listed in the *mishnah* embodies considered and orderly behavior.

Seven as the Symbol of Structure and Order

Objects have six sides: top, bottom, front, back, right and left. The six sides have no area in common with each other, but the center is a common point of reference for all sides (see diagram).

The center joins opposite sides and links the different directions together.

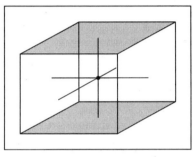

In summary, every physical object has seven parts: six sides and the center. The center is the reference point that links the other six parts together; it is the "seventh" part. For this reason the number 7 is used as the symbol of order.

∢§ שִׁבְעָה דְבָרִים — *Seven traits*

The *mishnah* draws our attention to the number 7 because it is the symbol of order and structure. Since a wise person demonstrates order, it is fitting for the *mishnah* to list seven traits.

∢§ שִׁבְעָה דְבָרִים בְּגֹלֶם — *Seven traits characterize a dullard*

The word **dullard,** גֹּלֶם, *golem,* denotes someone who does not have much common sense. The *mishnah* did not employ the more common term "ignoramus," עַם הָאָרֶץ, because that is used for one who lacks Torah, and that is not the point of this *mishnah.*

דִּבְרֵי חֲבֵרוֹ; וְאֵינוֹ נִבְהָל לְהָשִׁיב; שׁוֹאֵל כְּעִנְיָן וּמֵשִׁיב כַּהֲלָכָה; וְאוֹמֵר עַל רִאשׁוֹן רִאשׁוֹן וְעַל אַחֲרוֹן אַחֲרוֹן; וְעַל מַה שֶּׁלֹּא שָׁמַע אוֹמֵר: "לֹא שָׁמַעְתִּי"; וּמוֹדֶה עַל הָאֱמֶת. וְחִלּוּפֵיהֶן בְּגֹלֶם.

[י] שִׁבְעָה מִינֵי פֻּרְעָנִיּוֹת בָּאִין לָעוֹלָם

---

§ **וְאֵינוֹ נִבְהָל לְהָשִׁיב** — *he does not answer impetuously*

One should not be in a rush to respond, but should rather respond calmly and with due consideration.

---

§ **שׁוֹאֵל כְּעִנְיָן** — *he questions with relevance to the subject*

One should phrase a question by specifying precisely the premises on which the question is based.

It can also mean that one should ask only questions about the subject matter under discussion. Therefore, if people are studying one tractate of the Talmud, one should not ask about a different tractate, even if it is an intelligent question.

---

§ **וּמֵשִׁיב כַּהֲלָכָה** — *and he replies accurately*

An answer should be accurate enough that one could act upon it with confidence.

---

§ **שׁוֹאֵל כְּעִנְיָן וּמֵשִׁיב כַּהֲלָכָה** — *he questions with relevance to the subject and he replies accurately*

An intelligent manner in both questioning and answering is but a single trait, and is reckoned as just one of the seven traits.

---

§ **וּמוֹדֶה עַל הָאֱמֶת** — *and he acknowledges the truth*

"Order" is evenness, symmetry and balance, and anything that lacks these qualities is not in order. The ultimate evenness is the center, for it

the words of his fellow; he does not answer
impetuously; he questions with relevance to the
subject and he replies accurately; he discusses
first things first and last things last; about
something he has not heard he says: "I have not
heard"; and he acknowledges the truth. And the
reverse of these characterize a dullard.

10. Seven kinds of punishment come to the world

---

does not incline to any side. Therefore, the center point is the essence of order.

It is fitting that the seventh quality of a wise person is **truth,** because the seventh part is the center, the point of balance, and the essence of truth is its balanced perspective. The Hebrew word for truth, אֱמֶת, *emes,* is a portrait of its nature. The first letter of *emes* is the beginning of the Hebrew alphabet; the middle letter is the middle letter of the alphabet;[1] and the last letter is at the end of the alphabet. Therefore, the structure of the word א־מ־ת reflects the key attribute of truth, which is a balanced perspective between the most divergent positions. Truth gives expression to the extremes that define it, and is the common ground between them. Truth also embodies order, as reflected in the fact the letters of אֱמֶת are in alphabetical order.

By contrast, falsehood, שֶׁקֶר, *sheker,* is off balance. The letters of that word are all at one end of the alphabet, and even so do not include the full extreme of that end, the letter ת. Furthermore, the letters are out of order, and falsehood departs from the nature of truth in that way also.

Falsehood is associated with deterioration, for it is found near the end, like extinction. Truth, however, is associated with enduring existence. Like the center, it does not incline towards any end but is stable and hence enduring.

Mishnah 10

We explained in the previous *mishnah* that the number seven is associated with order and structure. This *mishnah* discusses the consequences of violating the structure that *mitzvos* build. A list of exactly seven transgressions emphasizes how *mitzvos* set bounds that give

---

1. The letter מ is the precise middle of the full alphabet which includes the final forms of the letters such as ך ,ם ,ן, ף and ץ.

עַל שִׁבְעָה גוּפֵי עֲבֵרָה: מִקְצָתָן מְעַשְּׂרִין וּמִקְצָתָן אֵינָן מְעַשְּׂרִין, רָעָב שֶׁל בַּצְּרֶת בָּא, מִקְצָתָן רְעֵבִים וּמִקְצָתָן שְׂבֵעִים; גָּמְרוּ שֶׁלֹּא לְעַשֵּׂר, רָעָב שֶׁל מְהוּמָה וְשֶׁל בַּצְּרֶת בָּא; וְשֶׁלֹּא לִטּוֹל אֶת הַחַלָּה, רָעָב שֶׁל כְּלָיָה בָּא;

ה/יא

[יא] דֶּבֶר בָּא לָעוֹלָם עַל מִיתוֹת הָאֲמוּרוֹת בַּתּוֹרָה שֶׁלֹּא נִמְסְרוּ לְבֵית דִּין וְעַל פֵּרוֹת שְׁבִיעִית; חֶרֶב בָּאָה לָעוֹלָם עַל עִנּוּי הַדִּין, וְעַל עִוּוּת הַדִּין, וְעַל הַמּוֹרִים בַּתּוֹרָה שֶׁלֹּא כַהֲלָכָה;

---

structure and stability to our lives. This also is the reason that precisely seven *mitzvos* were given to Adam.[1]

God created the world with perfect order, and without deficiency, but transgression breaks out of the set order and brings deficiency in its wake. Therefore, each of these seven sins brings about a loss that departs from the normal order of nature.

Tithes and Challah

Tithes are the tenth part of crops,[2] which Torah law requires be given to members of the tribe of Levi. *Challah* is a small portion of dough that is separated from large batches of dough and given to *Kohanim*.

Kohanim and Levites do not have family land holdings, and those who do have land must help support them, through tithes and *challah*. If they do not, then God likewise withholds their livelihood and brings famine.

---

§◈ *tumultuous famine* — רָעָב שֶׁל מְהוּמָה

This is a degree of famine so severe that people are crying out and are in feverish pursuit of sustenance. The famine of drought, which comes when some people tithe and others do not, is less severe, and even those who are hungry are not in a state of panic.

---

1. Maharal differs with Rambam's view in *Hilchos Malachim*, 9:1 that Adam was given only six *mitzvos*. Maharal proves his point in *Gur Aryeh* to *Bereishis* 9:3.
2. Grown in the Land of Israel.

for seven kinds of transgressions. (a) If some people tithe and others do not, a famine caused by lack of rain ensues, some go hungry and others are satisfied; (b) if all decided not to tithe, tumultuous famine caused by drought ensues; and (c) [if they also decided] not to separate the challah, a famine caused by destructive drought ensues;

11. (d) pestilence comes to the world for the death penalties prescribed by the Torah that were not carried out by the court and for [illegally using] the fruits of the Sabbatical year; (e) the sword [of war] comes to the world for the delay of justice, for the perversion of justice and for interpreting the Torah decision in opposition to the *halachah;*

Mishnah 11

Fruits of the Sabbatical year may be eaten. The following year, produce that was not consumed must be destroyed, by placing it where people and animals frequently walk. It is fitting that the punishment for not destroying Sabbatical year produce is pestilence, an epidemic of disease that destroys people and animals.

◆§ *(d) Pestilence* — דֶּבֶר בָּא לָעוֹלָם עַל מִיתוֹת . . . וְעַל פֵּרוֹת שְׁבִיעִית
comes to the world for the death penalties . . .
and for the fruits of the Sabbatical year

Pestilence has two attributes: It comes forcefully and it destroys without regard to innocence or guilt. The forcefulness of pestilence makes it a fitting punishment for not enforcing the harsh decree of law. The fact that pestilence attacks without discrimination befits the transgression of Sabbatical year produce which should have been put into a place where anyone or anything could get it.

◆§ *(e) the sword [of war]* — חֶרֶב בָּאָה לָעוֹלָם עַל עִנּוּי הַדִּין
comes to the world for the delay of justice

God punishes transgression in like kind. The various forms of improper execution of the law are punished through lawless execution by the sword.

ה/יא **חַיָּה רָעָה בָּאָה לָעוֹלָם עַל שְׁבוּעַת שָׁוְא וְעַל חִלּוּל הַשֵּׁם; גָּלוּת בָּאָה לָעוֹלָם עַל עוֹבְדֵי עֲבוֹדָה זָרָה, וְעַל גִּלּוּי עֲרָיוֹת, וְעַל שְׁפִיכוּת דָּמִים וְעַל שְׁמִטַּת הָאָרֶץ.**

ײַ — **חַיָּה רָעָה בָּאָה לָעוֹלָם עַל שְׁבוּעַת שָׁוְא וְעַל חִלּוּל הַשֵּׁם** ײַ
(f) wild beasts come upon the world for vain oaths and for desecration of God's Name

Using God's Name for a false or frivolous oath and desecrating God's Name are the same type of transgression. They both are a flagrant disregard for the honor due to the King of kings.

It is difficult to explain how a punishment of "wild beasts" would be a fitting punishment for these sins. Possibly, the expression **wild beasts** is an allusion to oppressive governments. If people do not demonstrate reverence and fear for the true King of kings, then God brings a king that they will fear.

ײַ **גָּלוּת בָּאָה לָעוֹלָם — עַל עוֹבְדֵי עֲבוֹדָה זָרָה, וְעַל גִּלּוּי עֲרָיוֹת, וְעַל שְׁפִיכוּת דָּמִים וְעַל שְׁמִטַּת הָאָרֶץ** — *(g) exile comes to the world for idolatry, for immorality, for bloodshed and for working the land during the Sabbatical year*

Exile is the fitting punishment for these transgressions for the following reason.

There are three unique attributes of the Land of Israel:

• God's Name is identified with the Land of Israel and hence those who dwell in the Land of Israel can especially recognize that He is God.
• The Land of Israel is called a holy land.
• The Land of Israel is called the land of life. It is the center of the world in the sense that it is the central point that gives meaning to all other aspects of life.
• Rest is suitable only for that which is complete, because that which is in need requires action to supply that need.

Israel is whole and fully actualized and for this reason, the Sabbatical year is unique to the holy Land of Israel.

Exile ensues from transgressions that undermine the unique attributes of the Land of Israel.

(f) wild beasts come upon the world for vain oaths and for desecration of God's Name; (g) exile comes to the world for idolatry, for immorality, for bloodshed and for working the land during the Sabbatical year.

- **Idolatry.** Serving other gods in God's land is unacceptable.
- **Immorality.** Holiness is characterized by being completely free of improper relationships. The holy land cannot accommodate such immorality.
- **Bloodshed.** Murder in the land of life is unacceptable.
- **Working the land** of Israel in the Sabbatical year declares the land as deficient and in continuous need of being worked. Hence, exile is a fitting punishment because the ensuing rest affirms the lofty stature of the land.

In summary, the Land of Israel has unique qualities that demand of the inhabitants suitable behavior. When the people do not behave appropriately, they are exiled to an ordinary country.

Another reason these four transgressions bring exile is based solely on the basis of the holiness of the Land of Israel. Scripture refers to all three — idolatry, sexual immorality and bloodshed — by the term טוּמְאָה, *tumah,* impurity.[1] Hence all three are the opposite of holiness and cannot be tolerated in the holy land. The Sabbatical year is itself based on the holiness of Israel and abrogating its observance abrogates the holiness of the land.

Still another approach to understanding why these four transgressions result in exile is based on the fact that the Land of Israel came to us through the merit of the forefathers, as it says,[2]

> Then I will remember My covenant with Yaakov and also My covenant with Yitzchak and also My covenant with Avraham will I remember and I will remember the land.

The *Midrash* explains,[3]

> Why does God mention the land at the same time as the forefathers? Rabbi Shimon ben Lakish said that the parable to explain it is of a king who had three sons and a maid to

---

1. *Shavuos* 7b.

2. *Vayikra* 26:42.

3. *Vayikra Rabbah,* Section 36.

raise them. Whenever the king would inquire after the welfare of his sons, he would inquire after the welfare of the maid as well.

In this parable the Land of Israel is compared to the maid. The land fostered the spiritual growth of the forefathers and hence the sanctity of the land and the sanctity of the forefathers are inseparable.

Only when the people of Israel are like their forefathers do they deserve to have the land. Each of the forefathers exemplified a particular quality for which he deserved to receive the Land of Israel.

- Avraham was the antithesis of **immorality.** He did not gaze at the beauty of even his own wife.[1] If the people of the Land of Israel are not careful about immorality, they act in the opposite way of Avraham, to whom the land was given.
- Yitzchak so dedicated himself to the service of God that he offered himself as a sacrifice. Therefore, one who would practice **idolatry** demonstrates the very opposite of Yitzchak's quality.
- Yaakov is the antithesis of **bloodshed.** Even semen emitted to no purpose is a form of bloodshed,[2] and Yaakov was so distant from any form of bloodshed that he avoided even an accidental flow of semen until his marriage. Therefore, any inclination of the people of Israel towards bloodshed would remove them from this quality of Yaakov and they would be exiled.
- The forefathers acquired the holy land through a covenant with God. Transgression of the **Sabbatical year** violates the holiness of the land and abrogates the covenant.

In the count of seven transgressions, which began with *mishnah* 10, the four sins for which exile comes count as one; namely, the corruption of the Land of Israel.

Mishnah 12

The phrase **pestilence increases** means that there is simply some increase over normal levels. It contrasts with the expression "pestilence comes" for unpunished capital transgressions, in *mishnah* 11, which refers to a major epidemic.

This *mishnah* deals with the consequences of withholding from the

1. Rashi to *Bereishis* 12:11.
2. *Niddah* 13b.

poor the gifts that the Torah specified. Produce of the Sabbatical year is also intended for the poor, as Scripture says,[1]

> And the seventh [year] you shall let it rest and lie fallow, that the poor of your people shall eat.

These gifts belong to the poor and their life depends on them. It is true that stealing is a sin whether the victim is rich or poor, but stealing from the poor engenders serious harm. To steal even a dollar from a poor person is comparable to taking his life, as Scripture says,[2]

> Do not rob the poor, for he is poor, and do not oppress the afflicted in the gate. For God will fight their quarrel and will rob the life of those who rob them.

Why should God take the life of a thief? Because any amount of theft from a poor person virtually robs him of his life.

By increasing pestilence, God denies a living to those who would deprive the poor of their sustenance.

◆§ **בְּאַרְבָּעָה פְּרָקִים הַדֶּבֶר מִתְרַבֶּה** — *At four periods . . . pestilence increases*

Why is there only an increase over normal levels of pestilence for withholding the tithe of the poor, while refraining from capital punishment causes a major epidemic?[3]

The sin of refraining from capital punishment does not bring immediate consequences. God waits for the people to repent and if He eventually does bring retribution, all the punishments that have been pending come at the same time. Therefore, the pestilence due to other transgressions is a severe plague, because it combines many accumulated punishments. In contrast, when a poor person cries out, God brings retribution swiftly. Therefore, punishments for oppressing the poor do not accumulate, and the ensuing pestilence is less severe.

---

1. *Shemos* 23:11.
2. *Mishlei* 22:22-23.
3. Previous *mishnah*.

וּבַשְּׁבִיעִית, וּבְמוֹצָאֵי שְׁבִיעִית וּבְמוֹצָאֵי הֶחָג
שֶׁבְּכָל שָׁנָה וְשָׁנָה. בָּרְבִיעִית, מִפְּנֵי מַעְשַׂר
עָנִי שֶׁבַּשְּׁלִישִׁית; בַּשְּׁבִיעִית, מִפְּנֵי מַעְשַׂר עָנִי
שֶׁבַּשִּׁשִּׁית; בְּמוֹצָאֵי שְׁבִיעִית, מִפְּנֵי פֵּרוֹת
שְׁבִיעִית; בְּמוֹצָאֵי הֶחָג שֶׁבְּכָל שָׁנָה וְשָׁנָה,
מִפְּנֵי גֶּזֶל מַתְּנוֹת עֲנִיִּים.

[יג] אַרְבַּע מִדּוֹת בָּאָדָם. הָאוֹמֵר: „שֶׁלִּי שֶׁלִּי
וְשֶׁלְּךָ שֶׁלָּךְ,״ זוֹ מִדָּה בֵינוֹנִית, וְיֵשׁ
אוֹמְרִים זוֹ מִדַּת סְדוֹם; „שֶׁלִּי שֶׁלָּךְ וְשֶׁלְּךָ

Mishnah 13

---

§ הָאוֹמֵר: „שֶׁלִּי שֶׁלִּי וְשֶׁלְּךָ שֶׁלָּךְ,״ זוֹ מִדָּה בֵינוֹנִית § — *(a) One
who says: "My property is mine and yours
is yours," is an average character type*

He is **average** because he has a perfect right to keep his property
to himself, according to Torah law. He is not generous enough to
be called "scrupulously pious," but neither is he covetous of other's
things.

---

§ וְיֵשׁ אוֹמְרִים זוֹ מִדַּת סְדוֹם § — *but some say that
this is characteristic of Sodom*

The people of Sodom hated giving of their things to help others. They
were so afraid of helping another person that they were willing to forgo
receiving help in their own time of need.

According to the view that this is an evil trait, he says, "What is mine
is mine," even if does not cost him anything,[1] because he simply
begrudges others benefiting. In the same vein, he does not say, "What is
yours is yours," out of genuine respect for their property, but rather as
a mere pretext to justify not helping others.

Whether "Mine is mine and yours is yours" is average or evil depends upon the intent of the person. The test of the person's intent

---

1. For example, lending an article that he does not need at the time.

in the seventh year, in the year following the Sabbatical year and annually following the Succos festival. In the fourth year, for [neglecting] the tithe of the poor in the third year; in the seventh year, for [neglecting] the tithe of the poor in the sixth year; in the year following the Sabbatical year, for [violating the laws of] the Sabbatical produce; annually at the conclusion of the festival of Succos, for robbing the poor of their gifts.

13. There are four character types among people: (a) One who says: "My property is mine and yours is yours," is an average character type, but some say that this is characteristic of Sodom; (b) "Mine is yours and yours

---

comes when someone wants to use something in a way that will not cause any loss to the owner. The person with evil intent will not lend the article, claiming, "My property is mine and yours is yours." The average person does not try to link respect for another's property to his own rights of ownership, and will lend things if causes him no loss.

וּ§ עַם הָאָרֶץ "שֶׁלִּי שֶׁלָּךְ וְשֶׁלְּךָ שֶׁלִּי,, — *(b) "Mine is yours and yours is mine," is an ignoramus*

This person does not mean "Mine is yours" as an act of generosity. If he were being generous, he would not add the condition that "yours is mine." This person is willing to give up his things only if he can share in the other's things. His end goal is for each party to be able to use the other's things, without limit and without distinguishing what belongs to whom.

Wise people ascertain whose possessions are whose. Conversely, one who says, "Mine is yours and yours is mine," is an ignoramus.

Another indication of this person's materialistic character is his willingness to receive from others, unlike the independent personality that reflects *sechel*, intellect.

ה/יד

שֶׁלִּי,״ עַם הָאָרֶץ; ״שֶׁלִּי שֶׁלָּךְ וְשֶׁלְּךָ שֶׁלָּךְ,״
חָסִיד; ״שֶׁלְּךָ שֶׁלִּי וְשֶׁלִּי שֶׁלִּי,״ רָשָׁע.

[יד] אַרְבַּע מִדּוֹת בַּדֵּעוֹת: נְוֹחַ לִכְעוֹס וְנְוֹחַ
לִרְצוֹת, יָצָא שְׂכָרוֹ בְּהֶפְסֵדוֹ; קָשֶׁה
לִכְעוֹס וְקָשֶׁה לִרְצוֹת, יָצָא הֶפְסֵדוֹ בִּשְׂכָרוֹ;
קָשֶׁה לִכְעוֹס וְנְוֹחַ לִרְצוֹת חָסִיד; נְוֹחַ לִכְעוֹס
וְקָשֶׁה לִרְצוֹת רָשָׁע.

⧉ שֶׁלִּי שֶׁלָּךְ וְשֶׁלְּךָ שֶׁלָּךְ,״ חָסִיד — (c) "Mine is yours
and yours is yours," is scrupulously pious

Some people find the praise of this trait as "pious" problematic, for he
will give all of his things to others and be left with nothing.

The truth is that this is a scrupulously pious quality only when
practiced within limits. The Rabbis instituted[1] that one must not
dispense more a fifth of his assets to charity, so that he will not become
dependent on society. The mishnah assumes that the practice of "mine
is yours and yours is yours" is limited to giving away no more than one
fifth, as is proper. The mishnah did not intend one to apply this trait to
everything he owns.

Mishnah 14

Whether one has a staunch character or a flaccid character, his
actions will be consistent with his nature. A strong-natured individual
will be difficult to anger and equally difficult to pacify. A weak
individual will be easily angered and just as easily pacified. It is highly
unusual for a person to be firm in one way, such as not getting angry,
and soft in another way, such as being easily pacified.

⧉ נְוֹחַ לִכְעוֹס וְנְוֹחַ לִרְצוֹת, יָצָא שְׂכָרוֹ בְּהֶפְסֵדוֹ — (a) One who is angered
easily and pacified easily, his gain is offset by his loss

This is a person who has a flaccid nature. His variability accounts
for the good quality of being easily pacified and for the bad quality
of being easily angered. The reason for his "gain" is the very same

1. Kesubos 50a.

is mine," is an ignoramus; (c) "Mine is yours and yours is yours," is scrupulously pious; (d) "Yours is mine and mine is mine," is wicked.

14. There are four types of temperament: (a) One who is angered easily and pacified easily, his gain is offset by his loss; (b) one who is hard to anger and hard to pacify, his loss is offset by his gain; (c) one who is hard to anger and easy to pacify is scrupulously pious; (d) one who is easily angered and hard to pacify is wicked.

reason for his "loss," and hence "his gain is offset by his loss."

⊷ קָשֶׁה לִכְעוֹס וְקָשֶׁה לִרְצוֹת, יָצָא הֶפְסֵדוֹ בִּשְׂכָרוֹ ⊷ — *(b) one who is hard to anger and hard to pacify, his loss is offset by his gain*

The same firmness of character that is responsible for his good nature is responsible for his bad nature of being hard to appease.

⊷ קָשֶׁה לִכְעוֹס וְנוֹחַ לִרְצוֹת חָסִיד ⊷ — *(c) one who is hard to anger and easy to pacify is scrupulously pious*

If this person is hard to anger by nature, he should also be hard to pacify. The reason he is easily pacified is that he makes a deliberate effort to shake off his anger. Conversely, if his nature is to be easily pacified, but he rarely gets angry, it must be the result of resisting his natural tendency. In summary, it is a scrupulously pious person indeed who loves and respects humanity enough to rise above his nature.

⊷ נוֹחַ לִכְעוֹס וְקָשֶׁה לִרְצוֹת רָשָׁע ⊷ — *(d) one who is easily angered and hard to pacify is wicked*

Similarly, one who is easily moved to anger should be easily appeased. This person does not allow himself to be pacified because of his hatred. Conversely, if by nature he is hard to appease, he should be hard to anger. The reason he is easily angered is that he hates people and that is truly wicked.

[טו] אַרְבַּע מִדּוֹת בְּתַלְמִידִים: מָהִיר לִשְׁמוֹעַ וּמָהִיר לְאַבֵּד, יָצָא שְׂכָרוֹ בְּהֶפְסֵדוֹ; קָשֶׁה לִשְׁמוֹעַ וְקָשֶׁה לְאַבֵּד, יָצָא הֶפְסֵדוֹ בִשְׂכָרוֹ; מָהִיר לִשְׁמוֹעַ וְקָשֶׁה לְאַבֵּד, זֶה חֵלֶק טוֹב; קָשֶׁה לִשְׁמוֹעַ וּמָהִיר לְאַבֵּד, זֶה חֵלֶק רָע.

[טז] אַרְבַּע מִדּוֹת בְּנוֹתְנֵי צְדָקָה: הָרוֹצֶה שֶׁיִּתֵּן וְלֹא יִתְּנוּ אֲחֵרִים, עֵינוֹ רָעָה בְּשֶׁל אֲחֵרִים; יִתְּנוּ אֲחֵרִים וְהוּא לֹא יִתֵּן, עֵינוֹ רָעָה בְּשֶׁלּוֹ;

§ נוֹחַ לִכְעֹס וְקָשֶׁה לִרְצוֹת רָשָׁע — *One who is easily angered and hard to pacify is wicked*

One could also explain this on the basis of the statement,[1]

It is known that anyone who gets angry has many sins.

In other words, we do not consider him wicked because of his anger, but rather we attribute his anger to his accumulation of evil deeds.

Mishnah 15

§ מָהִיר לִשְׁמוֹעַ וּמָהִיר לְאַבֵּד, יָצָא שְׂכָרוֹ בְּהֶפְסֵדוֹ — *(a) One who grasps quickly and forgets quickly, his gain is offset by his loss*

The expression "his gain is offset by his loss" conveys that the thing that is responsible for his gain is the same thing that is responsible for his loss. When a person retains something very quickly, without working at it, the knowledge is likely to quickly fade from active recall. Conversely, when a person expends great effort at acquiring information, that effort helps to ingrain it in his consciousness.

Mishnah 16

§ אַרְבַּע מִדּוֹת בְּנוֹתְנֵי צְדָקָה — *There are four types of donors to charity*

The expression "donors to charity" means those who are obligated to give, aside from whether they do or do not actually give.[2]

---

1 *Nedarim* 22b. In this explanation Maharal hints at matters of *Kabbalah*.

2. This statement serves to remove the difficulty of applying the term "donor" to the examples of people who do not give to charity.

5/
15-16

15. There are four types of students: (a) One who grasps quickly and forgets quickly, his gain is offset by his loss; (b) one who grasps slowly and forgets slowly, his loss is offset by his gain; (c) one who grasps quickly and forgets slowly, this is a good portion; (d) one grasps slowly and forgets quickly, this is a bad portion.

16. There are four types of donors to charity: (a) One who wishes to give himself but wants others not to give, he begrudges others; (b) that others should give but that he should not give, he begrudges himself;

---

§⊱ הָרוֹצֶה שֶׁיִּתֵּן וְלֹא יִתְּנוּ אֲחֵרִים — *(a) One who wishes to give himself but wants others not to give*

The *mishnah* refers to a person who is literally generous to a fault. He loves people so much that he is concerned for their loss if they give their money to charity. Because of his concern for their money, it actually bothers him if others give and therefore he wants to be the sole donor.

---

§⊱ הָרוֹצֶה שֶׁיִּתֵּן וְלֹא יִתְּנוּ אֲחֵרִים, עֵינוֹ רָעָה בְּשֶׁל אֲחֵרִים —
(a) One who wishes to give himself but wants others not to give, he begrudges others

---

Another explanation Is that this refers to a person who has a good trait and a bad trait. His bad trait is that he does not like to see people receive charity. His good trait is that he is very generous and he would, for example, give amply to the Temple. If his generosity prevails, he will give charity despite his resentment of people receiving something for free. However, he will begrudge the donations that others make, because it does not satisfy his personal generosity, while it does offend his conviction that people should not receive charity.

---

§⊱ יִתְּנוּ אֲחֵרִים וְהוּא לֹא יִתֵּן, עֵינוֹ רָעָה בְּשֶׁלּוֹ — *(b) that others should give but that he should not give, he begrudges himself*

The conclusion that "he begrudges himself" seems to be too mild. Why is his refusal to perform the *mitzvah* of charity not termed "wicked," just because he wants others to give?

יִתֵּן וְיִתְּנוּ אֲחֵרִים חָסִיד; לֹא יִתֵּן וְלֹא יִתְּנוּ
אֲחֵרִים רָשָׁע.

[יז] אַרְבַּע מִדּוֹת בְּהוֹלְכֵי בֵית הַמִּדְרָשׁ:
הוֹלֵךְ וְאֵינוֹ עוֹשֶׂה שְׂכַר הֲלִיכָה בְּיָדוֹ;

We must conclude that the *mishnah* is not dealing with the case of someone who merely says that he would like others to give. Rather, this must be someone who exerts his utmost energy and effort to get others to give to charity. His failing is that he resents giving up his own money, but the term רָשָׁע, *rasha*, a wicked person, is applied only to those who are wicked to people, and is not used for one who is wicked to God alone. This person is good to people, working at raising funds on their behalf, and hence is spared the designation of *rasha*.

---

§ יִתֵּן וְיִתְּנוּ אֲחֵרִים חָסִיד — *(c) that he should give and that others should give is pious*

What is pious about this person? He gives to charity, as he is obligated to do. That behavior is just normal, and merely wanting others to give is surely not enough to qualify as "pious."

We must say that this case also refers to a person who tries with his utmost energy and effort to get others to give to charity. He is not satisfied with just fulfilling the letter of the law with his own donation. Rather, he pursues the spirit of Torah as well, by energetically raising funds from others. This is the truly **pious** person.

Mishnah 17

---

§ הוֹלֵךְ וְאֵינוֹ עוֹשֶׂה שְׂכַר הֲלִיכָה בְּיָדוֹ — *(a) One who goes but does not accomplish has the reward for going*

Is it right that he should get a reward for merely going when, in the end, he did not study? Does one who goes to give charity, but does not give, merit a reward just for going?

Preparing for a *mitzvah* brings merit in its own right. Since learning Torah must be preceded by going to a teacher of Torah,[1] the travel itself

---

1. In the time of the *Mishnah*, there were no books of Oral Law. Torah was studied from the discourses of rabbis and then discussed among the students. The *mishnah* itself was not committed to writing until a substantial time had elapsed after its redaction.

(c) that he should give and that others should give
is pious; (d) that he should not give and that others
should not give is wicked.

17. There are four types among those who go to
the house of study: (a) One who goes but
does not accomplish has the reward for going;

---

is a preparatory act with its own merit. In this regard, Torah study is
unlike most other *mitzvos*, which do not inherently require preparation.
For example, going to acquire a *lulav* is quite incidental to the *mitzvah*
of shaking the *lulav*, for if there would be a *lulav* at hand, there would be
no value in going. Torah study is different, for the value of going to the
teacher is additional to the value of study itself. This thought is reflected
in the saying of the Rabbis,[1]

> These are the precepts whose fruits a person enjoys in this world,
> but whose principal remains intact for him in the World to
> Come: . . . early attendance at the house of study morning and
> evening . . . and the study of Torah is equivalent to them all.

In this passage, attendance at the house of study is listed separately
from the study of Torah because each has its own merit.

Another example of travel as a *mitzvah* in its own right is the act of
walking to the synagogue. Since there is merit in joining with the
community, the very act of going carries a separate reward.

There is another reason why the reward for going to study is separate
from the reward of the study itself. Going is a physical action, whereas
study is an intellectual action, and because the two actions are
inherently different they are rewarded independently. By contrast, for
most other *mitzvos*, the preparation is physical and the *mitzvah* is
physical. Consequently, the preparation is sufficiently similar to the
mitzvah that it does not have independent merit or reward.

◄§ הוֹלֵךְ וְאֵינוֹ עוֹשֶׂה — *(a) One who goes but does not accomplish*

The *mishnah* means that he does not accomplish anything because
the studies are too difficult to understand without tremendous effort. It
cannot mean that he does not want to understand, for the *mishnah* would
would have included such a person in the category of "wicked." It means

---

1. *Shabbos* 127a.

ה/יח עוֹשֶׂה וְאֵינוֹ הוֹלֵךְ שְׂכַר מַעֲשֶׂה בְּיָדוֹ; הוֹלֵךְ
וְעוֹשֶׂה חָסִיד; לֹא הוֹלֵךְ וְלֹא עוֹשֶׂה רָשָׁע.

[יח] אַרְבַּע מִדּוֹת בְּיוֹשְׁבִים לִפְנֵי חֲכָמִים:
סְפוֹג, וּמַשְׁפֵּךְ, מְשַׁמֶּרֶת וְנָפָה: סְפוֹג,
שֶׁהוּא סוֹפֵג אֶת הַכֹּל; וּמַשְׁפֵּךְ, שֶׁמַּכְנִיס בְּזוֹ

---

that he could have understood had he been willing to exert himself
sufficiently.

---

§ **וְאֵינוֹ עוֹשֶׂה — but does not accomplish**

Why does the *mishnah* say "does not accomplish" rather than "does
not learn"?

The words "does not learn" would include even someone who understood and then forgot right away, or someone who did not understand,
although he could repeat what he heard. In contrast, the expression
"does not accomplish" is much stronger, and means that he accomplished absolutely nothing. He does not understand the text nor can he
even repeat it. This statement emphasizes the point that even someone
who gains nothing from going to study will receive reward for his going.

---

§ **עוֹשֶׂה וְאֵינוֹ הוֹלֵךְ שְׂכַר מַעֲשֶׂה בְּיָדוֹ — (b) one who accomplishes
[at home] but does not go [to the house of study]
has the reward for accomplishment**

The *mishnah* chose the term "accomplish" rather than "learn" for the
instance of one who studies at home, because the term "learn" לוֹמֵד,
lomeid, is reserved for one who learns from another.

For this same reason, the text of the daily blessing on studying Torah
is ". . .and has commanded us to occupy, לַעֲסוֹק, ourselves in the words
of Torah." The blessing was not phrased ". . .to learn, לִלְמוֹד, Torah"
because that term implies learning from another, whereas the blessing
was formulated in reference to individual study.

---

§ **הוֹלֵךְ וְעוֹשֶׂה חָסִיד — (c) one who goes and accomplishes is pious**

The word "pious" connotes doing more than duty demands. He is
considered pious because he could fulfill his minimum duty by studying

5/ 18   (b) one who accomplishes [at home] but does not go [to the house of study] has the reward for accomplishment; (c) one who goes and accomplishes is pious; (d) one who does not go and does not accomplish is wicked.

18. There are four types among students who sit before the sages: a sponge, a funnel, a strainer and a sieve: a sponge, which absorbs everything; a funnel, which lets in from one end

---

at home. Instead, he makes the physical exertion to go to the house of study, and hence he deserves to be called "pious." Furthermore, his accomplishment is qualitatively better in the house of study, where he has colleagues with whom to discuss his studies and refine his understanding of the material.

◆§ **לֹא הוֹלֵךְ וְלֹא עוֹשֶׂה רָשָׁע** — *(d) one who does not go and does not accomplish is wicked*

This refers to someone who makes no effort to improve himself. He is rightly called wicked, for he has wasted his human potential by neither attending the discourses at the house of study, nor studying on his own at home.[1]

The epithet of "wicked" is applied only to those who are capable of study. Conversely, a person with no background, who cannot understand the subject being discussed, would not be called "wicked," for he will gain nothing from attendance at the house of study.

Mishnah 18

The Oral Law is rich and complex, and incorporates many opinions about each subject. Our *mishnah* discusses various ways of selectively retaining information.

The term **sponge** is an apt image for one who retains all of those opinions equally. He does not discern between teachings that are more sound and those that are less sound.

The one described as a **funnel** also does not distinguish between various opinions, but with the opposite result. The many opinions on

---

1. Maharal frequently makes the point that the term "wicked" connotes doing evil to people. In this case, he has done himself an injustice.

וּמוֹצִיא בְזוֹ; מְשַׁמֶּרֶת, שֶׁמּוֹצִיאָה אֶת הַיַּיִן
וְקוֹלֶטֶת אֶת הַשְּׁמָרִים; וְנָפָה, שֶׁמּוֹצִיאָה אֶת
הַקֶּמַח וְקוֹלֶטֶת אֶת הַסֹּלֶת.

---

each subject create a complexity that he cannot deal with, and hence everything escapes him.

Some students are like a **strainer** that lets the clear wine pass through while it retains the dregs. This student has not developed his thinking skills, and his logic is not clear and sound. He finds weak arguments to be reasonable. Opinions that have not been clearly and soundly thought through appeal to him, while opinions that are founded on positive and rigorous logic do not. He lets the more logical and relevant information pass by and retains the weaker opinions that do not find their way into practice. The great majority of people fall into this category.

The image of a **sieve** alludes to the process of preparing fine flour. Ground wheat is passed through a coarse strainer to remove the bran and particles from the flour. The flour is then passed through a fine **sieve** that lets the flour dust pass through and retains the full-bodied fine flour for further grinding. Therefore, the student who is blessed with exceptionally clear and positive logic is compared to a sieve. He registers completely reliable statements and lets statements that are not clearly reasoned go by.

Summary of Mishnayos 1-18:
The Numbers Ten, Seven And Four

Mishnayos 1 through 18 form a self-contained section of Chapter 5. The theme of this section is that God created the world and maintains its existence in conjunction with mankind.

The theme is introduced in *mishnah* 1. God placed Divine sanctity in the world, and He "exacts payment from the wicked who destroy the world and bestows reward upon the righteous who sustain the world." In other words, mankind is an active participant who is able to counter the Creation or to reinforce it.

God created the world at three levels. The lowest level is physical existence, and the highest level is spiritual existence. The intermediate level is the plane of form and concept, which, although intangible, are found only in conjunction with substance.

Mankind interacts with each level in the spiritual, conceptual and physical arenas of life. The righteous unify these levels into a complete

and lets out from the other; a strainer, which lets the wine flow through and retains the sediment; and a sieve, which lets the flour dust pass through and retains the fine flour.

---

and harmonious system, while those who turn away from God dismantle the structure of the universe and destroy the world as a result.

We will discuss how the numbers 10, 7 and 4 allude to each of these levels. The symbolism of numbers is the subject of the author's introduction to this chapter, but the messages that underlie these numbers will be reviewed here briefly.

The number 10 conveys sanctity and its extreme differentiation from physical matters. Hence, the number 10 represents the highest level, which is the domain of the absolutely holy and intangible, such as the essence of Torah.

The number 4 conveys the uniquely physical property of multiplicity and disparity, such as the four directions of the world. Hence, 4 represents the lowest level, the plane of physical existence.

The number 7 conveys intelligence, order and structure. It represents the intermediate level, lying halfway between the highest level (10) and the lowest level (4), for it integrates the spiritual and physical planes of existence.

Eight 10's; Two 7's; Seven 4's

It is worthy of note that there are eight mishnayos based on the number 10; two mishnayos[1] based on the number 7; and seven mishnayos based on the number 4. No other numbers appear in this section, because the redactor of the mishnayos was hinting at the characteristics of the three levels, as we will now explain.

Seven 4's

The mishnayos based on the number 4 are directed towards the lowest, most physical world, which is characterized by multiplicity and disparity. There are seven such mishnayos, based on the Scriptural use of 7 to express diversity, as we find in the verse[2] "your enemies. . . shall come out against you in one way and they will flee before you in seven ways."

---

1. It is clear that mishnah 10 and mishnah 11 of our text were originally a single mishnah.
2. Devarim 28:7.

ה/יט **[יט]** כָּל אַהֲבָה שֶׁהִיא תְּלוּיָה בְדָבָר, בָּטֵל דָּבָר, בְּטֵלָה אַהֲבָה; וְשֶׁאֵינָהּ תְּלוּיָה בְדָבָר, אֵינָהּ בְּטֵלָה לְעוֹלָם. אֵיזוֹ הִיא אַהֲבָה

Two 7's

There are two *mishnayos* based on the number seven for reasons presented[1] in depth in *mishnah* 9 and summarized here:

The number seven represents a physical structure of six sides (top, bottom, right, left, front, back) and the center of that structure. The absolute center is a conceptual point that does not, itself, take up space. It is the only thing that the sides have in common, and hence it consolidates the sides into a unified structure. The center has attributes of *kedushah,* holiness: It is non-physical; it is conceptual; it does not occupy space; and it unifies disparate physical elements into a whole.

It is the center that has these attributes of holiness, and the center is found only in conjunction with a physical structure. The inseparable combination of the sacred and the ordinary is characteristic of the number seven. For example, there are six workdays and the seventh day is the holy Shabbos. Another example is the seventh month, Tishrei, which is holy.[2] Likewise, there are six years of working the land and the seventh is the *Shemittah* year, which is holy.

Seven connotes the central point around which the physical revolves. Therefore, a seven-element structure has only two directions: inside and outside. Goodness is on the inside and evil is on the outside, just as one *mishnah* talked about 7 qualities of the wise person and one *mishnah* talked about the 7 sins that bring the destruction of pestilence.

In conclusion, there are two *mishnayos* based on the number 7, as befits the two directions, inwards and outwards, of a structure with holiness inside and the profane outside. The number two conveys that the middle level is associated with the union of such opposites as form and substance; tangible and intangible; and holy and profane.

Eight 10's

Maharal notes that there are eight *mishnayos* based on the number 10

---

1. See commentary to *mishnah* 9, section entitled "Seven as the Symbol of Structure and Order."

2. As the month in which God comes closest to mankind and therefore the time of the holy days of Rosh Hashanah, Yom Kippur and Succos.

19. Any love that depends on a specific cause, when that cause is gone, the love is gone; but if it does not depend on a specific cause, it will never cease. What sort of love

---

and alludes to a Kabbalistic reason. One way to understand why the highest world, represented by the number ten, should have 8 *mishnayos* is as follows.

Seven represents the order of nature in this world, for the six sides of physical existence are infused with a central core of holiness. The number 8, which is one higher than 7, belongs to the next level, the level higher than nature. That is the level of absolute holiness, with no physical qualities. Appropriately, this chapter has 8 *mishnayos* based on the number 10, to express that the absolutely holy level (10) transcends nature.

The purpose of this lengthy explanation is to demonstrate that the words of the Rabbis should not be construed as merely opinions or assumptions. Rather, the Rabbis of the *Mishnah* and Talmud based their words on the Divine wisdom of *Kabbalah*.

Mishnah 19

The preceding *mishnayos* were based on the numbers 10, 7 and 4, and now this *mishnah* explains the power that lies within the number one, for love is union, and unity endures.

Something that consists not of parts, but is an integral whole, has no weakness from within, and no vulnerable seam where destructive forces could take hold. Therefore a solid entity will endure, because there is no factor, internal or external, that will bring it to an end.

Love that is purely union with another, with no element of gain to be had from the relationship, is just such an entity. It has the internal strength of integrity, and it is immune to external attack. Such love endures forever.

Conversely, love that depends on some other thing will cease when the circumstance holding the relationship together ceases.

Selfless love endures even if it is not "for the sake of Heaven"[1] because unity itself is the essence of durability.

---

1. In contrast to the next *mishnah,* which states that opposing views can endure only if they are undertaken for the sake of Heaven. The reason there is that opposites can coexist only with God's support. Since selfless love is not internally fragmented, it endures even without special Divine support.

שֶׁהִיא תְּלוּיָה בְדָבָר? – זוֹ אַהֲבַת אַמְנוֹן
וְתָמָר. וְשֶׁאֵינָהּ תְּלוּיָה בְדָבָר? – זוֹ אַהֲבַת דָּוִד
וִיהוֹנָתָן.

◆§ — אֵיזוֹ הִיא אַהֲבָה שֶׁהִיא תְּלוּיָה בְדָבָר? – זוֹ אַהֲבַת אַמְנוֹן וְתָמָר —
*What sort of love depended on a specific cause? —
The love of Amnon for Tamar.*

The love of Amnon for Tamar was based only on physical desire.[1]
There was nothing more to their relationship, and when that was over, he
immediately hated her.

◆§ וְשֶׁאֵינָהּ תְּלוּיָה בְדָבָר? – זוֹ אַהֲבַת דָּוִד וִיהוֹנָתָן — *And what did not
depend on a specific cause? — The love of David and Yehonasan.*

The love of David and Yehonasan never waned, for there were no
considerations other than pure friendship.

It is rare that love completely "depends on a specific cause" or
completely "does not depend on a specific cause." Normally, a relationship has both an element of sincere love and an element of love that
hinges on some benefit. Although the relationship may be primarily
sincere, if the element that "depends on a cause" ceases, then the entire
relationship can be mitigated.

Man and Wife

The love of man and wife has both elements. In the main, their love is
not dependent on any benefit. It is a sincere relationship, one which is
fundamentally inherent in human nature, as Scripture declares,[2]

"a man. . .cleaves to his wife and they are one."

In addition, a man's love for his wife depends partly on benefits he
receives from her role as עֵזֶר,[3] *eizer,* a help. If the element of "help"

---

1. *II Shmuel* 13:1-15. Amnon's desire for Tamar culminated in his violating her. As
soon as his desire was fulfilled, he loathed her more than he had ever loved her.
2. *Bereishis* 2:24. The full concluding phrase "they are one flesh" has been truncated
in the adaptation to avoid the inference of sexual union. Maharal emphasizes that the
phrase cannot be referring to sexual union, because the phrase makes a much bigger
and more fundamental point; namely, that the natural bond between man and wife
was cast into human makeup as part of Creation.
3. *Bereishis* 2:20.

depended on a specific cause? — The love of Amnon for Tamar. And what did not depend on a specific cause? — The love of David and Yehonasan.

---

ceases and turns adversarial, then the primary, sincere love will be undermined as well.

In marriage, sincere love is at risk of being weakened by a breakdown in the pragmatic element of their love. However, the sincere love of David and Yehonasan did not have a pragmatic aspect and therefore it was more durable than even the love of husband and wife.[1]

God's love for Israel

Our *mishnah* says that love which does not depend on a specific cause will never cease. Since God's love for Israel is not contingent upon anything, we may take substantial consolation in knowing that His love for Israel will not cease and that eventually He will bring us back from this long and bitter exile.

Ramban[2] notes that Scripture relates how God chose Avraham to be His chosen one, before describing his righteousness and merit. Scripture wished to avoid any impression that Avraham was chosen for his righteousness, for that would have implied that God's love for Avraham and his children would cease if their righteousness ceased. Rather, the order chosen for the narrative assures us that God's love for Avraham's children does not depend on anything and hence will never cease.

Mishnah 20

Mishnah 18 categorizes students according to their ability to deal with differing opinions. The best category of student, described as a "sieve," fully retains the opinion that is sound enough to practice, while other opinions are merely noted. This *mishnah* presents an exception. The best students will retain and perpetuate both views, if those views were developed for the sake of Heaven.

There are three categories of disputes. Two of these are diametric opposites: personal conflict, which God abhors, and debate that is purely for the sake of Heaven, which God helps support. The intermediate category is a dispute that is sincerely motivated, but also has an element of pride or competition. In these, God does not intervene.

---

1. *II Shmuel* 1:26.

2. *Ramban's Commentary to Bereishis,* Chapter 12.

[כ] כָּל מַחֲלֹקֶת שֶׁהִיא לְשֵׁם שָׁמַיִם סוֹפָהּ
לְהִתְקַיֵּם; וְשֶׁאֵינָהּ לְשֵׁם שָׁמַיִם אֵין
סוֹפָהּ לְהִתְקַיֵּם. אֵיזוֹ הִיא מַחֲלֹקֶת שֶׁהִיא
לְשֵׁם שָׁמַיִם? — זוֹ מַחֲלֹקֶת הִלֵּל וְשַׁמַּאי.
וְשֶׁאֵינָהּ לְשֵׁם שָׁמַיִם? — זוֹ מַחֲלֹקֶת קֹרַח
וְכָל עֲדָתוֹ.

⊰§ **כָּל מַחֲלֹקֶת שֶׁהִיא לְשֵׁם שָׁמַיִם סוֹפָהּ לְהִתְקַיֵּם** — *Any dispute that is for the sake of Heaven will endure*

In general, God despises controversy and He brings about events in such a way that one side will prevail and the other side will cease. However, even a dispute that *is* for the sake of Heaven does not necessarily endure forever. The debate might be sustained for the lifetime of the two rabbis in contention arguing, or it may not endure even that long. God does not intervene to hasten the end of a sincere debate.

However, a dispute that is *purely* for the sake of Heaven, untinged by pride, competition or lack of effort, is different. God not only permits such debate to go unresolved, but He supports the continuation of both views indefinitely.

⊰§ **אֵיזוֹ הִיא מַחֲלֹקֶת שֶׁהִיא לְשֵׁם שָׁמַיִם? – זוֹ מַחֲלֹקֶת הִלֵּל וְשַׁמַּאי** —
What sort of dispute was for the sake of Heaven?
— The dispute between Hillel and Shammai.

The Rabbis say,[1]

> A heavenly voice went out and said: "These and these (i.e., the school of Hillel and the school of Shammai) are the words of the living God; but the *halachah* is in accordance with the school of Hillel."

Although Heaven designated that Hillel's view be adopted in practice, the validity of both schools of Torah was endorsed equally. The debates of Hillel and Shammai were beloved to God, because they were purely for the sake of Heaven. Their views are endorsed as "the

---

1. *Eruvin* 13b.

20. Any dispute that is for the sake of Heaven will endure; but one that is not for the sake of Heaven will not endure. What sort of dispute was for the sake of Heaven? — The dispute between Hillel and Shammai. And which was not for the sake of Heaven? — The dispute of Korach and his entire company.

---

words of the living God" because they arise from unsurpassed religious dedication.

Every aspect of their debate was for the sake of Heaven. There was no tinge of pride or competition. Furthermore, there was no lack of diligence to master the subject matter and no opportunity to seek a better-informed source was missed. The proof is that Heaven declared both opinions to be God's words, and surely no amount of further research could have proven wrong the words of God!

מַחֲלֹקֶת הִלֵּל וְשַׁמַּאי ‎ — *The dispute between Hillel and Shammai.*

Only disputes of the schools of Hillel and Shammai were acknowledged to be the "words of the living God." Later Rabbinical debates were sincere also, but they were not as perfectly "for the sake of Heaven" as those of Hillel and Shammai.[1] Had there been enough effort to research the point or to consult many rabbis, one viewpoint could have prevailed. The other side may not have been wrong, but the argument for one side could be shown to be more compelling.

וְשֶׁאֵינָהּ לְשֵׁם שָׁמַיִם? – זוֹ מַחֲלֹקֶת קֹרַח וְכָל עֲדָתוֹ ‎ — *And which was not for the sake of Heaven? — The dispute of Korach and his entire company.*

There was not a shred of religious intention in Korach's dispute. Indeed, in his quarrel with Moshe and Aharon, Korach "strove against

---

1. Maharal's view is that the opinions of *Tannaim,* such as Rabbi Meir and Rabbi Yehudah, were not necessarily on the plane of "these and these are the words of the living God." Rashi to *Kesubos* 57a (introductory words הֹאקמ״ל), apparently applying the principle of "these and these" in a somewhat different way, states that even the opinions of the *Amoraim* were "the words of the living God" if the dispute centered around principles rather than facts.

God."[1] Korach exemplifies the extreme degree of "not for the sake of Heaven." That dispute was terminated when the earth swallowed Korach and his men alive, as a fitting end for conflict that had no religious integrity at all.

All other religious controversy falls in between the diametric extremes of Hillel and Shammai's pure "for the sake of Heaven" and Korach's rebellious "not for the sake of Heaven." Most disputes centered around religious practice have some degree of religious motivation, even if they are tainted by arrogance. Those controversies endure to the extent of their religious sincerity.

---

§ *Any dispute* — כָּל מַחֲלֹקֶת שֶׁהִיא לְשֵׁם שָׁמַיִם סוֹפָהּ לְהִתְקַיֵּם
that is for the sake of Heaven will endure

How can two contrary views of one *halachah* be equally valid? God effects His will through opposites, just as fire and water both serve His purpose. To say that both sides of a dispute are the "words of the living God" is to say that both sides are equally effective vehicles to bring His will into practice. Truth is relative to the observer. From the perspective of Hillel or Shammai, the other side's view is totally incompatible; but from God's perspective, both sides are tenable. As a result, the study of Hillel's view counts as Torah study and the study of Shammai's view equally counts as Torah study.

Although both sides of their debate are correctly reasoned, we can practice only one approach. The criterion to select an opinion to follow is not based on the kind of logic used in debate. It is a higher, more Divine reasoning, based on the merits of the disputants' character rather than the merits of the argument. Hillel's opinion, in general, is practiced because his equanimity reflects the balance and directness that is appropriate for *halachah*.[2]

---

§ — אֵיזוֹ הִיא מַחֲלֹקֶת שֶׁהִיא לְשֵׁם שָׁמַיִם? — זוֹ מַחֲלֹקֶת הִלֵּל וְשַׁמַּאי
What sort of dispute was for the sake of Heaven? —
The dispute between Hillel and Shammai.

All the debates of the early Rabbis were for the sake of Heaven and expressed valid views on both sides. One view, however, was closer to God.[3] The debates of Hillel and Shammai are unique in

---

1. *Bamidbar* 26:9.
2. See Maharal's *Nesivos Olam, Nesiv HaKaas*, Chapter 1.
3. One view is a "preferred" vehicle to implement God's will.

that both opinions are equally close to God, and hence only their debates are described as "these and these are the words of the living God."

In the expression "the words of the **living** God," the Hebrew word חַיִּים, *chaim*, is plural, implying two. The message is that life can flow from God to the world through two vehicles, such as the opinions of Hillel and Shammai.

Conflict

Be alert to the consequences of conflict. Conflict is a powerful force that draws people as a magnet and brings about evil.

The Rabbis say that conflict and *Gehinnom* were both made on the second day of Creation. The Rabbis group them together because *Gehinnom* is the destruction of a person, and destruction is inherent in conflict. They were both made on the second day because the number 2 embodies the destructive power of divisiveness.[1] For example, an item which is useful when whole, such as a container, is destroyed when divided in two. So it is that conflict brings destruction unless the two factions are united by the sincere pursuit of God's will.

Mishnah 21

Why should the likelihood of sin depend on whether a person has helped the community? How can the ability to repent be denied even to one who has misled the community? The answers lie in understanding the distinction between a community and an individual, and the relation of the individual to the community.

A category is different from the members of the category. A category is a conceptual entity. Since it is not physical, it is not subject to change, and hence it endures indefinitely. In contrast, the physical members of the category can change, deteriorate or improve. For example, within the general category of "trees," individual trees grow and die. Woods flourish in some areas and languish in others; but the *category* of trees does not change. Likewise, the category of "community" is a stable concept, although individual members of the community might change for the better through merit, or for the worse through sin.

One who brings merit to the community develops a connection with the community. As a result, he acquires the stability associated with a community, and he loses an individual's tendency to change.

With this background, we may analyze the *mishnah*.

---

1. See *Derech Chaim,* page 24, London edition.

[כא] כָּל הַמְזַכֶּה אֶת הָרַבִּים אֵין חֵטְא בָּא עַל יָדוֹ; וְכָל הַמַּחֲטִיא אֶת הָרַבִּים אֵין מַסְפִּיקִין בְּיָדוֹ לַעֲשׂוֹת תְּשׁוּבָה. מֹשֶׁה זָכָה וְזִכָּה אֶת הָרַבִּים, זְכוּת הָרַבִּים תָּלוּי בּוֹ, שֶׁנֶּאֱמַר: „צִדְקַת יהוה עָשָׂה, וּמִשְׁפָּטָיו עִם יִשְׂרָאֵל." יָרָבְעָם בֶּן נְבָט חָטָא וְהֶחֱטִיא אֶת הָרַבִּים, חֵטְא הָרַבִּים תָּלוּי בּוֹ, שֶׁנֶּאֱמַר: „עַל חַטֹּאות יָרָבְעָם אֲשֶׁר חָטָא וַאֲשֶׁר הֶחֱטִיא אֶת יִשְׂרָאֵל."

⊷ כָּל הַמְזַכֶּה אֶת הָרַבִּים אֵין חֵטְא בָּא עַל יָדוֹ — *Whoever influences the masses to become meritorious shall not be the cause of sin* [1]

One who influences the public to become meritorious establishes a connection with the community. In so doing, he acquires the stability of the community, and he will not change from being meritorious to being wicked. One may ask: How can the masses become meritorious if the public is a category and unchangeable? In this case, it is not the concept of community that changes but rather the individuals of the community who become meritorious.

⊷ וְכָל הַמַּחֲטִיא אֶת הָרַבִּים אֵין מַסְפִּיקִין בְּיָדוֹ לַעֲשׂוֹת תְּשׁוּבָה — *but one who influences the masses to sin will not be given the means to repent*

Similarly, one who influences the public to sin establishes a connection with the community and is no longer open to the spirit of change that can prevail over a private individual. As a result, he is tied to the community that he led astray and cannot independently repent.

In summary, the destiny of the leader is tied to the destiny of the community and hence cannot change. The Rabbis said, [2]

What is the reason that: "Whoever influences the masses to become meritorious shall not be the cause of sin?" So that he

---

1. See Rashi to *Yoma* 87a, אֵין חֵטְא בָּא עַל יָדוֹ.
2. *Yoma* 87a.

21. Whoever influences the masses to become meritorious shall not be the cause of sin; but one who influences the masses to sin will not be given the means to repent. Moses was meritorious and influenced the masses to be meritorious, so the merit of the masses was to his credit, as it is said: "He performed the righteousness of Hashem, and His laws together with Israel." Yeravam ben Nevat sinned and caused the masses to sin, so the sin of the masses is charged against him, as it is said: "For the sins of Yeravam which he committed and which he caused Israel to commit."

---

should not be in *Gehinnom* (Purgatory) while his disciples are in *Gan Eden* (Paradise).

What is the reason that "one who influences the masses to sin will not be given the means to repent?" So that he should not be in *Gan Eden* while his disciples are in *Gehinnom*.

What is the connection between this *mishnah* and the preceding *mishnayos*? The previous *mishnayos* established the theme that unity endures. They taught that the union that comes of selfless love will not cease and that God joins with both sides of sincere debate to ensure its continuity. This *mishnah* extends that theme to the unity of the community and its leaders. Therefore, the righteousness of one who brings merit to the public will endure forever, and one who brings sin to the community will remain unrepentant and wicked all his life.

Mishnah 22

The *mishnah* contrasts Avraham and Bilam. Avraham is the paradigm of human maturity, while Bilam is the exact opposite.

The human soul consists of three major faculties:[1] the physical, the spiritual and the intellectual. The Rabbis call these, respectively, נֶפֶשׁ, רוּחַ, נְשָׁמָה, *ruach, nefesh,* and *neshamah.*

- The physical part of the soul, *ruach,* maintains the bodily functions such as the digestive system, the reproductive system and their physical desires.

---

1. This paragraph is essentially a repetition of the information presented *supra* in the commentary to 4:28.

[כב] כָּל מִי שֶׁיֵּשׁ בְּיָדוֹ שְׁלֹשָׁה דְבָרִים הַלָּלוּ
הוּא מִתַּלְמִידָיו שֶׁל אַבְרָהָם אָבִינוּ;
וּשְׁלֹשָׁה דְבָרִים אֲחֵרִים הוּא מִתַּלְמִידָיו שֶׁל
בִּלְעָם הָרָשָׁע. עַיִן טוֹבָה, וְרוּחַ נְמוּכָה וְנֶפֶשׁ
שְׁפָלָה תַּלְמִידָיו שֶׁל אַבְרָהָם אָבִינוּ. עַיִן
רָעָה, וְרוּחַ גְּבוֹהָה וְנֶפֶשׁ רְחָבָה תַּלְמִידָיו
שֶׁל בִּלְעָם הָרָשָׁע. מַה בֵּין תַּלְמִידָיו שֶׁל
אַבְרָהָם אָבִינוּ לְתַלְמִידָיו שֶׁל בִּלְעָם הָרָשָׁע?

- The spirit, *nefesh,* is responsible for will, motivation and emotions.
- Intellect, *neshamah,* embraces perception, thought and understanding.

Of these, two support our physical nature: The *ruach* and the *nefesh* are intrinsic to a living body. The *neshamah* is coupled to the other two parts of the soul, but it is not at all physical.

Avraham exercised his *neshamah* to discipline and direct the physical elements of the soul. This is the message of the Scriptural image of Avraham saddling his donkey:[1] He utilized his physical nature as a person would ride a donkey. As a result, even his physical qualities were elevated and refined: He was benevolent, humble and content with what he had.

Bilam was the opposite. His intellectual faculty was tightly bound to his physical nature. Scripture alludes to this fact by noting that Bilam rode a female donkey, and the Rabbis bring out the hint explicitly by commenting that he had relations with it.'[2] The point of the image is that Bilam's *neshamah* was intimately integrated with his physical faculties. The result was that all three parts of his being were base

---

1. *Bereishis* 22:3.

"And Avraham rose up early in the morning and saddled his donkey and took two of his young men with him." The "donkey" symbolizes the body and the "two young men" represent the two physical faculties, *ruach* and *nefesh,* that reside with the body. These physical aspects are a necessary part of daily life and accompanied Avraham on his journey to fulfill the greatest of his ten trials. As Avraham came within sight of the final ascent to fulfill God's will, he left the young men behind with the donkey; i.e., he had to temporarily dissociate himself from all physical influences to fully submit to God. When he returned from his mission, he resumed a normal association with the physical components of the soul.

2. *Avodah Zarah* 4b.

22. Whoever has the following three traits is among the disciples of our forefather Avraham; and [whoever has] three different traits is among the disciples of the wicked Bilam. Those who have a good eye, a humble spirit and a meek soul are among the disciples of our forefather Avraham. Those who have an evil eye, an arrogant spirit and a greedy soul are among the disciples of the wicked Bilam. How are the disciples of our forefather Avraham different from the disciples of the wicked Bilam?

---

and coarse and hence he was evil, arrogant and greedy.

עֵין טוֹבָה, וְרוּחַ נְמוּכָה וְנֶפֶשׁ שְׁפָלָה תַּלְמִידָיו שֶׁל אַבְרָהָם אָבִינוּ §◄
Those who have a good eye, a humble spirit and a meek soul are among the disciples of our forefather Avraham.

"A good eye" means benevolent. Avraham would draw travelers in to be guests in his home and he was kind and generous. We see his "humble spirit" when he refers to himself as dust and ashes[1] while pleading for the lives of the people of Sodom. "A meek soul" means that one is satisfied with what he has and not desirous of others' possessions. Avraham had every right to keep the spoils of war, but he rejected taking anything "from a thread to a shoelace; I will not take anything that is yours."[2]

עֵין רָעָה, וְרוּחַ גְּבוֹהָה וְנֶפֶשׁ רְחָבָה תַּלְמִידָיו שֶׁל בִּלְעָם הָרָשָׁע §◄
Those who have an evil eye, an arrogant spirit and a greedy soul are among the disciples of the wicked Bilam.

Bilam is the antithesis of Avraham. "An evil eye" means malevolent. This is the quality of one who resents others' good fortune. It follows from a corrupt *nefesh* that is filled with jealousy.[3] The *midrash* says[4]

---

1. *Bereishis* 18:27.
2. *Ibid.*, 14:23.
3. *Supra*, 4:28.
4. *Bereishis Rabbah*, section 82.

תַּלְמִידָיו שֶׁל אַבְרָהָם אָבִינוּ אוֹכְלִין בָּעוֹלָם הַזֶּה וְנוֹחֲלִין הָעוֹלָם הַבָּא, שֶׁנֶּאֱמַר: ,,לְהַנְחִיל אֹהֲבַי יֵשׁ וְאֹצְרֹתֵיהֶם אֲמַלֵּא.״ אֲבָל תַּלְמִידָיו שֶׁל בִּלְעָם הָרָשָׁע יוֹרְשִׁין גֵּיהִנֹּם וְיוֹרְדִין לִבְאֵר שַׁחַת, שֶׁנֶּאֱמַר: ,,וְאַתָּה אֱלֹהִים תּוֹרִדֵם לִבְאֵר שַׁחַת,

---

that Bilam surveyed the people of Israel dwelling harmoniously, tribe by tribe,[1] and wished for evil to come upon them.

Bilam was too **arrogant** to go to Balak unless accompanied by high-ranking officers.[2] This quality follows from a misguided intellectual faculty, the *neshamah.* His **"greedy soul"** was evident when he hinted that a house filled with gold and silver[3] would be appropriate payment for his services. Insatiable desire is a deficiency of the *ruach.*

These three traits are a direct consequence of the intimate connection between Bilam's spiritual and physical faculties. Bilam's soul was deficient in every characteristic because physical things are inherently deficient. **"An evil eye"** seeks destruction at every glance. **Arrogance** is a blemish;[4] it attracts its own downfall, just as every physical excess hastens its own destruction.[5] **Greed** is a sure sign of deficiency: He must be lacking or why would he want the possessions of others?

---

§ תַּלְמִידָיו שֶׁל אַבְרָהָם אָבִינוּ . . . וְנוֹחֲלִין הָעוֹלָם הַבָּא . . . אֲבָל תַּלְמִידָיו שֶׁל בִּלְעָם הָרָשָׁע יוֹרְשִׁין גֵּיהִנֹּם — ***The disciples of our forefather Avraham . . . inherit the World to Come. . . but the disciples of the wicked Bilam inherit Gehinnom***

Although history is replete with people who were more wicked than Bilam, the *mishnah* chose to discuss Bilam because he was the precise opposite of Avraham. While Avraham found fulfillment in this world

1. *Bamidbar* 24:2.
2. *Ibid.,* 22:15.
3. *Ibid.,* v. 18.
4. *Megillah* 29a.
5. This idea is the subject of the commentary to 2:8, supra.

5/ 22 The disciples of our forefather Avraham enjoy [the fruits of their good deeds] in this world and inherit the World to Come, as is said (*Mishlei* 8:21): "To cause those who love Me to inherit existence; and I will fill their storehouses." But the disciples of the wicked Bilam inherit Gehinnom and descend into the well of destruction, as is said (*Tehillim* 55:24): "And You, O God, shall lower them into the well of destruction,

---

and the Next, through spiritual pursuits, Bilam pursued only worldly desires.

∙§ תַּלְמִידָיו שֶׁל אַבְרָהָם אָבִינוּ אוֹכְלִין בָּעוֹלָם הַזֶּה וְנוֹחֲלִין הָעוֹלָם הַבָּא, שֶׁנֶּאֱמַר: ,,לְהַנְחִיל אֹהֲבַי יֵשׁ, וְאֹצְרֹתֵיהֶם אֲמַלֵּא'' — *The disciples of our forefather Avraham enjoy the fruit of their good deeds in this world and inherit the World to Come, as is said: "To cause those who love Me to inherit existence; and I will fill their storehouses."*

Physical needs can be satisfied with finite physical things. By contrast, desire is in the spirit. The spirit is not satisfied with physical things, and one whose spirit is in pursuit of physical desires will always be unsatisfied. Avraham's disciples can easily "eat" in this world and be satisfied. They **"inherit existence"** because they are fulfilled and free of want. **"I will fill their storehouses"** of those who used their life to grow to spiritual maturity. These are the storehouses of the Next World, that are concealed in this world.

∙§ אֲבָל תַּלְמִידָיו שֶׁל בִּלְעָם הָרָשָׁע יוֹרְשִׁין גֵּיהִנֹּם וְיוֹרְדִין לִבְאֵר שַׁחַת — *But the disciples of the wicked Bilam inherit Gehinnom and descend into the well of destruction*

Gehinnom is the opposite of existence; the term is synonymous with desolation. It is a fitting place for Bilam's disciples, who create a dependence on physical indulgences which are ultimately self-destructive. Indeed, they assimilate the physical attributes of dependence and deterioration into their very being. As a result, after the great day of judgment they descend further, to the well of destruction, which is worse yet than *Gehinnom*.

אַנְשֵׁי דָמִים וּמִרְמָה לֹא יֶחֱצוּ יְמֵיהֶם;
וַאֲנִי אֶבְטַח בָּךְ."

[כג] יְהוּדָה בֶּן תֵּימָא אוֹמֵר: הֱוֵי עַז
כַּנָּמֵר, וְקַל כַּנֶּשֶׁר, רָץ כַּצְּבִי

◆§ אַנְשֵׁי דָמִים וּמִרְמָה לֹא יֶחֱצוּ יְמֵיהֶם — *men of bloodshed and deceit will not live out half their days*

The destructive nature of Bilam's personality threatens the existence of those around him and results in his early demise, himself. His kind are referred to as **men of bloodshed,** for he attempted to devour the nation of Israel. Furthermore, Bilam himself did **not live out half his days,** dying at the age of 33.[1]

Structure of Chapter 5

This *mishnah* concludes a major section of Chapter 5, which begins with the Creation of the world and proceeds to explore level after level of spiritual emergence. *Mishnah* 21 dealt with strengthening the community and *Mishnah* 22 completes the thought by describing the qualities of Avraham, the forefather of the community of Israel, whose merit stands by community leaders even to this day.[2] After twenty generations of spiritual evolution, Avraham marked the end of Creation and the beginning of the world, for finally it was worthy of existence through serving God.

Avraham elevated the secular to the sacred, by dominance of the intellectual soul over the physical faculties. He infused the physical world with the spiritual level of the highest order and which is associated with *Gan Eden.*

Whereas Avraham secured the world's existence, Bilam is the antithetical force that drives towards non-existence. Because his physical nature dominated his soul, he initiated a culture of destruction that is associated with *Gehinnom.*

Since these *mishnayos* are not attributed to individual Sages, we see that they are intended as a unit. With the next *mishnah,* however, *Avos* reverts to *mussar* of individual rabbis.

---

1. *Sanhedrin* 106b.
2. *Supra,* 2:2.

men of bloodshed and deceit will not live out half their days; but as for me, I will trust in You."

23. Yehudah ben Teima said: Be bold as a leopard, light as an eagle, swift as a deer,

---

Mishnah 23

Yehudah ben Teima recognizes the lethargy that is inherent in the physical makeup of a person. He encourages one to be energetic in every step of performing *mitzvos,* since that is the purpose for which mankind was created.

There are four steps to action. We decide to do something, stand up, prepare and act. A *mitzvah* develops, from intent through to action, by way of these same four stages, each of which is exemplified by the four animals of our *mishnah.*

---

§ הֱוֵי עַז כַּנָּמֵר — *Be bold as a leopard*

In this context the word **bold** is to be understood as the opposite of "shy," which means that one is easily inhibited by others.

The advice to be **bold as a leopard** means that a person must not allow his wish to serve God to be swayed by others. Rather, he should be bold enough to perform the *mitzvah* in the face of those who mock him, and not just go elsewhere to do the *mitzvah.*

---

§ הֱוֵי עַז כַּנָּמֵר — *Be bold as a leopard*

A physical thing does not move by itself, and so it is that the body moves only in response to the will. Therefore, the first step to action is to **be bold**: have the will, the motivation, the desire, the excitement of an aroused leopard.

---

§ וְקַל כַּנֶּשֶׁר — *light as an eagle*

This refers to the next stage of action. Stand up swiftly and energetically, with no hint of inertia.

---

§ רָץ כַּצְּבִי — *swift as a deer*

Run to gather needed items and to go to the right place. At this stage the *mitzvah* is developing from thought into action.

וְגִבּוֹר כָּאֲרִי, לַעֲשׂוֹת רְצוֹן אָבִיךְ שֶׁבַּשָּׁמָיִם.

[כד] הוּא הָיָה אוֹמֵר: עַז פָּנִים לְגֵיהִנֹּם, וּבֹשֶׁת פָּנִים לְגַן עֵדֶן. יְהִי רָצוֹן מִלְפָנֶיךָ יהוה אֱלֹהֵינוּ וֵאלֹהֵי אֲבוֹתֵינוּ שֶׁיִּבָּנֶה בֵּית הַמִּקְדָּשׁ, בִּמְהֵרָה בְיָמֵינוּ, וְתֵן חֶלְקֵנוּ בְּתוֹרָתֶךָ.

---

§ **וְגִבּוֹר כָּאֲרִי** — *and strong as a lion*

This refers to actually doing the *mitzvah*. A *mitzvah* must be performed with determination and energy.

---

§ **לַעֲשׂוֹת רְצוֹן אָבִיךְ שֶׁבַּשָּׁמָיִם** — *to carry out the will of your Father in Heaven*

God is referred to here as "your **Father** in Heaven" to put the performance of *mitzvos* into context: God is our Father, Who brought us into being, and we must serve Him with the utmost of our energy.

Mishnah 24

The previous *mishnah* advised being bold, even brazen, but only **"to carry out the will of your Father in Heaven,"** and this characteristic is not intended in a worldly context.

---

§ **עַז פָּנִים לְגֵיהִנֹּם** — *The brazen goes to* Gehinnom

---

In metaphysical terms, we may say that things tend to eventually join with their like kind, as water flows to join water. Since the power and strength that underlie being brazen are qualities of fire, the fire of the brazen personality will by nature join with the fire of *Gehinnom*.

In simpler terms, we may explain that the wicked act energetically to go outside the bounds of decent behavior. Hence, it is fitting that they will experience the unconstrained power of the fire of *Gehinnom*.

---

§ **וּבֹשֶׁת פָּנִים לְגַן עֵדֶן** — *but the shamefaced goes to the Garden of Eden*

Being shamefaced is the opposite quality to being brazen. Such a person is passive and accommodating and hence belongs in the tranquil, stable repose of *Gan Eden*.

and strong as a lion, to carry out the will of your Father in Heaven.

24. He used to say: The brazen goes to *Gehinnom,* but the shamefaced goes to the Garden of Eden. May it be Your will, Hashem, our God and the God of our forefathers, that the Holy Temple be rebuilt, speedily in our days, and grant us our share in Your Torah.

יְהִי רָצוֹן מִלְפָנֶיךָ . . . שֶׁיִבָּנֶה בֵּית הַמִקְדָּש, בִּמְהֵרָה בְיָמֵינוּ, וְתֵן חֶלְקֵנוּ ⊸§
בְּתוֹרָתֶךְ — *May it be Your will . . . that the Holy Temple be rebuilt, speedily in our days, and grant us our share in Your Torah.*

It may seem rather surprising that this prayer for the Holy Temple and for Torah is in the same breath as the statement that "The brazen goes to *Gehinnom.*" However, the fact is that most people, especially among Jews, are brazen; that is, audacious and impudent, and hence there is a significant risk that a Jew's *chutzpah* will land him in *Gehinnom.* Therefore, the mention of "The brazen goes to *Gehinnom*" is immediately followed by a prayer for the Holy Temple and for Torah, for these two things protect us from *Gehinnom.*

In the following discussion, we must remember[1] that holiness is the central, conceptual point that ties together the otherwise disconnected physical dimensions. Hence, holiness imparts to the physical world the structure needed to form an effective unit, and the Temple is the entry point of holiness into this world. Also, in this discussion, "Torah" refers to the system of principles, relationships and values for which the world was created.

How do the Holy Temple and the Torah protect us from the destructive power of *Gehinnom*? This can be understood by comparing the Temple to the heart and the Torah to the brain, for the heart is the source of life, while the brain is the seat of intelligence, and both are principle components that are prerequisites to life.

The heart is central to the body and provides life to the limbs. Through the blood, the heart sends nourishment to the entire body, but it receives nourishment first, before the other organs. Analogously, the entire world is nourished by the Temple's holiness, but the land of Israel drinks first and from there the life force of holiness flows to the rest of the world.

---

1. See *supra,* Chapter 5, *mishnah* 9 and *mishnah* 18.

[כה] הוּא הָיָה אוֹמֵר: בֶּן חָמֵשׁ שָׁנִים לַמִּקְרָא;
בֶּן עֶשֶׂר שָׁנִים לַמִּשְׁנָה; בֶּן שְׁלֹשׁ
עֶשְׂרֵה לַמִּצְוֹת; בֶּן חֲמֵשׁ עֶשְׂרֵה לַגְּמָרָא; בֶּן
שְׁמוֹנֶה עֶשְׂרֵה לַחֻפָּה; בֶּן עֶשְׂרִים לִרְדּוֹף;

As human intelligence resides in the brain, so is Torah the repository of intellect for the world.

The heart and the brain together provide the principal functions of the human being, but one operates at a higher level than the other. So it is that the Temple supports prosperity, while Torah reaches to the upper world. The Temple and Torah join together to form a ladder that stands on the ground and reaches above the heavens. When the People of Israel are occupied with the Temple and with Torah, they have a ladder that leads away from *Gehinnom*.

In another metaphor, the Temple and Torah are two lights of existence, while *Gehinnom* is the darkness of non-existence. As long as the People of Israel cling to these two principal elements of existence, they are safe from the threat of extinction called *Gehinnom*.

י֙ שֶׁיִּבָּנֶה בֵּית הַמִּקְדָּשׁ ... יְהִי רָצוֹן מִלְפָנֶיךָ — **May it be Your will . . . that the Holy Temple be rebuilt**

The *mishnah* concludes with a prayer for the return of the Temple,[1] but until that prayer is fulfilled we must each strive to be like the Temple, rising to a high spiritual and intellectual plane to bring Divine blessing into the world.

Mishnah 25

Life is made up of phases, each of which is a ten-year unit, and so the different phases listed in the *mishnah* are generally ten years apart.

י֙ בֶּן חָמֵשׁ שָׁנִים לַמִּקְרָא; בֶּן עֶשֶׂר שָׁנִים לַמִּשְׁנָה ... בֶּן חֲמֵשׁ עֶשְׂרֵה לַגְּמָרָא — **A five-year-old begins Scripture; a ten-year-old begins Mishnah . . . a fifteen-year-old begins the study of Gemara**

Why do these phases take only five years? Since Torah study is shared with his teacher, five years of his own effort and five years of the teacher's effort produce ten years of development in a five-year span.

---

1. In the original *Derech Chaim,* this thought is at the beginning of the next *mishnah.*

25. He used to say: A five-year-old begins Scripture; a ten-year-old begins *Mishnah*; a thirteen-year-old becomes obliged to observe the commandments; a fifteen-year-old begins the study of *Gemara*; an eighteen-year-old goes to the marriage canopy; a twenty-year-old begins to pursue;

◆§ בֶּן שְׁלֹשׁ עֶשְׂרֵה לַמִּצְוֹת — *a thirteen-year-old becomes obliged to observe the commandments*

The ability to bear the weight of warnings and commandments comes with the strength of adulthood, which is characterized by the ability to have children.

◆§ בֶּן שְׁמוֹנֶה עֶשְׂרֵה לַחֻפָּה — *an eighteen-year-old goes to the marriage canopy*

A man is not a complete entity without a wife. As the Rabbis say:[1]

> Whoever does not have a wife is not an *Adam* (person), as it says:[2] "On the day that God created mankind. . .male and female He created them, and He blessed them and called their name *Adam*."

A man's physical growth is at its peak at eighteen, and then it is time to grow in another dimension, by expanding his life to include another. This stage of life begins at eighteen and continues until twenty, when he is ready to provide leadership in the household, as we will soon see.

It is noteworthy that eighteen years is a quarter of man's life span of seventy years.[3] In this way our lives parallel the sun, which reaches the zenith of its strength at noon, after one quarter of its 24-hour cycle.[4]

◆§ בֶּן עֶשְׂרִים לִרְדוֹף — *a twenty-year-old begins to pursue*

A person functions at three levels. The highest level is צֶלֶם, *tzelem*, a reference to mankind's "image of God" which gives rise to the independent spirit of individual existence. The lowest level is חוֹמֶר, *chomer*,

---

1. *Yevamos* 63a.
2. *Bereishis* 5:1-2.
3. Rounded to a whole number.
4. The motion of the sun is always referenced to the equinox, when the sun achieves full height in the sky 6 hours after sunrise.

which refers to physical, pragmatic existence. The middle level is called צוּרָה, *tzurah,* which literally means form. It is the aspect of personality that seeks to impose form and structure on other things, on oneself and on other people. *Tzurah* is the origin of the human drive to influence and to govern.[1]

A twenty-year-old begins to *pursue* means to pursue another person and to dominate him. After twenty years of age, one seeks to triumph over others and to govern them. Since the intent of war is to pursue one's enemies and to rule over them, Torah law prescribes that eligibility for military duty begins at age twenty.

During the formative years, *tzurah* is merged with *chomer.* At age eighteen, when physical growth is complete, *tzurah* comes into its own and a man seeks to exert influence over others. At this stage of life, one is ready to provide leadership in his own household.

At eighteen, he is ready to get married, and after that:[2]

> God waits for a man until twenty years of age. If he does not take a wife, He says, "Let his bones swell!"

⊷§ בֶּן עֶשְׂרִים לִרְדוֹף — *a twenty-year-old begins to pursue*

One who is ready to pursue others is ready to be pursued.[3] At twenty, the quality of *tzurah* is complete, and one is subject to punishment at the hands of Heaven. Until twenty, *tzurah* is dependent on *chomer,* the earthly level of existence, and only the earthly human court of law can judge and administer punishment. However, after twenty, *tzurah* is no longer dependent on the physical body, but has developed to its full, independent state. One is then subject to judgment and retribution from the heavenly court of law.

⊷§ בֶּן שְׁלֹשִׁים לַכֹּחַ — *a thirty-year-old attains full strength*

"Strength" refers to spiritual strength. The physical faculty, *chomer,*

---

1. Author's introductory paragraph, based on Maharal's various writings.
2. *Kiddushin* 29b.
3. Author's introductory comment.

a thirty-year-old attains full strength; a forty-year-old attains understanding; a fifty-year-old can offer counsel; a sixty-year-old attains seniority; a seventy-year-old attains a ripe old age;

---

matured at eighteen; *tzurah* matured at twenty; *tzelem* matures at thirty. At this stage, the spiritual faculties are completely developed.

בֶּן אַרְבָּעִים לַבִּינָה — *a forty-year-old attains understanding*

One can expand his knowledge by inference and analysis of what he has learned already. This talent is the "understanding" one attains at age forty. At thirty, the *physical* and *spiritual* components were complete. After ten more years, at age forty, the *intellect* begins to reach full maturity.

בֶּן חֲמִשִּׁים לְעֵצָה — *a fifty-year-old can offer counsel*

"Counsel" is deeper than "understanding." There are hidden matters that one does not perceive until this stage of intellectual maturity.

בֶּן שִׁשִּׁים לְזִקְנָה — *a sixty-year-old attains seniority*

The Rabbis use the word זִקְנָה, *ziknah,* to mean the advanced wisdom that comes with age.[1] As the physical faculties fade, the intellectual faculties bloom. As a result, God provides comprehension of purely conceptual matters that have no physical representation.

בֶּן שִׁבְעִים לְשֵׂיבָה — *a seventy-year-old attains a ripe old age*

He has achieved fullness of years, for we are normally granted seventy years. The term שֵׂיבָה, *sevah,* can be understood as שְׂבַע, meaning full and satisfied. This is related to the number seven, שִׁבְעָה, which connotes fullness, as we find in cycles that are complete in seven days and in seven years. It is possible to add to a full measure, and life can extend to a hundred years.

---

1. *Kinnim* 3:6, "the understanding of elderly Torah scholars gets clearer with age."

ה/כו בֶּן שְׁמוֹנִים לִגְבוּרָה; בֶּן תִּשְׁעִים לָשׁוּחַ; בֶּן מֵאָה כְּאִלּוּ מֵת, וְעָבַר וּבָטֵל מִן הָעוֹלָם.

[כו] בֶּן בַּג בַּג אוֹמֵר: הֲפָךְ בָּה וַהֲפָךְ בָּה דְּכֹלָּא בָה; וּבָה תֶּחֱזֵי; וְסִיב וּבְלֵה בָּה,

---

§ בֶּן שְׁמוֹנִים לִגְבוּרָה — *an eighty-year-old shows strength*

Exceptional people may have strength up to age eighty.

---

§ בֶּן תִּשְׁעִים לָשׁוּחַ — *a ninety-year-old becomes stooped over*

At ninety, all growth and maturity are past and hence deterioration sets in.

Man is made in the image of God. One way that finds expression is in mankind's erect posture, symbolizing kingship. The phrase **"becomes stooped over"** conveys that he has lost, to some degree, the unique stature of a human being.

Mishnah 26

---

§ הֲפָךְ בָּה . . . דְּכֹלָּא בָה — *Delve in it [the Torah] . . . for everything is in it*

Ben Bag Bag wishes to convey the importance of the Torah. **"Everything is in it"** means that the Torah describes the entire universe, but why would that be so?

Mankind is the point of Creation and hence all Creation is subsidiary to mankind. Furthermore, Torah is the conceptual structure that God established for human conduct. Since Creation exists to support human existence, the structure of Creation must follow from Torah's structure for mankind. Hence, Torah is the original premise of Creation, as the Rabbis said,[1]

> The Holy One, Blessed is He, looked in the Torah to create the world.

---

1. *Bereishis Rabbah*, section 1.

5/ 26   an eighty-year-old shows strength; a ninety-year-old becomes stooped over; a hundred-year-old is as if he were dead, passed away and ceased from the world.

26. Ben Bag Bag says: Delve in it [the Torah] and continue to delve in it [the Torah] for everything is in it; look deeply into it; grow old and gray over it,

---

If one could fully comprehend Torah, he would have in his grasp the structure of all existence.

---

§◆ דְּכֹלָּה בָהּ — *for everything is in it*

The fact that everything is in the Torah makes it an important field of study, even if one's studies do not yield that level of comprehension. The importance of a field of study depends on the subject. For example, one could be an expert in millstones, but millstones are just not an important subject. Indeed, an expert in millstones is insignificant compared to one who knows even a small amount about astronomy. So it is that even a limited knowledge of Torah is extremely important, for the subject of Torah is mankind. That subject must be more important than all the heavens, for they were created only because of man.

---

§◆ וַהֲפָךְ בָּהּ דְכֹלָּה בָהּ — *Delve in it [the Torah] and continue to delve in it [the Torah] for everything is in it*

Torah is worth scrutinizing over and over. Since everything is in it, there is always something new and interesting to learn.

---

§◆ וּבָהּ תֶּחֱזֵי — *look deeply into it*

One should turn to the Torah as the source of all delight and stimulation.

---

§◆ וְסִיב וּבְלֵה בָהּ — *grow old and gray over it*

Even if you are feeble from old age, do not turn aside from Torah study.

ה/כו

וּמִנָּהּ לָא תָזוּעַ, שֶׁאֵין לְךָ מִדָּה טוֹבָה הֵימֶנָּה.
בֶּן הֵא הֵא אוֹמֵר: לְפוּם צַעֲרָא אַגְרָא.

❊ ❊ ❊

---

§◈ שֶׁאֵין לְךָ מִדָּה טוֹבָה הֵימֶנָּה — *for you can have no better portion than it*

Torah is superior to everything else, for it brings one close to God as nothing else can. If those who dwell in the dark only understood what this *mishnah* is about! They would not forsake the Torah, in whose shelter we live, and waste their lives with the secular studies of other nations.

---

§◈ לְפוּם צַעֲרָא אַגְרָא — *The reward is in proportion to the exertion*

The Hebrew word צַעַר, *tsaar,* includes discomfort and distress.

The *mishnah* cannot mean that difficult *mitzvos* bring more reward than easy *mitzvos,* for in *Avos* 2:1 we learned that: "you do not know the reward given for the respective *mitzvos."*

The reward for *mitzvos* derives from the person coming close to God. Although we do not know which *mitzvos* are more effective in bringing one close to God, we do know that there is additional reward for additional effort, because the extra effort brings him even closer. This may be understood by considering a person who tries to visit another person, but there is an obstacle in his way. He exerts energy, effort and his full strength to remove the obstacle, and clearly only a very close friend would expend that effort to come. So it is with *mitzvos,* for God will reward one who is so close to Him as to exert such effort.

---

§◈ לְפוּם צַעֲרָא אַגְרָא — *The reward is in proportion to the exertion*

There is no extra reward for one who tries to do the *mitzvah* out of צַעַר, *tsaar,* duress, when he could have done the *mitzvah* without duress. Extra reward comes only when he overcomes an obstacle that would have prevented him from doing the *mitzvah.*

Hebrew and Aramaic

There are two levels of Torah. There is Torah as presented to this world and there is the Torah as it comes from the highest world.

The chapter begins with the Creation of this world. It was created with the Hebrew language and the Torah that was given to this world is

and do not stir from it, for you can have no better portion than it. Ben Hei Hei says: The reward is in proportion to the exertion.

❀ ❀ ❀

likewise written in the Hebrew language. The chapter concludes with the highest level of Torah, which has everything in it, for it transcends this world and hence the final *mishnah* is not in Hebrew but in the special language of Aramaic.

The physical world was created with the Hebrew language and hence Aramaic is not part of its structure. Rather it corresponds to the highest world, which is above the level of the angels, and for that reason angels do not understand Aramaic.

The fact that Torah has components in this world and in the highest world is demonstrated through the language of Torah. Scripture and *Mishnah* are written in Hebrew, but the highest level of Torah, the Talmud,[1] is written in Aramaic. Another example is the *mitzvah* to review the portion of the week in Hebrew twice and in Aramaic once. These three times correspond to the lower world, the middle world and the highest world, with the third review of the portion in Aramaic corresponding to the highest world.

⧓§ בֶּן הֵא הֵא אוֹמֵר . . . בֶּן בַּג בַּג אוֹמֵר — *Ben Bag Bag says . . . Ben Hei Hei says*

Rabbi Shmuel ben Meir points out that both Ben Bag Bag and Ben Hei Hei were offspring of converts to Judaism and spoke Aramaic.

Their names reflect the number five,[2] corresponding to the Hebrew letter ה, *hei*. Among letters it is unsurpassed as a symbol of the spiritual[3] for it is only the intangible strength of the life breath with no physical contribution from the throat, mouth or lips. Hence, the letter *hei* expresses the essence of conversion, for a convert leaves the nations of the world and takes on the power of holiness that is the strength of Israel. Indeed, the letter *hei* was added to the names of Avraham and Sarah when they entered into God's holy covenant.[4]

---

1. That Talmud is the highest form of Torah is explained in the commentary to Chapter 4, *mishnayos* 15-17.
2. בַּג = 5; הֵא = the letter ה = 5.
3. Creation is referred to in *Bereishis* 2:4 by the word בְּהִבָּרְאָם (when they were created), which can be understood as בְּהֵי בְּרָאָם — He created them with *hei*.
4. *Bereishis* 17:5, 15.

רַבִּי חֲנַנְיָא בֶּן עֲקַשְׁיָא אוֹמֵר: רָצָה הַקָּדוֹשׁ
בָּרוּךְ הוּא לְזַכּוֹת אֶת יִשְׂרָאֵל; לְפִיכָךְ
הִרְבָּה לָהֶם תּוֹרָה וּמִצְוֹת, שֶׁנֶּאֱמַר: „יהוה חָפֵץ
לְמַעַן צִדְקוֹ, יַגְדִּיל תּוֹרָה וְיַאְדִּיר.‟

It is appropriate that the two ideas of this *mishnah* are stated by converts, for the ability to convert reflects the high level of Torah. "Everything is in it" means that it embraces everything, including the nations of the world. Torah transcends everything and encompasses everyone. The nations did not want the Torah but, for God's part, it is relevant to everyone.

Relation of Mishnah 26 to Preceding Mishnayos

The *mishnayos* progress from the level of performing *mitzvos* — "Be bold as a leopard. . .to carry out the Will of your Father in Heaven"[1] — to the study of Torah, which is superior to doing *mitzvos*.[2] The next thought, "The **reward** is in proportion to the exertion," concludes the chapter with the highest level of all, for our ultimate destiny is the reward of the World to Come.

The level of "Be bold as a leopard, light as an eagle. . .to carry out the will of your Father in Heaven" is a plane of life that is shared by angels; indeed, they especially do God's will with love and reverence and rejoicing. In contrast, the final *mishnah* deals with study of Torah and acquiring the World to Come, which are available only to people and not to angels. That is another reason why they were phrased in Aramaic, a language which angels do not comprehend.

Torah was not given to angels[3] and they cannot earn reward for they do not change and improve, nor do they earn reward for duress, for they experience no difficulty in performing the will of their Creator.

Summary of Chapter Five

The chapter commences with the Creation of the world, and progresses through the structure of the world, level upon level. *Mishnah* 19 then describes the force that ties the world together: "Any love

---

1. Supra, *mishnah* 23.
2. *Kiddushin* 40b: . . .the study of Torah is greater because it leads to doing *mitzvos*.
3. *Shabbos* 88b-89a. The angels claimed that the Torah should not be given to mortals. Moshe responded: What is written in it? "I am the Lord your God Who has brought you out of the land of Egypt, out of the house of bondage." (*Shemos* 20:2). He said to them, "Did you go down to Egypt? Were you enslaved to Pharaoh? What would you do with the Torah?"

Rabbi Chanania ben Akashia says: The Holy One, Blessed is He, wished to confer merit upon Israel; therefore He gave them Torah and *mitzvos* in abundance, as it is said (*Yeshayahu* 42:21): 'Hashem desired, for the sake of His righteousness, that the Torah be made great and glorious."

---

that. . .does not depend on a specific cause will never cease." The opposite force is controversy, in *mishnah* 20. The power of the community is discussed in *mishnah* 21, followed by the exalted stature of Avraham, father of the Jewish community, in *mishnah* 22. Up to this point, the chapter discussed the world in general, and the authorship of the *mishnayos* was general; i.e., no specific sage is named. *Mishnah* 23, "Be bold as a leopard. . ." turns from the general to the specific. It addresses the individual, and from this point on the *mishnah* names the individual authors.

Yehudah ben Teima addresses the individual at both the *physical* and *spiritual* aspects of human existence. He offers advice to overcome *physical* lethargy: "Be bold as a leopard. . ." in the service of God; and he offers advice to counter aggression, which is *spiritual,* stemming from the *nefesh*: "The brazen goes to *Gehinnom*";[1] i.e., one should be gentle in worldly matters.

In *mishnah* 25 he then explores the development of the human being, stage by stage, from childhood to his demise. Nature dictates that people must die, but in *mishnah* 26 we learn that one whose life is Torah has eternal life, for Torah is from a higher world, which transcends nature. The chapter concludes with "The reward is in proportion to the exertion," a statement of mankind's ultimate destiny: the reward of the World to Come.

This is the conclusion of tractate *Avos,* for the sixth chapter is a later addition. It is most noteworthy that *Avos* began with Torah[2] —

They said three things: Be deliberate in judgment; develop many disciples; and make a fence for the Torah.

— and concludes with Torah and the reward of Torah. Torah is the origin of everything and Torah is the purpose of everything. Through Torah, we merit and achieve our ultimate goal.

Deliberate carefully on everything that we have said, and through your own efforts add wisdom, understanding and knowledge.

---

1. *Supra, mishnah* 24.
2. *Avos* 1:1.

פרק ששי ⸲
Chapter Six

כָּל יִשְׂרָאֵל יֵשׁ לָהֶם חֵלֶק לָעוֹלָם הַבָּא,
שֶׁנֶּאֱמַר: „וְעַמֵּךְ כֻּלָּם צַדִּיקִים; לְעוֹלָם
יִירְשׁוּ אָרֶץ, נֵצֶר מַטָּעַי, מַעֲשֵׂה יָדַי לְהִתְפָּאֵר.“

All Israel has a share in the World to Come, as it
is said (*Yeshayahu* 60:21): "And your people
are all righteous; they shall inherit the land
forever; they are the stem of My plantings, My
handiwork, in which to take pride."

שָׁנוּ חֲכָמִים בִּלְשׁוֹן הַמִּשְׁנָה. בָּרוּךְ שֶׁבָּחַר בָּהֶם וּבְמִשְׁנָתָם.
[א] רַבִּי מֵאִיר אוֹמֵר: כָּל הָעוֹסֵק בַּתּוֹרָה לִשְׁמָהּ זוֹכֶה לִדְבָרִים הַרְבֵּה;

Torah and *mussar* complement each other. Torah illuminates the path that leads to the World to Come, while *mussar* is advice to deal with worldly temptations that draw us away from that path. The living practice of the study of *mussar* is called *derech eretz* — the discipline of civilized behavior and good qualities of character. *Avos*, as a work of *mussar*, is clearly a close companion of Torah, as the Rabbis stated,[1]

> "If there is no Torah, there is no *derech eretz*; if there is no *derech eretz*, there is no Torah."

The redactors of the Mishnah composed *Avos* with five chapters, corresponding to the five books of the Torah, to emphasize how tightly *Avos* is intertwined with Torah. Indeed, the first chapter of *Avos* parallels the first book of the Torah. The Book of *Bereishis* traces the generations from Creation to the exile in Egypt, while the first chapter of *Avos* traces the generations of Torah leadership from the creation of the Jewish nation at Sinai to the current exile.

Chapter 6 is not part of the original tractate of *Pirkei Avos*. It is an addendum, dedicated to describing our Torah's exalted level. The entire chapter cements the connection between Torah and *derech eretz*, while making it clear that *derech eretz* paves the way for the ultimate goal of Torah.

§ בִּלְשׁוֹן הַמִּשְׁנָה — *in the language of the Mishnah*

This chapter is composed of *baraisos*, redacted in a later period than the *mishnah*. In general, *baraisos* expound the Scriptural sources of law and are not as terse as the *mishnah*.

§ בָּרוּךְ שֶׁבָּחַר בָּהֶם — *Blessed is He Who chose them*

God chose the **Sages** to promulgate Torah. He sanctioned their interpretation of Torah as being the definitive one, as the verse says,[2]

> According to the Torah which they (the Sages of the Rabbinical

1. *Supra*, 3:21.
2. *Devarim* 17:11.

The Sages taught [this chapter] in the language of the Mishnah. Blessed is He Who chose them and their teaching.

1. Rabbi Meir says: Whoever engages in Torah study for its own sake merits many things;

Court) teach, shall you. . . do; you shall not deviate . . .to the right or to the left.

◆§ **וּבְמִשְׁנָתָם** — *and their* teaching

That He loves their **teaching** is evident from the *Midrash,* [1]

The words of the [early] Rabbis are more dear [to God] than the words of the Torah.[2]

◆§ **בָּרוּךְ שֶׁבָּחַר בָּהֶם וּבְמִשְׁנָתָם** — *Blessed is He Who chose them and their teaching.*

The *baraisa* expresses love and praise for these *Avos* — the Rabbinical fathers of the Jewish nation — by drawing attention to God's own pleasure in them and their teachings.

Mishnah 1

The term "Torah" is used in different contexts to refer to various aspects of the Torah. It may refer at times to a Torah scroll; to all Scripture; or to the laws of the Torah. In this chapter, Maharal considers Torah in its fullest scope, as an entity that embodies all truth. Here, "Torah" refers to ontology and law; theory and practice; values, principles and relationships; history and philosophy; as articulated or implied by God's communication to mankind through Moshe. All we know about God is in the Torah, and within Torah lies even more about God than we will ever comprehend.

◆§ **כָּל הָעוֹסֵק בַּתּוֹרָה לִשְׁמָה זוֹכֶה לִדְבָרִים הַרְבֵּה** — *Whoever engages in Torah study for its own sake merits many things*

A person who engages in Torah study for its own sake becomes

---

1. *Shir HaShirim Rabbah,* 1:18.
2. This may be compared to parents who have taught their children good manners. They delight in their son and daughter finding their own ways of practicing polite behavior and teaching it to others. It should be noted that the Rabbis' teachings are more **dear** to God than is Torah. They are not necessarily superior to the Torah.

intimately connected with Torah. When he achieves Torah's exalted level, he acquires **many things** that flow from Torah, such as wealth, honor and length of days, in addition to the other blessings detailed in the *mishnah*.

Only a person who studies Torah for its own sake reaches Torah's level, and therefore it is only he who merits these things. Certainly, anyone whose studies are not for the sake of Torah, but for the sake of earning the title "Rabbi" or some other personal benefit, has not achieved the exalted level of Torah and does not deserve these blessings.

שֶׁכָּל הָעוֹלָם כֻּלּוֹ כְּדַאי הוּא לוֹ — *[the Creation of] the entire world is worthwhile for his sake* **alone**

Torah's conceptual systems infuse this material world with purpose and worth.[1] By endowing time and substance with such attributes as *sacred*, *sanctioned* and *profane*, Torah creates institutions such as Shabbos, *kashrus* and other vehicles for spiritual growth and eternal life.

A single concept can find expression in a thousand actions and objects. Torah's concepts are so fundamental and far reaching that only 613 laws suffice to govern the details of all affairs of all social roles — king, *Kohen,* rabbi and layperson — all day, all year, in all circumstances, while providing spiritual growth to enjoy eternity in the World to Come. Indeed, Torah stands in a transcendent relationship towards the entire world, for it provided the world's conceptual blueprint and it continues to support its existence on every plane.[2]

Chapter 19 of *Tehillim* hints at the fact that Torah transcends the world. The first seven verses (in an allusion to the seven days of Creation) declare how the grandeur of Creation is testimony to God's glory. The number 8 connotes that which transcends the seven-day Creation and fittingly, the eighth verse states: "God's Torah is perfect." Thus, the Torah's transcendence of nature is embedded into the very structure of the psalm.

---

1. These two paragraphs are the author's explanation of Maharal's thesis that Torah is a conceptual שִׂכְלִי (*sichli*) system.

2. See *supra*, 1:2, "The world depends on three things: on Torah study, on the service [of God] and on kind deeds," and commentary *ad loc.*

Similarly, Chapter 119 of *Tehillim,* which is dedicated to Torah, consists of 8-verse stanzas, to convey that Torah transcends the seven-day Creation.

The primacy of Torah relative to material Creation is also alluded to by the fact that the Ten Commandments begins with א (אָנֹכִי ה׳ אֱלֹהֶיךָ), the first letter of the Hebrew alphabet, whereas the Creation of the world begins with the subsequent letter ב (בְּרֵאשִׁית).

In summary, the entire world is worthwhile for one who learns Torah for its own sake, because one who achieves the stature of Torah transcends the world, just as Torah transcends the world.

≈§ נִקְרָא רֵעַ — *He is called, "Friend"*

One who learns Torah for its own sake is called a **friend** of both God and people.

≈§ נִקְרָא . . . אָהוּב — *He is called, ". . .Beloved"*

Love is superior to friendship. To be a "friend" means to associate with another. To "love" another means that one's very soul is bound up with the soul of the beloved. We conclude that **beloved** is a higher quality than **friend,** רֵעַ, from the verse,[1] "And you shall love your fellow, רֵעֲךָ, as yourself."[2]

≈§ אוֹהֵב אֶת הַמָּקוֹם, אוֹהֵב אֶת הַבְּרִיּוֹת — *He loves the Omnipresent, he loves people*

We said that one who learns Torah for its own sake is a "friend" and "beloved" of both God and people. It is the study and practice of Torah that infuse the world with its values. Since Torah flows from God, and Torah lives in people, a person who is the embodiment of Torah is tightly bound up with both God and mankind.

Indeed, one who learns Torah for its own sake is the vehicle through

---

1. *Vayikra* 19:18.

2. The reasoning is that the quality of love cannot be at a par with the quality of friendship, or the exhortation to "love your friend" would be trivial.

אֶת הַבְּרִיּוֹת; מְשַׂמֵּחַ אֶת הַמָּקוֹם, מְשַׂמֵּחַ אֶת
הַבְּרִיּוֹת. וּמַלְבַּשְׁתּוֹ עֲנָוָה וְיִרְאָה; וּמַכְשַׁרְתּוֹ
לִהְיוֹת צַדִּיק, חָסִיד, יָשָׁר וְנֶאֱמָן. וּמְרַחַקְתּוֹ

which the spiritual and physical planes of existence unite.[1]

> **מְשַׂמֵּחַ אֶת הַמָּקוֹם, מְשַׂמֵּחַ אֶת הַבְּרִיּוֹת** — *he gladdens the Omnipresent, he gladdens people*

Happiness flows from completeness, just as grief is the result of loss and deficiency. Since this world was created to provide us with oppornities to enrich our lives through Torah, it is clear that Torah brings completeness into our lives and hence to the entire world. A person who engages in sincere Torah study **gladdens the Omnipresent**, for he fulfills the verse "God shall rejoice in His works"[2] by bringing completeness to His works.

> **מְשַׂמֵּחַ אֶת הַבְּרִיּוֹת** — *he gladdens people*

Why does learning Torah for its own sake gladden other people? Torah perfects every aspect of the world and hence we are glad that this person improves the world we live in, through his Torah studies.

> **וּמַלְבַּשְׁתּוֹ עֲנָוָה** — *[The Torah] clothes him in humility*

Arrogance imposes barriers on a person. He is no longer free to act in a way that is beneath his perceived dignity and station. Furthermore, his intellectual integrity is compromised and his intellectual freedom is limited; he cannot be open to an idea that may prove his opinion wrong and undermine his arrogant self-image. In contrast, true humility leaves a person unencumbered by a preconceived self-image that must be maintained, and hence he is free to pursue all goals.[3]

The arrogant person therefore shares the attribute of finite size that defines physical entities, whereas the humble person has not imposed upon

---

1. Creation has both spiritual and physical components. Spiritual qualities and physical qualities are opposites, as explained in the Author's Introduction dealing with Maharal's system of thought. The human being, however, has both spiritual and physical components which are integrated by applying the spiritual principles of Torah to daily life.

2. *Tehillim* 104:31.

3. Author's explanatory comments, based in part on Maharal's writings elsewhere.

people; he gladdens the Omnipresent, he gladdens people. [The Torah] clothes him in humility and fear [of God]; it makes him fit to be righteous, pious, fair and faithful. It moves him away

---

himself any limitations at all, which is a characteristic of the conceptual.

Consequently, it is the humble person who is most capable of assimilating Torah, for they both operate in the unbounded realm of the conceptual. Indeed, Moshe Rabbeinu, who was the most humble person on earth, was more spiritual than any other human being and he was also the most deserving of Torah, as the Rabbis said:[1]

> Moshe said, "Who am I that God should give me the Torah?". . . God said to him, "Since you have considered yourself minor, it will be called by your name, as it is said:[2] Remember the Torah of Moshe My servant."

Humility and Torah are intertwined. Humility brings success in Torah and Torah wisdom brings humility.

◆§ וּמַלְבַּשְׁתּוֹ עֲנָוָה וְיִרְאָה § — *[The Torah] clothes him in. . .fear [of God]*

Another two qualities that go hand in hand are wisdom and the fear of Heaven. This is explained above in the commentary to *mishnah* 3:21, "If there is no wisdom, there is no fear of God; if there is no fear of God, there is no wisdom." See also the commentary to *mishnah* 2:6: "A boor cannot be fearful of sin, and an unlearned person cannot be scrupulously pious."

◆§ וּמַלְבַּשְׁתּוֹ עֲנָוָה וְיִרְאָה § — *[The Torah] clothes him in humility and fear [of God]*

The refined and lofty qualities of humility and fear of God are well compared to clothes. Like fine clothes, they are readily noticed and draw esteem.

◆§ וּמַכְשַׁרְתּוֹ לִהְיוֹת צַדִּיק, חָסִיד, יָשָׁר וְנֶאֱמָן § — *[The Torah] . . . makes him fit to be righteous, pious, fair and faithful*

What is the difference between these very similar terms? A person is called **righteous,** צַדִּיק, *tzaddik,* for doing the decent thing, even if not

---

1. *Shabbos* 89a.
2. *Malachi* 3:22.

ו/א מִן הַחֵטְא וּמְקָרַבְתּוֹ לִידֵי זְכוּת. וְנֶהֱנִין מִמֶּנּוּ עֵצָה וְתוּשִׁיָּה, בִּינָה וּגְבוּרָה, שֶׁנֶּאֱמַר: "לִי עֵצָה וְתוּשִׁיָּה, אֲנִי בִינָה, לִי גְבוּרָה." וְנוֹתֶנֶת לוֹ מַלְכוּת וּמֶמְשָׁלָה וְחִקּוּר דִּין;

demanded by Torah law, such as giving clothes to one in need. A person is called **fair,** יָשָׁר, *yashar,* if he precisely fulfills his duty as prescribed by Torah law. One who fulfills *mitzvos* in a way that surpasses the requirements of law is called **pious,** חָסִיד, *chassid.*

The terms, **righteous, pious** and **fair,** characterize behavior ranging from basic goodness, to religious duty, to supererogation. In contrast, **faithful,** נֶאֱמָן, *ne'eman,* describes the essential character of a person, not the way in which a *mitzvah* was performed. The faithful person is reliable. He is a person of substance, who would not betray his integrity and would not prevaricate.

All of these good qualities flow from the earnest study of Torah.

⏤§ וּמְרַחַקְתּוֹ מִן הַחֵטְא — *It moves him away from sin*

This is a higher quality than that conveyed in the earlier statement that: "[The Torah] . . . makes him fit to be righteous." **"It moves him away from sin"** means that if one clings to the Torah, it will provide him with some protection against committing even an accidental sin.

⏤§ וּמְקָרַבְתּוֹ לִידֵי זְכוּת — *and draws him near to merit*

Even if he had not set out with the intention of doing a *mitzvah*, God will bring to him the opportunity to do a *mitzvah*.

⏤§ וְנֶהֱנִין מִמֶּנּוּ עֵצָה וְתוּשִׁיָּה, בִּינָה וּגְבוּרָה — *From him people enjoy counsel and wisdom, understanding and strength*

Torah endows him with counsel and understanding and he uses it to benefit others. If one follows the counsel he receives from this scholar, God will grant him **strength** over his enemies.

from sin and draws him near to merit. From him people enjoy counsel and wisdom, understanding and strength, as it is said (*Mishlei* 8:14): "Mine are counsel and wisdom, I am understanding, mine is strength."[1] [The Torah] gives him kingship and dominion and analytical judgment;

---

1. The speaker is "wisdom" personified.

וְנוֹתֶנֶת לוֹ מַלְכוּת וּמֶמְשָׁלָה ‎§ *— [The Torah] gives him kingship and dominion*

Kingship befits the Torah, as the Rabbis say,[1]

From where do you say that Rabbis should be called kings? As it is written:[2] 'Through me (wisdom), kings will reign."

Like a king, one who is distinguished in intellect commands people's respect, and in this way Torah gives "dominion." For example, people comply with a Rabbi's decrees because of their respect for Torah scholars, as the Talmud says,[3]

[The apparently redundant word] אֶת in the verse[4] "You shall fear אֶת the Lord your God" includes the [requirement to fear] the Rabbis.

In summary, "[The Torah] gives him kingship and dominion" means that Heaven instills in people reverence for sincere, dedicated Torah scholars, such as they might have for a king, and gives those scholars the dominion to declare decrees.

וְנוֹתֶנֶת לוֹ . . . וְחִקּוּר דִּין ‎§ *— [The Torah] gives him. . . analytical judgment*

This means that Heaven bestows upon him the ability to discern and comprehend the deepest aspects of cases that he judges.

---

1. *Gittin* 62a.
2. *Mishlei* 8:15. A king is distinct from the rest of the nation, and from that vantage point he rules the people and is feared. The *sechel*, intellect, is likewise a "king": It is distinct from the material aspect of our existence and governs our physical actions.
3.*Pesachim* 22b.
4. *Devarim* 6:13.

ו/ב וּמְגַלִּין לוֹ רָזֵי תוֹרָה; וְנַעֲשֶׂה כְּמַעְיָן
הַמִּתְגַּבֵּר וּכְנָהָר שֶׁאֵינוֹ פוֹסֵק. וְהֹוֶה
צָנְוּעַ, וְאֶרֶךְ רוּחַ וּמוֹחֵל עַל עֶלְבּוֹנוֹ. וּמְגַדַּלְתּוֹ
וּמְרוֹמַמְתּוֹ עַל כָּל הַמַּעֲשִׂים.

[ב] אָמַר רַבִּי יְהוֹשֻׁעַ בֶּן לֵוִי: בְּכָל יוֹם
וָיוֹם בַּת קוֹל יוֹצֵאת מֵהַר חוֹרֵב,

---

§ וּמְגַלִּין לוֹ רָזֵי תוֹרָה — *the secrets of the Torah are revealed to him*

If one studies Torah for the essence of Torah itself, then the Torah's very essence — its secrets — are revealed to him.

---

§ וְנַעֲשֶׂה כְּמַעְיָן הַמִּתְגַּבֵּר וּכְנָהָר שֶׁאֵינוֹ פוֹסֵק — *he becomes like a steadily strengthening fountain and like an unceasing river*

These two metaphors refer to two aspects of the scholar who posits a statement and brings proof after proof without limit. The unending stream of proofs is described as **"a steadily strengthening fountain"** and the sheer volume of proofs and sources is described as **"an unceasing river."** Torah has no beginning, no end and no bounds. The Torah scholar acquires that same characteristic, becoming like "a steadily strengthening fountain and an unceasing river."

---

§ וְהֹוֶה צָנְוּעַ — *He becomes modest*

"Modest" here means private. Torah comes from the upper world, which is hidden and private. One who learns Torah acquires its hidden nature, and he is modest in all his ways.

---

§ וְאֶרֶךְ רוּחַ – *He becomes . . . patient*

Anger is the sign of a fool, as it is written:[1]

"for anger rests in the bosom of fools."

The opposite is also true: Patience is a sign of intellectual strength.

---

1. *Koheles* 7:9.

the secrets of the Torah are revealed to him; he becomes like a steadily strengthening fountain and like an unceasing river. He becomes modest, patient and forgiving of insult to himself. [The Torah] makes him great and exalts him above all things.

2. Rabbi Yehoshua ben Levi said: Every single day a heavenly voice emanates from Mount Horeb,

---

◆§ **וּמוֹחֵל עַל עֶלְבּוֹנוֹ** — *He becomes. . .forgiving of insult to himself*

He forgives an insult after the person who insulted him asks for forgiveness and pacifies him, and not before that. He should not take the honor due to Torah so lightly as to forgive an insult before the guilty party expresses regret.

◆§ **וּמְגַדַּלְתּוֹ וּמְרוֹמַמְתּוֹ עַל כָּל הַמַּעֲשִׂים** — *[The Torah] makes him great and exalts him above all things*

Torah transcends all existence and is exalted above all existence. That high level brings greatness to one who studies Torah and it exalts him above all things.

Mishnah 2

Mount Horeb is another name for Mount Sinai, famous as the site where God gave the Torah. The word Horeb, חוֹרֵב, comes from the same Hebrew root as does חוּרְבָּן, churban, meaning "destruction." Why does Rabbi Yehoshua ben Levi refer to Mount Sinai by the term that designates "Mount Destruction"? We would have expected the opposite, for Torah brings structure and security to the world, fashioning it into an edifice. Indeed, he should have referred to Mount Sinai as "Mount Edifice"!

The truth is that Torah has a double-edged power. For people who seek Torah, it brings fulfillment and structure to their lives. Conversely, to people who distance themselves from Torah, it brings destruction. Rabbi Yehoshua ben Levi finds the name Mount Horeb appropriate because destructive qualities are more prominent than positive qualities.

◆§ **בַּת קוֹל יוֹצֵאת מֵהַר חוֹרֵב** — *a heavenly voice emanates from Mount Horeb*

Since we certainly do not hear this voice, why should it emanate each

וּמַכְרֶזֶת וְאוֹמֶרֶת: ,,אוֹי לָהֶם, לַבְּרִיּוֹת,
מֵעֶלְבּוֹנָה שֶׁל תּוֹרָה!" שֶׁכָּל מִי שֶׁאֵינוֹ עוֹסֵק
בַּתּוֹרָה נִקְרָא נָזוּף, שֶׁנֶּאֱמַר: ,,נֶזֶם זָהָב בְּאַף
חֲזִיר אִשָּׁה יָפָה וְסָרַת טָעַם." וְאוֹמֵר: ,,וְהַלֻּחֹת
מַעֲשֵׂה אֱלֹהִים הֵמָּה וְהַמִּכְתָּב מִכְתַּב אֱלֹהִים

day? And since it is improbable that Rabbi Yehoshua ben Levi heard the voice, how did he know that it emanates from Mount Horeb?

This is not a voice that is heard with the ears; rather, it is a heavenly voice that is heard with the heart. When a person allows his Torah studies to lapse, Heaven sends this message through a feeling of ominous hollowness. His intuition compels him to resume his Torah studies and this *baraisa* warns that all who ignore the intuitive imperative of goodness will pay the price.

This nature of Torah is illustrated by the Rabbis,[1]

> Why are the words of Torah compared to a prince, in the verse "Hear, for I will speak princely things"?[2] Just as a prince carries the power of life and death, so do the words of Torah have the power [to influence] life and death.

If a person cultivates a close relationship with the prince and complies with his wishes, the prince will elevate his station. If a person defies his wishes, the prince will demote him. Similarly, a person who does not conduct himself in accordance with the demands of the Torah deserves to be punished and humbled.

In conclusion, the source of the "heavenly voice" is the Divine decree against those who insult the Torah through willful neglect.

§◆ ,,אוֹי לָהֶם, לַבְּרִיּוֹת, מֵעֶלְבּוֹנָה שֶׁל תּוֹרָה — *"Woe to them, to the people, because of [their] insult to the Torah!"*

This warning of **"Woe to them"** is directed only to people whose lack of Torah study implies an **insult to the Torah**; namely, to those who are able to study and do not. These harsh words are not directed at a person who is not capable of studying Torah,[3] for no insult is implied when the situation is beyond control.

1. *Shabbos* 98b.
2. *Mishlei* 8:6.
3. For example, due to illness, or lack of education and teachers, or responding to an emergency.

6/2 proclaiming and saying, "Woe to them, to the people, because of [their] insult to the Torah!" For whoever does not occupy himself with the Torah is called "Rebuked," as it is said (*Mishlei* 11:22): "Like a golden ring in a swine's snout is a beautiful woman who turns away from good judgment." And it says (*Shemos* 32:16): "The Tablets are God's handiwork and the script was God's script

---

עֵ§ שֶׁכָּל מִי שֶׁאֵינוֹ עוֹסֵק בַּתּוֹרָה נִקְרָא נָזוּף — *For whoever does not occupy himself with the Torah is called "Rebuked"*

A man who does not engage in Torah study is **rebuked** by God, Who censures and distances him. He is banished, נָזוּף, from God's Presence.

עֵ§ שֶׁנֶּאֱמַר: ,,נֶזֶם זָהָב בְּאַף חֲזִיר אִשָּׁה יָפָה וְסָרַת טָעַם'' — *as it is said: "Like a golden ring in a swine's snout is a beautiful woman who turns away from good judgment."*

The cited verse illustrates why the *baraisa* says "Woe to them" who do not engage in Torah study. The image "Like a golden ring in a swine's snout" conveys that even an extremely precious article becomes disgusting when it is attached to something so repulsive as a swine. Similarly, the beauty of even the most attractive woman becomes repugnant if she is inane.

The golden ring and the beauty of the woman are metaphors for the intellect, for intelligence shines in a person's face with the same radiance as beauty. The pig's snout is a metaphor for the physical component of a human being. The verse tells us that if the precious intellect is not applied to Torah, it is an irrelevant accessory of the physical body. It becomes as worthless as a golden ring attached to a snout that pokes around in the garbage heap.

This image is invoked also in an earlier *mishnah*[1] which compares a meal without Torah to a table filled with vomit and filth.

By engaging in Torah study, a person extricates the intellect from the materialistic plane of existence.

---

1. *Supra*, 3:4.

הוּא חָרוּת עַל הַלֻּחֹת.״ אַל תִּקְרָא
„חָרוּת״ אֶלָּא „חֵרוּת,״ שֶׁאֵין לְךָ בֶּן חוֹרִין
אֶלָּא מִי שֶׁעוֹסֵק בְּתַלְמוּד תּוֹרָה. וְכָל מִי

⧉ וְאוֹמֵר: . . . „חָרוּת עַל הַלֻּחֹת״ . . . שֶׁאֵין לְךָ בֶּן חוֹרִין אֶלָּא מִי שֶׁעוֹסֵק
בְּתַלְמוּד תּוֹרָה — *And it says:. . . "and the script was. . . engraved
on the Tablets". . . for you can have no freer man than one who
engages in the study of the Torah.*

We might have expected the *baraisa* to cite a proof that one who does
not engage in Torah study is called "rebuked." Rather, it cites a verse
that takes the point even further. It would be bad enough if he were
banished from God, but still a free man. This verse declares that one who
shuns Torah is enslaved to the mundane.

⧉ אַל תִּקְרָא „חָרוּת״ אֶלָּא „חֵרוּת״ — *Do not read
"charus" (engraved) but "cheirus" (freedom)*

This interpretation appears to be an irrelevant play on words, but in
truth it conveys a remarkable idea.

The mind conceives a picture of an object, but that conceptual
representation, of course, is not the object itself. Similarly, the Torah is
a picture of the world — indeed, it is the blueprint of Creation and a
prescription for how the world should be — but it is not the world itself.
Script is a parallel to Torah, for script is also a graphical representation
of words, not the words themselves.

Script is form, rather than matter. When script is written in ink, it has
a minor physical aspect to it, but the letters of the Tablets of Law, of the
Luchos, were not formed by ink. They were engraved right through the
stone tablets and hence they were purely form without material. The
very letters of the *Luchos* reflected an essential characteristic of Torah;
namely, that Torah is purely conceptual and its concepts stand independently of physical implementation.[1]

External forces act only upon substance, not upon form. Hence, only
the physical can be subjugated and not the conceptual. Such is Torah,[2]

---

1. The Torah's *mitzvos* are practiced in the physical world, but the Torah's truths are
not dependent on actual practice. The vision of perfection is not altered by its
implementation or lack thereof.

2. The following two paragraphs are taken from Maharal's introduction to *Derech Chaim*
and serve to demonstrate that Torah principles stand firm even when not practiced.

6/ 2 *charus* (engraved) on the Tablets." Do not read "*charus*" (engraved) but "*cheirus*" (freedom), for you can have no freer man than one who engages in the study of the Torah. And anyone who

---

for even when the *mitzvos* are abrogated through neglect or through persecution, the principles of Torah are unchanged. As the Rabbis said,[1]

> Rabbi Shimon bar Yochai said: When King Shlomo took an excessive number of wives, the book of *Devarim* went up and prostrated itself before the Holy One, Blessed is He, and said: Master of the World! King Shlomo has uprooted me and invalidated me. A contract that is breached in part is null and void, and King Shlomo uprooted my [Hebrew letter] *yud*.[2] The Holy One, Blessed is He, replied: Shlomo and a thousand like him may be nullified but even a single *yud* (the smallest Hebrew letter) will never be invalidated.

Even if all the kings of the nations attempt, as they have done, to uproot the Torah from Israel through their decrees, Torah will not be uprooted.

In summary, the word *charus*, meaning engraved, is truly connected to *cheirus*, meaning freedom. True freedom comes only when the intellect is unencumbered by physical vulnerability and limitation.

---

§⊷ שֶׁאֵין לְךָ בֶּן חוֹרִין אֶלָּא מִי שֶׁעוֹסֵק בְּתַלְמוּד תּוֹרָה —
for you can have no freer man than one who engages in the study of the Torah

---

It is true that many Torah scholars are not free in terms of material burdens and government oppression. However, the *baraisa* means only that Torah study would lead to freedom if everything else would be in order. In practice, other factors such as the sins of individuals and of the community produce a different result. Nonetheless, within the

---

1. Maharal paraphrases the *midrash* in *Vayikra Rabbah*, section 19.
2. With reference to *Devarim* 17:16-17, "He (the king) shall not take יַרְבֶּה, *yarbeh*, many horses for himself. . . he shall not take, יַרְבֶּה, many wives for himself. . . he shall not take, יַרְבֶּה, much gold and silver. . ."
   The commentary *Matanos Kehunah* explains that the letter *yud* of יַרְבֶּה makes the word a commandment. This *midrash* interprets Shlomo's violation of these three commandments as erasing the *yud* of יַרְבֶּה.

שֶׁעוֹסֵק בְּתַלְמוּד תּוֹרָה הֲרֵי זֶה מִתְעַלֶּה,
שֶׁנֶּאֱמַר: ,,וּמִמַּתָּנָה נַחֲלִיאֵל, וּמִנַּחֲלִיאֵל
בָּמוֹת.''

[ג] הַלּוֹמֵד מֵחֲבֵרוֹ פֶּרֶק אֶחָד, אוֹ הֲלָכָה אֶחָת,
אוֹ פָּסוּק אֶחָד, אוֹ דִבּוּר אֶחָד, אוֹ אֲפִילוּ
אוֹת אֶחָת — צָרִיךְ לִנְהָג בּוֹ כָּבוֹד. שֶׁכֵּן מָצִינוּ
בְּדָוִד, מֶלֶךְ יִשְׂרָאֵל, שֶׁלֹּא לָמַד מֵאֲחִיתְפֶל
אֶלָּא שְׁנֵי דְבָרִים בִּלְבָד, וּקְרָאוֹ רַבּוֹ, אַלּוּפוֹ,
וּמְיֻדָּעוֹ, שֶׁנֶּאֱמַר: ,,וְאַתָּה אֱנוֹשׁ כְּעֶרְכִּי,
אַלּוּפִי וּמְיֻדָּעִי.'' וַהֲלֹא דְבָרִים קַל וָחֹמֶר: וּמַה
דָּוִד מֶלֶךְ יִשְׂרָאֵל, שֶׁלֹּא לָמַד מֵאֲחִיתְפֶל
אֶלָּא שְׁנֵי דְבָרִים בִּלְבָד, קְרָאוֹ רַבּוֹ אַלּוּפוֹ

---

intellectual domain only Torah study can provide true freedom from
physical constraints.

∞§ שֶׁאֵין לְךָ בֶּן חוֹרִין אֶלָּא מִי שֶׁעוֹסֵק בְּתַלְמוּד תּוֹרָה — *for you can have*
no freer man than one who engages in the study of the Torah

Even a king is not as free as one who engages in Torah, for his
kingship is dependent on his subjects and hence he is vulnerable to
revolt. This thought is conveyed in the later *baraisa* [1] "Do not desire the
table of kings, for your table is greater than theirs and your crown is
greater than their crown."

∞§ וְכָל מִי שֶׁעוֹסֵק בְּתַלְמוּד תּוֹרָה הֲרֵי זֶה מִתְעַלֶּה — *And anyone*
who engages in the study of the Torah becomes elevated

When a person engages in the study of Torah he is more than free; he
is elevated above this lowly world that is limited in every dimension.
That growth emerges through the quality of humility, which frees us
from the fear of being ridiculed and from trying to attract admiration.
Once we are free of arrogance, we can think and grow without limit. [2]

---

1. *Infra, baraisa* 5.
2. Adapted from Maharal's *Nesiv HaTorah*, page 11, London edition.

engages in the study of the Torah becomes elevated, as it is said (*Bamidbar* 21:19): "From Mattanah to Nachaliel, and from Nachaliel to Bamos."

3. He who learns from his fellowman a single chapter, a single halachah, a single verse, a single Torah statement, or even a single letter, must treat him with honor. For thus we find in the case of David, king of Israel, who learned nothing from Achitophel except for two things, yet called him his teacher, his guide, his intimate, as it is said (*Tehillim* 55:14): "You are a man of my measure, my guide and my intimate." One can derive from this the following: If David, king of Israel, who learned nothing from Achitophel except for two things, called him his teacher, his guide,

---

Mishnah 3

▷ דָּוִד, מֶלֶךְ יִשְׂרָאֵל, שֶׁלֹּא לָמַד מֵאֲחִיתֹפֶל אֶלָּא שְׁנֵי דְבָרִים בִּלְבָד — *David, king of Israel, who learned nothing from Achitophel except for two things*

Rashi explains that the two things are:

- not to study alone, but with another.
- not to enter into the house of study or House of God with a proudly erect posture.

▷ אֱנוֹשׁ כְּעֶרְכִּי — *You are a man of my measure*

We do not explicitly find that David called Achitophel his teacher, *Rav*. It is implied in the statement "You are a man of my measure"; i.e., you are equally deserving of honor. David meant to say: Just as you owe me honor as the king, I owe you honor as my teacher.

▷ אַלּוּפוֹ — *his guide*

The Hebrew אַלּוּפוֹ connotes "his superior," showing that the honor for Torah is superior to the honor for a king.

וּמְיֻדָּעוֹ – הַלּוֹמֵד מֵחֲבֵרוֹ פֶּרֶק אֶחָד, אוֹ הֲלָכָה אֶחָת, אוֹ פָסוּק אֶחָד, אוֹ דִבּוּר אֶחָד, אוֹ אֲפִילוּ אוֹת אֶחָת, עַל אַחַת כַּמָּה וְכַמָּה שֶׁצָּרִיךְ לִנְהָג בּוֹ כָּבוֹד! וְאֵין כָּבוֹד אֶלָּא תוֹרָה, שֶׁנֶּאֱמַר: "כָּבוֹד חֲכָמִים יִנְחָלוּ"; "וּתְמִימִים יִנְחֲלוּ טוֹב" וְאֵין טוֹב אֶלָּא תוֹרָה, שֶׁנֶּאֱמַר: "כִּי לֶקַח טוֹב נָתַתִּי לָכֶם, תוֹרָתִי אַל תַּעֲזְבוּ."

‌‌§ וּמְיֻדָּעוֹ — *his intimate* —

David was constantly aware of his reverence for Achitophel.

§ אוֹ אֲפִילוּ אוֹת אֶחָת, עַל אַחַת כַּמָּה וְכַמָּה שֶׁצָּרִיךְ לִנְהָג בּוֹ כָּבוֹד — *or even a single letter, how much more so must he treat him with honor*

This appears to be illogical. How can we draw an inference about someone who learns even **a single letter**, from David who learned **two things** from Achitophel?

The logic is based on the fact that the knowledge of Torah Law is more deserving of honor than the knowledge of good conduct. The two things that Achitophel taught David are merely points of good conduct, neither of which is demanded by Torah Law. However, a matter which is in the Torah itself — even if it is but a single letter of Torah — is greater than Achitophel's lessons and hence is certainly more deserving of honor.

§ עַל אַחַת כַּמָּה וְכַמָּה — *how much more so*

If even a king gives honor to his teacher, how more so should others honor their teachers.[1]

1. Since the superficial reading — if David gave honor because he learned two things, then all the more so must we give honor to someone from whom we learn a single letter — is illogical, Maharal applies the logic of "how much more so" to the comparison of king and layman.

his intimate — one who learns from his fellowman
a single chapter, a single halachah, a single verse,
a single Torah statement, or even a single letter,
how much more so must he treat him with honor!
And honor is due only for Torah, as it is said
(*Mishlei* 3:35, 28:10): "The wise shall inherit
honor," ". . .and the perfect shall inherit good."
And only Torah is truly good, as it is said (*Mishlei*
4:2): "I have given you a good teaching, do not
forsake My Torah."

⊷ וְאֵין כָּבוֹד אֶלָּא תוֹרָה, שֶׁנֶּאֱמַר: ,,כָּבוֹד חֲכָמִים יִנְחָלוּ'' — *And honor is
due only for Torah, as it is said: "The wise shall inherit honor."*

The wise refers to Torah scholars. Hence, Maharal prefers a text of our
baraisa which reads: "And honor is due only for Torah scholars."[1]

Achitophel was not really David's teacher, guide and intimate. David
conferred those titles on Achitophel only out of honor for his Torah
wisdom.

This point is a continuation of the thought introduced in *baraisa* 2 that,
"And anyone who engages in the study of Torah becomes elevated."
Therefore, we must honor a Torah scholar even if we have not learned
anything from him.

Mishnah 4

This *baraisa* provides advice for those who endeavor to acquire and
integrate the holy Torah into their very being.

The physical realm is completely opposite in nature to the conceptual
realm.[2] How then can we, as physical beings, successfully pursue,
integrate and retain Torah studies, which are purely conceptual?

We may answer this by considering that every object has form and
substance, which also are opposite in nature. Form and substance can
unite when the physical is subordinate, and conforms to shape. Likewise,
this is the principle behind our *baraisa*, which advises us to subordinate
the physical to the spiritual. When the intellect supersedes physical

---

1. Consistent with the proof-verse "The wise [Torah scholars] shall inherit honor."
2. Physical things are limited, specific and temporary, whereas concepts are
unbounded, general and timeless.

[ד] כָּךְ הִיא דַרְכָּהּ שֶׁל תּוֹרָה: פַּת בַּמֶּלַח תּאֹכַל, וּמַיִם בַּמְּשׂוּרָה תִּשְׁתֶּה, וְעַל הָאָרֶץ תִּישָׁן, וְחַיֵּי צַעַר תִּחְיֶה — וּבַתּוֹרָה אַתָּה עָמֵל! אִם אַתָּה עוֹשֶׂה כֵן, "אַשְׁרֶיךָ וְטוֹב לָךְ." "אַשְׁרֶיךָ" — בָּעוֹלָם הַזֶּה, "וְטוֹב לָךְ" — לָעוֹלָם הַבָּא.
[ה] אַל תְּבַקֵּשׁ גְּדֻלָּה לְעַצְמְךָ, וְאַל תַּחְמֹד

desires, then the intellect is primary and our physical plane of existence will not interfere with Torah.

פַּת בַּמֶּלַח תֹּאכֵל, וּמַיִם בַּמְּשׂוּרָה תִּשְׁתֶּה, וְעַל הָאָרֶץ תִּישָׁן, וְחַיֵּי צַעַר תִּחְיֶה — *Eat bread with salt, drink water in small measure, sleep on the ground, live a life of deprivation*

The *baraisa* is addressed only to those who can endure such a lifestyle and not be so weakened as to interfere with their studies.

כָּךְ הִיא דַּרְכָּהּ שֶׁל תּוֹרָה: פַּת בַּמֶּלַח תֹּאכֵל — *This is the way of Torah: Eat bread with salt*

If a person is very wealthy and can afford a comfortable life, then the lifestyle suggested in this *baraisa* will not help his studies. **The way of Torah** is to sacrifice the physical for the spiritual, but if one can afford to eat meat, then eating bread and salt is not a sacrifice for the sake of Torah. What can a wealthy person sacrifice, which *will* enhance his pursuit of Torah? He can give up all involvement with his investments, and dedicate all of his time and attention to Torah study.

כָּךְ הִיא דַּרְכָּהּ שֶׁל תּוֹרָה: פַּת בַּמֶּלַח תֹּאכֵל — *This is the way of Torah: Eat bread with salt*

This may appear to be contradicted by the following:[1]

> Rava said to the rabbis, "Please do not appear before me during Nissan (the grain harvest) and Tishrei (the time of wine and olive pressing) so that you will not be anxious about your food supply the entire year."

1. *Berachos* 35b.

4. This is the way of Torah: Eat bread with salt, drink water in small measure, sleep on the ground, live a life of deprivation — but toil in the Torah! If you do this, "You are praiseworthy, and all is well with you" (*Tehillim* 128:2). "You are praiseworthy" — in this world; "and all is well with you" — in the World to Come.

5. Do not seek greatness for yourself, and do not

Clearly, Rava took a break from his Torah studies to earn a living. Did he not accept the teaching of our *baraisa*, which implies that the dedicated Torah scholar ought not to leave his studies as long as he has some bread and salt?

The answer is that the Torah scholar may take a small, limited break from his Torah studies, perhaps one or two months a year, to support himself. However, if there is no fixed limit to the intermission, then he should not interrupt his studies as long as there is still bread in the house.

◆§ "אַשְׁרֶיךָ וְטוֹב לָךְ,, — *"You are praiseworthy" — in this world*

The Hebrew אַשְׁרֶיךָ, *ashrecha*, translated here as "praiseworthy," also denotes "confirmed," meaning strong and durable. Although he lives on bread and salt, and does not have the things that make life comfortable, he is free of the needs that come from a material focus in life. As a result, he has the good cheer that comes with the strength and durability of a resilient character.

◆§ "וְטוֹב לָךְ,, – לָעוֹלָם הַבָּא — *"and all is well with you" — in the World to Come*

Since he was not drawn after the material attractions of this world, he will be unencumbered by physical qualities and ready to enjoy the non-physical life of the World to Come.

Mishnah 5

◆§ אַל תְּבַקֵּשׁ גְּדֻלָּה לְעַצְמְךָ — *Do not seek greatness for yourself*

"Greatness" refers to a position of high rank, such as a president or an officer.

כָּבוֹד; יוֹתֵר מִלִּמּוּדֶךָ עֲשֵׂה. וְאַל תִּתְאַוֶּה
לְשֻׁלְחָנָם שֶׁל מְלָכִים, שֶׁשֻׁלְחָנְךָ גָּדוֹל
מִשֻּׁלְחָנָם, וְכִתְרְךָ גָּדוֹל מִכִּתְרָם; וְנֶאֱמָן הוּא
בַּעַל מְלַאכְתְּךָ שֶׁיְּשַׁלֶּם לְךָ שְׂכַר פְּעֻלָּתֶךָ.

[ו] גְּדוֹלָה תוֹרָה יוֹתֵר מִן הַכְּהֻנָּה וּמִן

⇛ יוֹתֵר מִלִּמּוּדֶךָ עֲשֵׂה — *let your performance exceed your learning*

This translation is in accordance with Rashi. However, Maharal finds it problematic that the *baraisa* would interrupt the flow of "Do not seek greatness," "do not crave honor," and "Do not lust for the table of kings" with this extraneous thought. Indeed, the thought is out of context for the chapter, which does not deal with *mitzvos* but with the qualities that accompany Torah scholarship.

Maharal prefers to group the words "honor" and "learning" in one phrase, while "perform" and "do not lust for the table of kings" are grouped in the next phrase. Maharal would translate: וְאַל תַּחְמֹד כָּבוֹד יוֹתֵר מִלִּמּוּדֶךָ. עֲשֵׂה וְאַל תִּתְאַוֶּה לְשֻׁלְחָנָם שֶׁל מְלָכִים, *and do not crave honor beyond that to which your learning entitles you. Perform and do not lust for the table of kings.*

This is still a surprising statement, because it implies that one may indeed crave *as much* honor as his learning entitles him to. Yet that is unthinkable, for then his studies would be for the sake of his own honor, and not for the sake of Torah.

In truth, the *baraisa* does not at all condone a person craving honor. However, one's Torah learning will unavoidably bring him honor, as quoted in *baraisa* 3: "The wise shall inherit honor."[1] Hence, the message of our *baraisa* is: The honor of Torah is the only true and valid honor, and there is no justification to crave more honor than that.

Alternatively, this statement may be seen as a way to appease the evil inclination's drive for honor. In that interpretation, the *baraisa* tells us that one can be satisfied with the honor that comes from Torah and there is no need for more than that.

⇛ וְאַל תִּתְאַוֶּה לְשֻׁלְחָנָם שֶׁל מְלָכִים — *Do not lust for the table of kings*

The phrase **table of kings** alludes to great wealth.

---

1. *Mishlei* 3:35.

crave honor; let your performance exceed your learning. Do not lust for the table of kings, for your table is greater than theirs, and your crown is greater than their crown; and your employer is trustworthy to pay you remuneration for your deeds.

6. Torah is even greater than priesthood or

Not only is the wealth of Torah superior to the material wealth of kings, but it is more durable. Material wealth is always vulnerable to loss. In contrast, the Torah we possess is safe from loss and it endures for the eternity of the World to Come.

As indicated before, Maharal groups "perform" and "do not lust for the table of kings" together: עֲשֵׂה וְאַל תִּתְאַוֶּה לְשֻׁלְחָנָם שֶׁל מְלָכִים.

He explains the phrase to mean: **Perform** your Torah studies ceaselessly. Do not tire of it **and do not lust for the wealth of kings,** because the wealth of Torah is superior.

◆§ וְכִתְרְךָ גָּדוֹל מִכִּתְרָם — *and your crown is greater than their crown*

A crown symbolizes the highest level, for it rests upon the top of the head, which is the highest part of the body. Similarly, the crown of Torah rests upon the head, in the sense that it is the place of the *neshamah*, which transcends the physical body.

A king's crown demonstrates that he is beyond the rest of the nation. Indeed, a king of Israel has a Divine quality and for that reason he is anointed with holy oil. Yet one who engages in Torah study has a higher, more Divine quality than a king of Israel. The crown of Torah is higher than the crown of the king, for the Torah scholar rises above physical, material constraints, while the position of king is but a pragmatic role.

◆§ וְנֶאֱמָן הוּא בַּעַל מְלַאכְתְּךָ שֶׁיְשַׁלֶּם לְךָ שְׂכַר פְּעֻלָּתֶךָ — *and your employer is trustworthy to pay you*

The payment is tendered for "Perform your Torah studies ceaselessly" according to Maharal's explanation of עֲשֵׂה וְאַל תִּתְאַוֶּה in the previous segment of the commentary.

הַמַּלְכוּת, שֶׁהַמַּלְכוּת נִקְנֵית בִּשְׁלֹשִׁים מַעֲלוֹת,
וְהַכְּהֻנָּה נִקְנֵית בְּעֶשְׂרִים וְאַרְבָּעָה, וְהַתּוֹרָה
נִקְנֵית בְּאַרְבָּעִים וּשְׁמוֹנָה דְבָרִים, וְאֵלּוּ הֵן:[1]

---

1. *Maharal's text of the baraisa* differs widely from our text. There are differences in the qualities to be included among the forty-eight, and in the order in which the qualities are listed.

Mishnah 6

---

§ — **שֶׁהַמַּלְכוּת נִקְנֵית בִּשְׁלֹשִׁים מַעֲלוֹת, וְהַכְּהֻנָּה נִקְנֵית בְּעֶשְׂרִים וְאַרְבָּעָה** — *for royalty is acquired along with thirty prerogatives, and the priesthood with twenty-four [gifts]*

The *baraisa* does not list the prerogatives of royalty nor the privileges of priesthood, because the subject of this chapter is Torah. The privileges of royalty and priesthood are enumerated only to show that Torah is greater than these two offices.

---

§ **שֶׁהַמַּלְכוּת . . . בִּשְׁלֹשִׁים . . . וְהַכְּהֻנָּה . . . בְּעֶשְׂרִים וְאַרְבָּעָה, . . . וְהַתּוֹרָה . . . בְּאַרְבָּעִם וּשְׁמוֹנָה** — *for royalty . . . with thirty . . . and the priesthood . . . with twenty-four . . . but the Torah. . . by. . . forty-eight*

The three offices of royalty, priesthood and Torah leadership were symbolized in the Holy Temple by three sacred articles, each of which was graced by a "crown" of gold work surrounding the upper border. These are: the *Shulchan*, Table; the *Mizbei'ach HaZahav*, Golden Altar; and the *Aron*, Ark.

The crown upon the Table, which carries the show-bread, corresponds to the crown of kingship, because it is the king's role to ensure the nation's sustenance. The smallest perimeter of any plane of the Table is thirty *tefachim*,[1] corresponding to the thirty prerogatives of the king.[2]

The crown upon the Incense Altar corresponds to the crown of the priesthood. The upper surface of the Altar has a perimeter of twenty-four

---

1. A *tefach* is a handbreadth, approximately 4 inches.
2. The Table is one and a half *amos* high and one *amah* wide. Since there are six *tefachim* in an *amah*, the plane is nine *tefachim* by six *tefachim*, and the perimeter is thirty *tefachim*.

6/ 6   royalty; for royalty is acquired along with thirty prerogatives, and the priesthood is acquired with twenty-four [gifts], but the Torah is acquired by means of forty-eight qualities, which are:

---

tefachim, corresponding to the twenty-four privileges of the priesthood.[1]

The crown upon the Ark containing the Ten Commandments corresponds to the crown of Torah. The perimeter of the upper surface is forty-eight *tefachim*, corresponding to the forty-eight qualities of Torah listed in this *baraisa*.[2]

⋖§ שֶׁהַמַּלְכוּת נִקְנֵית בִּשְׁלֹשִׁים מַעֲלוֹת — *for royalty is acquired along with thirty prerogatives*

Thirty is an appropriate number for royalty. The corresponding Hebrew letter ל is the tallest letter of the alphabet and hence symbolizes majesty and exaltation. Fittingly, the letter ל is the middle letter of the Hebrew word מֶלֶךְ, *melech*, king, because ל symbolizes greatness, and the middle is the most exalted position.

⋖§ וְהַתּוֹרָה נִקְנֵית בְּאַרְבָּעִים וּשְׁמוֹנֶה דְבָרִים — *but the Torah is acquired by means of* forty-eight *qualities*

The number forty-eight is integrally associated with Torah. For example, each page of a Torah scroll has at least forty-eight lines.[3] Furthermore, the Hebrew for "brain" — מֹחַ, *mo'ach* — has a numerical value[4] of 48, for Torah knowledge resides in the brain, the location of the *neshamah*.

---

1. The minimum perimeter of the Altar is along the length and width, which are each one *amah*. Since there are six *tefachim* in an *amah*, the perimeter is twenty-four *tefachim*.

2. The two *Keruvim* atop the Ark are included in the height of the Ark. Hence, any plane which includes the height has a large perimeter, and the plane of minimum perimeter is that defined by the length and the width. The Ark is two-and-a-half *amos* long by one-and-a-half *amos* wide. Hence, the perimeter is 8 *amos*, or 48 *tefachim*.

3. Rambam, *Laws of Sefer Torah*, 7:10. The Vilna edition of Tractate *Sofrim*, 2:6 reads "42 lines." However, the commentary *Maadnei Yom Tov* on Rabbeinu Asher's *Hilchos Kattanos*, near the end of the laws of *sefer* Torah, cites *Sofrim* 2:6 as the source of the 48-line minimum. The author of *Maadnei Yom Tov* was R' Yom Tov Lipman Heller, a disciple of Maharal.

4. מ = 40; ח = 8.

The Forty-Eight Qualities

---

1. תַּלְמוּד — *study*

He must learn from his *Rav*, teacher, and not rely on his own intelligence.

---

2. שְׁמִיעַת הָאֹזֶן — *attentive listening*

He must take care to catch every word, for missing a single phrase or even a single word can distort the entire point being studied.

---

3. עֲרִיכַת שְׂפָתַיִם — *articulate speech*

Articulating the words carefully and deliberately helps to understand and to retain the material. One should not study silently, and certainly not hurriedly.

---

4. בִּינַת הַלֵּב — *intuitive understanding*

He must pay attention to the meaning of his studies until he comprehends it well.

---

5. אֵימָה — *awe*

He must sit in front of the *Rav* with awe, for that establishes the relationship necessary for a student to be receptive. Awe comes from appreciating the greatness of the *Rav*.

---

6. יִרְאָה — *reverence*

Reverence comes from recognizing his own inadequacy. A person who thinks he is already an accomplished scholar is not prepared to be receptive to his studies.

---

7. עֲנָוָה — *modesty*

Modesty is the origin of effective Torah studies. Despite Moshe Rabbeinu's many fine qualities, he received the Torah because of his modesty. The Rabbis say,[1]

> Rabbi Chanina bar Idi said: Why is Torah compared to water?[2] . . . Just as water flows from a high place to a low place, so do the words of Torah remain only with one who is humble.

8. שִׂמְחָה — *joy*

Joy is associated with spiritual fulfillment. One who knows joy is ready to receive Torah, for it is the fulfillment of a human being. The Talmud relates:[3]

> Rabbi Zeira met Rav Yehudah standing by the door of his father-in-law's house. He saw that he was in a cheerful mood and that if he would ask any secret of the universe he would reveal it to him.

9. שִׁמּוּשׁ חֲכָמִים — *ministering to the sages*

When the student ministers to the *Rav*, he forms a relationship that opens the way for Torah to flow to him from the *Rav*. Studying with the *Rav* does not by itself create this relationship and will not by itself transmit Torah as effectively. The Rabbis say,[4]

> Rabbi Yochanan said in the name of Rabbi Shimon bar Yochai: ministering to Torah is greater than studying it, for it is said,[5] "Here is Elisha, the son of Shafat, who poured water on the hands of Eliyahu." It is not said "who learned [from Eliyahu]" but "who poured water [for Eliyahu]." This teaches that service is greater than study.

---

1. *Taanis* 4a.
2. *Yeshayahu* 55, "Ho, everyone that thirsts, go to the water."
3. *Shabbos* 77b.
4. *Berachos* 7b.
5. *II Melachim* 3:11.

בִּדְבוּק חֲבֵרִים, בְּפִלְפּוּל הַתַּלְמִידִים, בְּיִשׁוּב, **ו/1**
בְּמִקְרָא, בְּמִשְׁנָה, בְּדֶרֶךְ אֶרֶץ, בְּאֶרֶךְ אַפַּיִם,
בְּלֵב טוֹב, בֶּאֱמוּנַת חֲכָמִים, בְּקַבָּלַת הַיִּסּוּרִין,

When a student comes close to his *Rav*, it is like a wick coming close to a flame: It is certain that the fire will jump the gap and ignite the wick.

10. בִּדְבוּק חֲבֵרִים — *closeness with colleagues*

Torah is intended to be studied with another person, and otherwise it is not fully considered Torah study. The Rabbis say,[1]

> Rabbi Yose bar Chanina said: What is the meaning of the passage,[2] "A sword upon the liars (Hebrew: *baddim*) and they shall become fools"? [It means] "A sword upon Torah scholars[3] who sit separately (Hebrew: *bad bebad*) and study Torah." Furthermore, they become foolish, as it says: "and they shall become fools."

11. פִּלְפּוּל הַתַּלְמִידִים — *sharp discussion with students*

The sharp questions of young students stimulate the senior scholars to fuller understanding. The Rabbis say,[4]

> Rav Nachman bar Yitzchak said: Why are the words of Torah likened to wood?[5] Just as a small piece of wood can kindle a large log, so do the young Torah scholars sharpen the senior Torah scholars. This is the same as Rabbi Chanina said: I learned much from my teachers; and from my colleagues more than from my teachers; and from my students most of all.

12. יִשׁוּב — *deliberation*

This refers to mental composure; one who is flustered cannot learn.

---

1. *Taanis* 7a.
2. *Yirmeyahu* 50:36.
3. Literally, "the enemies of Torah scholars," a common form of Talmudic euphemism.
4. *Taanis* 7a.
5. *Mishlei* 3:18, "It (Torah) is a tree of life."

closeness with colleagues, sharp discussion with students, deliberation, [knowledge of] Scripture, *Mishnah, derech eretz,* slowness to anger, a good heart, faith in the sages, acceptance of suffering,

---

13. מִקְרָא — *[knowledge of] Scripture*

---

14. מִשְׁנָה — *Mishnah*

---

15. דֶּרֶךְ אֶרֶץ — *derech eretz*

This refers to good qualities of deportment.

16. אֶרֶךְ אַפַּיִם — *slowness to anger*

If one gets angry, his wisdom departs from him.[1]

---

17. לֵב טוֹב — *a good heart,*

Torah is called "good."[2] It comes to one whose heart is likewise "good" and remains with him.

---

18. אֱמוּנַת חֲכָמִים — *faith in the sages*

Trusting in the Rabbis creates a close bond which forms the basis of acquiring their wisdom. If one does not trust the sages, he himself will certainly not become a sage.

---

19. קַבָּלַת הַיִּסּוּרִין — *acceptance of suffering*

Intellect is constrained by the physical. Only by reducing the importance of the physical aspects of life can the intellect fully develop. "Acceptance of suffering" means reducing the constant neediness that accompanies dependence on the material things in life.

---

1. *Pesachim* 66b.
2. *Mishlei* 4:2, "For I give you **good** doctrine; do not forsake My Torah."

בְּמִעוּט שֵׁנָה, בְּמִעוּט סְחוֹרָה, בְּמִעוּט שִׂיחָה,
בְּמִעוּט תַּעֲנוּג, בְּמִעוּט שְׂחוֹק, בְּמִעוּט דֶּרֶךְ
אֶרֶץ, הַמַּכִּיר אֶת מְקוֹמוֹ, וְהַשָּׂמֵחַ בְּחֶלְקוֹ,

20. מִעוּט שֵׁנָה — *limited sleep*

Sleep is the least intellectual, most physical part of life. When you sleep, you cannot learn, whereas the nature of Torah is that it should be studied day and night, as it says,[1] "and you shall meditate in it day and night."

21. מִעוּט סְחוֹרָה — *limited business activity*

This refers to buying and selling. The point is explained *supra* in the commentary to 2:6, "anyone excessively occupied in business cannot become a scholar."

22. מִעוּט שִׂיחָה — *limited conversation*

Speaking distracts the higher intellect, and profuse speech brings silliness. Therefore, limiting conversation is an important foundation of wisdom.

23. מִעוּט תַּעֲנוּג — *limited pleasure*

Physical indulgence counters the acquisition of wisdom. However, the expression "limited pleasure" implies that some pleasure is acceptable.

Although the Rabbis extolled the virtue of a life of "bread and salt" in *baraisa* 4, the benefit arises only if the deprivations are necessary in order to learn Torah and only if there is no alternative. There is no benefit to be had if he can continue to learn without giving up normal comforts. On the other hand, he should avoid *extra* physical pleasures, for that goes against the nature of Torah, and that is the practice of limited pleasure.

24. מִעוּט שְׂחוֹק — *limited laughter*

The laughter referred to is שְׂחוֹק, *sechok*: derisive laughter that arises from vapid sarcasm. One who laughs frequently will not acquire the

---

1. *Yehoshua* 1:8.

limited sleep, limited business activity, limited conversation, limited pleasure, limited laughter, limited work, knowing one's place, being happy with one's lot, making a

crown of Torah because שְׂחוֹק is the opposite of intellect. It is a kind of laughter that arises from hollow jokes, while intellect is true and substantial.

This laughter is not to be confused with joy. Joy is spiritual, and hence it is in the heart. This laughter, by contrast, is a physical expression.

25. מְעוּט דֶּרֶךְ אֶרֶץ — *limited work*

Even though "All Torah study that is not joined with work will cease in the end,"[1] work must not be his principal concern. This point is slightly different from "limited business activity" in article 21. "Business activity" refers to buying and selling, which can be done from time to time and hence is not likely to occupy a person continuously, as does labor.

26. מַכִּיר אֶת מְקוֹמוֹ — *knowing one's place*

This means that he can accurately assess his accomplishments and his faults. If he does not evaluate himself accurately, but overestimates himself, then he is in error. Because Torah is truth, it will elude one who is in error. Conversely, if one can objectively recognize his personal faults, he will be able to recognize the shortcomings in his studies and rectify them.

27. שָׂמֵחַ בְּחֶלְקוֹ — *being happy with one's lot*

This is one whose happiness comes from his accomplishments, and not from monetary possessions. He can feel fulfillment because he is free of the gnawing need that comes from material dependence. Articles 26 and 27 belong together, for one who **knows his place** — recognizing the need for self-improvement — will crave the fulfillment that Torah can bring, while one who is **happy with his lot** is able to appreciate fulfillment as Torah brings it.

---

1. *Supra,* 2:2.

ו/1 וְהָעוֹשֶׂה סְיָג לִדְבָרָיו, וְאֵינוֹ מַחֲזִיק טוֹבָה לְעַצְמוֹ,
אָהוּב, אוֹהֵב, מְשַׂמֵּחַ אֶת הַמָּקוֹם מְשַׂמֵּחַ אֶת
הַבְּרִיּוֹת, אוֹהֵב אֶת הַצְּדָקוֹת, אוֹהֵב אֶת
הַמֵּישָׁרִים, אוֹהֵב אֶת הַתּוֹכָחוֹת, וּמִתְרַחֵק מִן

---

28. עוֹשֶׂה סְיָג לִדְבָרָיו — *making a protective fence around his words*

This refers to one who takes all necessary precautions to avoid being misunderstood. Confusion in one's speech causes confused and erroneous thought as well as forgetfulness.

---

29. אֵינוֹ מַחֲזִיק טוֹבָה לְעַצְמוֹ — *claiming no credit for himself*

One who thinks that he deserves credit for his Torah study believes that it is something he does not have to do and hence will not take it seriously. If he takes credit for study, eventually he will feel that he has studied more than is necessary and will stop. Conversely, one who realizes that Torah study is his duty will never cease his studies, but rather he will embrace Torah with his full energy.

---

30. אָהוּב — *being beloved*

Beloved includes being beloved to God as well as beloved to people. Clearly, if one is not beloved to God, God will not give him His Torah and share with him His wisdom.

Being beloved to people is part of being beloved to God, for He is close to the community, and one who is beloved to people is well integrated with the community.

---

31. אוֹהֵב — *loving*

He loves God, clings to Him and is ready to accept His Torah, and he loves God's creations.

---

32. מְשַׂמֵּחַ אֶת הַמָּקוֹם מְשַׂמֵּחַ אֶת הַבְּרִיּוֹת — *causing both the Omnipresent and people to be happy*

This is different from article 30, **being beloved** to God and man. One is **beloved** for the pleasing things he does for another. One **makes God**

6/6 protective fence around his words, claiming no credit for himself, being beloved, loving, causing both the Omnipresent and people to be happy, loving righteous ways, loving justice, loving reproof, keeping far from

---

"happy," not for what he does, but for what he is. One who is of fine and pleasant character makes God happy that He created such a being, and he makes people happy to have him as part of the community. Being close to people and to God is reflected by the Torah being close to him, and hence he receives Torah readily.

---

33. אוֹהֵב אֶת הַצְּדָקוֹת — *loving righteous ways*

---

34. אוֹהֵב אֶת הַמֵּישָׁרִים — *loving justice*

---

35. אוֹהֵב אֶת הַתּוֹכָחוֹת — *loving reproof*

Torah is built on these three foundations. Righteousness, justice and reproof embrace all the ways of Torah:

- Torah has *mitzvos* that are **righteous**, such as honoring parents or giving charity.
- "The ways of God are **justice**."[1] The Torah dictates what is just and unjust in legal judgments.
- Torah Is **reproof**, such as laws that incur a penalty of exile, death or bringing a sacrifice.

One who does not love all three ways will not succeed in Torah, for they are the foundations and ways of Torah.

---

36. מִתְרַחֵק מִן הַכָּבוֹד — *keeping far from honor*

Honor flees from one who chases it, and it pursues one who flees from it. It follows that one must flee honor to succeed in Torah, for only then will true honor — that of Torah[2] — follow of itself. Conversely, one who does not flee from honor is denied Torah, because he is unworthy of the honor that Torah would bring.

---

1. *Hoshea* 14:10.
2. *Supra, baraisa 3.*

הַכָּבוֹד, וְלֹא מֵגִיס לִבּוֹ בְּהוֹרָאָה, נוֹשֵׂא
בְּעֹל עִם חֲבֵרוֹ, וּמַכְרִיעוֹ לְכַף זְכוּת,
וּמַעֲמִידוֹ עַל הָאֱמֶת, וּמַעֲמִידוֹ עַל הַשָּׁלוֹם,
וּמִתְיַשֵּׁב לִבּוֹ בְּתַלְמוּדוֹ, שׁוֹאֵל וּמֵשִׁיב
שׁוֹמֵעַ וּמוֹסִיף, הַלּוֹמֵד עַל מְנָת לְלַמֵּד,

---

37. לֹא מֵגִיס לִבּוֹ בְּהוֹרָאָה — *not being arrogant with his halachic decision-making*

Arrogance is demonstrated by making quick halachic decisions, as we learned in *mishnah* 4:9: "One who is too self-confident in handing down legal decisions is a fool, wicked and arrogant of spirit." Since this person is a fool, he is not fit for the wisdom of Torah.

38. נוֹשֵׂא בְּעֹל עִם חֲבֵרוֹ — *sharing his fellow's yoke*

If one's fellow is in a situation that is burdensome, requiring him to expend great effort to save himself from the situation, a Torah personality will get involved to help shoulder his fellow's burden. Such behavior demonstrates his readiness for Torah, because of his personal goodness and his association with the community.

39. מַכְרִיעוֹ לְכַף זְכוּת — *judging him favorably*

40. מַעֲמִידוֹ עַל הָאֱמֶת — *setting him on the truthful course*

41. מַעֲמִידוֹ עַל הַשָּׁלוֹם — *setting him on the peaceful course*

These three along with "sharing his fellow's yoke" make him worthy of Torah because he is "good." If he is "good" and Torah is "good," then goodness will join with goodness. The Rabbis say,[1]

Let good come and receive good from Good for the good. [What do these words refer to?] "Let good come" refers to Moshe, as it

---

1. *Menachos* 53b.

honor, not being arrogant with his halachic decision-making, sharing his fellow's yoke, judging him favorably, setting him on the truthful course, setting him on the peaceful course, thinking deliberately in his study, asking and answering, listening and contributing to the discussion, learning in order to teach,

is written,[1] "and she saw that he was good." "And receive good" refers to Torah, as it is written,[2] "For I give you good doctrine; do not forsake My Torah." "From Good" refers to God, as it is written,[3] "God is good to all." "For the good" refers to the nation of Israel, as it is written,[4] "Do good, Hashem, to those who are good. . .peace shall be upon Israel."

42. מִתְיַשֵּׁב לִבּוֹ בְּתַלְמוּדוֹ — *thinking deliberately in his study*

He does not rush into a "peppery" question-and-answer analysis until he is sufficiently familiar with the subject matter to be at ease with it.

Thinking deliberately also implies that he does not bring a hurried manner to his study.

43. שׁוֹאֵל וּמֵשִׁיב שׁוֹמֵעַ וּמוֹסִיף — *asking and answering, listening and contributing to the discussion*

These four together are a single quality; namely, expanding the comprehension of Torah. If there is a question to ask, he asks it, thereby bringing out another point of Torah. Likewise, if he is asked, he answers and improves his fellow's comprehension. When someone speaks, he pays careful attention to what is said and then adds to it. All of these activities have a single goal: to expand Torah knowledge at every opportunity.

44. הַלּוֹמֵד עַל מְנָת לְלַמֵּד — *learning in order to teach*

Torah is meant to be taught, and not to stagnate within the individual.

---

1. *Shemos* 2:2. The verse states that at Moshe's birth, his mother saw that he was good.
2. *Mishlei* 4:2.
3. *Tehillim* 145:9.
4. *Ibid.* 125:4-5.

וְהַלּוֹמֵד עַל מְנָת לַעֲשׂוֹת, הַמַּחְכִּים אֶת רַבּוֹ, וְהַמֵּבִין אֶת שְׁמוּעָתוֹ, וְהָאוֹמֵר דָּבָר בְּשֵׁם אוֹמְרוֹ. הָא לָמַדְתָּ: כָּל הָאוֹמֵר דָּבָר בְּשֵׁם אוֹמְרוֹ מֵבִיא גְאֻלָּה לָעוֹלָם, שֶׁנֶּאֱמַר: „וַתֹּאמֶר אֶסְתֵּר לַמֶּלֶךְ בְּשֵׁם מָרְדְּכָי."

---

45. הַלּוֹמֵד עַל מְנָת לַעֲשׂוֹת — *learning in order to practice*

Similarly, practice is integral to Torah. Indeed, one who does not practice Torah does not deserve to receive it.

---

46. הַמַּחְכִּים אֶת רַבּוֹ — *making his teacher wiser*

This refers to the student sharpening his *Rav's* understanding through questions, as a small piece of kindling, when lit, can ignite a large piece of wood. Since that process is the nature of Torah, one who does not participate is not deserving of Torah.

---

47. הַמֵּבִין אֶת שְׁמוּעָתוֹ — *pondering over what he has learned*

One should not just accept a point he has heard. Rather, he must ponder it until he understands it and sees how it fits into the subject matter overall. No matter how difficult the point is to grasp, it is not adequate to just remember it and not fully understand it.

---

48. הָאוֹמֵר דָּבָר בְּשֵׁם אוֹמְרוֹ — *repeating a saying in the name of the one who said it*

One should repeat a point of Torah in the name of the one who said it, and not plagiarize.

Even God says Torah in the name of the one who said it, for the *Midrash* tells us[1] that God would repeat a particular law of the red heifer in the name of Rabbi Eliezer. The point of the story is that everyone has a personal viewpoint which, if sincerely developed, is valid. The viewpoint is not necessarily unique, but Rabbi Eliezer's intellect was so powerful and the subject of the red heifer is so deep that

---

1. *Bamidbar Rabbah,* section 19.

learning in order to practice, making his teacher wiser, pondering over what he has learned, and repeating a saying in the name of the one who said it. For this you have learned: Whoever repeats a saying in the name of the one who said it brings redemption to the world, as it is said (*Esther* 2:22): "And Esther said to the king in the name of Mordechai."

---

his viewpoint *was* unique and deserved to be identified by his name.

Each person was created with a unique aptitude which surfaces in his perception of Torah. Since Torah includes all of these personal viewpoints, if one omits the name of the person whose opinion he states, he has altered the Torah.

On a more practical level, one may explain the requirement to "repeat a saying in the name of the one who said it" as being careful not to gloss over or change any detail of his studies.

⊷§ כָּל הָאוֹמֵר דָּבָר בְּשֵׁם אוֹמְרוֹ מֵבִיא גְאֻלָּה לָעוֹלָם — *Whoever repeats a saying in the name of the one who said it brings redemption to the world*

How does the author of the *baraisa* know that the redemption in the days of Esther came because of this point? Indeed, why *should* this quality bring about redemption?

When God brings redemption, he wants people to know that He caused it, and that redemption did not come through their own might and wisdom or by some accident. When Esther cited the one who said it, God saw that she was fit to bring about the redemption, for she would accurately attribute the redemption to God and not to her own efforts.

Purim is the most appropriate illustration of this principle. More than any other redemption, Purim was a concealed miracle which, if not for Esther's fine quality, could easily have been misrepresented as a human triumph.

Maharal's Views on Torah Education

Maharal uses this *baraisa* as the springboard for an evaluation of the educational system in his time, over four hundred years ago.

Yehudah ben Betzalel[1] said:

Now that we have explained the forty-eight qualities through which Torah is acquired, it is worthwhile to examine the educational system of our generation. Which of these are necessary for the Torah of *this* generation? None! for today's educational system has failed so grievously that little Torah is left.

Nonetheless, if the young and capable students would summon the strength to disregard today's educational practices, they could far surpass all the rabbis of the generation.

Reviewing Studies

People today do not try to maintain their Torah knowledge by reviewing their studies. They learn to their full capacity today and they have forgotten by tomorrow, because they do not review. Worse yet, however, is that failing to review Torah studies demonstrates disdain for God's word.[2]

If we do not desist from this practice, what will happen at the end of our stay in this world? How will we face God when we are deficient in wisdom because we were not accustomed to reviewing our studies of Scripture, *Mishnah* or Talmud? Can people be oblivious to the reward of Torah in the afterlife?

The Talmud and the *Midrash* make it clear that in the afterlife there is a great qualitative difference between those who come to that world with a firm grasp of their Torah studies, and those who do not have their Torah studies in hand when they come. Those whose Torah is with them are confident and comfortable in a purely spiritual existence. Those without Torah are disgraced by their obvious lethargy and are uneasy to participate in that lofty spiritual world.

Furthermore, Rabbi Yehoshua ben Karchah said,[3]

> "One who learns and does not review is like one who sows and does not reap."

Let us understand this image. Like the ground, a human being is a physical, fertile place for growth. A seed that is placed in the ground becomes part of the ground, and even after it takes root and grows, it remains part of the ground until it is harvested. Indeed, crops do not come into their own existence — they are of no use — until they are separated from the earth.

---

1. Maharal's full name. "Maharal" is an acronym for *M*oreinu *H*a*R*av Yehudah *L*oew of Prague. He lived from 1512 to 1609. This section is a synopsis of Maharal's comments.

2. *Sanhedrin* 99a.

3. *Ibid.*

Is there anything more shameful than to allow crops to rot in the ground, never having provided the food for which they were planted? So it is when a person takes in wisdom but does not harvest it through review. It never takes on its own existence, but remains buried within the person until it dissipates. Only through review does knowledge emerge as a source of sustenance for the soul.

Throughout our history and even for many generations after the [12th-century] *Tosafos*, people were fluent in every part of the *Mishnah* and Talmud. The reason is that Torah did not cease from their lips morning, noon or night as they constantly reviewed their studies.

Study of Mishnah

It is unnecessary to discuss the *review* of *Mishnah,* because we do not even *study Mishnah* seriously today. We are unconcerned about the *baraisa* in which Rabbi Nosson said[1] that the verse:[2] "For he has despised the word of God," applies to one who is lax in the study of Mishnah.

The cases of the *Mishnah* are meant to focus the legal principles of the Talmud, and hence the two go together as a unit. All the earlier generations studied in the intended order: Scripture, followed by *Mishnah* and then Talmud. An intelligent person should be dumbfounded to realize what *our* educational practices are. In this generation we begin with Talmud! We educate a lad of six or seven in Talmud, and later he progresses to *Mishnah!* Even then, the intent is not to know the *Mishnah,* but to be able to search around for clear-cut cases.

If they would teach *Mishnah* early in a child's education, at least the *Mishnah* would remain with him. The way they go about it today, nothing remains: neither Talmud, nor *halachah* nor the ability to ascertain *halachah* without searching for similar cases.

Pilpul — Hypothetical Discourses

The reason that no one in this generation pays attention to *Mishnah* is a false premise that gives rise to a perverse conclusion. People believe that one can develop into a Torah scholar only through the mental gymnastics of *pilpul,* פִּלְפּוּל. *Pilpul*[3] is a very sharp, iterative method of Talmudic analysis which posits theories of *halachah* and then analyzes these empty, contrived hypotheses. They create new explanations of Torah that are unfounded, claiming that this method is necessary to sharpen the mind. How can they think like that? A person should tear his heart out over this practice of turning truth into falsehood in order to

---

1. *Ibid.*
2. *Bamidbar* 15:31.
3. Literally "pepper."

sharpen the mind. Such a thing should not be found in Israel — to sharpen the mind with falsehood or to even spend time on falsehood — for the Torah is a Torah of truth.

As a result, they become more foolish, rather than wiser. It would be better to learn carpentry[1] or another trade, or to sharpen the mind by playing chess. At least they would not engage in falsehood, which then spills over from theory and into practice.

The spicy give-and-take of *pilpul* has great appeal and as a result people ignore *Mishnah*. Yet *Mishnah* is especially called the "word of God,"[2] for it is the body of *halachah*. They, however, do not seek to know the commandments of God and therefore they disregard *Mishnah* and focus only on acquiring wisdom.

Focus on Halachah[3]

How will we not hide our faces in shame when we come to the next world empty handed! The situation has not been this bad since the day that Torah was given on Mount Sinai.

Furthermore, the earlier generations fulfilled the Torah from conditions of great financial duress and under oppression from the nations. Today, we sit tranquilly in our houses, and when a matter of *halachah* arises, or a halachic decision needs to be rendered, we search every nook and cranny to find relevant references. We search through topics until we find what we are looking for, or something close to it, and then proudly invoke the Rabbinical dictum: "Believe one who says: I labored and I found it."[4]

And now there is a new short cut: *Shulchan Aruch*. [5] The table is set[6] and everyone, great and small, is invited. Rabbis today issue halachic rulings based on the rulings in *Shulchan Aruch,* without knowing the theory behind those rulings or their context. Since they do not know the sources of law, it is likely that the case at hand will be

---

1. In contrast to wasting aptitude on *pilpul*, this may be a reference to the creativity and skill of fitting things together that carpentry offers.

2. Referring to the earlier quote: "For he has despised the word of God," which continues, "he has nullified His commandment."

3. *Halachah* is the practical application of the legal principles discussed in the Talmud.

4. *Megillah* 6b.

5. Rabbi Yosef Karo's codification of Jewish law, *Shulchan Aruch,* appeared when Maharal was middle-aged; about 25 years before *Derech Chaim* was printed.

6. *Shulchan Aruch* means "arranged table."

compared to a dissimilar ruling in *Shulchan Aruch*. Worse yet, Torah students feel that they no longer need to take their Talmudic studies seriously, while in truth Talmud is the principal element of Torah study.

[If only our youth would have studied the basics as children, they would be fluent in many tractates by the time they are married. Instead, they come away from their education with nothing to show for it. This is the result of their learning *Tosafos*, which is an addition, rather than the basic body of the Talmud. Rather than placing the commentary of *Tosafos* on the same page as the Talmud, they should have printed the halachic decisions of Rabbeinu Asher, or other commentaries with a focus on *halachah*.][1]

Now you, my dear students, be concerned for this affront to Torah and do not trust in your desires or in your teachers who tell you that these methods are a good thing. I have seen children with the aptitude to receive the entire Torah who were subjected to these methods. In the end they were lost and became but common ignoramuses. As God lives! Should we not rend our clothes in mourning over this, as for a Torah scroll which is burnt!

Is anyone willing to remove himself from this false path and to direct himself, and others with him, along the straight and true path? If so, the Torah will protect him in this world and in the World to Come, and of him it is said,[2]

> ". . .if you will bring out the precious from the worthless, you will be as My mouth; let them return to you, but do not return to them."

Mishnah 7

⋄§ גְּדוֹלָה תוֹרָה, שֶׁהִיא נוֹתֶנֶת חַיִּים — *Great is Torah, for it confers life*

Maharal's text of the *baraisa* has seven proofs that Torah confers life. His text omits the eighth statement: And it says: "For lengthy days and years of life, and peace shall they add to you." Also, his text places the statement, "Indeed, through me [Torah] your days shall be increased,

------

1. This paragraph is actually from Maharal's *Nesiv HaTorah,* Chapter 5 (page 25 in the London edition).

2. *Yirmeyahu* 15:19.

בָּעוֹלָם הַזֶּה וּבָעוֹלָם הַבָּא, שֶׁנֶּאֱמַר: „כִּי
חַיִּים הֵם לְמֹצְאֵיהֶם, וּלְכָל בְּשָׂרוֹ מַרְפֵּא."

and years of life shall be added to you," at the end of the *baraisa,* as the seventh proof.

Why are seven proof-verses required? Would the first verse not suffice to prove that Torah confers life upon its practitioners?

The answer is that there are seven levels of life, from the lowest plane of life in this world to the highest plane of eternal life in the World to Come. The seven verses correspond to each level of life, and each verse demonstrates that it is Torah which confers life to the corresponding plane of existence.

Some of these levels of life are of shorter duration, some are of longer duration, and one is the eternal life of the World to Come. The first three verses pertain to life in this world; the last three verses pertain to life in the World to Come; and the middle verse pertains to a level which bridges this world and the World to Come, as will be explained.

We will preface the commentary on this *baraisa* with an explanation of how Torah supplies life to this world and the Next.

God is One and there is none besides Him. Nothing exists of itself, for there is only the existence that He confers. Hence, all existence and life, including human existence and life, is from Him, for He is the living God, Who gives life.

God is called the Source of life.[1] His existence emanates to all existence, which is joined to Him as branches are joined to a tree and receive life from the tree. This metaphor is used in the verse: "It (Torah) is a tree of life to those who grasp it."[2] It is through Torah that mankind joins with his Creator, for nothing is closer to God than Torah. Indeed, Torah is derived from God.

Let us better understand the metaphor of Torah as a tree, whose structure emerges from the root, to the tree trunk, and to the branches. The root is the source of the tree's life and existence. The branches are joined to the tree and receive life from it; indeed, if a branch is severed, it dies. In the same way, Torah is a tree, and its root is God Himself. The tree of Torah receives existence and life from God, and transmits it to people who, within this metaphor, are the branches.

---

1. *Tehillim* 36:10, "For with You is the fountain of life; in Your light we see light."
2. *Mishlei* 3:18.

practitioners, both in this world and in the World to Come, as it is said (*Mishlei* 4:22): "For they [the teachings of the Torah] are life to those who find them, and a healing to his entire flesh."

When a person is connected to Torah, then "It is a tree of life to those who grasp it," for it brings life from God, the root and source of life.

גְּדוֹלָה תוֹרָה — *Great is Torah*

The greatness of Torah, in the context of this *baraisa*, is that it gives life in this world and in the World to Come. The *baraisa* chose the term גְּדוֹלָה, *gedolah*,[1] (great) which has a numerical value of 48, to allude to the power of life which appears through the 48 qualities of Torah scholarship enumerated in *baraisa* 6.

כִּי חַיִּים הֵם לְמֹצְאֵיהֶם — *"For they [the teachings of the Torah] are life to those who find them*

Why does the verse use the phrase "to those who **find** them" rather than "to those who **learn** them"? The point may be understood by comparison with someone who finds an article. When he picks it up it becomes his, but he will never feel as attached to it as something he had earned or otherwise been involved with. The phrase "to those who **find** them" refers to the aspect of Torah that so transcends mundane human life that our involvement with it remains tenuous. That high level of Torah is the level from which life originates, and which endows Torah with its ability to confer life to those who **find** it.

וּלְכָל בְּשָׂרוֹ מַרְפֵּא" — *and a healing to his entire flesh"*

This refers to the first, minimal level of life. The phrase "to his entire **flesh**" implies that this is a very limited degree of life. It gives life to his flesh only, and not to the entire person. This level is the minimal spark of life that flows to a person, enough to just sustain life.

The *baraisa* proceeds to the next level with the verse:

---

1. גְּדוֹלָה = 3 + 4 + 6 + 30 + 5 = 48.

וְאוֹמֵר: ,,רְפְאוּת תְּהִי לְשָׁרֶךָ, וְשִׁקּוּי לְעַצְמוֹתֶיךָ." וְאוֹמֵר: ,,עֵץ חַיִּים הִיא לַמַּחֲזִיקִים בָּה, וְתֹמְכֶיהָ מְאֻשָּׁר." וְאוֹמֵר: ,,כִּי לְוְיַת חֵן הֵם לְרֹאשֶׁךָ, וַעֲנָקִים לְגַרְגְּרוֹתֶיךָ." וְאוֹמֵר: ,,תִּתֵּן לְרֹאשְׁךָ לִוְיַת חֵן, עֲטֶרֶת תִּפְאֶרֶת תְּמַגְּנֶךָּ." וְאוֹמֵר: ,,כִּי בִי יִרְבּוּ יָמֶיךָ,

---

§ ,,רְפְאוּת תְּהִי לְשָׁרֶךָ, וְשִׁקּוּי לְעַצְמוֹתֶיךָ" — *'It shall be healing to your body, and marrow to your bones.''*

This refers to full, healthy life. The Torah is the source of "healing" for the entire body. Torah is to human life as marrow is to the bones: It provides life that spreads from the center to the entire body.

---

§ ,,עֵץ חַיִּים הִיא לַמַּחֲזִיקִים בָּה, וְתֹמְכֶיהָ מְאֻשָּׁר" — *'It is a tree of life to those who grasp it, and its supporters are praiseworthy.''*

Torah provides *length* of life as well as good health. Since no living thing surpasses the longevity of a tree, the image of a "tree" is appropriate, conveying durability in the extreme. Therefore we also find this image in the verse,[1] "for as the days of a tree shall the days of my people be."

---

§ ,,כִּי לְוְיַת חֵן הֵם לְרֹאשֶׁךָ, וַעֲנָקִים לְגַרְגְּרוֹתֶיךָ" — *'They are a garland of grace for your head, and necklaces for your neck.''*

This next level is the good *spiritual* life that the soul receives from Torah. The imagery of the verse is to be understood as follows:

The נְשָׁמָה, *neshamah*, soul, resides in the head; hence, "a garland of grace for your **head**" is a reference to life that flows to the soul. Torah endows it with "grace," an intangible, spiritual quality.

A **"necklace"** is an ornament, and hence symbolizes an ethereal, transcendent level.[2] "Necklaces for your **neck**" is a reference to speech, which emanates from the throat. The image of "necklaces for your neck"

---

1. *Yeshayahu* 65:22.
2. There are different levels of existence. Substance is the lowest. Form, which is imposed on substance, is a higher level. Beauty is an intangible aura that transcends even form.

6/ 7   And it says (*Mishlei* 3:8): "It shall be healing to your body, and marrow to your bones." And it says (*Mishlei* 3:18): "It is a tree of life to those who grasp it, and its supporters are praiseworthy." And it says (*Mishlei* 1:9): "They are a garland of grace for your head, and necklaces for your neck." And it says (*Mishlei* 4:9): "It will give to your head a garland of grace, a crown of glory it will deliver to you." And it says (*Mishlei* 9:11): "Indeed, through me [the Torah] your days shall be increased,

---

therefore refers to the highest level of this world, for speech epitomizes human life.[1]

The complete metaphor expressed in this verse is thus:

Torah gives a person two things: (a) "a garland of grace for your head." It endows the soul with the transcendent quality of "grace," which induces a bond between man and God. (b) "necklaces for your neck." Torah also endows the faculty of speech with a transcendent, spiritual, quality.

This fourth level is a bridge between the life of the first three levels, which are in this world, and the last three levels, which are in the World to Come. The cited verse combines the highest level of physical life — speech — with the *baraisa's* first reference to spiritual life. At this level, Torah brings into our lives a measure of the goodness, tranquillity and rest such as those of the World to Come, just as Shabbos reflects the nature of the World to Come.

---

§ תִּתֵּן לְרֹאשְׁךָ לִוְיַת חֵן, עֲטֶרֶת תִּפְאֶרֶת תְּמַגְּנֶךָּ,, — *"It will give to your head a garland of grace, a crown of glory it will deliver to you."*

This verse is a metaphor for the fifth level: purely spiritual life in the World to Come. This verse mentions only spiritual metaphors of "head" and "grace," with no reference to the physical metaphors of "neck" and "necklace." There is an additional metaphor of ornament: a "crown of glory," which refers to transcendent existence as described in rabbinical metaphor[2] as well:

---

1. This may be seen in *Onkelos'* Aramaic rendering of "man became a living soul" [*Bereishis* 2:7] as "man had a speaking soul."
2. *Berachos* 17a.

וְיוֹסִיפוּ לְךָ שְׁנוֹת חַיִּים.״ וְאוֹמֵר: ״אֹרֶךְ יָמִים בִּימִינָהּ, בִּשְׂמֹאולָהּ עֹשֶׁר וְכָבוֹד.״ וְאוֹמֵר: ״כִּי אֹרֶךְ יָמִים וּשְׁנוֹת חַיִּים, וְשָׁלוֹם יוֹסִיפוּ לָךְ.״

[ח] רַבִּי שִׁמְעוֹן בֶּן יְהוּדָה מִשּׁוּם רַבִּי שִׁמְעוֹן בֶּן יוֹחַאי אוֹמֵר: הַנּוֹי, וְהַכֹּחַ, וְהָעֹשֶׁר,

---

The World to Come has neither eating nor drinking. . . Rather, the righteous sit with crowns on their heads.

So far, the verses cited tell us only that Torah brings one to some existence in the World to Come, but for how long? The World to Come itself certainly lasts a long time, but entry to the World to Come does not ensure that one's life there will be long.[1]

One might think that only *mitzvos* and good deeds will ensure long life. The next verse proves that Torah itself brings long life in the World to Come.

≈§ ״אֹרֶךְ יָמִים בִּימִינָהּ, בִּשְׂמֹאולָהּ עֹשֶׁר וְכָבוֹד״ — *"Lengthy days are at its right, and at its left are wealth and honor."*

The subject of the verse is Torah. The expression **at its right** refers to the study of Torah for its own sake, while **at its left** refers to study for some ulterior motive. **Lengthy days** can refer only to the World to Come, for life in this world never reaches "lengthy days." A hundred years is not "lengthy days" and yet after a hundred years in this life one is considered as good as dead.[2] Hence, we know that "lengthy days" can only be in the World to Come.

Still, the image of "days" is not as strong a metaphor for long life as is "years" and hence the next verse alludes to the highest level of life that Torah can bring:

≈§ ״כִּי אֹרֶךְ יָמִים וּשְׁנוֹת חַיִּים וְשָׁלוֹם יוֹסִיפוּ לָךְ״ — *"For lengthy days and years of life, and peace shall they add to you.*

Length of **days** implies a long but finite time, whereas the phrase **"years** of life" is the next and ultimate level: eternity.

---

1. There are levels of life in the World to Come, and not all of them are eternal. The entry level, according to Maharal, is the revival of the dead. There are successive levels after that and only the highest is truly eternal.

2. *Supra,* 5:25.

6/ 8 and years of life shall be added to you." And it says (*Mishlei* 3:16): "Lengthy days are at its right, and at its left are wealth and honor." (And it says [*Mishlei* 3:2]: "For lengthy days and years of life, and peace shall they add to you.")

8. Rabbi Shimon ben Yehudah says in the name of Rabbi Shimon ben Yochai: Beauty, strength, wealth,

---

In summary, this *baraisa* presents the different levels of life that Torah can endow, from the lowest level to the highest level, which is eternal life in the World to Come.

Mishnah 8

Variations of the text of this *baraisa* abound, citing different Rabbis and with differences in the number and order of the qualities. Maharal does not include "hoary age" as one of the qualities, and he explains the *baraisa* in the following order: Beauty, strength, wealth, wisdom, children, old age and honor.

Are there only seven qualities that befit the righteous and no others?

The number seven is a symbol of completeness, just as Creation was completed in seven days. Each of the qualities listed here is representative of a *type* of quality and there are seven types altogether. All other good qualities are included in these seven types or are similar to them.

הַנּוֹי, וְהַכֹּחַ — *Beauty, strength*

The essence of a person is just what he is born with: body and spirit. The first quality listed is **beauty**, a quality associated with the physical aspect of the body. The next quality listed is **strength**, which pertains to the spirit that animates the body, for the spirit is the origin of strength.

וְהָעשֶׁר וְהַחָכְמָה — *wealth, wisdom*

In addition to our essential body and soul, we have possessions that we acquire throughout life. We acquire physical possessions, represented by the quality of **wealth**, and we also acquire intangible possessions such as **wisdom**.

ו/ח וְהַכָּבוֹד, וְהַחָכְמָה, וְהַזִּקְנָה, וְהַשֵּׂיבָה,
וְהַבָּנִים — נָאֶה לַצַּדִּיקִים וְנָאֶה לָעוֹלָם,
שֶׁנֶּאֱמַר: "עֲטֶרֶת תִּפְאֶרֶת שֵׂיבָה, בְּדֶרֶךְ
צְדָקָה תִּמָּצֵא." וְאוֹמֵר: "עֲטֶרֶת זְקֵנִים בְּנֵי
בָנִים, וְתִפְאֶרֶת בָּנִים אֲבוֹתָם." וְאוֹמֵר:
"תִּפְאֶרֶת בַּחוּרִים כֹּחָם, וַהֲדַר זְקֵנִים שֵׂיבָה."

֍ וְהַכָּבוֹד — *and honor*

Honor that comes from God is a superior, spiritual level.

֍ וְהַזִּקְנָה — *old age*

Old age conveys the fulfillment that comes of wisely spent days: wholeness, and freedom from material desires. It is a unique quality that comes as the body weakens, permitting a person to rise above his physical nature.

֍ וְהַבָּנִים — *children*

"**Children** is a quality that lies in between the previous two qualities of essential existence and possessions. To some degree, offspring are a person's own flesh and blood, and to some degree they are obligated to serve their parents.

֍ נָאֶה לַצַּדִּיקִים — *these befit the righteous*

In what way do these qualities 'befit' the righteous?
The righteous must earn these qualities and therefore each quality **befits** the righteous before it is granted.

֍ נָאֶה לַצַּדִּיקִים וְנָאֶה לָעוֹלָם — *these befit the righteous and befit the world*

When righteous people have these qualities, they wish to benefit the world and share their blessing with others. By contrast, when the wicked

honor, wisdom, old age, hoary age,[1] and children — these befit the righteous and befit the world, as it is said (*Mishlei* 16:31): "Ripe old age is a crown of splendor, it can be found in the path of righteousness." And it says (*Mishlei* 17:6): "The crown of the aged is grandchildren, and the splendor of children is their fathers." And it says (*Mishlei* 20:29): "The splendor of young men is their strength, and the glory of old men is hoary age."

---

1. The conclusion of the *baraisa* makes it clear that there are seven qualities listed; our text has eight. Maharal's text indeed has seven, omitting "hoary age." Maharal says that in those texts that list both old age and hoary age, the two are a single expression of old age, and together count as a single quality.

---

have these qualities they become arrogant and in their arrogance they want to use their advantage to harm others.

Furthermore, when the righteous have these qualities, the world runs according to its Divine intent and hence these qualities befit the righteous and the world together.

These seven qualities are derived from the cited verses as follows.

◆§ "עֲטֶרֶת תִּפְאֶרֶת שֵׂיבָה, בְּדֶרֶךְ צְדָקָה תִּמָּצֵא" — *"Ripe old age is a crown of splendor, it can be found in the path of righteousness."*

One who walks in *the path of righteousness* is the subject of the *baraisa*, **the righteous** who have the enumerated qualities.

A crown is the adornment of a king, and refers to **wealth**.

Splendor refers to **beauty**.

Ripe old age refers to literal **old age**.

In summary, this verse demonstrates that: "Beauty, wealth and old age befit the righteous."

◆§ "עֲטֶרֶת זְקֵנִים בְּנֵי בָנִים, — *"The crown of the aged is grandchildren*

"The aged," זְקֵנִים, in this verse must refer to old men literally, and not to sages, for what logical connection is there between grandchildren and sages? As explained in the first verse, old age befits the righteous and this verse similarly means that **grandchildren** befit the righteous.

וְאוֹמֵר: ,,וְחָפְרָה הַלְּבָנָה וּבוֹשָׁה הַחַמָּה, כִּי
מָלַךְ יהוה צְבָאוֹת בְּהַר צִיּוֹן וּבִירוּשָׁלַיִם, וְנֶגֶד
זְקֵנָיו כָּבוֹד.″ רַבִּי שִׁמְעוֹן בֶּן מְנַסְיָא אוֹמֵר:
אֵלּוּ שֶׁבַע מִדּוֹת, שֶׁמָּנוּ חֲכָמִים לַצַּדִּיקִים,
כֻּלָּם נִתְקַיְּמוּ בְּרַבִּי וּבְבָנָיו.

[ט] אָמַר רַבִּי יוֹסֵי בֶּן קִסְמָא: פַּעַם אַחַת
הָיִיתִי מְהַלֵּךְ בַּדֶּרֶךְ, וּפָגַע בִּי אָדָם אֶחָד.
וְנָתַן לִי שָׁלוֹם, וְהֶחֱזַרְתִּי לוֹ שָׁלוֹם. אָמַר לִי:
,,רַבִּי, מֵאֵיזֶה מָקוֹם אָתָּה?″ אָמַרְתִּי לוֹ:
,,מֵעִיר גְּדוֹלָה שֶׁל חֲכָמִים וְשֶׁל סוֹפְרִים אָנִי.″

─────────────

§◦— ,,תִּפְאֶרֶת בַּחוּרִים כֹּחָם, וַהֲדַר זְקֵנִים שֵׂיבָה.″ — *"The splendor of young men is their strength, and the glory of old men is hoary age."*

Strength, of course, is the Scriptural source for the enumerated quality of **strength**.

Old men refers to **wise people**. The phrase "old men" זְקֵנִים, *zekainim*, is used in the sense of "sages,"[1] and hence the verse means that the glory of *sages* is old age.[2]

─────────────

§◦— וְנֶגֶד זְקֵנָיו כָּבוֹד″ — *and honor shall be before His elders"*

Again, "elders" refers to the righteous; hence the verse says that **honor** befits the righteous.

Mishnah 9

Through a brilliant analysis, which the reader may wish to pursue in Maharal's *Derech Chaim*, Maharal brings to light many subtle details which are only implied in this tersely phrased *baraisa*. The full story is as follows.

───────

1. *Kiddushin* 33a: The Hebrew word for an elder — זָקֵן, *zakein* — is considered as a short form for *zeh shekanah chochmah*, "one who acquired wisdom," זֶה שֶׁקָּנָה חָכְמָה, referring to a sage.
2. "Old men" cannot be understood literally, or the verse would be making the trivial and redundant statement that "the glory of *old men* is *old age*."

And it says (*Yeshayahu* 24:23): "The moon will grow pale and the sun be shamed, when Hashem, Master of Legions, will have reigned on Mount Zion and in Jerusalem, and honor shall be before His elders." Rabbi Shimon ben Menasya says: These seven qualities, that the Sages attributed to the righteous, were all realized in Rebbi[1] and his sons.

9. Rabbi Yose ben Kisma said: Once I was walking on the road, when a certain man met me. He greeted me, and I returned his greeting. He said to me: "Rabbi, from what place are you?" I said to him: "I am from a great city of scholars and sages."

---

1. Rabbi Yehudah HaNasi, redactor of the six Orders of *Mishnah*.

Rabbi Yose ben Kisma was walking alone on the road and contemplating Torah as he went, in accordance with Jewish dictates for one who travels alone. Since he was traveling alone, he enjoyed a solitude that enabled him to become deeply engrossed in his studies. Indeed, he was so engrossed that he did not notice a certain man on the road until the man interrupted his thoughts with a greeting. Rabbi Yose then responded to the greeting, as one is obligated to do even when deeply involved in Torah study.

The man on the road was honest, of fine character, and perceptive enough to recognize Rabbi Yose as an accomplished Torah scholar by his utter immersion in his studies. He wanted to ask Rabbi Yose to move to his town, but he knew that the success of that request would depend on whether or not Rabbi Yose was from a place of Torah. If he *was*, then it would take some effort to persuade him to come. Therefore, he immediately asked Rabbi Yose from which place he comes.

Rabbi Yose realized what the man's intention was, for why else would the first topic of conversation be a query of from where he comes? For this reason, he responded with a description of how strong his town's Torah scholarship is, rather than the name of the town. He wanted to make it clear that there would be little point in asking him to move into the man's community.

The man persisted, asking if Rabbi Yose would live "with us, in our place." The request was not for Rabbi Yose to come and teach them Torah. Rather, they were in need of the advice and wisdom that an

אָמַר לִי: „רַבִּי, רְצוֹנְךָ שֶׁתָּדוּר עִמָּנוּ
בִּמְקוֹמֵנוּ? וַאֲנִי אֶתֵּן לְךָ אֶלֶף אֲלָפִים דִּינְרֵי
זָהָב, וַאֲבָנִים טוֹבוֹת וּמַרְגָּלִיּוֹת.״ אָמַרְתִּי לוֹ:
„אִם אַתָּה נוֹתֵן לִי כָּל כֶּסֶף וְזָהָב, וַאֲבָנִים
טוֹבוֹת וּמַרְגָּלִיּוֹת שֶׁבָּעוֹלָם, אֵינִי דָר אֶלָּא
בִּמְקוֹם תּוֹרָה.״ וְכֵן כָּתוּב בְּסֵפֶר תְּהִלִּים עַל
יְדֵי דָוִד, מֶלֶךְ יִשְׂרָאֵל: „טוֹב לִי תוֹרַת פִּיךָ
מֵאַלְפֵי זָהָב וָכֶסֶף.״ וְלֹא עוֹד, אֶלָּא שֶׁבִּשְׁעַת
פְּטִירָתוֹ שֶׁל אָדָם, אֵין מְלַוִּין לוֹ לְאָדָם לֹא
כֶסֶף, וְלֹא זָהָב, וְלֹא אֲבָנִים טוֹבוֹת וּמַרְגָּלִיּוֹת,

---

accomplished Torah scholar has to offer. The connotation of the Hebrew
עִמָּנוּ, with us, is that Rabbi Yose would be there to serve the needs of the
townspeople. He would be a resource rather than a leader.[1]

Rabbi Yose would indeed have agreed to come if they needed him to
teach Torah, but he was not willing to leave his strong Torah community
solely to become an adviser. He refused the post because of his complete
commitment to Torah study; indeed, his soul was bound up with love for
Torah.

Alternative approaches to explaining this story are based on prece-
dents where the expression אָדָם אֶחָד, "a certain man," may refer to Satan,
or to Eliyahu the prophet.

If it is a reference to Satan, then he was trying to distract Rabbi Yose's
concentration from his Torah studies with promises of wealth. He
said, "Rabbi, would you be willing to live with us in our place? I would
give you thousands upon thousands of golden dinars, precious stones
and pearls."

If it was Eliyahu, he wanted to increase Rabbi Yose's reward. He gave
him the opportunity to resist the temptation of wealth and be loyal to a
Torah environment. Eliyahu was confident that Rabbi Yose would reply
as he did. There is a possible precedent for Eliyahu appearing to Rabbi
Yose, if this is the same Rabbi Yose for whom Eliyahu stood guard when
he entered a dilapidated building to pray.[2]

---

1. The fact that they did not want a leader is derived from the expression "with us in
our place." Rabbi Yose would be subservient to the community as it existed.
2. *Berachos* 3a.

He said to me, "Rabbi, would you be willing to live with us in our place? I would give you thousands upon thousands of golden dinars, precious stones and pearls." I replied: "Even if you were to give me all the silver and gold, precious stones and pearls in the world, I would dwell nowhere but in a place of Torah." And so it is written in the Book of *Psalms* by David, king of Israel (*Tehillim* 119:72): "I prefer the Torah of your mouth above thousands in gold and silver." Furthermore, when a man departs from this world, neither silver, nor gold, nor precious stones nor pearls escort him,

---

§ שֶׁבִּשְׁעַת פְּטִירָתוֹ שֶׁל אָדָם, אֵין מְלַוִּין לוֹ לְאָדָם לֹא כֶסֶף, וְלֹא זָהָב, וְלֹא אֲבָנִים טוֹבוֹת וּמַרְגָּלִיּוֹת — *when a man departs from this world, neither silver, nor gold, nor precious stones nor pearls escort him*

Does anyone think that silver and gold will accompany him to the World to Come? Certainly not, but some people do think that the penchant for success that they enjoyed in this world will continue with them into the Next World. Rabbi Yose advises that having been a successful person in worldly matters does not carry on into the Future World. The good fortune that came his way ceases at his departure from this life.

---

§ אֵין מְלַוִּין לוֹ לְאָדָם לֹא כֶסֶף, וְלֹא זָהָב, וְלֹא אֲבָנִים טוֹבוֹת וּמַרְגָּלִיּוֹת — *neither silver, nor gold, nor precious stones nor pearls escort him*

In a Kabbalistic interpretation, **silver** and **gold** are metaphors for the best that the lowest world has to offer, while **precious stones** and **pearls** are a metaphor for the best of the more refined middle world.

A person must realize that the substance that remains in the afterlife does not originate from either of these lower, finite worlds. Only through Torah, which originates from the highest and eternal world, can a person bring out eternal value from the finite worlds.[1]

---

1. A human being spans all three worlds and unifies them, as explained *supra*, in the commentary to 5:18.

אֶלָּא תוֹרָה וּמַעֲשִׂים טוֹבִים בִּלְבָד, שֶׁנֶּאֱמַר:
„בְּהִתְהַלֶּכְךָ, תַּנְחֶה אֹתָךְ; בְּשָׁכְבְּךָ, תִּשְׁמֹר
עָלֶיךָ, וַהֲקִיצוֹתָ, הִיא תְשִׂיחֶךָ.״ „בְּהִתְהַלֶּכְךָ,
תַּנְחֶה אֹתָךְ״ — בָּעוֹלָם הַזֶּה; „בְּשָׁכְבְּךָ,
תִּשְׁמֹר עָלֶיךָ״ — בַּקֶּבֶר; „וַהֲקִיצוֹתָ, הִיא
תְשִׂיחֶךָ״ — לָעוֹלָם הַבָּא. וְאוֹמֵר: „לִי הַכֶּסֶף,
וְלִי הַזָּהָב, נְאֻם יהוה צְבָאוֹת.״

---

§⠄ אֵין מְלַוִּין לוֹ לְאָדָם לֹא כֶסֶף, וְלֹא זָהָב, וְלֹא אֲבָנִים טוֹבוֹת וּמַרְגָּלִיּוֹת, אֶלָּא
תּוֹרָה וּמַעֲשִׂים טוֹבִים בִּלְבָד — neither silver, nor gold, nor precious
stones nor pearls escort him, but only Torah study and good deeds

This phrase highlights the difference between our temporal form and
substance in the finite world, and the eternal form and substance that
develop even while we still inhabit the finite world.

The symbolism of the phrase is as follows. **Silver** and **pearls** represent
the finest of material substance. The gleam of **gold** and **precious stones**
is a metaphor for the finest, intangible "form" that graces substance. Yet
even the intangible beauty of the finest material will not persist into
eternity.

A person consists of body and soul. The body, of course, is substance.
The soul is form: It animates the body, imparts character and provides
the ability to live purposefully. Both the body and the soul of a human
being merit the afterlife. Only **good deeds** provide the kind of *bodily*
substance that continues into the World to Come, and only **Torah** provides the kind of *spiritual* substance that carries into the World to Come.

---

§⠄ וְאוֹמֵר: „לִי הַכֶּסֶף, וְלִי הַזָּהָב, נְאֻם ה׳ צְבָאוֹת״ — And it says: "Mine is
the silver, and Mine is the gold, says Hashem, Master of Legions."

Silver and gold belong to God. A human being may take control of
them, and consider them a possession; however, their special beauty is
never his but God's.

Torah, by contrast, comes from God, but in the end it belongs to man,
as the Rabbis say,[1]

---

1. *Avodah Zarah* 19a.

but only Torah study and good deeds, as it is said (*Mishlei* 6:22): "When you walk, it shall guide you; when you lie down, it shall guard you; and when you awake, it shall speak on your behalf." "When you walk, it shall guide you" — in this world; "when you lie down, it shall guard you" — in the grave; "and when you awake, it shall speak on your behalf" — in the World to Come. And it says (*Chaggai* 2:8): "Mine is the silver, and Mine is the gold, says Hashem, Master of Legions."

Rava said: At first Torah is called by God's Name, but then it is called by the name of the one who learns it, as it says,[1] "But his desire is in the Torah of Hashem, and in **his** Torah he meditates day and night."

◆§ לִי הַכֶּסֶף, וְלִי הַזָּהָב ,, — *"Mine is the silver, and Mine is the gold*

The simple reason that "silver" comes before "gold" in the verse is that it is normal to first give praise for a lesser thing and then build up to even higher praises.

A deeper thought is based on the concept of "simplicity." "Simplicity," פְּשִׁיטוּת, in Maharal's lexicon denotes that which is not mixed with anything else; hence, that which is "simple" is pure, independent and self-sufficient. Since silver is not a color, but neutral and pure, it is a symbol of "simplicity." Gold, however, has a reddish color and hence does not have the same simple purity as silver.

This symbolism subtends the deeper reason why silver is mentioned before gold in the verse "Mine is the silver, and Mine is the gold." As a symbol of simplicity, silver is a more appropriate emblem of God's absolute existence than is gold. He is the ultimate of simplicity, in the sense of being pure and not joined with anything else. This is the reason that the Jews in the desert constructed the Calf of gold, for they recognized that silver is appropriate only for the true God. Similarly, the High Priest wore only white clothes into the Holy of Holies in the Temple, but none of his gold attire.

---

1. *Tehillim* 1:2.

[י] חֲמִשָּׁה קִנְיָנִים קָנָה הַקָּדוֹשׁ בָּרוּךְ
הוּא בְּעוֹלָמוֹ, וְאֵלּוּ הֵן: תּוֹרָה,
קִנְיָן אֶחָד; שָׁמַיִם וָאָרֶץ, קִנְיָן אֶחָד;

Mishnah 10

Does God own exactly five things? Does He not own everything?

The *baraisa* enumerates five things that are of the highest degree of possession, for possession has many degrees, as we will now explain.

What determines the degree at which someone possesses an article? There are three factors to consider:[1]

1. How complete is the owner's **control**?
2. How intensely does the **owner** want to own the item?
3. To what degree does the **item** fully satisfy the owner's desire to own it?

To explain more fully:

1. A possession is within the owner's domain of control. If it is not fully within the owner's domain, it is not fully owned. For example, the degree to which a person can own a slave is limited, because only the slave's productivity is owned, not the slave himself. Hence, a slave may be considered a possession to only a nominal degree.
2. Ownership implies a desire to own the article. Naturally, the more necessary an article is, the more the owner wants it. A residence, for example, is so essential that anyone without a residence would certainly acquire one. Hence, a person possesses his residence at a superior degree.
3. Even if an article fills an essential need, it is essential only if nothing else fills the need. For example, a person who has two residences,[2] and lives in only one at a time, does not consider the unoccupied house to be an essential possession. Indeed, neither house is essential as long as he could live in the other house. Because uniqueness is a characteristic of an essential possession, the *baraisa* lists each possession with the epithet **one possession**.

---

1. These points can be profitably applied for a fuller appreciation of Maharal's frequent assertion that knowledge and understanding are a possession (*supra,* 1:18; 2:10-14; 4: 1).
2. The author has substituted an example of two residences, rather than Maharal's example of two slaves, in the belief that this may be a more effective example for the modern reader.

10. Five possessions did the Holy One, Blessed is He, acquire for Himself in His world, and they are: Torah, one possession; heaven and earth, one possession;

It may appear contradictory to say that a possession is of the highest degree only if it is unique, and yet say that God has five possessions of the highest degree. However, the rule that a possession is essential only if it is unique means only that it is uniquely able to fulfill its role. There can indeed be two essential possessions if neither one can substitute for the other. For example, a field and a house can both be essential possessions, because neither can fulfill the other's role. The *baraisa* identifies five essential possessions, and each fulfills its role by itself.

Now we can understand the statement that God has five possessions. Only these five things are distinguished as God's possessions, because they are so thoroughly pertinent to Him, so absolutely within His domain, and without lapse or duplication.

These five things, each in its own way, serve God's role as the Deity. We will now show how the recognition of God as the Deity rests upon these five things.

◆§ תּוֹרָה — *Torah*

Torah is the set of His Divine decrees upon all created. His Name as the Deity is declared in the opening words of the Ten Commandments,[1] "I am Hashem, your God."

◆§ שָׁמַיִם וָאָרֶץ — *heaven and earth*

Heaven and earth are the entire world. His Name is declared upon them, for He is called "the God of heaven and God of the earth."[2]

How can both heaven and earth be called a possession, if something must be unique to be called God's possession? The proof-verse "The heaven is My throne, and the earth is My footstool" shows that heaven and earth are a single unit, just as a footstool is found only in conjunction with a chair. Heaven and earth were created together;[3] they are as inseparable as a circle and its center.

---

1. Maharal uses the term "Torah." The verse is *Shemos* 20:2.
2. *Bereishis* 24:3
3. *Chagigah* 12a.

אַבְרָהָם, קִנְיָן אֶחָד; יִשְׂרָאֵל, קִנְיָן אֶחָד; בֵּית הַמִּקְדָּשׁ, קִנְיָן אֶחָד. תּוֹרָה מִנַּיִן? דִּכְתִיב: "יהוה קָנָנִי רֵאשִׁית דַּרְכּוֹ, קֶדֶם מִפְעָלָיו מֵאָז." שָׁמַיִם וָאָרֶץ מִנַּיִן? דִּכְתִיב: "כֹּה אָמַר יהוה: הַשָּׁמַיִם כִּסְאִי, וְהָאָרֶץ הֲדֹם רַגְלָי; אֵי זֶה בַיִת אֲשֶׁר תִּבְנוּ לִי, וְאֵי זֶה מָקוֹם מְנוּחָתִי?" וְאוֹמֵר: "מָה רַבּוּ מַעֲשֶׂיךָ, יהוה, כֻּלָּם בְּחָכְמָה עָשִׂיתָ, מָלְאָה הָאָרֶץ קִנְיָנֶךָ." אַבְרָהָם מִנַּיִן? דִּכְתִיב: "וַיְבָרְכֵהוּ וַיֹּאמַר, בָּרוּךְ אַבְרָם לְאֵל עֶלְיוֹן, קֹנֵה שָׁמַיִם וָאָרֶץ." יִשְׂרָאֵל מִנַּיִן? דִּכְתִיב: "עַד יַעֲבֹר עַמְּךָ יהוה, עַד יַעֲבֹר – עַם זוּ קָנִיתָ"; וְאוֹמֵר: "לִקְדוֹשִׁים אֲשֶׁר בָּאָרֶץ הֵמָּה וְאַדִּירֵי – כָּל חֶפְצִי בָם." בֵּית הַמִּקְדָּשׁ מִנַּיִן? דִּכְתִיב:

---

§◉ אַבְרָהָם — *Avraham*

God's Name is called upon Avraham, for He is called "the God of Avraham."[1] Although God's Name was connected with the other forefathers as well, it is primarily associated with Avraham.[2]

Avraham is unique in that he was the first fully complete being.[3]

---

§◉ יִשְׂרָאֵל — *Israel*

God's Name is called upon the nation of Israel, for He is called "the God of Israel."[4]

Israel is unique, for it is God's chosen nation.

---

1. *Bereishis* 26:24.
2. As we find in prayer. The blessing which identifies God as the God of Avraham, Yitzchak and Yaakov begins with Avraham and concludes with Avraham alone: 'Blessed are You, Hashem, Shield of Avraham."
3. A Kabbalistic concept explained *supra*, 5:3.
4. *Yehoshua* 7:13, among many other places.

6/ 10   Avraham, one possession; Israel, one possession; the Holy Temple, one possession. From where do we know this about the Torah? Since it is written (*Mishlei* 8:22): "Hashem acquired me [the Torah] at the beginning of His way, before His works in times of yore." From where do we know this about heaven and earth? Since it is written (*Yeshayahu* 66:1): "So says Hashem: The heaven is My throne, and the earth is My footstool; what House can you build for Me, and where is the place of My rest?" And it says (*Tehillim* 104:24): "How abundant are Your works, Hashem, with wisdom You made them all, the earth is full of Your possessions." From where do we know this about Avraham? Since it is written (*Bereishis* 14:19): "And He blessed him and said: Blessed is Avram of God the Most High, Who acquired heaven and earth." From where do we know this about the people Israel? Since it is written (*Shemos* 15:16): 'Until Your people passes through, Hashem, until it passes through — this people You acquired," and it [also] says (*Tehillim* 16:3): "But for the holy ones who are in the earth and for the mighty — all my desires are due to them." From where do we know this about the Holy Temple? Since it is written

---

◆§ בֵּית הַמִּקְדָּשׁ — *the Holy Temple*

His name is called upon the Temple as it says,[1] "this house is called by Your Name."

The Holy Temple is unique, for it is the chosen of all places in the land of Israel.

In summary, these five things are God's possessions because they are fully in His domain; they are pertinent to God as the Deity; and they are unique in fulfilling that role.

---

1. *II Divrei HaYamim* 6:33.

„מָכוֹן לְשִׁבְתְּךָ פָּעַלְתָּ יהוה, מִקְּדָשׁ אֲדֹנָי
כּוֹנְנוּ יָדֶיךָ"; וְאוֹמֵר: „וַיְבִיאֵם אֶל גְּבוּל קָדְשׁוֹ,
הַר זֶה קָנְתָה יְמִינוֹ."

[יא] כָּל מַה שֶּׁבָּרָא הַקָּדוֹשׁ בָּרוּךְ הוּא
בְּעוֹלָמוֹ, לֹא בְרָאוֹ אֶלָּא לִכְבוֹדוֹ,

Mishnah 11

Since this chapter deals solely with Torah, it is clear that the point of
this *baraisa* is that **His glory** is found in the study of Torah and the
concomitant observance of the Creator's *mitzvos*. Since Torah study is
God's glory, it follows that one must not study Torah for the sake of his
own glory. Better not to have been created than to use the instrument of
God's glory for one's own glory![1]

כָּל מַה שֶּׁבָּרָא הַקָּדוֹשׁ בָּרוּךְ הוּא בְּעוֹלָמוֹ, לֹא בְרָאוֹ אֶלָּא
לִכְבוֹדוֹ — **All that the Holy One, Blessed is He,
created in His world, He created solely for His glory**

This message is an appropriate conclusion to the chapter that
deals with Torah study. It teaches that our Torah studies must bring
glory to God. Therefore, Torah study must be accompanied by proper
conduct, so that God will be glorified through His Torah. Conversely,
even if it is for the sake of Heaven, purely academic Torah study, without putting the knowledge gleaned into practice, is insufficient. The
Rabbis say,[2]

> [The verse,] "And you shall love the Lord your God,"[3] [includes
> an obligation] that the name of Heaven shall be beloved [to
> others] through you. Who can bring others to love God? One
> who studies Scripture and law and ministers to Torah scholars.
> This individual speaks gently. When making a purchase, he is
> pleasant in his dealings. He deals with integrity in his business
> relationships. What do people say about him? "How fortunate
> he is that he learned Torah! Happy is the teacher who taught

---

1. *Berachos* 17a, "If one does [Torah study] for other than the sake of Heaven, it
would be better had he not been born."
2. *Yoma* 86a.
3. *Devarim* 6:5.

6/ 11 (*Shemos* 15:17): "Your dwelling place which You, Hashem, have made; the Sanctuary, my Lord, that Your hands established." And it says (*Tehillim* 78:54): "And He brought them to His sacred boundary, to this mountain which His right hand acquired."

11. All that the Holy One, Blessed is He, created in His world, He created solely for His glory,

---

him Torah! Woe to those people who did not learn Torah! See this person who learned Torah: How nice are his ways, how proper are his deeds."

Of him Scripture says,[1] "And He said to me: You are My servant, Israel, in whom I will be glorified."

◆§ כָּל מַה שֶׁבָּרָא הַקָּדוֹשׁ בָּרוּךְ הוּא בְּעוֹלָמוֹ, לֹא בְרָאוֹ אֶלָּא לִכְבוֹדוֹ — *All that the Holy One, Blessed is He, created in His world, He created solely for His glory*

Another reason that God's glory is a fitting subject with which to end *Avos* is that God's glory is the end goal of everything. Since everything was created for His glory, there is nothing else in life. For this reason, Shlomo *HaMelech* concludes his work of *mussar, Koheles,* with the same message:[2]

"The end of the matter, all having been heard: Fear God and keep His commandments; for that is the whole of man."

This verse means that the fear of God is the sole point of all creation.

The essence of the "fear of God" is the recognition of how utterly dependent we are on Him for our very existence.

The world was created only for mankind, and mankind was created only to fear God and to observe His commandments. All of creation leads up to that goal, and the book of *Koheles* parallels life by leading up to that conclusion. The author of this chapter, following the precedent of *Koheles,* likewise concludes with the purpose of life; namely, that everything which God created, He created for His glory.

---

1. *Yeshayahu* 49:3.
2. *Koheles* 12:13.

ו/יא שֶׁנֶּאֱמַר: ,,כֹּל הַנִּקְרָא בִשְׁמִי וְלִכְבוֹדִי בְּרָאתִיו, יְצַרְתִּיו אַף עֲשִׂיתִיו"; וְאוֹמֵר: ,,יהוה יִמְלֹךְ לְעוֹלָם וָעֶד."

❧ ❧ ❧

_____

◆§ **כֹּל הַנִּקְרָא בִשְׁמִי וְלִכְבוֹדִי בְּרָאתִיו** — *"All that is called by My Name, indeed, it is for My glory that I have created it*

"All that is **called by My Name**" refers to those people who are righteous and holy, for God is called Righteous and Holy.

"All that. . . for **My glory** that I have created it," refers to the rest of Creation. Even though His Name is not directly associated with them, every thing He created is His glory.

_____

◆§ **בְּרָאתִיו, יְצַרְתִּיו אַף עֲשִׂיתִיו** — *I have created it, formed it and made it."*

These three expressions emphasize different aspects of created things.

- "Created" refers to totally intangible form. It is not physical form; i.e., the shape to which substance conforms. It is a Divine, intangible aura, such as the beauty of a rainbow or the radiance of a joyful face. It is part of every created thing, but it is most evident in the totality of heaven and earth, and in man as the "image of God."[1] This Divine aspect was also prominent in the extraordinary dimensions of the great sea monsters, the *Tanninim*.[2]
- "Formed" refers to form that is imposed upon substance, as an artist might paint or sculpt in some medium. All physical creations have form; it is remarkable in animals, and it is most striking in the human being.
- "Made" emphasizes physical substance. This term is used in conjunction with the firmament and the luminaries, because they are prominent only as luminous bodies, without discernible shape.

The following analysis of the account of Creation shows that these three terms are applied to different parts of creation, but all three terms are applied to the creation of mankind.

The expression "created" is applied to heaven and earth: "God **created**

_____

1. *Bereishis* 9:6.
2. *Ibid* 1:21.

6/ 11   as it is said (*Yeshayahu* 43:7): "All that is called by My Name, indeed, it is for My glory that I have created it, formed it and made it." And it says (*Shemos* 15:18): "Hashem shall reign for all eternity."

❧ ❧ ❧

---

the heaven and the earth."[1] It is also applied to the great sea monsters, the *Tanninim*[2] and to man.

The expression "formed" is applied to animals[3] and to man, and there are no other instances of the term in Creation.

The expression "made" is applied to the firmament,[4] to the luminaries,[5] to animals[6] and to man.

All three acts of Creation — to create, to form and to make — were involved in every creation, because everything has substance, form and a Divine aura. Scripture uses only one or two of the terms for each thing, as appropriate to its prominent characteristic. The human being exists fully at every level of creation, and so all three terms are used in the account of man's creation: "And God said, Let us **make** man."[7] "And God **created** man."[8] "And Hashem. . .**formed** man."[9]

In summary, the verse, "for My glory that I have **created** it, **formed** it and **made** it," alludes to the fact that God created the entire world with these three aspects.

◆§ "וְאוֹמֵר: ,,ה׳ יִמְלֹךְ לְעוֹלָם וָעֶד'' — *And it says:*
"*Hashem shall reign for all eternity.*"

Why is this additional verse necessary? This verse defines the nature of the "glory" that accrues to God from His Creation. It is the glory of being King over His subjects.[10] His subjects are all created things, and

---

1. *Bereishis* 1:1.
2. *Ibid* 1:21.
3. *Ibid* 2:6.
4. *Ibid* 1:7.
5. *Ibid* 1:16.
6. *Ibid* 1:25.
7. *Ibid* 1:26.
8. *Ibid* 1:27.
9. *Ibid* 2:7.
10. The king fills a venerable role of leadership and responsibility for his subjects. Maharal's point is that God's glory does not come from the praise He receives from His own Creation. His glory comes through caring for His Creation.

רַבִּי חֲנַנְיָא בֶּן עֲקַשְׁיָא אוֹמֵר: רָצָה הַקָּדוֹשׁ
בָּרוּךְ הוּא לְזַכּוֹת אֶת יִשְׂרָאֵל; לְפִיכָךְ
הִרְבָּה לָהֶם תּוֹרָה וּמִצְוֹת, שֶׁנֶּאֱמַר: ,,יהוה חָפֵץ
לְמַעַן צִדְקוֹ, יַגְדִּיל תּוֹרָה וְיַאְדִּיר."

without them He would not be King over anything. All created things, through their very existence, bring Him the glory due to a King.

Maharal's Response to the Philosophers

Rambam[1] disputes the view that God made everything so that mankind might serve Him. Rambam makes the point that God does not benefit from our service, nor would He lack anything if there were no Creation. Why then did He create the world? Because such was His will. His will is His essence, and since God's essence is unknowable, we cannot state a purpose for Creation.

Based on this approach, Rambam adopts a different interpretation of the word "glory" in the verse, "All that is called by My Name, indeed it is for My **glory** that I have created it,"[2] He maintains that God's "glory" is His essence, as His will is His essence. Hence the verse means: Everything that God made in His world has been made for the sake of His will.

Rambam likewise understands the verse,[3] "God has made everything for His Own sake"[4] to mean "God has made everything for the sake of His will."

Rambam is forced to advance these explanations to resolve the difficulty posed by the philosophical tenet that God does not receive glory from others.

Rambam's opinion that God does not have any benefit from His Creation is not shared by our Rabbis. The Rabbis indicate[5] that all of Creation was created to serve mankind, and mankind was created to serve the Creator. That sentiment implies that God's glory emerges through His creations, as confirmed in our baraisa: "All that the Holy One . . . created in His world, He created solely for His glory."

It is true that God does not receive glory from others. It is true that He is not better off for a man's righteousness, nor is He worse off for a man's sin. God made mankind because it is appropriate for God to be King over

---

1. *Guide for the Perplexed,* Part 3, Chapter 13.
2. *Yeshayahu* 43:7.
3. *Mishlei* 16:4.
4. According to others, the phrase means "His praise" or "His glory."
5. See *Kiddushin* 82a, *mishnah.*

Rabbi Chanania ben Akashia says: The Holy One, Blessed is He, wished to confer merit upon Israel; therefore He gave them Torah and *mitzvos* in abundance, as it is said (*Yeshayahu* 42:21): 'Hashem desired, for the sake of His righteousness, that the Torah be made great and glorious."

---

him. The glory of being a King does not come from the subjects but from the dominion. When a person is righteous, God is King and rewards him. When a person sins, God is King and metes out punishment. God's glory does not depend on mankind but on ruling over Creation. It is for this reason that the *baraisa* adduces the additional verse, "Hashem shall reign for all eternity."[1]

The point that Rambam finds so difficult is addressed by the Rabbis in the *mishnah,* [2] "against your will you were created; against your will you were born; against your will you live; against your will you die, and against your will you are destined to give an account before the King Who rules over kings." In other words, God receives nothing from mankind; He imposes everything upon man. The statement of the Rabbis[3] that man was created to serve God means that God's kingship is upon him.

Still, we may wonder why God, Whose glory is in His essence, would make the world. He has no need to be King! The answer is that God is perfect, and that which is perfect is actualized, not just capable in potential. God's perfection is actualized through Creation.

There is no need for Rambam's explanations. The approach of the Rabbis is unquestionably certain, clear and pure. It is my[4] opinion that Rambam explained the verses as he did because the people of his generation were drawn after the philosophers — gentile scholars, upon whom the light of Torah had never dawned. Rambam found a method to explain Scripture in a way that aligned with their opinions. He deviated from the explanations of the earlier Rabbis because there was risk of a more serious loss: The people might not have accepted Scripture at all. This is the reason he explained Scripture in accordance with their views, but be assured that the genuine explanation did not elude him or anyone with wisdom in his heart.

Blessed is the Name of His glorious kingdom for all eternity. Amen.

---

1. *Shemos* 15:18.
2. *Supra,* 4:29.
3. *Kiddushin* 82a, *mishnah.*
4. Maharal is speaking.

This volume is part of
THE ARTSCROLL SERIES®
an ongoing project of
translations, commentaries and expositions
on Scripture, Mishnah, Talmud, Halachah,
liturgy, history, the classic Rabbinic writings,
biographies, and thought.

For a brochure of current publications
visit your local Hebrew bookseller
or contact the publisher:

Mesorah Publications, ltd

4401 Second Avenue
Brooklyn, New York 11232
(718) 921-9000